CONTEMPORARY POLITICAL IDEOLOGIES

Movements and Regimes

CONTEMPORARY POLITICAL IDEOLOGIES

Movements and Regimes

SIXTH EDITION

Roy C. Macridis
&
Mark Hulliung
Brandeis University

HarperCollins*CollegePublishers*

Acquisitions Editor: Leo A. W. Wiegman
Project Coordination and Text Design: York Production Services
Cover Design: Wendy Ann Fredericks
Cover Illustration: Morgan Russell, Four Part Synchomy, Number 7, 1914–15. Four sections, overall: 15¾ x 11½ inches. Collection of Whitney Museum of American Art. Gift of the artist in memory of Gertrude V. Whitney 51.33.
Photo Researcher: Leslie Coopersmith
Electronic Page Makeup: R. R. Donnelley and Sons Company, Inc.
Printer and Binder: R. R. Donnelley and Sons Company, Inc.
Cover Printer: Color-Imetry Corp.

Contemporary Political Ideologies, Sixth Edition.

Library of Congress Cataloging-in-Publication Data

Macridis, Roy C.
    Contemporary political ideologies: movements and regimes / Roy C. Macridis and Mark Hulliung. — 6th ed.
        p.   cm.
    Includes bibliographical references and index.
    ISBN 0-673-52458-2
    1. Political science—History.   2.   Comparative government.
    I. Hulliung, Mark. II. Title.
JA81.M316   1996
320.5'09—dc20   95-41488
                                                                                    CIP

95 96 97 98   9 8 7 6 5 4 3 2 1

*This book is dedicated to
the memory of my late son, Peter.*

R.C.M

To my students

M.H

One person with a belief is a social power equal to ninety-nine who have only interests.

JOHN STUART MILL

Contents

Preface xiii

Chapter 1
POLITICAL IDEOLOGIES: INTRODUCTION   *1*
What Is an Ideology?   2
Political Ideology: The Building Blocks   4
The Uses of Political Ideology   9
The Intellectuals   13
Types of Political Ideologies   14
The Major Political Ideologies   16
Bibliography   18

Part One
DEMOCRACY: MANY ROOTS AND FAMILIES   21
Contemporary Democracy: Major Phases   22

Chapter 2
DEMOCRACY AND LIBERALISM   *25*
The Three Cores of Liberalism   26
The State and the Individual   40
Achievements: The Expansion of Liberalism   44
Conclusion   47
Bibliography   48

Chapter 3
DEMOCRAY AND THE ECONOMY: SOCIALISM, THE WELFARE STATE, . . . CAPITALISM AGAIN?   51

Radical Democrats   52

Liberal and Radical Democrats: Reconciliation   54

The Socialist Impulse   55

Reforming Capitalism   62

Back to Capitalism?   66

Political Parties and the Shift to Capitalism   70

Capitalism: Problems and Prospects   74

Bibliography   76

Chapter 4
THE CONSERVATIVE TRADITION   79

Classic Conservatism: The British Model   80

American Conservatives and the British Model   87

The American Conservative Ideology   90

Bibliography   93

Part Two
COMMUNISM: THE VISION AND THE REALITY   95

Chapter 5
THE THEORY AND THE VISION: MARXISM   97

The Legacy of Marx   98

The Dynamics of the Communist Revolution   103

Bibliography   108

Chapter 6
THE REALITY: LENINISM AND STALINISM   **110**

Leninism   110

Stalinism   115

Soviet Domination: The Comintern   119

Stalinism: Contradictions and Stagnation   120

Bibliography   123

Chapter 7
THE COLLAPSE OF COMMUNISM   **125**

Decline of the Communist Ideology   126

The "Opening": *Glasnost* and *Perestroika*   129

The Collapse of Communism in Eastern Europe   134

The Last Bastions   138

Epilogue: A World Without Communism?   141

Bibliography   142

Part Three
THE AUTHORITARIAN RIGHT   **145**

Chapter 8
THE INTELLECTUAL ROOTS OF FASCISM   **147**

Fascists and Marxists   148

Fascists and Syndicalists   151

Fascists and the Volk   156

Fascist Ideology: Its Significance and Consequences   164

Bibliography   166

Chapter 9
THE NAZI IDEOLOGY AND POLITICAL ORDER   *168*

The Road to Power   169

The Nazi Ideology   172

Authoritarianism: Interpretations and Prospects   180

The Return of the Extreme Right in Europe   184

The Extreme Right in the United States   186

Bibliography   193

Part Four
OLD VOICES AND NEW   195

Chapter 10
NATIONALISMS   *197*

Nationality, Nation–States, States, and Nationalism   198

German Nationalism: The 1990 Version   203

Nationalism in Action: A Historical Overview   204

Black Separatism in the United States   211

Beyond Nationalism—Internationalism?   216

Internationalism and Internationalist Arrangements   220

Conclusion   220

Bibliography   221

Chapter 11
THE RELIGIOUS IMPULSE: LIBERATION THEOLOGY AND RELIGIOUS FUNDAMENTALISM   *223*

Liberation Theology   224

The Philosophy of Liberation Theology   226

Religious Fundamentalism   231

Bibliography   242

Chapter 12
RED FLAGS/BLACK FLAGS:
  MARXISTS AGAINST ANARCHISTS   **244**

Organization: What Is to Be Done?   245

The Paris Commune: What Is to Be Remembered?   251

Theory: What Is to Be Conceptualized?   258

Art: What Is to Be Created?   264

Final Thoughts   269

Bibliography   270

Chapter 13
STUDENT REBELLION IN THE LATE 1960s:
  AMERICA AND FRANCE   **272**

That Remarkable Year, 1968   272

America and France: The Similarities   276

America and France: The Differences   283

The Legacy of 1968   291

Bibliography   294

Chapter 14
MULTICULTURALISM AND THE
  POLITICS OF IDENTITY   **295**

Unveiling the Problem   295

The Revolt against Universalism   299

The Revolt against Science   303

Multiculturalism and Liberalism   307

Bibliography   312

Chapter 15
WHITHER LIBERAL DEMOCRACY?   **313**

Index   321

Preface

Roy Macridis died after preparing the fifth edition of *Contemporary Political Ideologies*. Responsibility for this, the sixth edition, is mine. I have edited and updated two of the essays written by Professor Macridis, deleted four other chapters, and added five of my own.

The chapters I edited are "The Collapse of Communism" and "Nationalisms." Gorbachev was still in power and Yugoslavia had not yet disintegrated at the time that Roy Macridis finished the last edition. Obviously some changes in the text had to be made, and I have acted accordingly.

Among the deleted chapters are those on feminism and environmentalism. In a future edition I hope to restore these topics in a single chapter dealing with the politics of "causes." Readers familiar with Professor Macridis' essays on feminism and environmentalism will recall that he repeatedly expressed doubts whether either chapter addressed a full-fledged ideology. I share both his doubts and his conviction that women's issues and environmental questions are matters of fundamental significance. A chapter on the politics of causes strikes me as a fitting way to place feminism and environmentalism in the larger context of contemporary ideological struggles.

Aware how adept Professor Macridis was at bringing his book up to date, I have written a chapter on "Multiculturalism and the Politics of Identity" for this edition. My final essay, "Whither Liberal Democracy?", serves much the same purpose of addressing a recent controversy: the furor over Samuel Huntington's essay bearing the title "The Clash of Civilizations?"

Because students remain fascinated with the rebellions that shook the universities in the late 1960s, and because the New Left did permanently alter the way politics is conducted, I have written a chapter comparing campus rebellions in French and American schools. I argue that although the events in the two nations were much the same, the meanings and consequences were quite different; and that the only way to understand what happened is to study the contrasting ideological and cultural traditions of France and America.

The long history of battles between Marxists and anarchists is possibly both the most important and the least studied aspect of leftist thought. My chapter on the conflict between bearers of the red flag and those waving the contending black flag aims primarily to do justice to a neglected but vital and fascinating chapter of intellectual, cultural, and political history. A secondary objective is to set the stage for the following chapter on student rebellion where I argue that only on the surface were the New Lefts of France and America similar.

Any book devoted to the study of political ideologies, it seems to me, should contain a chapter on fascist thought. Accordingly I have written an essay on "The Intellectual Roots of Fascism," which covers both Italian Fascism and German National Socialism. In the usual textbook account, Italian Fascism is treated as little more than a warming up exercise for the Nazi ideology; I have done my best to treat Mussolini seriously.

Except where updating was unavoidable I have left the essays of Professor Macridis as they were. This is not to say that I am in full agreement with this viewpoint or that I shall hesitate in future editions to write new chapters setting forth my own interpretations. To cite just one example, readers will almost certainly discover a new treatment of the welfare state in future editions. Perhaps because Roy Macridis was so much a classic laissez-faire liberal, he offered little by way of explaining the liberal justification for a welfare state. I intend to articulate a full-scale account of the liberal welfare state, its philosophical rationale, its actual practice, and its prospects in an age when it is under sharp attack.

I am the author of Chapters 8, 12, 13, 14, and 15; the rest belong to my fallen comrade, Roy C. Macridis.

Mark Hulliung

CONTEMPORARY POLITICAL IDEOLOGIES

Movements and Regimes

Chapter
1

Political Ideologies

Introduction

Olympian bards who sung
Divine ideas . . .
Which always find us young
And always keep us so

Ralph Waldo Emerson The Poet

Whether we know it or not, all of us have an ideology, even those who claim openly that they do not. We all believe in certain things. We all value something—property, friends, the law, freedom, or authority. We all have prejudices, even those who claim to be free of them. We all look at the world in one way or another—we have "ideas" about it—and we try to make sense out of what is going on in it. Quite a few of us are unhappy, discontented, critical of what we see around us as compared to what we would like to see. Some become alienated—rejecting the society and its values, sulking into their separate and private tents but ready to spring forth into action.

People with the same ideas about the world, our society, and its values band together. We are attracted by those with similar values and ideas, who like the same things we do, who have prejudices similar to ours, and who, in general, view the world in the same way we do. We talk of "like-minded" people, individuals who share certain beliefs and tend to congregate—in clubs, churches, political parties, movements, various associations, and so on. No matter how independent we claim to be, we all are influenced by ideas. We are sensitive to appeals made to us—to our honor, patriotism, family, religion, pocketbook, race, or class—and we can all be manipulated and aroused. We are creators and creatures of ideas, of ideologies, and through them we manipulate others or are ourselves manipulated.

Ideologies are very much a part of our lives; they are not dead and they are not on the decline anywhere, as some authors have argued.

Ah, but a man's reach should exceed his grasp,
Or what's a Heaven for?

wrote Browning in 1885. Almost a century later, a strong upsurge in ideological and utopian movements made powerful governments totter as many sought their own vision of heaven on earth. "Be rational; think of the impossible" was one of the slogans of intellectuals and students in the late 1960s.

Not only are ideologies surviving, their all-embracing importance is again being recognized. "Neo-Marxists" now agree that a drastic revolutionary overhaul of the society, if there is to be one, must be above all a moral and intellectual revolution: a revolution in the *ideology* of society. It must create its own "countercon-sciousness," its own "counterculture"—a new set of beliefs and values and a new style of life that will eat, like a worm, into the core of prevailing liberal–capitalist orthodoxy. Only with its ideological core gone can the old society be changed and replaced.

But "ideologies" are resilient; they persist. The core is far more resistant to change than most people had thought. Established ideas and values cannot be pulled out like a rotten tooth. They have deep roots in the soil in which they grew. While there has been so much emphasis and discussion on ideologies that either brought about change or command change, little attention has been given to the complex of values, habits, and practices that resist change—to the phenomenon that may be called *ideological conservation.* The family, the church, attachment to property and nationalisms continued to defy, as we have seen recently in the break up of Communist regimes, the Communist-revealed and imposed truths. Ideological "formation" has been continuously in conflict with ideological "preservation."

WHAT IS AN IDEOLOGY?

Ideology has been defined as "a set of closely related beliefs, or ideas, or even attitudes, characteristic of a group or community."[1] Similarly, a *political* ideology is "a set of ideas and beliefs" that people hold about their political regime and its institutions and about their own position and role in it. Political ideology accordingly appears synonymous with "political culture" or "political tradition." The British or the Americans or the French or the Russians pattern their political life on the basis of different sets of interrelated ideas, beliefs, and attitudes.

Various groups, however, within one and the same political community may, and often do, at given times and under given conditions, challenge the prevailing ideology. Interests, classes, and various political and religious associations may develop a "counter-ideology" that questions the status quo and attempts to modify it. They advocate change rather than order; they criticize or reject the political regime and the existing social and economic arrangements; they advance schemes for the restructuring and reordering of the society; and they spawn political movements in order to gain enough power to bring about the changes they advocate. In

---

[1]John Plamenatz, *Ideology,* p. 15.

this sense, a political ideology moves people into action. It motivates them to demand changes in their way of life and to modify the existing political, social, and economic relations, or it mobilizes them on how to preserve what they value. In discussing ideologies—all ideologies—we must always bear in mind these two all-important characteristics: a given political ideology rationalizes the status quo, whereas other, competing ideologies and movements challenge it.

Philosophy, Theory, and Ideology

A distinction should be made between philosophy or theory on the one hand, and ideology on the other. *Philosophy* literally means love of wisdom—the detached and often solitary contemplation and search for truth. In the strictest meaning of the terms, *theory* is the formulation of propositions that causally link variables to account for or explain a phenomenon, and such linkages should be empirically verifiable. This is, of course, true for natural scientists. They operate within a clearly defined framework of rules accepted by them all. However, in the social sciences there is not as yet an accepted framework of rules, and it is very difficult to come up with empirical verifications.

What separates theory or philosophy from ideology is that, while the first two involve contemplation, organization of ideas, and whenever possible, demonstration, ideology shapes beliefs that incite people into action. Men and women organize to *impose* certain philosophies or theories and to realize them in a given society. Ideology thus involves action and collective effort. Even when they originate (as they often do) in philosophy or theory, ideologies are inevitably highly simplified, and even distorted, versions of the original doctrines. It is always interesting to know the philosophy or the theory from which an ideology originates. But it is just as important to understand ideology as a distinct and separate entity to be studied in terms of its own logic and dynamics rather than in terms of the theory from which it stems or of how closely it resembles that theory.

It is difficult to understand when and under what circumstances a theory or a philosophy becomes transformed into an ideology—that is, into an action-oriented movement. Important theories and philosophic doctrines remain unnoticed and untouched for generations before they are "discovered." The well-known German sociologist Max Weber makes the point by indicating that theories or philosophies are "selected" to become transformed into ideologies without, however, explaining precisely how, when, and why. History may be compared to a freezer where ideas and theories are stored for use at a later time. Different works of Plato, for example, have been at various times the origin of different ideological movements. Similarly, whereas a powerful ideological movement developed from the major works of Karl Marx, it is his early works—the "early Marx"or the "young Marx"—that have been adapted to suit some contemporary movements and tastes. The same is the case with powerful religious or nationalist movements that pick and choose from different parts of the Bible or the Koran. There is a dialectic between ideas, as such, and social needs; both are indispensable in order to have an ideology. Heartfelt demands arising from the social body may fail for the lack of ideas; and ideas may go begging for a long time for the lack of relevance to social needs.

POLITICAL IDEOLOGY: THE BUILDING BLOCKS

The debt most political ideologies owe to political speculation and philosophy is quite obvious when we look at some of the major themes that political ideologies address: (1) the role and the nature of the individual (human nature); (2) the nature of truth and how it can be discovered; (3) the relationship between the individual and the group, be it the tribe, the small city–state, or the contemporary state as we know it; (4) the characteristics of political authority—its source and its limits, if any; (5) the goals and the mechanics of economic organization and the much-debated issue of material and economic equality as it relates to individual freedom. Normative judgments about each of these themes and many more are the very "stuff" of contemporary political ideologies. Some have been hotly debated over many centuries and will continue to be debated.

The Individual

Political ideologies are addressed to each one of us; they all begin with one preconception or another about us—about human nature. Some believe that we are the creatures of history and the environment, that our nature and characteristics are interwoven with the material conditions of life and ultimately shaped by them. Human nature is plastic and ever-changing and with the proper "social engineering"—another term for education—it can be shaped into a pattern. Many ideologies assume that, with the proper changes in our environment and the proper inculcation of new values, "new" men and women can be created. There is nothing sacrosanct, therefore, in our present institutions and values; on the contrary, some of them are downright bad.

On the other hand, many well-known philosophers, especially those in the period of the Enlightenment and in the nineteenth century, have presented a different notion of human nature. People have some innate characteristics: we are born with traits of sociability, goodness, and rationality. We are also endowed with rights, such as life, liberty, and property. Institutions are but a reflection of these human traits and rights, and a political organization must respect them; indeed, it must provide the best means for protecting them. Therefore, the state that protects these rights cannot invade them—the state is limited. Finally, other political philosophers have argued that human nature is "greedy," "selfish," and "bellicose" and that it is the duty of the state to curb our ignoble drives. Political power and coercion are what make social life possible and safe.

Of particular interest are psychological theories of individual motivation, generally associated with economic liberalism, which we examine in Chapter 2. Rejecting the notion of natural rights, British philosophers and economists postulated an individual driven by desire who seeks only the gratification of pleasure. Each and all of us are motivated by the pursuit of pleasure and the only constraints are external—the pleasures and drives of others. Competition in a free market provides such constraints. Similar notions about the "political man," thirsty for power and glory, led to the formulation of theories of checks and balances—each power checking the other to provide for a balance that preserved the freedom of all. It

Plato (c. 427–347 B.C.)

The Greek philosopher Plato was a disciple of Socrates and the founder of philosophic idealism, according to which ideas exist in themselves and by themselves, forming a perfect and harmonious universe. As a political philosopher, Plato wrote *The Republic,* a work describing an ideal state with a strict class structure ruled by philosopher–kings who divested themselves of property and family ties in order to rule for the common good.

was because of the depravity of human nature that James Madison, one of the authors of The Federalist Papers and our fourth president, considered government to be necessary.

The Nature of Truth

Is there one truth? Or is truth progressively discovered as many ideas and points of view compete with each other—every generation adding something to it? The notion that there is one truth revealed only to some or perceived authoritatively by them requires us to submit to it. We must hew as closely as possible to what is given, and obey those who speak for it. Human beings are thus deprived of the freedom to seek truth, to experiment with new ideas, to confront each other with different points of view, and to live in a system that tolerates different ways.

On the other hand, there are those for whom a constant exploration of the universe by human beings and a constant inquiry into the foundations and conditions of life are the only ways to discover truth. "Such is the nature of the understanding that it cannot be compelled to the belief of anything by outside force," wrote John Locke. People who hold this view favor competition of ideas, advocate tolerance for all points of view, and want to assure the conditions of freedom that are indispensable for ongoing inquiry. This is what we call *pluralism*. If one Absolute Truth did exist, pluralists would have none of it for fear that it would deprive human beings of the challenge of discovering it!

The Individual and Society

For some social scientists there is no such entity as an "individual." The individuals are perceived as part of a herd or a group whose protection and survival require cooperation. The individual is considered helpless outside the group or the state. The group or the state then makes the rules of conduct and establishes the relationship between rulers and ruled. The individual is a "social being"—first and last!

The other point of view stresses the opposite—the primacy of individuals. They are perceived as having originally lived in the state of nature and endowed with reason and natural rights. To protect themselves and their belongings, these individuals contrive to create a political society that protects their lives and their property. The political system—the state—is made up of individuals, by the individuals, and for the individuals. It is the result of a contract—freely entered upon.

As with theories about human nature, our view of the relationship between the individual and the society often determines our political ideology. Those who give primacy to the group show an inclination to emphasize the "organic" nature of society and the political system: it is a whole, like our body, and the individuals are like the cells of our organism. They are only parts that fit into the whole; they have no freedoms and rights. The "organic" theory puts the accent on the whole and the close interdependence of the parts that is required to make it function. This theory leaves little room for change, unless it is very gradual. Sudden change shifts the balance of existing relationships among the parts and hence endangers the whole—the society. The "organic" theory also is totalitarian in the name of society's overriding purpose to which all parts and individuals remain subservient.

Those who assume the primacy of the individual reach diametrically opposite conclusions. *The individual is what counts most.* Individuals *make* the political society in which they live, and they can change it. Political life is an act of will and political authority is based on consent. The society consists of a maze of overlapping, cooperating, or conflicting wills and units—both individuals and groups— participating in the political system. Change, reform, experimentation, and even revolution must spring from the will and the consent and the common effort and action of the individuals. If, as Thomas Jefferson did, revolution is to be envisaged, it must stem from the will of the majority of the people.

Political Authority

Basic divisions on the nature and organization of political authority derive from theories about the nature of truth and about the relationship between the individual and the group. Belief in one overriding truth leads almost always to an authoritarian position. It is *elitist.* It assumes that a small group "knows" and is capable of governing on the basis of certain qualities. For Plato these qualities were *intellectual:* the philosopher–king; for some they are *prescriptive:* based on inheritance. The qualities deemed necessary for governing could also be *charismatic:* appeal and personality, or *class*—either the property owners or the working class—having a historical mission of ruling or transforming the society.

On the other hand, those who postulate that political authority derives from the will of individuals favor limiting political authority in order to allow for participation and open deliberation. They advocate freedom of thought and expression, respect for individual freedoms, and freedom for associations, political parties, and all other organizations. *No claims to rule based on birth, heredity, wealth, intellectual superiority, or prescriptive titles are accepted.* No "monopoly of truth" is conceded—to anybody.

Equality and Property

Many of the most important political ideologies can be distinguished in terms of the answers they try to provide to the following questions: *Who produces and who decides what is produced? Who gets what and how much?* The answers are complex, and all the more so since the very concepts and questions, let alone the answers, are laden with emotions and values; they are steeped in ideology.

The central issue remains that of equality. For the early liberals, equality was interpreted narrowly to mean equality before the law, or equality of all to vote and participate in the choice of political leaders. Yet, unless people have equal access to education and material living standards (even if minimal), equality before the law is a fiction. Throughout the twentieth century, as we will see, those who advocated political or legal equality above all clashed with the proponents of material equality. There is a constant tension between material and economic equality on the one hand and formal legal and political equality on the other.

Property and the right of individual property have been the subject of intense ideological conflicts, as we will see. Few theorists and philosophers have given to individual property their unqualified blessing. Whenever they did, as it was the case with Aristotle and John Locke, among others, property was considered in physical terms—that which individuals managed by their labor to bring under their direct control. From Plato, who would have none of it, through the Christian fathers, down to many Utopian Socialists, and of course including Marxists, property was viewed, especially when unevenly distributed, as something disruptive of the community and social life. Property set one against another. It was not a natural right, but the result of forceful exploitation—the source of and the reason for inequality that accounts for social strife.

Liberal democracies have emphasized property rights—even when they have been forced to qualify them for the sake of greater material equality. Socialism and communism, on the other hand, have favored the socialization of property. Throughout the twentieth century, virtually all political regimes and all political ideologies have come to terms with the need for providing greater material opportunities and equality. Even when individual property is accepted, its uneven distribution has been a source of profound concern and a reason for reconsideration of property rights. How does a political system avoid excessive differences and inequalities? Taxation—in many cases steep progressive income taxes—has been used and the monies procured have been redistributed to the poor and the needy in the form of services and outright grants. This is the essence of the welfare state that became the political formula of all liberal democracies, until very recently.

Property is no longer defined only in terms of land or the real estate one owns or even in terms of liquid wealth and high salaries, although they are still important. For many people in most societies, "property" has now become "public" in the sense that it consists of claims against the state that individuals have for service and benefits to which they are entitled. Education, health, housing, transportation, old age pensions, unemployment benefits, and special assistance programs have become rights—"entitlements"—and they are just as important as property rights. Whatever the justification or the adequacy of such entitlements, they have significantly changed the distribution of material benefits and the nature of property in most all societies. For many people, such services and benefits have provided a cushion just as important as ownership.

Notions about human nature, truth, political authority, freedom, property and equality, and the production and distribution of goods and services outlined here are present in each and every ideology we will study in this book. They are the major building blocks of all contemporary ideologies and movements. Men and women organize behind their respective visions of a just and better world or barricade themselves to defend their own visions of justice. Political philosophy gives us all a chance to contemplate these notions in a detached and objective way; political ideologies and movements often transform them into a battle cry.

THE USES OF POLITICAL IDEOLOGY

An *ideology*, then, is a set of ideas and beliefs held by a number of people. It spells out what is valued and what is not, what must be maintained and what must be changed, and it shapes the attitudes of those who share it accordingly. In contrast to philosophy and theory, which are concerned with knowledge and understanding, ideologies relate to social and political behavior and action. They incite people to political action and provide the basic framework for such action. They infuse passion and call for sacrifice.

Legitimization

As pointed out earlier, one of the most important functions of a political ideology is to give value to a political regime and its institutions. It shapes the operative ideas that make a political regime work. It provides the basic categories by which the people know the political regime, abide by the rules, and participate in it. To perform this all-important role, a political ideology must have a *coherent set of rules* and must set them forth as clearly as possible. Although a constitution is a political document that embodies these rules, it cannot function well unless it is valued by the people. A political ideology shapes these values and beliefs about the constitution and lets the people know of their roles, positions, and rights within their own political regime.

Solidarity and Mobilization

A common sharing of ideas integrates individuals into the community, a group, a party, or a movement. Commonly held ideas define the things that are acceptable and the tasks to be accomplished, excluding all others. Ideologies play the same role that totems and taboos play in primitive tribes, defining what is common to the members and what is alien. The Soviet Communist ideology purported to unify those who adhered to it by branding the outside world of capitalism as the enemy. The same is increasingly so with Islamic fundamentalism. All ideologies perform this function of unifying, integrating, and giving a sense of identity to those who share it, but they do so with varying degrees of success. Nationalism as an ideology, for instance, has provided the unifying and integrating force that has made it possible for nation–states to emerge and retain their positions. The greater the integration sought and the stronger the solidarity to be maintained, the greater the emphasis on unifying symbolisms.

Leadership and Manipulation

Although ideologies incite people to action, what kind of action and for what purpose depend very much on the content and substance of an ideology. Manipulation of ideas, a special case, often involves the conscious and deliberate formulation of propositions that incite people to action for ends that are clearly perceived only by those in power or attempting to get political power. They may promise peace in order to make war, freedom in order to establish an authoritarian system, socialism in order to consolidate the position and privileges of the property holders, and so on.

Ideology can often be used as a powerful instrument of manipulation. Usually in times of social distress and anxiety, or when society seems divided into warring groups and frustration warps daily life, simple propositions and promises on how to remove the evils besetting society fall upon receptive ears and minds. Ideologies are great simplifiers. For instance, "Islam is the solution" is the cure-all slogan of Islamic fundamentalists. The demagogue, the leader, the self-professed savior is lurking somewhere in all societies at such times to spread his or her message and to manipulate those who seem to have nowhere else to turn.

Communication

A coherent set of ideas—an ideology—shared by a given number of people makes communication among them much easier. It provides a *common, highly simplified, special language*, like shorthand. Words have special meaning—"the Reds," "the bleeding-heart liberals," "the pigs," "the Establishment," "fat cats," "the power elite," "the chosen people," or "Communist conspiracy." These are terms easily understood by those who belong to a given group, and they help others to place them within a given ideological family. They are, of course, very crude terms, and ideologies usually provide more sophisticated ones. "The last stage of capitalism," "neocolonialism," "avant-garde of the working class," "democratic centralism," "democratic pluralism," "human rights," and "gradual change"are commonly understood by those who use them in their own respective political group or party. These terms can help the outsider to identify the ideological family to which the speaker belongs. A common ideology simplifies communication and makes common effort easier for all those who accept it.

Communication is also made easier because people with a common ideology look upon the outside world with the same preconceptions. They all have the same binoculars! People receive messages from the world outside and have to put these messages into some kind of order—into concepts. These concepts, in terms of which messages for the outside world are sorted out, depend on ideology. For some, the condition of the poor calls for study and concern; for others, it is a bore—the situation of the poor is attributed to innate laziness. This, however, is an extreme case. More frequent are cases of interpretation or evaluation, where the same event is seen from a different viewpoint—a different ideological perspective. The assassination of a political leader is applauded by some and mourned by others. During the Cold War, any Soviet move anywhere in the world was an indication of Communist aggression for some; for others, it was an inevitable reaction to American provocation! People may also reject messages because of their ideology. A mystic is blind to the world outside; for a scientist, the world is a constant source of wonder to be studied and explained.

Emotional Fulfillment

Some have argued that the primary function of an ideology is to rationalize and protect material interests or to provide for a powerful medium for their satisfaction. Thus, liberal democracy has been viewed as the rationalization of the interests of the rich and the relatively well-to-do, while socialism is an instrument for the satisfaction of the demands of those without property, the workers, and the poor. But it is not only interest that spawns an ideology. Emotional drives and personality traits are expressed through different ideologies. Not only do ideas simplify, they also tap emotions and often arouse the public into a frenzy. Nationalism and religious fundamentalism, Islamic or other, are but two illustrations among many. In recent years, the fight for or against abortion in the United States has reached a level of emotional crescendo that brooks no rational discourse and no easy compromise.

There also may be some correlation between ideology and personality types. There may be, for instance, an "authoritarian personality" that finds expression and fulfillment through being subject to rank and authority. An ideology can provide a form of expression to people with similar personality traits. Animal rights activists, environmentalists, proponents or opponents of the Equal Rights Amendment, as well as Democrats, Communists, and Fascists, all may give vent to their emotions through a particular ideology that fits their personality.

Ideology, then, provides for emotional fulfillment. People who share it are closely knit together; they share the same ambitions, interests, and goals and work together to bring them about. A person who has an ideology that is shared with a group of people is likely to be happy and secure: basking in the togetherness of a common endeavor. Identifying with it, he or she is never alone.

Criticism, Utopia, and Conservation

Ideologies often embody social criticism. Critical examination of social and political beliefs has played an important role in the development of new ideologies and the rejection of others. Many beliefs have yielded to it, to be replaced by others. Institutions like slavery, property, hereditary monarchy, bureaucratic centralization, and many others have been critically challenged and accordingly abandoned or qualified.

In certain instances, criticism may be pushed to extremes. Certain ideologies are like a *dream,* an impossible and unrealizable quest: world government, perfect equality, abundance for all, elimination of force, and abolition of war. Many political ideologies have something of this quality, but those that have it in an exaggerated form are called *utopias,* a word derived from the Greek for "nowhere." If we give this particular meaning to the term, we are implying that an "ideologue" is either naive or dangerous or a little bit crazy, ignoring Shakespeare's pithy remark that dreams are the stuff that life is made of! The opposite of an individual who dreams of utopia is one who accepts the existing state of affairs—the conservation of the status quo—of the values and ideas that we inherited.

The noted German sociologist Karl Mannheim made the distinction between "ideology," the set of values and beliefs we share about our society, and "utopia," the critical exposition of new ideas for its restructuring. It is hard—except in the extreme cases—to know when we deal with an "ideology" or a "utopia." While ideas constantly emerge to criticize existing values and beliefs, there are also ideologies dedicated to the preservation of values. Conservatives and fundamentalists extol with passion the past and romanticize it. In so doing, however, they, too, often verge on utopia, since a return to past traditions, values, and beliefs is cast in terms of a critical evaluation and rejection of the existing ideology. Most all ideologies, even conservative and preservative ones, include elements of criticism of the present. Moreover, most all utopias share elements of the prevailing truths and values, even if they propose to recast them. The kingdom of God or of the Prophet is part of the values and beliefs of many, but few would like to sacrifice themselves to bring it about; the greed and selfishness of human nature are acknowledged by most, but few would call for a revolution to transform it.

Ideology and Political Action

Above all, ideology *moves* people into concerted action. Sometimes it moves a whole nation; sometimes it is a group, a class, or a political party that unites people behind certain principles to express their interests, demands, and beliefs. In France, socialism is still for many the vindication of a long-standing quest for equality—material equality. In the United States, on the other hand, it is political and economic liberalism—the freedom to produce, consume, think, and worship—that seems to be the major rallying point for many political movements. An example of a single-issue organization motivated by ideology to take political action is the environmentalist group Greenpeace, which both in the United States and elsewhere seeks to put an end to the despoliation of our physical environment; it shares many of the same objectives as the various "No Nuke" organizations. Other powerful single groups want to reintroduce religious teaching and prayers in the schools, while still others mount a fierce campaign against abortion. "Welfare liberals" continue to reconcile freedoms with state intervention and welfare legislation to mitigate the harshness of economic competition. Communism—whether adopted by a nation, a movement, or a party that challenges the existing political order—is an ideology that projects a vision of abundance, equality, and peace. Most of the Communist movements have viewed the former Soviet Union as the legitimate advocate of a new social order that would replace the existing one. With the weakening of communism, many are searching now for a substitute.

The dynamics of politics, therefore, lie in the ideas people develop. But the same is true with political institutions, movements, social groups, and political parties. We have to focus on the ideologies they represent, and the beliefs they propagate and legitimize. The same is true for political attitudes. They, too, are fashioned by political ideologies. It is in terms of different constellations of attitudes that major political movements and ideologies can be identified and described. Liberals share common attitudes with regard to race relations, economic policy, prayers in the school, the United Nations, taxes, the draft, nuclear weapons, food stamps, social security, and so on. Conservatives can be identified in terms of a set of different attitudes with regard to some of the same issues; so can Socialists or Communists.

In studying political ideologies, we are also studying the dynamics of political systems—the type of political regime, its constitution, and institutions—the degree to which the regime is accepted, the existing conflicts within the regime, and the manner in which conflicts can be resolved. Compatibility of ideological outlooks makes for stability and acceptance; incompatibility always presages conflict, instability, and possibly revolution.

THE INTELLECTUALS

Most ideologies have been shaped by "intellectuals"—the clergy, lawyers, professors, writers. The American historian R. R. Palmer in his book *Twelve Who Ruled,* which discusses the "Committee of Public Safety" that was responsible for the terror and the use of the guillotine against opponents in the last year of the French Revolution, finds that all twelve members of the committee had one thing in common—they were intellectuals. They came from different classes and had different professions, had different careers and lifestyles. Those who engineered the Bolshevik Revolution were also intellectuals, versed in philosophy, economics, and history, conversant in three or four languages. The only exception was Stalin, who survived them all after disposing of them all! The road to both the American and French revolutions had been paved by intense literary and philosophic work, with the writing of Benjamin Franklin, Thomas Paine, and Thomas Jefferson, and in France by the remarkable body of literature produced by a new school of intellectuals—the Encyclopedists.

Who are the intellectuals, and why do they play such an important role in the creation of ideas associated with the formulation of a new political ideology? There are no easy answers. But if we assume that most ideologies reflect interest, class, or status and rationalize given positions in the society, then ideas are directly linked with them. Rarely can ideologies rise above such positions or be dissociated from the interests with which they are linked—be they material or spiritual ones. The intellectuals, however, represent a group of people with no such positions and no such linkages or attachments to interests. They float somehow between, among, and above them. In this sense they have more freedom than all others to criticize and dream. They can use the word, written and spoken, the typewriter, the radio, the press, and the TV better than others—that is why they are intellectuals—and can therefore direct new messages where they wish. For example, it was a group of intellectuals in Britain who at the end of the nineteenth century introduced socialism.

Intellectuals criticize and manage to elevate their criticism to new ideological heights that transcend the existing formulations. In the same way that inventors or talented managers may renovate the state of the art in a trade or industry, intellectuals attempt to renovate society, its life, and its values, but with a far wider impact. The intellectuals influence profoundly and reshape our views and perceptions, and one of the reasons they do not dominate the society—except in some extreme cases—is that they are not a coherent group with common ideas, like a party. In fact, they are constantly at odds with each other. Another reason is that their messages are resisted by those to whom they are addressed—people don't like change. For instance, there has been a shared distrust between left-wing intellectuals and workers in liberal democracies. Workers feared that the ideology of intellectuals was but a device for them to gain power without necessarily providing to the workers the benefits they had promised. Workers feared that the Marxists intellectuals would become a "new class."[2] There has been little love lost, too, between the British Socialist intellectuals and the British trade unions. Similarly, during the uprisings against the "Establishment" in many liberal democracies in the late 1960s, which were spearheaded by intellectuals and students, the workers were reluctant to join in the protests. When they did, it was to improve their wages and conditions of work, not to change the society. As for the intellectuals in liberal capitalist regimes that purport to be democratic, they never made their peace with property and the free-market economy and more generally with the materialistic ethics of capitalism. For many of them, Marxism became the major weapon of criticism. It became a passionate commitment to save us all by creating a new society. It became in the words of another intellectual, Raymond Aron, an opium—intoxicating the intellectuals and opiating the people.[3]

Whether they dispense lifesaving drugs or opium pills, it is the function of intellectuals to stir up our thinking and our ideas about the world. They are a thorn in the flesh of every established order and prevailing ideology. Socrates was the first of many thousands to pay the price with his life. Scratch each and all of the intellectuals and you will find an ideologue. But by and large, they remain divided and therefore harmless. Only those among them who begin to develop a common set of beliefs geared to a common goal and who are in search of a new order may play an important role. They become "organic" intellectuals, assembling and synthesizing existing beliefs, compromising among many, rejecting others, and suggesting new ones until they form a "bloc."[4]

By and large, intellectuals perform a critical and innovative role that all societies need. They criticize the old and constantly open up new horizons of thought and social endeavor. As long as they exist, the formation of ideology will flourish.

TYPES OF POLITICAL IDEOLOGIES

Political ideologies address themselves to values: the quality of life, the distribution of goods and services, freedom and equality. If there were agreement on each of these values, there would be a single ideology shared by all. But there is no agreement within any society nor, needless to say, among the various political societies of the world. People hold different views; nations project different values and beliefs.

---

[2]Daniel Bell, *The End of Ideology*, pp. 355–357. Djilas, *New Class, An Analysis of the Communist System.*
[3]Raymond Aron, *The Opium of the Intellectuals.*
[4]The terms were used by the Italian Communist intellectual Antonio Gramsci.

It is precisely here that we see the role of political ideologies: they mobilize men and women into action in favor of one point of view or another, and in favor of one movement or party or another. Their aim is invariably either the preservation of a given point of view or the overhaul of the existing state of things, including the political system itself. British squires who defended their privilege and property; the workers who formed trade unions or parties to defend their interests; the American conservatives—all have had a common set of ideas that united them into a common posture. The same is true for the small terrorist bands who seize planes. They want to destroy what they despise most—the complacency of an orderly society interested in material satisfaction.

We can divide political ideologies into three broad categories.

1. Those that defend and rationalize the existing economic, social, and political order at any given time in any given society, which we call *status quo* ideologies.
2. Ideologies that advocate far-reaching changes in the existing social, economic, and political order, which we call *radical* or *revolutionary* ideologies.
3. In between there is, of course, a large gray area favoring change. We may call these the *reformist* ideologies.

One way to state the difference between *status quo, reformist,* and *revolutionary* ideologies is to think of maps and mapmaking. Someone who diligently learns to read a map and to travel by following given routes and signals may be considered to represent a status quo mentality or ideology: he or she simply follows the rules and the signs and is guided by them. On the other hand, a person who attempts to trace his or her own route and to change the signals, but not the destination, is a reformist. There is an agreement that the means must change, not the end. *But a revolutionary changes both the map and the destination.*

This classification is merely a formal one because ideologies shift and change not only in content but also in the particular functions and roles they perform. A revolutionary ideology, for instance, may become transformed into one of status quo when it succeeds in imposing its own values and beliefs. Similarly, the same ideology may be a status quo ideology, protecting the existing order of things in a given place at a given time, and a revolutionary one in a different place or at a different time. Communism in the former Soviet Union was a status quo political ideology, while in other countries communism was considered to be a revolutionary one. While workers in the nineteenth century were protesting in the name of socialism against Western European liberalism, which had become a status quo ideology, liberalism was very much a revolutionary ideology in the eyes of many in Central Europe and Russia.

Status quo, reformist, and revolutionary ideologies can also be distinguished by the tactics used to realize goals. These include persuasion, organization, and force. Few, if any, ideologies rely exclusively on any one to the exclusion of others. Most use, in different proportions, all these tactics. The more fundamental and comprehensive the goals are and the more an ideology challenges the status quo, the greater the chances that it will be translated into a political movement that will resort to organized force, without, of course, neglecting organization and persuasion. A political ideology, on the other hand, that has limited and incremental goals, as is the case with reformist ideologies, is more likely to resort to political organization and persuasion.

In general, political ideologies and movements that challenge the status quo are more likely to use force at the time when they confront it. This was the case with liberalism before it overthrew the aristocratic and monarchical regimes in the eighteenth century and after, and with the Communist and other revolutionary movements first in Russia and later in other countries. Yet, when such political ideologies succeed—when they have been transformed into political regimes and have implemented their major goals and consolidated their position—persuasion and organization are likely to take the place of force.

There is one qualification to these generalizations. According to some analysts, there are some political ideologies for which force is a necessary and permanent characteristic. And there are others for which persuasion and political organization, rather than force, are inherent characteristics. Some authoritarian systems—and Communist regimes are included—institutionalize the use of force in order to bring about and maintain compliance. On the other hand, liberal and democratic regimes, committed to political competition and pluralism, eschew the use of force. If it is to be used, it is only as a last resort.

THE MAJOR POLITICAL IDEOLOGIES

Criteria of Choice

If we look at the spread of contemporary political ideological movements, we have a rich choice of subjects: liberalism, capitalism, democratic socialism, socialism, communism, national communism, consociationalism, corporatism, Eurocommunism, anarchism, Gaullism, Stalinism and post-Stalinism, communalism, self-determination in industry, Titoism, Maoism, welfarism, to say nothing of variations that come from the Third World under various labels. Which ones do we discuss, and why? We obviously need some criteria to help, and I suggest four: *coherence, pervasiveness, extensiveness,* and *intensiveness.*

Coherence   By coherence I have in mind the overall scope of an ideology, along with its internal logic and structure. Is it complete? Does it clearly spell out a set of goals and the means to bring them about? Do its various propositions about social, economic, and political life hang together? Is there an organization—a movement or a party—to promote the means of action envisaged?

Pervasiveness   Pervasiveness refers to the length of time that an ideology has been "operative." Some ideologies may be in decline over a period, only to reappear. Others have been operative over a long period, despite variations and qualifications. Whatever the case, the basic test is the length of time during which an ideology has been shared by people, affected their lives, and shaped their attitudes and actions.

Extensiveness   The criterion of extensiveness refers simply to a crude numerical test. How many people share a given ideology? One can draw a crude "ideological map" showing the number of people sharing common political ideologies.

The larger the "population space" of a given ideology, the greater its extensiveness. How many people are influenced today by communism? By liberalism? By socialism? By anarchism? By religious fundamentalism? An estimate of numbers will answer the question of extensiveness.

Intensiveness   Finally, by intensiveness I mean the degree and the intensity of the appeal of an ideology—irrespective of whether it satisfies any of the other three criteria. Does it evoke a spirit of total loyalty and action? "Interest is sluggish," wrote John Stuart Mill. Ideas are not! They are like weapons, which in the hands of even a small minority may have a far greater impact on society than widely shared interests. Intensiveness implies emotional commitment, total loyalty, and unequivocal determination to act even at the risk of one's life. It was this kind of intensiveness that Lenin managed to impart to his Bolsheviks and to the Communist party.

Ideally, we should choose among various ideologies only those that satisfy *all* the criteria set forth here—coherence, pervasiveness, extensiveness, and intensiveness. However, this would fail to do justice to some ideologies that have played or are playing an important role in our political life, even though they may satisfy only one or two of these criteria, and so I intend to take several such movements into account. (See Table 1.1 for a sampling of ideologies and how they fare according to these four criteria.)

Table 1.1   THE POLITICAL IDEOLOGIES DISCUSSED

	Coherence	Pervasiveness	Extensiveness	Intensiveness
Democratic liberalism	Strong	Long	Wide	Weak
Democratic socialism	Weak	Long	Wide	Mediocre
Utopian socialism	Weak	Sporadic	Limited	High
Communism	Strong, but rapidly weakening	Long, but in the process of being questioned	Wide, but in the process of being regionalized	High, but increasingly weakening
Conservatism	Weak	Long	Wide	Weak
Fascism/nazism	Weak	Sporadic	Uncertain	High
Nationalism	Weak	Long	Wide	High
Anarchism	Weak	Sporadic	Limited	High
Religious fundamentalism	Strong	Sporadic	Selective, regional	Very high
Feminism	Weak	Gaining	Progressively widening	Uncertain
Environmentalism	Weak	Recent	Widening	Mediocre, but increasing

For each ideology discussed, I begin by examining the basic theoretical formulations to which it owes a major debt and describe its transformation into a political movement and, in some cases, into a political regime. We should never lose sight of the fact that we are dealing with ideas that become political movements and lead people to political action; and the fact that their "influence" can be assessed in terms of the strength of the movements and parties through which ideas become readied and armed for a struggle for supremacy. Ideologies are not disembodied entities; they are not abstractions. They exist because men and women share them and adopt them as part of their own lives. Ideologies are weapons when men and women make them so; but they are also havens that produce companionship, cooperation, and fufillment.

Value Judgment   One last remark is in order. If there are so many ideologies, and if all of us share different ideologies to help us "know" the outside world and to prompt us to act in one way or another, which one of them is "correct"? If all ideologies provide us with different views and perceptions of the world, how do we know what the world is really like? How can we describe the landscape if we use different binoculars? This is the nagging question throughout the book—the question of the validity of a given ideology. When it comes to political ideologies, there is really no authoritative test to produce definitive proof of validity. We can only present the various political ideologies in terms of their internal logic, their coherence, their relevance to the outside world, and the passion and intensity for action they infuse.

This book does not ask, therefore, which ideologies are "true" and which are "false." Instead, our approach will be expository: Where does an ideology come from? What does it posit? What does it purport to achieve? What have been its accomplishments or failures?

BIBLIOGRAPHY

Abercrombie, N., et al. *The Dominant Ideology*. London: Allen and Unwin, 1980.

Apter, David (ed.). *Ideology and Its Discontents*. Englewood Cliffs, N.J.: Prentice-Hall, 1964.

Aristotle. *Politics*. Translated by Ernest Barker. New York: Oxford University Press, 1962.

Aron, Raymond. *The Opium of the Intellectuals*. New York: Norton, 1962.

Bailyn, Bernard. *The Ideological Origins of the American Revolution*. Cambridge, MA.: Harvard University Press, 1967.

Bell, Daniel. *The End of Ideology*, rev. ed. New York: Free Press, 1965.

Benda, Julien. *The Betrayal of the Intellectuals*. Boston: Beacon Press, 1955 (Transl. by Richard Aldington).

Bluhm, William T. *Ideologies and Attitudes: Modern Political Culture*. Englewood Cliffs, N.J.: Prentice-Hall, 1974.

Bracher, Karl D. *The Age of Ideologies: A History of Political Thought in the Twentieth Century*. London: Weindenfeld and Nicolson, 1982.

Brown, L. B. *Ideology*. New York: Penguin, 1973.

Cox, Richard H. *Ideology, Politics and Political Theory*. Belmont, Calif.: Wadsworth, 1968.

Djilas, Milovan. *The New Class: An Analysis of the Communist System*. New York: Holt, 1957.

Feuer, L. *Ideology and the Ideologists*. Oxford: Basil Blackwell, 1975.

Gramsci, Antonio. *Selections from the Prison Notebooks*, edited and translated by Quintin Hoare and Geoffrey N. Smith. London: Lawrence and Wishart, 1971.

———— *Selections from Political Writings*. edited and translated by Quintin Hoare and Geoffrey N. Smith. London: Lawrence and Wishart, 1977.

Grimes, Alan, and Robert Horowitz (eds.). *Modern Political Ideologies*. New York: Oxford University Press, 1959.

Habermas, J. *Legitimation Crisis*. London: Heinemann, 1976.

Hartz, Louis. *The Liberal Tradition in America*. New York: Harcourt, 1955.

Hill, Christopher. *The World Turned Upside Down: Radical Ideas During the English Revolution*. London, England: Penguin, 1975.

Jenkins, Thomas. *The Study of Political Theory*. New York: Random House, 1955.

Kramnick, I., and Frederick Watkins. *The Age of Ideology—Political Thought 1950 to the Present*. Englewood Cliffs, N.J.: Prentice-Hall, 1964.

Lefebre, Georges. *The Coming of the French Revolution*. Princeton, N.J.: Princeton University Press, 1967.

Lerner, Max. *Ideas Are Weapons: The History and Uses of Ideas*. New York: Viking, 1939.

Lichtheim, George. *The Concept of Ideology and Other Essays*. New York: Random House, 1967.

Mannheim, Karl. *Ideology and Utopia*. New York: Harcourt, 1955.

Marx, Karl. *Theses on Feuerbach*. In Robert C. Tucker: *The Marx-Engels Reader*, 2nd Ed. W. W. Norton, New York, 1978, pp. 143–146.

McLellan, D. *Marxism after Marx*. London: Macmillan, 1980.

————. *Ideology*. Minneapolis: University of Minnesota Press, 1986.

Oakeshott, Michael. *The Social and Political Doctrines of Contemporary Europe*. New York: Cambridge University Press, 1942.

Palmer, R. R. *Twelve Who Ruled*. Princton, N.J.: Princeton University Press, 1961.

Plamenatz, John. *Ideology*. New York: Praeger, 1970.

Rude, George. *Ideology and Popular Protest*. London: Lawrence and Wishart, 1980.

Schumpter, Joseph. *Capitalism, Socialism and Democracy*, 3rd ed. New York: Harper & Row, 1950.

Shklar, Judith N. *Political Theory and Ideology*. New York: Macmillan, 1966.

Thompson, J. *Studies in the Theory of Ideology*. *Cambridge University Press*, Cambridge, England: 1984.

Trigg, Roger. *Ideas of Human Nature: An Historical Introduction*. Cambridge, Mass.: Basil Blackwell, 1988.

Watkins, Frederick. *The Age of Ideology: Political Thought from 1750 to the Present*. Englewood Cliffs, N.J.: Prentice-Hall, 1964.

Wolin, Sheldon. *Politics and Vision*. Boston: Little, Brown, 1960.

One

DEMOCRACY: MANY ROOTS AND FAMILIES

Our constitution is called a democracy because power is in the hands not of the few but of the many.

Thucydides *Funeral Oration of Pericles*

*D*emocracy literally means "the government of the people." It comes from the Greek words *demos,* people, and *kratos,* government or power. The concept developed first in the small Greek city–states, the Athenian democracy (roughly between 450 B.C. and 350 B.C.) is what we usually point to as the principal early example. Pericles, the great Athenian statesman, speaking in 431 B.C., defined democracy in the following terms:

> Our constitution is named a democracy, because it is in the hands not of the few but of the many. But our laws secure equal justice for all in their private disputes and our public opinion welcomes and honors talent in every branch of achievement . . . on grounds of excellence alone. . . . Our citizens attend both to public and private duties and do not allow absorption in their various affairs to interfere with their knowledge of the city's. . . . We decide or debate, carefully and in person, all matters of policy, hold-ing . . . that acts are foredoomed to failure when undertaken undiscussed.[1]

In this classic formulation, Pericles identifies the following characteristics of a democracy:

---

[1]Thucydides, *The History of the Peloponnesian War.* Edited and translated by Sir Richard Livingston. New York: Oxford University Press, 1951, pp. 111–113.

1. Government by the people with the full and direct participation of the people.
2. Equality before the law.
3. Pluralism—that is, respect for all talents, pursuits, and viewpoints.
4. Respect for a separate and private (as opposed to public) domain for fulfillment and expression of an individual's personality.

Participation, equality before the law, pluralism, and individualism for everyone (except for women and also the many slaves)—these were the cornerstones of early democracy, before it disappeared from Greece and the then known world after a relatively short revival in Rome.

CONTEMPORARY DEMOCRACY: MAJOR PHASES

Contemporary democratic thought can be traced back to the sixteenth century and earlier. It has many roots: feudal practices and institutions, theories about natural law and natural rights, the religious wars and the demand for toleration, the assertion of property rights and freedom to pursue individual economic ventures, the notion of limitations upon political authority—to name the most important of them. The basic landmark is provided by the English philosopher John Locke who, writing in the latter part of the seventeenth century, developed in some detail four of the cardinal concepts of democracy: *equality, individual rights and freedoms, including property, government based upon consent of the governed,* and *limitations upon the state.* Locke's theories led to the development of representative and parliamentary government.

The second historical landmark—the emergence of economic liberalism—came with the works of Adam Smith, especially his *Wealth of Nations* (1776), and of a new school of radical philosophers known as the *utilitarians.* In the first half of the nineteenth century, they developed the theory of the "economic man" who is driven by twin impulses: to satisfy pleasure and avoid pain. In line with Adam Smith, they constructed a theoretically limited state that would allow individuals freedom to pursue their own interests. The utilitarians became the exponents of economic individualism—that is, capitalism.

Throughout the nineteenth century, Locke's theory of consent and representative government was broadened, but economic liberalism and economic individualism came constantly under scrutiny and criticism. The works of the French philosopher Jean-Jacques Rousseau, especially his *Social Contract* (1762), were used to broaden the theory of participation so as to include everybody. The role of the state was reassessed to favor more intervention in economic and social matters for the better protection of the poor, the unemployed, the old, the young, and many disadvantaged groups. For the first time the notion of a *positive state*—one that acts to provide social services and to guarantee economic rights—appeared. Finally, beginning in the twentieth century and extending well into the present, socialists and a growing number of democrats have begun to broaden the notion of a positive state. They ask for sweeping reforms of the economic system so that the state assumes the obligation of providing an ever-increasing number of services. This has come to be known as the *welfare state*.

Socialists question economic individualism and want to replace it with a system in which the major productive resources are owned and managed by the state itself. The economy is to be run by the state, no longer for the purpose of profit, but to further social and community needs. Many of the Socialist parties were committed to this position until very recently, representing a synthesis that combined democratic political and individual rights with massive state intervention in the economy and socialization of some of the major units of production. In this part we do not include, of course, Marxism and the Communist regimes since they rejected democratic political practices and committed themselves to the socialization and management by the state of every branch of the economy—including trade, agriculture, and services.

In discussing democracy as an ideology, we are dealing therefore with a very rich and comprehensive body of thought and action—one that has undergone shifts and changes in the past three centuries and has produced a great variety of political movements. We will look at the liberal phase of democracy, its political and economic doctrine and institutions, its welfarist, socialist, or collectivist phase, and again the most recent reassertion of economic liberalism—capitalism.

Chapter
2

Democracy and Liberalism

Give me the liberty to know, to utter, and to argue freely according to conscience.

John Milton *AREOPAGITICA*

Laissez-faire, laissez-passer.

*T*he individual—his or her experiences and interests—is the basic concept associated with the origin and growth of liberalism and liberal societies. Knowledge and truth are derived from the judgment of the individual, which in turn is formed by the associations his or her senses make of the outside world—from experience. There is no established truth, nor any transcendental values. Individual experience becomes the supreme value in itself, and the joining of many individual experiences in deliberation is the best possible way for a community to make decisions.

In its earliest phase, individualism is cast in terms of natural rights—freedom and equality. It is steeped in moral and religious thought, but already the first signs of a psychology appear that considers material interests and their satisfaction to be important in the motivation of the individual. In its second phase, it is based on a psychological theory according to which the realization of interest is the major force that motivates individuals. In its third phase, it becomes "economic liberalism"—generally referred to as capitalism.

Interest, in turn, is related to satisfaction of pleasure. Liberalism is anchored on this simple proposition: men and women strive to maximize pleasure and minimize pain. But it is not up to the collectivity to impose pleasure or pain; it is not up to a philosopher or a political party to determine it. On the contrary, it is up to individuals to pursue it and in so doing fulfill themselves. Knowledge that stems from experience and education will presumably set limits beyond which the maximization of pleasure will not be pushed; similarly, competition in an open market will set limits to individual enrichment.

The propositions of early liberalism were directed against eighteenth-century absolutism and the many feudal practices that lingered on. Absolutism, supported by a landed aristocracy, stifled human activity while maintaining the feudal privileges of the nobility at a time when the growth of manufacturing and commerce (even if ever so gradual) had begun to open up new vistas of individual effort, exploration, wealth, and change. National communities were divided internally into many jurisdictions with different laws, different standards, different tariffs, different regulations, and different weights and measures, all of which impeded communication, trade, and individual freedoms. The famous expression *laissez-faire, laissez-passer* was the battle cry of the burghers, the tradesmen, the money-lenders, the small manufacturers. "Let us do, let us pass" was the motto of the new middle classes. This liberalism was a challenge to the existing order, because laissez-faire capitalism, as we still call it, was the ideology that expressed the interests of the middle class; it stood against absolutism, and especially against political and economic constraints.

Liberals proclaimed individualism and individual freedoms—especially freedom of movement and trade; they borrowed from the past to develop what gradually became a comprehensive theory of individual rights to challenge and to limit absolute political power; they appealed to and represented the new rising classes and the new forms of wealth that began to appear in Western Europe. They also received the support of the peasants, against the landed aristocracy, and the workingmen, who became attracted by the promise of freedoms and equality. As a political ideology, liberalism appealed to large sectors of the society, while being opposed by the monarchy, the landed aristocracy, and the church.

THE THREE CORES OF LIBERALISM

Liberalism consists of three cores. One is moral, the second is political, and the third is economic. The *moral* core contains an affirmation of basic values and rights attributable to the "nature" of a human being—freedom, dignity, and life—subordinating everything else to their implementation. The *political* core includes primarily political rights—the right to vote, to participate, to decide what kind of government to elect, and what kind of policies to follow. It is associated with representative democracy. The *economic* core has to do with economic and property rights. It is still referred to as "economic individualism," the "free enterprise system," or "capitalism," and pertains to the rights and freedoms of individuals to produce and to consume, to enter into contractual relations, to buy and sell through a market economy, to satisfy their wants in their own way, and to dispose of their own property and labor as they decide. Its cornerstones have been private property and a market economy that is free from state controls and regulations.

The Moral Core

Long before Christianity, the notion had developed that the individual human being has innate qualities and potentialities commanding the highest respect.

Because each individual is imparted with a spark of divine will or reason, each should be protected, respected, and given freedom to seek fulfillment.

The Stoics and the Epicureans put individuals—their freedom, their detachment, their personal life—above all considerations of social utility or political expediency. Early Christians went a step further to proclaim that all individuals are the children of God, that we are all brothers and sisters, that our first duty is to God, and that salvation is the ultimate fulfillment. Temporal powers cannot impinge on this, but even if they did (in order, for example, to collect taxes or to maintain order), there were still many things that belonged *only* to God.

A number of inferences stem from this notion of the moral and rational nature of the individual. Many of them have been institutionalized in the practice of liberalism and continue to be essential to it. Recent proclamations supporting human rights in the United Nations and elsewhere represent one of the oldest battle cries of liberalism.

Personal Liberty   Personal liberty consists of all those rights guaranteeing the individual protection against government. It is the requirement that men and women live under a known law with known procedures. Locke wrote: "Freedom is . . . to have a standing rule to live by, common to everyone of that society and made by the legislative power erected in it."[1] Such a law protects all and restrains the rulers. It corresponds to individual "freedoms"—freedom to think, talk, and worship. No police officer will enter one's home at night without due authority; no individual, even the poorest or lowest, will be thrown into prison without a chance to hear the charges and argue before a judge; no citizen will have to discover one Sunday morning that his or her church is closed, or that a son or daughter has disappeared, and so forth. To American students such freedoms appear self-evident and naturally due. Unfortunately, this is not quite so; in fact, they are in constant jeopardy everywhere.

Civil Liberty   While personal liberties in general define a set of protections, civil liberties indicate the free and positive channels and areas of human activity and participation. In liberal ideology and practice, they are equally valued. Basic to the liberal faith is the concept of freedom of thought. The only way to define this positively is to state it as the right of individuals to think their own thoughts and learn in their own ways from experience, with no one impeding the process. Freedom of thought is closely associated with freedom of expression, freedom of speech, freedom to write, freedom to publish and disseminate one's thoughts, freedom to discuss things with others, and freedom to associate with others in the peaceful expression of ideas. We find these freedoms enshrined in the First Amendment to the U.S. Constitution, and also in many solemn documents in British and European political history—the Bill of Rights, the Petition of Rights, the Declaration of the Rights of Man, and so on.

The achievement and implementation of full civil liberties in the societies of Western Europe and the United States took time. Until the end of the nineteenth

---

[1]John Locke, *Second Treatise on Civil Government*, chap. 4.

century, there were countries where people were excluded from political partici-pation because of their ideas, religion, or race. Censoring the books, pamphlets, and the press was a common practice long after Milton wrote his famous pamphlet against censorship, *The Areopagitica,* in 1644. Freedom of the press had a partic-ularly shaky existence until the end of the nineteenth century, and freedom of asso-ciation—to form clubs, groups of like-minded people, political parties, trade unions, and religious sects—was hedged and qualified until almost the same time.

What is more, at no time could civil liberties be taken for granted. There were and still are constant exceptions and setbacks. There is always an inclination on the part of certain groups to deny to others what they do not like, and there is a perva-sive suspicion on the part of political authorities of nonconformist and dissenting groups.

Social Liberty   Freedom of thought and expression and protections against government in the form of personal and civil rights have little value if individuals are not given proper recognition so that they can work and live in accordance with their talents and capabilities. Social liberty corresponds to what we refer to today as opportunities for advancement or social mobility. It is the right of all individu-als, irrespective of race and creed and irrespective of the position of their parents, to be given every opportunity to attain a position in society commensurate with their capabilities. Personal liberties may become empty or purely formal prescrip-tions otherwise. There is little hope in the lives of disadvantaged Mexican Ameri-cans, African Americans, or the poor if they know that they and their children will always remain tied to the same occupation, status, education, and income. Only when equal opportunities are provided for all can there be freedom for all.

The Economic Core

As already pointed out, liberalism was the ideology of the middle classes, which rose to replace the old landed aristocracy. Their purpose was to liberate individual economic activity, to establish large trading areas that expanded to the nation–state and if possible the world, and to do away with all obstacles to the transport and trade of goods. It was their aim to reorganize the economy, to introduce new meth-ods (the market), and to invest capital in factories and machines.

Economic liberties, and in general the economic core of liberalism, assumed at least as great an importance as what we have called the moral core. The right to property, the right of inheritance, the right to accumulate wealth and capital, free-dom to produce, sell, and buy—all contractual freedoms—became an essential part of the new social order. Emphasis was put on the voluntary character of the relations between various economic factors, whether the employer, the worker, the lender, the producer, or the consumer. Freedom of contract was more valued than freedom of speech. A pattern of social life in which people were born and belonged in certain social categories or groups was shattered, and the individuals became free to shape their own situation by voluntary acts and contractual rela-tions with others. One great British historian, Sir Henry Maine, claimed that the essence of liberalism lay precisely in this transition from "status" (fixed group relations) to "contract" (individual self-determination).

The meeting point of various individual wills, where contractual relations are made, is the market. Here the individual—the famous "economic man"—propelled by self-interest, buys and sells, hires laborers, borrows or loans money, invests in joint-stock companies or maritime ventures, and finds employment. The market reflects the supply and demand for goods, and this in turn determines their prices. The market is the best barometer to register economic activity, because demand obviously pushes prices up, and hence incites production until the demand is met and prices begin to level off. Since the market does not sanction the incompetent and the inefficient, goods produced that do not meet a demand or are not widely desirable fall in price, until the producer is driven out of business, and replaced by a shrewder one.

Thousands of individual entrepreneurs face not only millions of consumers, who compare quality and prices, but also each other. If a given product sells well and fast, other manufacturers will produce it, increasing the supply and thus bringing prices down. The system is supposed to be both sensitive to consumer demand as well as entirely open, allowing for the entry of new competitors and the exit of unsuccessful ones. Prices faithfully register the volume of demand and supply adjusted to it.

It is a system that at least in theory favors the consumer: prices cannot be fixed, the volume of production cannot be controlled, competition makes monopolies or cartels impossible. But the gains for the producers are also great; they can take advantage of the same law of supply and demand in hiring or dismissing workers, in settling on the wages to be paid, and in setting the prices of new products. It is a system that provides the best mechanism both for production and the satisfaction of wants, and its classic formulation was provided by Adam Smith.

Adam Smith and *The Wealth of Nations*   The bible of liberal economic theory was, and still remains, Adam Smith's *The Wealth of Nations*. Smith's purpose was to open the channels of free individual economic effort and to defend the free-market economy as the best instrument for the growth of wealth—individual, national, and worldwide. Each person, he assumed, is the best judge of his or her actions and interests. If people are allowed a free hand to pursue these interests they will, and by so doing will improve the wealth of the society and the nation as a whole. What counts above all is to give free rein to individual action. Adam Smith was what we would call today a moral and compassionate man. He was not particularly happy with the notions of greed and self-enrichment associated with the materialistic ethic that was emerging. But he believed, nonetheless, that self-interest—the profit motive—was the best vehicle for economic growth and the well-being of society as a whole. The cure to self-interest, even to greed, was to make it available to all through the market and competition! Let businessmen raise prices with an eye to high profits, others will be attracted to manufacture the same goods, and the supply will increase and the prices fall. High prices, in general, attract producers and lead to competition that will bring about lower prices and increase efficiency in production by reducing costs. In this way, private

Adam Smith (1723–1790)

Adam Smith, a social philosopher and political economist, is best known for his major work, *An Inquiry into the Nature and Causes of the Wealth of Nations* (1776), in which he developed his theories of economic liberalism, competition, and free trade. His major plea was to release human activity from all state administrative and economic controls, allowing the individuals to seek individual profit and the satisfaction of wants. Adam Smith claimed that there were fundamental economic laws, such as the law of supply and demand, that provided for the self-regulation of the economy. He is the father of economic liberalism.

property and profit in a free market benefit all. This is the famous "paradox": private gain becomes translated into public good.

Adam Smith favored a limited state. The government, he argued, should limit itself to three major tasks: defense, internal order and justice, and "certain public works or certain public institutions, which can never be for the interest of any individual, or small number of individuals, to erect and maintain." This last task looks like a big hole in the wall between the state and the economy that he erects, and we return to it later. But it is safe to say that what he had primarily in mind for the government was education, roads, a postal service, control of certain natural monopolies (i.e., water), and a program of public assistance for the poor. He was adamantly opposed to government interference in the market. The market alone would determine prices. He was against price-fixing, direct and indirect subsidies, protectionist devices, and outright grants and preferences for some industries and goods, as opposed to others.

Adam Smith was also the staunchest advocate of a worldwide free trade. It could provide for competition and, hence, efficiency and lower prices that ultimately would mean wealth for those across borders. In a famous passage, he pointed out that wine could be grown in Scotland instead of importing it from France. Special soil could be brought in, hothouses could be built, special moisture mechanisms developed. And the wine produced might even taste the same as the French versions—but the cost would be thirty times higher than French imports! His arguments are still heard today in meetings of the GATT (General Agreement on Trade and Tariffs), in which about a hundred nations are represented, as they try to promote free trade.

Though Adam Smith spoke of the "Divine Hand of Providence" bringing order and wealth out of the myriad individual wills and interests that compete with each other in trying to satisfy their respective interests, his faith was not in divine providence. Rather, he believed that a social and economic harmony would result from the free competition and interplay of economic interests and forces. In his words, natural order would be promoted in every country by the natural inclinations of the individuals if political institutions had never thwarted those natural inclinations. If all systems of restraint were completely taken away, natural liberty would establish itself. Or as one of Smith's followers put the matter even more succinctly:

> As soon as a need becomes the object of public service the individual loses part of his freedom, becomes less progressive and less man. He becomes prone to moral inertia which spreads out to all citizens.[2]

Jeremy Bentham and Utilitarianism   But the real father of liberalism was Jeremy Bentham. His philosophy, followed also by James Mill and John Stuart

---

[2]Cited by Harold Laski, *The Rise of European Liberalism*, p. 203.

Jeremy Bentham (1748–1831)

Jeremy Bentham was the founder of the Utilitarian School, which proposed that people maximize pleasure and minimize pain (the so-called *felicific calculus*), and that these impulses were the source of human motivation. His various works, such as *Fragment on Government* and *Defense of Usury,* and most particularly his *Introduction to the Principles of Morals and Legislation,* expounded the theories of individualism and economic freedom. Benthamite liberals were extremely influential through the nineteenth century in England in pushing for administrative, criminal law, taxation, and economic reforms.

Mill, is known as *utilitarianism,,* from the term utility. Its basic elements can be summarized as follows:

1. Every object has a utility—that is, every object can satisfy a want.
2. Utility, as the attribute of an object, is subjective. It is what we like or do not like. It is amenable only to some crude quantifiable criteria that relate to the duration, the intensity, and the proximity of the pleasure that a given object can provide. There are no qualitative criteria that can be established

by anybody but the user. For some, a poem has a greater "utility" than a hot dog. For others, the hot dog comes first. The market ultimately registers utility as a reflection of the volume of goods in demand.

3. The purpose of our lives is to increase pleasure (that is, to use goods that have utility for each one of us) and to avoid pain. This is the *hedonistic* or the *felicific calculus* that applies not just in economic life but also in any other aspect of an individual's existence.

In order to work, this utilitarian model must be allowed to operate freely. If every man and woman were free to maximize pleasure and avoid pain, "the greatest happiness for the greatest number" would result. More people would be happy than unhappy!

The concept of utility and the utilitarian ethic are not restricted to the economy. It applies to everything. Social institutions, artistic works, education, philosophy—all must meet the test of utility and provide pleasure, in varying degrees, to some, or conversely result in pain if they are absent. *Utility* as a criterion of social, political, and economic life replaces moral and natural *rights*.

Thus, millions of individuals armed with small calculators, so to speak, constantly measure the pleasurable and the painful helping us to maximize the first and to minimize the second. The calculations are always directly related to self-interest, but they are not necessarily simple. The individual will have to balance a number of requirements—for example, the immediate utility an object may have compared to the far greater utility it may represent in five or ten years; the possibility of suffering deprivation and even pain *now* in order to enjoy pleasure later on; the pain that may be suffered in order to derive pleasure from protecting loved ones; the intensity of a given pleasure as opposed to its duration; and finally, overall considerations of peace and tranquility at home and national defense against outside enemies. The latter, too, represent a utility, no matter what the immediate pain of providing for them may be.

These considerations show that, while self-interest and the pleasure-maximizing calculations are the motivating force for all of us, a point comes when considerations other than the pure and immediate satisfaction of interest enter into the equation of social, political, and economic life. Self-interest gives way to *enlightened* self-interest.

John Stuart Mill and Enlightened Self-interest   Enlightened self-interest becomes an important criterion to guide the individual. For instance, someone who forgoes an immediate pleasure in order to derive a greater one later on shows enlightenment. Enjoying smaller pleasures in order to maintain a *fairly* pleasurable existence, rather than insisting on the maximum pleasure possible and in the process risking the loss of everything, also shows enlightenment. The same criteria apply to groups or classes of people. If they act in terms of enlightened self-interest, they may consider concessions to other social groups or classes rather than risk the loss of all they have.

John Stuart Mill came to grips with this problem by redefining utility. He introduces qualitative standards and establishes a hierarchy of pleasures on the basis of criteria that are *not* subjective. Some pleasures are better than others

John Stuart Mill (1806–1873)

John Stuart Mill was an English philosopher, who had studied under the strict tutelage of his father, a foremost utilitarian, James Mill. John Stuart Mill considerably modified utilitarian thought to abandon the simple pleasure-maximizing, pain-avoiding formula and to seek qualitative and "objective" criteria instead. In his essay *On Liberty* (1859) he developed the theory of moral (as opposed simply to economic) individualism and linked it to requirements of education and enlightenment. He was forced to introduce collective and social considerations and thus had to allow, contrary to what he seemed to profess, for state intervention. Many consider Mill, because of this to be one of the precursors of socialism; however, he is most well known as a strong advocate of individualism.

because of their intrinsic quality, not because of the particular pleasure they give to an individual. A poem has more utility than a hot dog!

There is therefore a necessary gradation in the utility of different goods. Some have a higher value even if they give pleasure to only few; others may, in the long run, prove to be painful even if they give pleasure to many. What then? Should we introduce a dictator or a philosopher–king who will impose his hierarchy of pleasures upon society and make it produce goods and services that correspond to it? Or should we expect individuals to make the right choice?

The last question is not speculative. It is right before us. Driving a car is pleasurable, but by depleting our energy resources American drivers weaken the country to the point where it may be unable to defend many of the values that are equally pleasurable to us—our freedoms, for instance. A comprehensive scheme of public transportation would be preferable to private ownership of cars. But how can the people be led to make the right decision?

The utilitarians, and particularly John Stuart Mill, put their hopes in education, and in the wisdom and self-restraint of the middle classes. It was the obligation of the state to establish education, and it was the function of education to *enlighten* self-interest in terms of collective, group, social, and national interests and considerations. Education would transform an essentially hedonistic society into a body of civic-minded individuals—who in the last analysis would choose public transportation! They would put the general good above their own particular pleasure.

The Political Core

Four basic principles make up the political core of liberalism: *individual consent, representation and representative government, constitutionalism,* and *popular sovereignty.*

Individual Consent   As we noted, beginning with the seventeenth century, there was a shift from the notion of 'status' to that of "contract." Contractual theories became the basis of political authority as men and women consented to bind themselves in a political system and to accept its decisions. The Mayflower Compact of 1629—the Pilgrims' "constitution"—is the best illustration.

It was John Locke who developed the theory of consent in detail. Men and women, he pointed out, live in the state of nature with certain natural rights: life, liberty, and property. At a given time, they discover that it is difficult to safeguard these rights without a common authority committed to them and to their protection. They agree to set up a political society consisting of a common legislature, a common judge, and a common executive. The first will interpret and safeguard the natural rights, the second will adjudicate conflicts about these rights, and the third will provide for enforcement. The contract is made by all individuals, and those who do not agree are not bound by it. They can leave! *The source of political authority and of the powers of state over those who stay is the people's consent.* The purpose of the state is the better preservation of the natural rights of life, liberty, and property.

John Locke (1632–1704)

John Locke was an English philosopher generally considered one of the founders of empiricism. His principal works include *Letters on Toleration* (1689–1692), *Essay Concerning Human Understanding* (1690), and *Thoughts on Education* (1693). As a political philosopher, Locke developed in his *Two Treatises on Government* (1690) the contract theory of the state, according to which the state is the custodian of natural rights and is founded upon the consent of the governed in order to protect these rights—specifically, the rights of life, liberty, and property. Contract theory led to the elaboration of institutions of limited state and a limited government.

Representation   But who can make decisions within this system? According to Locke, it is the legislature elected by the people (at the time, to be sure, on a very limited franchise). However, the legislature must accept certain restraints, all of them implicit or explicit in the original contract setting up the political system. It cannot deprive individuals of their natural rights, cannot abolish their freedom, and cannot do away with their lives or take away their property. The political authority—the legislature—is restrained by the very nature of the compact that originally established it.

Locke's idea of representative government, then, is based on the notion that political authority derives from the people. But moral, civil, economic, or property rights cannot be transgressed. The majority and its elected representatives can make all and any decisions, but the original contract and the good sense of the people who made it, as well as of their representatives, restrain it from violating the people's natural rights. Thus, the British tradition establishes parliamentary sovereignty and majority rule rather than checks and balances and judicial review, as in the United States.

It should be noted, however, that while Locke gave to the legislature the right to make decisions without any limitations, his theory of representation and representative government applied only to a small number—those who held property. They represented the middle classes and the landed aristocracy. It was only much later, when the franchise was expanded to most citizens (and ultimately to all), that the problem of how to limit the majority—which might decide to take away the property of the few—assumed particular importance.

Theories of representation and representative government also stemmed directly from utilitarian premises that led ultimately to the "one man, one vote" principle. At first the utilitarians attacked the vested interests, the aristocracy, the landowners, the church, and the well-to-do, and discarded the notion that these groups, more than others, had a special stake in the country and hence had a special right to represent the community and govern it. John Stuart Mill argued that the best individual protection was to allow each and all to select their representatives. "Human beings," he pointed out, "are only secure from evil at the hands of others in proportion to their ability to protect themselves,"[3] and he believed that representation was the best protection.

However, Mill did not quite accept the notion of the supremacy of the representatives—the legislature—and with it the right of the majority to govern. He and many other liberals feared that, if all the people were given the right to vote and to elect their own representatives, and if decisions in the representative assembly were to be made by majority vote, then the poor would use their numerical strength to take care of *their* interests at the expense of the middle classes and all others. There were, therefore, a number of direct and indirect restraints. One was the proposition that representative government could function well only when the educational level of the voters had improved. Citizens should learn to think of the

---

[3]J. S. Mill, "Considerations on Representative Government," in *Utilitarianism,* chap. 3, p. 43.

"general prosperity and the general good" rather than their own immediate interest; in other words, the system could work well only when people as a whole acted according to their enlightened interest. Mill wrote:

> The positive evils and dangers of representative government can be reduced to two: general ignorance and incapacity, and the danger of its being under the influence of interests not identical with the general welfare of the community.[4]

He mentioned specifically the "body of unskilled laborers" who were ignorant and likely to act at the expense of the general welfare.

Mill also had an aversion to the development of large national political parties that could mobilize the vote and capture a majority through the organization and discipline of its members. Moreover, he was in favor of property and age qualifications. He favored these at least for the candidates for election, who in this way would come from the middle classes and would have the proper level of maturity and moderation. He also favored giving a great weight—more votes—to people with education. Finally, he was in favor of a second chamber, the House of Lords, representing "personal merit" and acting as a "moral center of resistance" against the decisions of a popularly elected assembly—that is, against the majority.

Despite their insistence on representation and elections, the liberals hedged and hemmed at the power of the legislature and the right of the majority to decide. They did not have enough confidence in the people. Yet, notwithstanding their fears of the poor, the ignorant, and "the many," the utilitarian premises led gradually to universal suffrage. Representation and representative government gradually spread, and with it majoritarianism, the right of the majority to form a government and make decisions for all, gained legitimacy.

Constitutionalism   The notion of restraints on political authority, as proposed by Locke, influenced the framers of the U.S. Constitution. They feared arbitrary and absolute power so much that they rejected a concentration of power in the hands of any one body, whether it be the legislature, or even the majority of the people. While stressing the idea of natural rights, individual freedoms, and the derivation of authority from the people, they wanted to find a way to make it impossible for any single organ or government to become truly sovereign and overwhelm the others. Their emphasis was more on how to restrain political power, even when it was based on the will of the people, than on how to make it effective.

The answer was a written Constitution that limits power, sets explicit restraints (including the ten amendments) on the national government and the individual states, and institutionalizes the separation of powers in such a manner that one power checks another. At no time would it be possible for one branch—executive, legislative, or judicial—to overwhelm and subordinate the others. Having accepted the idea of fully representative government through periodic elections, the founders of the American Constitution put heavy restraints upon it.

This is essentially what we mean by constitutionalism. Constitutionalism provides solid guarantees for the individual by explicitly limiting government; it also

---

[4]J. S. Mill, "Considerations on Representative Government," in *Utilitarianism,* chap. 6, p. 86.

provides clear procedures for the implementation of the government's functions. In many cases it establishes a watchdog, in the form of a judicial body, to safeguard the Constitution and all the restraints written into it. In addition, it provides procedures through which the responsibility of the governors to the governed is maintained by periodic elections. The government is both *limited* and *responsible.* But the idea of limitations is far more important than that of popular sovereignty. The U.S. Constitution established a republic, not a democracy.

Popular Sovereignty   It was Jean-Jacques Rousseau who set up the model of a popular democracy before the French Revolution of 1789. He too found the source of political authority in the people. They were sovereign, and their sovereignty was "inalienable, infallible, and indestructible."[5] In contrast to those who favored representation and representative government, Rousseau believed in direct government by the people. There were to be no restraints on the popular will. He called it "the general will" and claimed that under certain conditions it was always right and that representation would only distort it. In the last analysis, he argued, nobody could really represent anybody else. Something like town meetings in small communities would be the only appropriate instruments for the expression of the general will.

Rousseau's affirmation of the absolute power of the general will, that many interpreted to be the will of the people, had revolutionary implications. It pitted an extreme doctrine of popular sovereignty against absolutism, which was current in France and many other continental countries in the eighteenth century. But it also antagonized liberals who believed in representative government with restraints and who were particularly reluctant to see all the people participate directly or indirectly in decisions.

Consent, representation, popular sovereignty leading to majority rule, and constitutional restraints on the state and its government (even on a majority) obviously emphasize different forms of liberal thought and put the accent on different values. They inevitably lead to different political institutions. Emphasis on constitutional restraints and the protection of individual and minority rights—economic rights at first—led to the type of liberalism, still very much in evidence in the United States, that restricts the majority and allows the judiciary to act as the supreme umpire. On the other hand, emphasis on the Rousseauian idea of popular sovereignty leads to unrestricted majority rule, either directly by the people or by their representatives. In between these two extremes, liberals and liberal institutions attempted, not always successfully, to find a solution that reconciled the idea of majoritarianism with the notion of restraints. Limitation on representative assemblies, various voting qualifications, a bicameral legislature in which one chamber is not directly elected by the people but represents wealth or birth or some other attribute of "moderation," and the veto of the monarch or a president were the devices most often used to deny a numerical majority the power to make decisions.

---

[5]Jean-Jacques Rousseau, *The Social Contract,* book 2.

Throughout the nineteenth century, the main stresses within the political core of liberalism lay in the conflict between those who, in line with Locke and some of the utilitarians, advocated restraints on the legislature and the majority, and those who, in line with Rousseau's theory of popular sovereignty, pressed for uninhibited majority rule.

THE STATE AND THE INDIVIDUAL

Liberalism was an antistate philosophy and remains one in the sense that, all other things being more or less equal, it values the individual and his or her initiative more than the state and its intervention. Nowhere has this position been better set forth than in John Stuart Mill's essay *On Liberty,* published in 1859. To approach it, let us set forth two models, the totalitarian and the liberal. According to the first, the individual and the civil society (i.e., the family, economic organizations, school and universities, and so on) are controlled by the state. It is therefore the state that shapes the social institutions on the basis of a predetermined scheme of values. The state exacts conformity and obedience.

The liberal model presents an entirely different order of things. Individuals and their social institutions are separate from the state. Strictly speaking, they constitute two different spheres of life and action. But when the two spheres do intersect, the intersection should cover only a limited and recognized area. Spontaneity, creativity, experimentation, and the search for truth are within the domain of individuals and their social institutions. It is at best and at most the function of the state to maintain order, to see that nobody in his or her relations with others uses force, to protect civil liberties and personal freedom, and at the same time to maintain the economic freedom of the individual. In other words, the role of the state is to protect the individual.

In his essay *On Liberty* Mill summarizes this by asserting:

1. That every restraint imposed by the state is bad.
2. That even if the individual cannot do certain things well, the state should not do them for fear that it might undermine the individual's independence and initiative.
3. That any increase in the powers of state is automatically bad and prejudicial to individual freedoms: it decreases individual freedom.

Thus Mill views the state on the one hand, and society and the individual on the other, in a mechanical and antithetical kind of relationship. The increase of powers of the state necessarily involves the decrease of powers of the individual; correspondingly, people must be extremely vigilant not to allow an increase in the power of state.

The most crucial problem for liberal thought has been the identification of exactly where the lines separating the state, on the one hand, and society and individuals, on the other, intersect. One might develop an elastic concept, allowing a fairly wide area within the intersecting lines, in which the state can intervene (numbers 2 and 3 in Figure 2.1). Or, in line with the thinking of early liberals, one

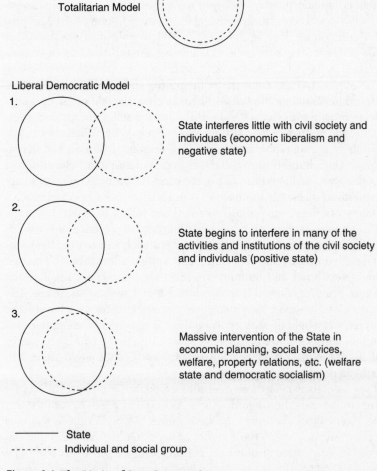

Totalitarian Model

Liberal Democratic Model

1.

State interferes little with civil society and individuals (economic liberalism and negative state)

2.

State begins to interfere in many of the activities and institutions of the civil society and individuals (positive state)

3.

Massive intervention of the State in economic planning, social services, welfare, property relations, etc. (welfare state and democratic socialism)

—————— State
- - - - - - - - Individual and social group

Figure 2.1 **The Limits of State Intervention.**

might allow for the minimum area of intersection in which the state can intervene (number 1 in Figure 2.1). Here the intersection would encompass only order and protection. In this latter case, the state becomes something of a police officer or a "night watchman," making sure that the factory does not burn down and no thieves break in but otherwise allowing full autonomy within the factory, the university, the home, or the school. The smaller the area included within the intersecting lines of Figure 2.1, the closer we are to laissez-faire liberalism; the larger the area, the more we move in the direction of the *positive state* or the *welfare state*, perhaps even getting close to socialism.

Self-regarding and Other-regarding Acts

Different periods in the history of liberalism tell us where the lines have been drawn. War, for example, necessitates state intervention. But this was considered an exception, since there is an understanding that with the passing of such a national emergency the situation would revert to the original liberal model. John Stuart Mill provided us with a criterion for drawing the lines. To Mill, all individual acts that affect the individual—*self-regarding acts,* as he called them—are acts that cannot be controlled or regulated by the state. However, acts that concern and affect others—*other-regarding acts*—can and should come under the control and regulation of the state. Thus, the area within our intersecting circles should include the other-regarding acts.

But "affect" provides no clean standard. Is smoking self-regarding or other-regarding? Is the use of drugs self-regarding or other-regarding? What about alcoholism? What about pornographic literature? Violence on television? The manufacture of drugs? The administration and the high cost of hospitals? The additives put in our foods? Ownership and use of private cars? Nuclear energy? These are just the first questions that come to mind.

The second set of questions is more complex, and relates to exactly *when* the state should bring into its purview other-regarding acts (if we have managed to define exactly what they are). Can it do so only *after* an act is *shown* to affect others, or can the state exercise control because an act *might* affect others? The first would provide a very strict and limiting criterion. The state could regulate the manufacturing of drugs only when it is shown that they have caused cancer. The second interpretation, however, provides a very generous criterion whereby the state can intervene. It would do so every time there is some doubt about the consequences certain drugs can have upon individuals. Drugs that *might* cause cancer should be taken off the market. Whenever certain acts or goods *might* affect others, they should be regulated and controlled.

Mill did not have to answer these questions explicitly, because of the way he defined self-regarding and other-regarding acts. *All individual acts, he claimed, are self-regarding except those that cause harm to others. The criterion in terms of which other-regarding acts are defined is that of harm. Only if harm is done can the state intervene.* Commerce, production, consumption are self-regarding.[6] The state should not intervene. But so, of course, are freedom of thought and expression and freedom of association. The state should not intervene here either. So, in the last analysis, the individual has the right to get drunk and to use drugs. However, your actions become other-regarding, and hence invite state intervention, when they cause harm to others. You can stay in your attic drinking beer as long as you want; you are free to indulge in this self-regarding act. But if you start throwing the empty cans out of a window and you endanger passersby, then the act becomes other-regarding.

---

[6]J. S. Mill, "Of the Limits of the Authority of Society over the Individual," in his essay *On Liberty,* ch. 4 in *Utilitarianism.*

But the moment we give a more relaxed definition of what is other-regarding, and introduce the concept of *effect* or *influence* rather than *harm,* we move in the opposite direction to favor state intervention and regulation. The police officer may try to save you from too much beer or drugs, even if you have not harmed anybody! The question should be raised at this point about apparently self-regarding acts that nonetheless "affect" the society as a whole. Costs of production concern the entrepreneurs and come within their discretion. Suppose, however, people and whole communities are affected by the manner in which production is carried out. Streams may become polluted, the water supply becomes unhealthy, pollutants spread into the air. Undoubtedly, people will then say that these actions are other-regarding and must be controlled. But who will pay the *social cost* involved—the harm caused to others.

Pluralism   The liberal ethic and the liberal ideology are intensely individualistic. However, liberalism is used also to refer to the rights and freedoms not only of individuals but also of groups and associations. Replace the individual with the group or an association to which he or she belongs and you have pluralism. Groups demand and expect the same treatment in regard to tolerance, representation, and participation that the individuals have. With the breakdown of rigid class and religious or ethnic solidarities in many modern systems, thousands of groups have mushroomed. Groups organize; they make their demands. Public policy, it is expected, will then be made in response to their demands. As David Apter writes, "The notion of individual competitions is replaced [under pluralism] by a network of organizational competition, influence, accountability and information in which groups can organize and, by exercising rights, realize interests to affect policy outcomes."[7]

But groups may make claims that go beyond the mere satisfaction of interest. They may claim the same autonomy that the individuals claim. These are claims for ethnic, racial, local, functional, occupational, and economic autonomy. Their implementation requires a great deal of decentralization of the democratic state. Very often demands on the part of certain groups even go beyond decentralization to assert separation and independence from the state. Sometimes pluralism is used to justify economic democracy—that is, the rights of certain groups and organizations to decide by themselves on the economic activities in which they are engaged without any intervention from the state.

As long as there is a basic agreement in the political society on the rules that determine political competition, pluralism and liberalism can coexist. But the moment a group or a combination of groups subordinate others, they will dominate the society and coerce the individual. This may clearly be the case with industrial corporations, trade unions, other economic groups, ethnic groups, and even religious sects. The early liberal theorists feared group dominance and tried in one

---

[7]David Apter, *Introduction to Political Analysis,* pp. 314–315.

way or another to make it difficult for groups to develop and to supplant the individuals. They argued that a group is not a moral entity like the individual. It overshadows the individuals and subordinates them to the imperative of group solidarity. As a result, groups pose the danger of subverting individual freedoms.

ACHIEVEMENTS: THE EXPANSION OF LIBERALISM

If we take a fairly thick brush and paint onto the canvas of the nineteenth century all the liberal achievements in the realm of economic rights, civil liberties, and political rights, the picture that emerges is breathtaking. The liberals and the liberal movements and parties changed the economic, social, and political structure of Europe, and drastically modified the international community as well. Some of the major achievements are listed here.

Slavery was outlawed. In the United States it continued until the Civil War, but the importation of slaves after 1808 had been declared illegal. In England the slave trade was banned in 1807, and slavery was abolished in the British Empire in 1833. France followed in 1848; the Netherlands in 1869; Argentina in 1853; Portugal in 1858; Brazil in 1888. Serfdom was abolished in Russia in 1861.

Gradually *religious disabilities* against holding political or other offices were abandoned virtually everywhere. Catholics, Protestants, Jews, Quakers, and nonconformist religious minorities were allowed full participation by the end of the nineteenth century.

After bitter controversies, *toleration* was granted, and church and state separated in many countries. Religious affiliation and worship became personal rights.

Freedom of press, speech, and *association* were granted. By the end of the nineteenth century, in Western Europe, Britain and its dominions, and the United States, rare were the cases where people could not express their views or were penalized for the views they did express, no matter how heretical or subversive.

The state began to provide *education* and to require children to attend school up to the age of ten, twelve, or fourteen.

The vote was gradually extended to all males first, and to women only after World War I. There was universal male suffrage in England by 1884; in France in 1848; in Italy by the end of the century; in Russia in 1905 (but not for long); and in Germany and the Scandinavian countries in varying degrees by the end of the century. In the United States, male universal suffrage (limited to whites) was established in the 1820s. Property qualifications for voters and candidates were eliminated, but some other qualifications—literacy, age, or residence—remained. All in all, the prediction of Lord Macaulay that "universal suffrage is utterly incompatible with the existence of civilization" proved quite wrong!

Nothing illustrates the force of liberalism better than the reforms undertaken in France after the revolution of 1830. The second chamber was changed from a hereditary one to one in which members sat for life; the electorate was broadened by lowering the age qualifications to twenty-five instead of thirty; property qualifications were reduced from three hundred francs to two hundred. Candidates for office were to be thirty years old instead of forty, censorship was abolished, extraordinary tribunals were eliminated, schools were set up in every commune by the state, and the control of church over the schools was put to an end. These reforms were modest; indeed, they stopped far short of what democrats wanted to accomplish. But they were moving in the direction of democracy. It took, for example, just eighteen years (after another revolution) before universal suffrage was introduced to France, in 1848.

Similarly, the liberal Reform Act of 1832 in England provided for a property qualification of ten pounds a year, thus excluding the poor and the workers from voting but allowing the middle classes to do so. The act increased the electorate to about 750,000 out of a total population of about 13.5 million. Further extensions in 1867 and 1884 followed, bringing the workers into the political system.

Constitutions, constitution-making, and *constitutionalism* were everywhere in the air. Even where a constitution had only symbolic character it still echoed the aspirations of citizens to limit government and establish the rules that made the holders of power responsible to the people or their representatives.

In Russia, a movement for a constitution that would limit the powers of the czar emerged in 1824; in Greece, liberal constitutions were promulgated in 1827 and again in 1843; in Germany, a liberal constitution was prepared by a convention that met in Frankfurt in 1848; in France, liberal constitutions were promulgated (after the failure of the ones established during the French Revolution) in 1830, 1848, and 1871. In Spain, Portugal, Italy, and in many Latin American republics, constitutional documents came into force by the end of the nineteenth century and often earlier. Even Poland, the Austro-Hungarian Empire, and the Ottoman Empire experienced liberal reforms that were embodied in constitutional documents or charters.

These reforms were not granted easily; occasionally, they were granted only to be withdrawn. Frequently liberal political movements were repressed, but the overall impact was the same—broadening and safeguarding civil liberties and extending political participation to an ever-growing number of people in every political system. Above all, they imposed responsibility and restraints, no matter how fragile and temporary, upon the holders of political power. This in itself helped to erode the claims of absolutism.

Representative government became increasingly accepted throughout Europe and in the English-speaking countries. With the exception of Russia (with a notable interval between 1905 and 1914), there was hardly a political system in the nineteenth century that did not introduce representative assemblies and did not give them some (often considerable) power over decisions. In many cases, the assembly was given the power to censure the government and force it out of office. Representative assemblies participated in the formulation of laws and decided on taxation and expenditures. Within limits (and sometimes without any restriction) debate was free and representatives were not liable for their words and actions in the legislature.

As the suffrage expanded to new groups, *political parties* began to emerge, seeking the vote in order to govern on the basis of pledges they offered to the electorate. They became transmission belts between the people and the government, making the latter increasingly responsive to popular demands and aspirations and helping translate demands and wants into policy and action. Parties emerged, at first in the United States where male universal suffrage was introduced as early as 1824, with platforms, leadership, organization, and ideological loyalties. In England, they gradually evolved from factions and cliques, manipulated and controlled by the king and the landed gentry, into national organizations representing the new towns and the middle classes. The Liberals and Conservatives, the two large parties, established national headquarters, designated candidates, prepared their platforms, solicited membership, and vied for office against each other after the middle of the nineteenth century. The Conservatives followed the logic of liberalism and enacted legislation enfranchising new groups by lowering property qualifications. Their leader, Benjamin Disraeli, spoke of the union between "the cottage and the throne," an expression that symbolized the reconciliation of the aristocracy with the principles of democracy and the needs of the common man.

In France, the nobility continued to influence the vote, and political parties were numerous, badly organized, regional rather than national, and without clearcut platforms. Until 1880 their differences were about the political regime: some favoring the republic, others a return to the monarchy, and still others aspiring to Bonapartism. It was only by the very end of the nineteenth century that the Socialists became unified into one party; the centrist groups—republican, anticlerical, and liberal—formed the Radical-Socialist party.

In Germany, the powerful Social Democratic party had the best organization and the largest membership and became revisionist and reformist rather than a revolutionary party. It was opposed by the Center party (liberal but appealing to Catholic groups), the Liberals (a middle-class party), and the Conservatives.

Almost everywhere the development of political parties strengthened liberal democratic principles and institutions. Parties allowed the people to opt directly for candidates and policies and brought the governments that emerged from elections closer to their control.

Liberalism had, of course, a profound impact on *economic life*. Freedom of movement (a simple right in our eyes) became a reality for the first time. Journeymen, merchants, manufacturers, and farmers could move not only their produce and goods but themselves without any prior permission or restraint. They could dispose of their property and do as they pleased with it. Individuals became free to change professions just as easily as they could change their domiciles; they could enter into partnership or agree to provide their services on the basis of mutually binding agreements. Not only their home but also their property became a "castle" against intervention, regulation, and confiscation by an arbitrary ruler.

There was (though not everywhere) a *trend against all forms of tariffs* and all indirect restrictions on the movement of goods—first felt against internal tariffs that allowed cities, municipalities, or regional authorities to tax goods at the point of their entry or exit. But beyond these internal tariffs, a great movement was under way, spearheaded by British industrial and trading groups, to reduce and even to eliminate all external tariffs that taxed goods coming into or moving out of a state. It favored worldwide free trade. As Richard Cobden, one of Adam Smith's disciples, stated in 1846:

There is no human event that has happened in the world more calculated to promote the enduring interests of humanity than the establishment of the principle of free trade.[8]

Despite their aversion to state intervention in social and economic matters, liberals were forced to consider *limited interventions*. "Poor laws" were introduced to keep the destitute from starvation. As unemployment assumed menacing proportions in the 1840s, public workshops were established in France, and at one time they employed as many as a quarter of a million people. Child labor legislation gradually began to prohibit the employment of children under certain ages and required them to go to school. A ten-hour working day was decreed in England in 1846, and factory laws began to provide for the safety of workers. Now workers were to receive compensation for accidents caused by their work. By the end of the century, many of these measures had been expanded to provide added protection, including the first steps in the direction of health insurance.

In the name of liberalism, a vast movement in favor of *national self-determination* and national independence spread over Europe. It culminated in the Wilsonian principles of self-determination. Throughout the nineteenth century, dynasties disintegrated and new nations came into being. Greece (1827), Norway (1830), and Belgium (1830) became independent. In Poland, a liberal national uprising in favor of independence took place in 1831. Italy became a unified national state in 1870, and Germany followed in 1871. The Ottoman Empire, encompassing the Balkans, Turkey, and the Middle East, cracked wide open, allowing for the emergence of a number of independent states, some late in the nineteenth century and the beginning of the twentieth. Bulgaria, Romania, part of Yugoslavia, and Albania became new national states. The Austro-Hungarian Empire evolved into Hungary, Serbia, and ultimately Czechoslovakia. Powerful liberal independence movements manifested themselves within the Czarist Empire. Most of these new states undertook constitutional reforms, providing for individual rights, election and popular participation, and restraints on the government.

CONCLUSION

In overall terms, nineteenth-century liberalism shows a remarkable record in bringing forth and institutionalizing civil rights, political rights, and economic freedoms. It was equally potent in causing a profound reconsideration of the position of the aristocracy, the church, and many unreconstructed traditionalists. But the century was also remarkable for the growth and the unprecedented development

---

[8]Cited by Donald Read, *Cobden and Bright*, p. 65.

of technology and production. This, despite the many miseries that continued to afflict the workers, gave credence to some of the assertions of Adam Smith and the utilitarians. Economies grew; world population began a rapid climb; water and rail communications were established, bringing people closer together in their national community as well as in the world; new cities developed rapidly while many old ones were literally torn apart and rebuilt; currency in gold or paper money and new banking practices facilitated exchange; and savings were channeled into new investments. Nations mushroomed in the name of self-determination. The best eulogy on the spirit of the innovation and the modernity that bourgeois liberalism exemplified was given by its greatest critic, Karl Marx, in the *Communist Manifesto*.

> Constant revolutionizing of production, uninterrupted disturbance of all social relations, everlasting uncertainty and agitation, distinguish the bourgeois epoch from all earlier times. All fixed, fast-frozen relationships, with their train of venerable ideas and opinions, are swept away, all new-formed ones become obsolete before they can ossify. All that is solid melts into air, all that is holy is profaned.

By the end of the century, a new factor was injected into the liberal philosophy—social justice. It was needed to support individuals in one form or another when their self-reliance and initiative could no longer provide them with protection, or when the market did not show the flexibility or the sensitivity it was supposed to show in satisfying basic wants. A new spirit of mutual aid, cooperation, and service began to develop. It became stronger with the coming of the twentieth century.

BIBLIOGRAPHY

Apter, David. *Introduction to Political Analysis*. Cambridge, MA.: Winthrop, 1978.

Bentham, Jeremy. *An Introduction to the Principles of Morals and Legislation.* New York: Harper & Row, 1952.

Berlin, Isaiah. *Four Essays on Liberty.* New York: Oxford University Press, 1969.

Black, Eugene (ed.). *Posture of Europe, 1815–1940.* Homewood, IL.: Dorsey Press, 1964.

———. *Victorians: Culture and Society.* New York: Harper & Row, 1973.

Briggs, Asa. *The Age of Improvement.* London: Longmans, 1959.

Clark, G. Kitson. *An Expanding Society: Britain 1830–1900.* New York: Cambridge University Press, 1967.

Dahl, Robert A. *A Preface to Democratic Theory.* Chicago: University of Chicago Press, 1956.

Dahl, Robert A. *Democracy, Liberty, and Equality* New York: Oxford University Press, 1988.

"Declaration of the Rights of Man and of the Citizen." In Paul H. Beik, *The French Revolution.* New York: Harper & Row, 1970.

Dicey, A. V. *Lectures on the Relationship Between Law and Public Opinion in England During the 19th Century.* New York: Macmillan, 1952.

Dinwiddy, John. *Bentham.* New York: Oxford University Press, 1989.

Gray, John. *Liberalism.* Minneapolis: University of Minnesota Press, 1986.

Halevy, E. *The Growth of Philosophic Radicalism.* London: Faber, 1952.

Hallowell, John H. *The Moral Foundations of Democracy.* Chicago: University of Chicago Press, 1954.

Hamilton, Alexander, James Madison, and John Jay. *The Federalist Papers.* New York: New American Library, 1961.

Hartz, Louis. *The Liberal Tradition in America.* New York: Harcourt, 1962.

Hobhouse, L. T. *Liberalism.* New York: Oxford University Press, 1964.

Jefferson, Thomas. *Drafts of the Declaration of Independence.* Washington, D.C.: Acropolis, 1963.

Laski, Harold J. *The Rise of European Liberalism.* Atlantic Highlands, N.J.: Humanities Press, 1962.

Levine, Andrew. *Liberal Democracy: A Critique of Its Theory.* New York: Columbia University Press, 1981.

Lively, Jack. *Democracy.* Oxford, England: Basil Blackwell, 1975.

Locke, John. *Two Treatises on Government.* Edited by Peter Laslett. New York: New American Library, 1965.

MacPherson, C. B. *The Political Theory of Possessive Individualism.* Oxford, England: Hobbes and Locke, 1962.

———. *The Real World of Democracy.* Oxford, England: Clarendon Press, 1966.

———. *Democratic Theory: Essays in Retrieval.* Oxford, England: Clarendon Press, 1973.

———. *The Life and Times of Liberal Democracy.* New York: Oxford University Press, 1977.

Mill, John Stuart. *Utilitarianism, Liberty,* and *Representative Government,* Everyman's Library, J. M. Dent and Sons, London, 1940. (With an introduction by A. D. Lindsay.) There have been many publications of these three essays by John Stuart Mill with critical introductory comments.

Palmer, R. R. *The Age of the Democratic Revolution,* 2 vols. Princeton, N.J.: Princeton University Press, 1959.

Palmer, R. R., and Joel Colton. *A History of the Modern World Since 1815.* New York: Knopf, 1971.

Read, Donald. *Cobden and Bright.* London: St. Martin's Press, 1968.

Rees, John C. *John Stuart Mill's On Liberty.* New York: Oxford University Press, 1985.

Revel, Jean-Francois. *Without Marx and Jesus: The New American Revolution Has Begun.* New York: Doubleday, 1971.

Rousseau, Jean-Jacques. *The Social Contract and Discourse on Inequality.* New York: Washington Square Press, 1967.

Ruggiero, E. *The History of European Liberalism.* Boston: Beacon Press, 1959.

Sartori, Giovanni. *Democratic Theory.* New York: Praeger, 1965.

Sidorsky, David. *The Liberal Tradition in European Thought.* New York: Putnam, 1970.

Smith, Adam. *The Wealth of Nations: Representative Selections.* New York: Bobbs-Merrill, 1961.

Tawney, R.H. *Religion and the Rise of Capitalism.* New York: New American Library, 1954.

Thomson, David. *Europe Since 1815,* 2nd rev. ed. New York: Knopf, 1957.

———. *Democracy in France Since 1870,* 4th ed. New York: Oxford University Press, 1964.

Thurman, Arnold. *The Folklore of Capitalism.* New Haven, CT.: Yale University Press, 1937.

Weber, Max. *The Protestant Ethic and the Spirit of Capitalism.* New York: Scribner's, 1958.

Chapter
3

Democracy and the Economy

Socialism, the Welfare State, . . . Capitalism Again?

But man in society not only lives his individual life: he also modifies the form of social institutions in the direction indicated by reason—in such a manner . . . that will render them more efficient for securing freedom.

Sydney Oliver *Fabian Essays in Socialism*

Our freedom of choice in a competitive society rests on the fact that, if one person refuses to satisfy our wishes, we can turn to another. But if we face a monopolist we are at his mercy. And an authority directing the whole economic system would be the most powerful monopolist conceivable.

F. A. Hayek *The Road to Serfdom*

*T*he year 1848 represents a watershed for European liberalism. From it, powerful and divergent currents began to flow. From Paris to Palermo, from Frankfurt and London to Budapest, Vienna, and Madrid, the poor, the workers, and the peasants who had left the countryside for the urban centers, led by students and intellectuals at their side, rose to take power away from the propertied classes in the name of *radical democracy* and *socialism*. Writing in the same year, John Stuart Mill commented on the industrial and technological achievements of the period and pointed out that they had improved the living standard of the middle classes only. "They have not as yet," he added, "begun to effect those great changes in human destiny, which it is their nature . . . to accomplish."[1]

---

[1]Cited by Asa Briggs, *The Age of Improvement*, p. 303.

The middle classes found themselves wavering. Some sided with radical democrats and the socialists and joined forces with them in an alliance that could not last. Others backed conservative groups—the nobility, the church, the landowners—that had resisted liberalism.

Using the three basic cores of the liberal democratic ideology as a guide, it is relatively easy to map out its evolution throughout the nineteenth century and to reassess its present position.

RADICAL DEMOCRATS

Radical democrats accepted the moral core of liberalism—civil rights, individual freedoms, freedom of press, religion, and association (though they insisted on the secularization of many of the functions that the church provided, such as education, and favored outright expropriation of its landed domains). They also supported the political core but interpreted it in Rousseauian terms: all political power should come directly from the people and a majority could make all decisions directly or through sovereign representative assemblies. They were against all voting qualifications and against any restraints on the exercise of popular will. They also began to express fundamental reservations about the economic core about capitalism.

Radical Democrats in England and France

A strong radical democratic movement developed in England roughly between 1830 and 1850. This was *Chartism,* a movement of middle-class reformers with working-class support. Their program (the Charter) seemed to be primarily political, calling for universal manhood franchise, equal electorate districts, "one man, one vote," annual parliaments, elimination of all property qualifications, and the secret ballot. The leaders, Feargus O'Connor, Francis Place, and William Lovett, attempted time after time to pressure Parliament into passing legislation in accordance with Charter, but without success.

But in addition to political reform, a strong group among the Chartists urged for social and economic reform. Sometimes they came close to the socialist ideas that were circulating in England and the Continent at the time. They demanded the regulation of work hours and wages as well as social benefits for the workers.

> Eight hours to work; eight hours to play
> Eight hours to sleep; eight bob [shillings] a day

was one among many Chartist slogans. Some of the Chartist leaders openly advocated socialist measures:

> It is the duty of the Government to appropriate its present surplus revenue, and the proceeds of national and public property, to the purchasing of lands, and the location thereon of the unemployed poor. . . .
> The gradual resumption by the State . . . of its ancient, undoubted, inalienable domain, and sole proprietorship over all the lands, mines, tributaries, fisheries, etc., of

the United Kingdom and our Colonies; for the same to be held by the State, as trustee in perpetuity, for the entire people. . . .

It is the recognized duty of the State to support all those of its subjects, who, from incapacity or misfortune, are unable to procure their own subsistence.[2]

In France during the same period, radical democracy took a more extreme form. Louis Blanqui, one of the early social reformers, moved very close to revolutionary socialism and led a number of armed uprisings against the governmental authorities. Louis Blanc, another social reformer, came closer to the Chartist position. He believed political reforms were essential, but it was the duty of the state to safeguard the "right to work." He urged the government to set up national workshops to employ workers, and he believed that such workshops would compete successfully with privately owned firms. As time went on, radical democracy in France increasingly moved in the direction of economic and social reforms—especially after 1848 when universal manhood suffrage, one of the major demands, was adopted. It raised the electorate overnight from a quarter million to nine million voters.

Thus, many radical democrats parted company with liberals on the definition of the economic core. They questioned the laissez-faire model of capitalism as it had been portrayed by Adam Smith. They were in favor of using the state in order to correct some of the evils and the uncertainties of the market, but they went beyond the mere search for corrective measures. They emphasized the importance of social and collective goals that could best be implemented by collective (i.e., state) action. They favored extensive state intervention not simply through legislation but through direct action and performance. Not just laws regulating child labor, but inspection and enforcement were demanded; not only poor laws providing for relief, but the actual operation of state workshops to provide employment to the poor. They demanded that the provision of social services be implemented directly by the public authorities.

Most radical democrats, however, stopped short of socialism. Their position was that the state should act and intervene where major social services and needs were involved, but without reaching out to expropriate property or to directly take over economic activities such as production and trade. They favored wide regulations and occasional direct controls but not the socialization of the means of production.

If we situate the radical democrats in terms of our basic cores of liberalism, we find them strong on the political core (leaning all the way to majoritarianism and popular sovereignty), strong on the moral core, but faithful to only a few of the basic principles defined as the economic core of early liberalism. In 1869, the French politician Jules Gambetta summed up the *political* program of radical democrats everywhere in his Belleville Manifesto and intimated at the same time the need for economic reform:

I think that there is no other sovereign but the people and that universal suffrage, the instrument of this sovereignty, has no value and basis unless it be radically free.

---

[2]Cited in G. D. H. Cole and A. W. Filson, *Working Class Movements: Selected Documents,* p. 79.

He asked for

> the most radical application of universal suffrage;. . . individual liberty to be . . . protected by law;. . . trial by jury for every kind of political offense; complete freedom of the Press;. . . freedom of meeting . . . with liberty to discuss all religious, philosophical, political, and social affairs;. . . complete freedom of association . . . separation of church and state; free, compulsory, secular primary education;. . . suppression of standing armies;. . . abolition of privileges and monopolies.[3]

LIBERAL AND RADICAL DEMOCRATS: RECONCILIATION

With the exception of those who remained attached to the economic philosophy of Adam Smith, most liberals, and what we have called radical democrats, gradually came to terms. Liberals have accepted the full logic of democracy. Today the franchise has been extended in almost all democracies to cover all citizens, male and female, above eighteen. All of the many qualifications for voting based on literacy, age, residence, income, and so on, have been eliminated. Restraints on representative assemblies have been virtually lifted, except in cases where the chief executive is also elected directly by the people. In all existing constitutional monarchies, the monarch has become a mere figurehead.

The people were mobilized into large mass parties and these parties, in many countries, exercise a controlling influence over their representatives. In some instances provisions for referenda give the people an additional measure of direct democracy. Popular democracy and majority rule expressed through direct elections for or against the members and candidates of large national political parties have been accepted by all liberals and democrats to be the major source of policymaking. At the same time, the moral core of liberalism in the form of individual and minority rights has been reaffirmed.

There has also been a similar reconciliation between radical democrats and liberals with regard to economic matters. The liberals, as well as many other parties, even when they call themselves conservatives, have found themselves increasingly in agreement. State intervention to support economic activities in the form of price and other controls is deemed acceptable; state intervention through direct or indirect means to stimulate economic activity is again deemed desirable; state regulation of a growing number of economic activities is viewed as indispensable; direct state involvement in providing for unemployment assistance and indirect and direct state action to provide for employment are now taken for granted in most democracies. Thus, the functions of the state are viewed not only as supportive or regulatory; they have actually become complementary to the private sector. This is the welfare state to which we return.

---

[3]Cited in David Thomson, *Democracy in France Since 1870,* pp. 315–316.

THE SOCIALIST IMPULSE

Socialism as a philosophy of life and as a scheme for the organization of society is as old as (perhaps older than) democracy or any other form of social, economic, or political organization. Some consider it, in fact, to have been prevalent among primitive societies where it has been suggested that land was collectively owned.

Socialism also represents an ethic diametrically opposed to that of private ownership and private profit and the inequalities that the free market may lead to. It is an ethic of an egalitarian and free society, from which the words "mine" and "yours" are eliminated.

Utopian Socialism

Utopian Socialists, beginning with Thomas More (1478–1535), through Francis Bacon (1561–1621) and Tommaso Campanella (1568–1639), down to some of the most important French and British Utopian Socialists of the nineteenth century, shared a set of common ideas.

1. They had an aversion to private property and the exploitation of the poor by those who owned the wealth, whether landed, commercial, or industrial. "Property is theft" was the curt aphorism of the French Socialist Proudhon. The Romantic poet Shelley voiced these early nineteenth-century socialist beliefs:

   The seed ye sow, another reaps,
   The wealth ye find, another keeps,
   The robes ye weave, another wears,
   The arms ye forge, another bears.

2. A passionate commitment to collectivism—the common ownership of wealth—was partly based on notions about primitive communism, and partly on ideas of mutual cooperation and social solidarity. Thus, socialism was seen as the way to extirpate strife, antagonisms, and selfishness. Utopian Socialists shared the nostalgic vision of the Roman poet Virgil about bygone ages:

   No fences parted fields, nor marks nor bounds
   Divided acres of litigious grounds,
   But all was common.

   In a famous passage, Rousseau expressed similar thoughts:

   The first man, who after enclosing a piece of ground, took it into his head to say, *this is mine,* and found people simple enough to believe him, was the real founder of civil society. How many crimes, how many wars, how many murders, how many misfortunes and horrors, would that man have saved the human species, who pulling up the stakes or filling up the ditches should have cried to his fellows:

> Beware of listening to this impostor; you are lost, if you forget that the fruits of the earth belong equally to us all, and the earth itself to nobody![4]

3. A passionate belief in what might be called "social collectivism" empha- sized the interdependence and solidarity of social life—the "social nature" of men and women, as opposed to the individualistic or utilitarian ethic. Communitarianism was the supreme value; individualism, competition, and self- interest were detested.
4. There were divergent opinions among the early Utopian Socialists on *how* to bring about socialism. Some believed in violence and revolution, but did not spell out any details; others believed in persuasion and example. For instance, the British Socialist Robert Owen (1771–1856) set up a model textile factory in East Lanark, Scotland, where good working conditions and wages, and the participation of the workers in some of the profits, were to become a model to convince other businessmen that it was in their own interests to follow the same pattern. Most Utopian Socialists, however, believed in education. If men and women were properly educated, they would opt for socialism, and it was the task of the intellectuals to provide this kind of education.
5. Many, especially among the French Utopian Socialists, were what we would call today social engineers. In their opinion, society should be con- trolled and manipulated so that, under proper conditions and with the proper social organization, human beings could attain perfection—both moral and material.

Most of the Utopian Socialists were not democrats. They paid lip service to the moral core of liberalism but argued that liberal political and economic principles and practices could not bring about a just social order. A "new ideology" had to be imposed first or inculcated through education by an elite—by philosophers and intellectuals. The Utopian Socialists never managed to form a party or even a polit- ical movement, but their writings had a profound influence on the development of socialist thought.

Democratic Socialism

We have already noted that by the end of the nineteenth century there developed a gradual reconciliation between the proponents of liberalism and the radical democrats in the form of political democracy. A similar reconciliation was also beginning to take shape between democracy and socialism—one that developed throughout the twentieth century and accounts for what today is generally called *democratic socialism.*

Nineteenth-century democrats endorsed popular sovereignty and majoritari- anism, while accepting the individual and civil rights that we have discussed as the moral core of liberalism. This set the tone for state intervention to regulate the

---

[4]Jean-Jacques Rousseau, *The Social Contract and Discourses,* book 1.

market, to correct malfunctioning, and to provide social service. But socialism, as first propounded by Marx and some Utopian Socialists, rejected the political core of liberalism. It favored revolution. However, revolutionary Marxism gave way by the end of the nineteenth century to "revisionism." In France, in Germany, especially in England, but also in Belgium, Holland, and the Scandinavian countries, socialist parties began increasingly to accept the logic and the techniques of democracy. Their goal was modified to bringing about social change through peaceful political means and established democratic procedures, and they became attached to the moral core of liberalism and its stress on individual and civil rights. Socialists began to consider these ideals as ends in themselves rather than as means to be used for the conquest of power. They became increasingly attracted to electoral politics, especially when Socialist candidates won appreciable numbers of votes at the polls. They began to see the proper instrument for change in democracy and realized that they could substitute democratic process for revolution and force.

The Fabians   By the end of the nineteenth century in England, a number of intellectuals were expounding on socialism. Most important were the Fabians (who took their name from the Roman general Fabius, whose defensive "wait and see" tactics gradually weakened Hannibal's invading forces until they were defeated). The Fabians and the Fabian Society, which they established in 1884, relied on three forces: *time,* which meant that socialism would come about gradually; *education,* to persuade the elites and the people that socialism was a superior system, morally and economically, to capitalism; and *political action* in the context of democratic and parliamentary institutions. This meant the formation of a Socialist party that would present its socialist doctrine to the people for their approval. There was not even a mention of the use of force, and nothing about revolution: in fact, many of their socialist principles were inspired by the Bible. British socialism was steeped in moral, egalitarian, and humanistic values and sought human dignity and freedom in a society from which profit and selfishness had been removed.

The philosophic foundations of Fabian socialism were set forth in the *Fabian Essays,* published in 1889. George Bernard Shaw, one of the movement's leaders, wrote:

> It was in 1885, that the Fabian Society . . . set . . . two definite tasks; first, to provide a parliamentary program for a Prime Minister converted to Socialism . . . and second, to make it as easy and matter-of-course for the ordinary respectable Englishman to be a Socialist.[5]

The Fabians favored socialization of the means of production, state controls, and broad welfare measures to bring about as much social equality as possible. They had no regard whatsoever for the economic core of liberalism and advocated drastic overhaul of the economy; in doing so, they went well beyond the simple regulation of social legislation advocated by radical democrats (and increasingly accepted by liberals). They favored the abolition of property and of the free enterprise system. Socialism was declared, however, to be an advanced form of individualism:

---

[5]George Bernard Shaw (ed.), *Fabian Essays in Socialism,* p. 33.

Sidney (1859–1947) and Beatrice Webb (1858–1943)

Sidney Webb, an Englishman of petit bourgeois background, spent over ten years in the service of the Colonial Office. In 1885, the year he joined the bar, he also joined the Fabian Society, a group of British socialists dedicated to the education of the British people in socialist principles. In 1889, Webb, along with other notable Fabians such as George Bernard Shaw and Graham Wallas, issued the *Fabian Essays in Socialism,* a book which was to become a classic of non-Marxist socialist thought. In 1887, Sidney Webb was married to Beatrice Potter, a woman of similar views. Both were heavily involved with social issues and active in the formation of the British Labour party. Sidney drafted its manifesto—*Labour and the New Social Order*—which served as the party's platform in the elections of 1918, 1922, and 1924.

"Socialism is merely individualism rationalised, organised, clothed, and in its right mind."[6]

At the beginning of this century, in 1901, the Fabians and the leaders of the major British trade unions formed the Labour party and, by 1906, were running their own independent candidates for election. In the same year, they won 323,195 votes and secured twenty-nine seats in the House of Commons. Socialism had begun to gain the respectability that the Fabians wanted to give it (Table 3.1).

[6]Shaw, p. 99.

Table 3.1   THE RISE OF THE LABOUR PARTY VOTE

General election	Seats contested	Members returned	Labour vote
1900	15	2	62,698
1906	50	29	323,195
1910 (Jan.)	78	40	505,690
1910 (Dec.)	56	42	370,802
1918	361	57	2,244,945
1922	414	142	4,236,733
1923	427	191	4,348,379
1924	514	151	5,487,620
1945	**640**	**393**	**11,632,891**

In 1918, Fabian intellectuals provided a definitive platform for the Labour party. The party declared the need for

the gradual building up of a new social order based, not on internecine conflict, inequality of riches, and dominion over subject classes, subject races, or a subject sex, but on the deliberately planned cooperation in production and distribution, the sympathetic approach to a healthy equality, the widest possible participation in power, both economic and political, and the general consciousness of consent which characterise a true democracy.[7]

Socialism was explicitly and proudly endorsed by the Labour party, in order

to secure for the producers by hand or by brain the full fruits of their industry, and the most equitable distribution thereof that may be possible, *upon the basis of the common ownership of the means of production* and the best obtainable system of popular administration and control of each industry and service [emphasis added].[8]

European Revisionism   In Western Europe it was revolutionary Marxism that remained the dominant intellectual force and inspiration of working-class Socialist movements, but in the latter part of the nineteenth century, democratic socialism (in the name of "revisionism") began to gain the upper hand.

Revisionism became a distinct ideological movement, based on the works of Eduard Bernstein, a German Socialist who produced the most comprehensive criticism of Marx and Marxism. He pointed out that:

1. The liberal capitalist system was not about to collapse, as Marx had anticipated.
2. The number of capitalists and property owners was increasing absolutely, rather than decreasing as Marxist theory stipulated it would. Thanks to the corporations and the stock exchange, a greater number of people began to "own" property in the form of stocks.

---

[7]Quoted in G. D. H. Cole, *A History of the Labour Party Since 1914*, p. 65.
[8]Cole, p. 72.

3. The capitalistic economy was generating an ever-increasing number of jobs as production became more specialized. The middle classes were, in fact, growing in number and changing in character. They no longer consisted of people who owned property, as in the past, but of new salaried personnel: technicians, engineers, white-collar workers, service personnel, civil servants, those in the liberal professions, teachers, and so on. Thus, instead of a pyramid with a huge base and sharp apex, the changing class structure under liberal capitalism was beginning to resemble a stepped pyramid in which blocks of decreasing width were superimposed upon each other.

According to Bernstein, class structure could be schematized, as shown on the left in Figure 3.1, as a stepped pyramid made up of many intermediate layers. This was contrary to Marx's view (to the right), which represents society as a smooth-sided pyramid, with the capitalist class at the apex.

4. As societies democratized, allowing for equal and universal franchise, associational freedoms, and the formation of political parties, strong working-class parties would be able to assume political power against the capitalist class, to use the state as an instrument for their own protection, and to secure a better allocation of goods and services. This would be accomplished through legislation and nationalizations. Bernstein felt that Marx had seriously underestimated the capabilities of the democratic state to intervene in favor of the workers and the underprivileged.

In light of these observations, Bernstein concluded that *Evolutionary Socialism* (the title of his book, published in 1899—ten years after the *Fabian Essays* were published) and not revolutionary socialism was to gain ascendancy. It was step-by-step and stage-by-stage development of socialism that would gradually replace capitalism.

Bernstein's analysis was persuasive. Revisionism was gradually adopted by the Socialist parties, and revolutionary socialism and its tactics were abandoned. Socialism became synonymous with *democratic socialism*. It accepted parliamentary government and elections and emphasized, almost exclusively, political activity within the framework of bourgeois legality and democracy. It signified the abandonment of revolutionary class struggle. The workers were to devote themselves to improving their working conditions, their pension benefits, and their wages within the capitalistic economy, and to see to it that a larger share of the national wealth

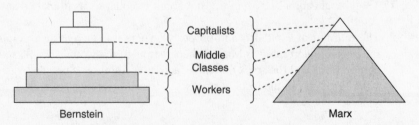

Figure 3.1 **Bernstein's schematization of capitalist society (left) compared to Marx's (right).**

went to them and their families. The trade unions and democratic political action were to become the instruments for the realization of such tasks.

The Socialist movements and parties in Europe began to move, therefore, close to the position of the British Labour party. They, too, accepted the logic of democracy and began to rely more and more on elections, votes, and the conquest of political power through elections. In so doing, they endorsed fully both the moral and the political cores of liberalism but remained hostile to private property and the market economy, promising to socialize the means of production when they achieved full power. But, as with the British Labour party, their approach became gradualistic, even eclectic and pragmatic. Socialists on the Continent, especially the German Social Democrats (Table 3.2), began to propose only specific and selective measures, dealing primarily with the major industries. Small shopkeepers, manufacturers, farmers, and also many large industrial firms and groups would be allowed to operate on their own.

Revisionism thus mobilized a large percentage of the workers to favor democratic change and convinced them (not always completely) that they could promote and defend their interests within the democratic political institutions. Socialism, as such, remained the ultimate end, and strong Socialist parties, supported by the vote of the workers, were expected to press for, or undertake comprehensive measures for, the welfare and well-being of the workers. Even if Socialist parties would not gain a majority, they could still carry great weight within representative assemblies and could directly influence governments to adopt measures favoring the working class. Broad educational reforms, health, accident, and unemployment insurance, retirement benefits, paid holidays, the reduction of work hours, paid

Table 3.2   THE STRENGTH OF THE GERMAN SOCIAL DEMOCRATS[a]

	Votes	Seats in Parliament (Reichstag)
1890	1,427,298	35
1893	1,786,738	44
1898	2,107,076	56
1903	3,010,771	81
1907	3,259,029	43
1912	4,250,401	110
1919	13,000,000	177
1920	11,100,000	184
1924	6,008,900	100
1928	9,153,000	153
1933[b]	**7,181,000**	**120**

[a]Since 1949, when the Federal Republic of Germany was established, the party has averaged about 37 percent of the vote.

[b]Last relatively free election before Hitler assumed full control.

vacations, collective bargaining, welfare measures for the poor and the incapaci-
tated, public works, reform in tax policies favoring low-income groups, and progressively higher taxes on middle and high incomes—these were essential and
beneficial measures to ameliorate the conditions of the workers within the broad
framework of both capitalism and democracy. Nationalizations could wait or be
selectively undertaken under propitious political and economic circumstances.
Gradually, a consensus evolved in the acceptance of the welfare state and of a
mixed economy—combining state economic controls and social services with the
market economy.

REFORMING CAPITALISM

Efforts to reform capitalism come from a variety of nonsocialist sources. The
premise of a free market and a price mechanism reflecting the law of supply and
demand gave way gradually to regulation. Overriding questions of health, education, unemployment, and poverty required regulatory legislation. Wild fluctuations
in prices in the market called for controls, especially when they affected the prices
of essential commodities like food and housing. Monopolies, which gave private
owners control over needed commodities and hence freedom to adjust prices to
satisfy the insatiable profit motive, had to be dealt with. Gradually, and especially
in the twentieth century, economic liberalism underwent major reforms.

Keynesian Economics   Reliance on the automatic performance of the market—for the adjustment of prices, savings, and employment—came under serious
reconsideration, thanks to the theoretical insights of the English economist John
Maynard Keynes (1883–1946). According to Keynes, the market by itself could
not provide a full utilization of resources, and the state should move into the picture with indirect controls.

By increasing the flow of money and decreasing the interest rates, there could
be renewed investments, which would snowball into the creation of new jobs and
hence more revenue to stimulate further demand. Thus unemployment would be
absorbed and resources fully utilized. In the process, inflationary pressures would
be avoided with appropriate tax measures. In this manner, capitalism would be
both reformed and salvaged. The public authorities would become its guardian
angel, and no structural modifications involving property rights, entrepreneurial
freedoms and incentives, or state planning in the allocation of resources or in
price-fixing would be required. "Keynesianism" resulted in policies adopted in a
number of countries ever since the 1930s, including Nazi Germany and the United States, especially through the development of public works projects, public
spending, and more generally through fiscal policy—including deficit financing.
Today when we talk about "capitalism," we virtually always have in mind reformed
capitalism, in which the public authorities, through fiscal policy and spending, play
a determining role in the market.

The Welfare State   The major instrument for ensuring social and economic
rights became the welfare state—the complex of public services and payments

John Maynard Keynes (1883–1946)

Considered by many as the greatest economist of the twentieth century, Keynes questioned the fundamental assumption of classic economists about the autonomy of the "economic laws" and opened the door for indirect state intervention. In both his *Treatise on Money* (2 volumes, 1930) and his *General Theory of Employment, Interest and Money* (1936), Keynes stressed the importance of monetary policy in providing for the full utilization of all resources, including labor. By manipulating the volume of money and the rate of interest through a central bank, the government could stimulate investment and employment (or, if needed, avert inflation). By lowering interest rates, for instance, it could stimulate investment, production, and employment. If this failed, and Keynes was particularly concerned in the years of the Great Depression with unemployment, the government could stimulate demand through "public works" that would simply put money in the pockets of many and thus stimulate demand, which in turn would stimulate investment and production. Keynes was not a socialist; he simply provided the best cure for the ailing free-market economy.

that correspond to "entitlements." The very magnitude of these entitlements is staggering. In the late 1970s, total government payments to individuals in various forms and through various services amounted to from 19 percent of the gross national product in the United States to as much as 40 to 60 percent in countries such as France or Sweden.

In all contemporary democracies the growth of social and economic rights calls for a series of choices, and this is what public policy is all about. Which services should be provided for everybody? What groups merit special attention? What are the limits below which poverty exists and should be prevented? The list is long, but by and large most democratic regimes have followed a similar route in establishing priority choices. Children and education have been at the top of the list, with minimal educational services provided. However, with ever-expanding requirements for schooling, a free college education was added in some countries, the United States being the first to do so.

The aged came next, with emphasis on pensions. In many countries today the age limit for retirement is set at sixty for women and sixty-two for men.

The third step came with legislation requiring the state to provide for employment or to cover the unemployed through special benefits (unemployment insurance). It is presently financed through compulsory contributions and public funds, and public subsidies have steadily grown. In Europe after World War II, a comprehensive scheme was developed, which provided for uniform payments and minimum income levels. In the United States, since the Social Security Act of 1935, an ever-expanding number of employees have been included, contributions have been raised steadily, and benefits have increased.

Health care was the fourth step. Originally undertaken by private and religious organizations, it has been increasingly assumed by government agencies either through insurance programs or through direct payments and services. Germany was the first country to develop a nationwide health program even before the turn of the century. England followed after the turn of the century, and in 1948 it introduced a most comprehensive medical care program: it nationalized all health services and hospitals and incorporated almost all the doctors into the National Health Service. Health care became free, a right of all citizens. In Sweden, a health insurance plan is mandatory, and every citizen receives health care free of charge. In France, medical expenses are covered through a system that combines insurance paid for by individuals with direct payments by the employer and the state. In the United States, it is only after age sixty-five that citizens become directly covered through the Medicare programs.

Although education, health, retirement, and unemployment coverage do provide some safeguards against unaffordable costs, the so-called safety net in the United States, is full of holes. Despite this supplementary income, there are millions who find themselves without adequate income—they are the poor. It is to plug these holes and support the poor that the income maintenance and public assistance programs have been developed everywhere. They are aimed at raising minimal income levels to tolerable ones. Minimum wages become a matter of public policy, and most democratic regimes have set a minimum floor below which wages cannot fall. But with a family to support, a minimum wage is often inadequate.

Various income maintenance programs are used to raise the family income. Tax exemptions, special benefits in the form of cash payments, rent allowances, food subsidies, special allowances for children, day care centers for working mothers, school lunches, maternity benefits, and all sorts of other free services are calculated to do so.

Public assistance programs and related special treatment and payments are afforded to special segments of society. Although these programs also vary from one country to another, they are almost always available, at least for a given time. However, their purpose is to provide a family with a minimum income, not to equalize income, even if they lessen the distance between the rich and the poor. Security and often a small cushion of adequacy are all that can be expected.

Mixed Economy   *Capitalism,* as we have seen, is a system of social organization in which the means of production is controlled by private persons and firms who make all decisions on how and what to produce and on how benefits are to be distributed. In direct contrast, *socialism* calls for all decisions about production, distribution, and benefits to be made by publicly owned and publicly managed firms. These, of course, are only definitions—"ideal types." When some ownership, management, and decision making is in the hands of the state and some is in the hands of private persons and firms, we have what is referred to as a *mixed economy.*

Virtually all the so-called free-market capitalist economies, including the United States and Japan, are mixed economies. The state plays a critically important role, even when it does not own any of the means of production, which it often does, in deciding what and how much will be produced, how the distribution benefits will be made, and what they will be.

The state widely promotes business ventures and provides a great number of services (i.e., highway and airport construction, air traffic controllers, medical inspection and vaccines, and so forth). In all capitalist democracies, the state is a big employer—providing employment for 15 to 30 percent of those gainfully employed; it is the biggest contractor—for goods and services; it is the biggest spender. In all of these governments, the state plays a critical role in the determination of services and benefits. This has not changed appreciably either in England or the United States in the last decade. Similarly, and particularly in France, despite privatizations of many socialized firms, the state participates directly or indirectly in their operation. In Italy, Japan, and Germany many major industrial firms operate under the control of state-owned banks or under semipublic financial and industrial "umbrella" organizations through which investment and production policies are made. Capitalism, in other words, as it developed in Western Europe and elsewhere, has included powerful ingredients of statism and socialism. Not so incidentally, a kind of "people's capitalism" has been developing in which workers own stocks through their pension funds or profit-sharing arrangements with their employers.

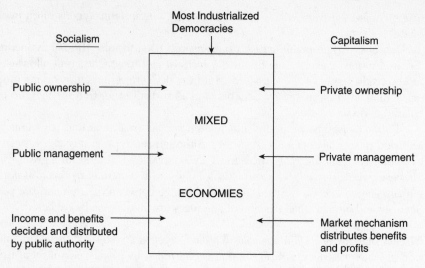

Figure 3.2 **The socialist/capitalist mix.**

How mixed is a mixed economy? The greater the portion of the economy owned by individual firms who make decisions about production and the distribution of benefits, the closer we move in the direction of capitalism, and vice versa (Figures 3.2 and 3.3). In most capitalist economies the "mix" is there. Just to give you an idea, in the seven largest OECD countries,[9] public spending is now about 39 percent of the gross national product (GNP); it was only 29 percent in 1960. The state takes the following percentage of the GNP in taxes: Sweden, 57 percent; France, 43 percent; Britain, 39 percent; Italy, 38 percent; Japan and the United States, about 30 percent. In many of these countries, significant areas of economic activity—public transportation, including the airlines, electricity and gas, nuclear energy, steel—are either owned and operated by public agencies or are subsidized by the state.

For many, the welfare state and the growth of mixed economies represented a synthesis that has put an end to the bitter conflicts between capital and labor and has transcended the ideological conflicts between Socialists on the one side and liberals or conservatives on the other. This trend was one of the reasons that prompted the noted sociologist Daniel Bell to announce the end of ideology in the early fifties.

BACK TO CAPITALISM?

Some Recent Trends

Democracy, liberalism, radical democracy, democratic socialism, the welfare state—in successive waves, through the nineteenth century and into the twentieth,

---

[9]OECD stands for the Organization of Economic Cooperation and Development, and provides, among many other services, the best surveys of current economic trends.

Extent of State Ownership

	Posts	Telecommunications	Electricity	Gas	Oil production	Coal	Railways	Airlines	Motor industry	Steel	Ship building
Australia	●	●	●	●	○	○	●	◑	○	○	NA
Austria	●	●	●	●	●	●	●	●	●	●	NA
Belgium	●	●	◕	◕	NA	○	●	●	○	◑	○
Brazil	●	●	●	●	●	●	●	◔	○	◕	○
Britain	●	◑	○	○	◕	●	●	●	●	○	●
Canada	●	◔	●	○	○	○	◔	◑	○	○	○
France	●	●	●	●	NA	●	●	◔	◑	◔	○
West Germany	●	●	◕	◑	◕	◑	●	●	◔	◕	◕
Holland	●	●	◕	◕	NA	NA	●	◕	◔	◕	○
India	●	●	●	●	●	●	●	●	○	◕	●
Italy	●	●	◕	●	NA	NA	●	●	◔	◕	●
Japan	●	●	○	○	NA	○	◔	◕	○	○	○
Mexico	●	●	●	●	●	●	●	●	◑	◔	◕
South Korea	●	●	◕	○	NA	◔	●	○	○	◔	○
Spain	●	◑	○	◔	NA	◑	●	●	◑	◑	◕
Sweden	●	●	◑	●	NA	NA	●	◑	○	◔	◔
Switzerland	●	●	●	●	NA	NA	●	◕	○	○	NA
United States	●	○	◕	○	○	○	◔*	○	○	○	○

○ Privately owned all or nearly all ● Publicly owned all or nearly all ◕ 75% ◑ 50% ◕ 25%

* Including Conrail,
NA- Not applicable or negligible production.

Figure 3.3

This appeared in *The Economist* (December 30, 1978). I have adjusted the original table to include major privatizations that have taken place in England in the 1980s: aerospace, oil, Jaguar, telecommunications, Rolls Royce, British Airways, British Steel, electricity were privatized. In France, after a wave of nationalizations in 1981–1982, major sectors of the economy were denationalized in 1988. In all, 30 major banking and industrial units were returned to private hands. Thus, France's economy was becoming clearly "mixed" and moving in the direction of a free market. Extensive privatizations have been taking place throughout the whole of Eastern Europe. In Italy, Sweden, Mexico, Spain, Austria, and Brazil, privatizations are in process, while in China free market zones have been established and farmers have been freed from state controls. Reprinted by permission.

these movements have shaped a new consensus. Its major feature has been the reconciliation of individual and political rights and freedoms with direct state intervention in the economy and the provision of social services.

The concept of the triple core of liberalism helps us identify the consensus. Early liberalism stressed personal rights and civil rights—the moral core. This was retained by democracy, which also expanded the political core of liberalism by institutionalizing majoritarianism, organizing political parties, eliminating voter qualifications, and minimizing restraints on the power of the representative assemblies. Socialism maintained respect for individual and civil rights (the moral core), accepted the political core, and squarely introduced the question of comprehensive economic controls and social services. This is the essence of the welfare state. It is this consensus that is being shaken by the resurgence of capitalism.

Inspired by some of the works of F. A. Hayek, Ludwig von Mises, and more recently Milton Friedman, the "neo-liberals" or "neo-liberal conservatives," as they are often referred to, restate forcefully the tenets of the early economic liberals that we surveyed in Chapter 2. They argue that political, moral, and economic freedoms—the three cores of liberalism—are inextricably and organically linked. These freedoms stand or fall together. State economic controls inevitably invite political controls that lead to an authoritarian system of government.

William Buckley, reemphasizing capitalism as an ideology, makes the linkage between economic freedom and political freedoms:

> Economic freedom is the most precious temporal freedom, for the reason that it alone gives to each one of us, in our comings and goings in our complex society, sovereignty—and over that part of existence in which by far the most choices have in fact to be made, and in which it is possible to make choices, involving oneself, without damage to other people. And for the further reason that without economic freedom, political and other freedoms are likely to be taken from us.[10]

The arguments presented by neo-liberals are clear and pointed: bureaucracy leads to inefficiency; state controls and regulations stifle competition and are wasteful because they increase the cost of production. Furthermore, we become dependent upon bureaucratic and impersonal services for which nobody is responsible. In 1946, F. A. Hayek, a professor of economics at the University of Chicago, wrote *The Road to Serfdom*, in which he sounded the alarm. State intervention and economic planning, he argued, and the end of individual economic freedoms would result in moral degradation for all of us and the ultimate loss of our political freedoms as well. The bureaucratic state would make choices for us—what to produce and what to consume, where to work and where to live, what income to make, and so on. The same theme is repeated by Buckley:

> What all conservatives in this country fear, and have plenty of reason to fear, is the loss of freedom by attrition. It is therefore for the most realistic reasons, as well as those of principle, that we must resist every single accretion of power by the State.[11]

---

[10]William F. Buckley, Jr., *Up From Liberalism*, p. 166.
[11]Buckley, p. 179.

Buckley provides the following list of particulars:

> to maintain and wherever possible enhance the freedom of the individual to acquire property and dispose of that property in ways that he decides on. To deal with unemployment by eliminating monopoly unionism, featherbedding, and inflexibilities in the labor market, and be prepared, where residual unemployment persists, to cope with it locally, placing the political and humanitarian responsibility on the lowest feasible political unit.[12]

In the last decade, no one has better expressed the position of the neo-liberals than Nobel Prize winner and economist Milton I. Friedman. One of his books, *Free to Choose* (written with his wife Rose), popularized the basic arguments against state intervention in the economy and the belief that such intervention will inevitably lead to controls that will undermine the moral autonomy of individuals and erode political freedoms.

Alongside the neo-liberal position, a second major argument has gained ground and relates to the efficiency of a free-market economy—where competition and free enterprise reign and where economic decisions are made in the market. It is an argument that has gained strength for two reasons. First, the economic crisis in many free-market democracies in the 1970s—with growing unemployment, inflation, and low rates of growth—was attributed to state regulation, the exorbitant growth of the welfare state, and government spending that did not stimulate the economy, as Keynes would have it. On the contrary, government produced, without taking into account the "defense establishment," a large bureaucracy to which resources were diverted; dependent upon this bureaucracy was now a growing number of recipients of welfare services. Second, the 1980s witnessed chaos in the socialist "command economies" of Eastern Europe, the Soviet Union, and China, where the means of production had been socialized and where the state had become virtually the sole manager. This growing disarray in socialist economies reinforced the arguments of those who favored a return to capitalism. Without individual property linked to responsibility and risk, and without the market to reflect accurately consumer demands and to regulate prices, their economies, it was argued, had entered a period of chronic stagnation—far worse than that of capitalism during the Great Depression of the thirties. This economic crisis also undermined private incentives and motivations, causing what some called an "egalitarian lethargy"! Unlike the Great Depression, however, it was a systemic collapse, and the socialist economies were unable to provide the seeds of their recovery.

Capitalism, therefore, simultaneously became the battle cry against mixed economy and the welfare state in many industrialized democracies and the driving ideology for many in Eastern Europe and even the Soviet Union who sought economic and political reform. For the industrialized democracies, the state had to be cut down to size; for Eastern Europe and the Soviets, it had to be thoroughly overhauled and democratized by disgorging the economy it had swallowed without being able to digest it.

---

[12]Buckley, p. 202.

The resurgence of capitalism is associated with the years of the Reagan presidency (1980–1988), the government of Margaret Thatcher in England (1979–1990), and the remarkable turnaround of the French Socialist party between 1982 and 1983. In the first case, the Reagan ideology was antistate and antiwelfare, emphasizing deregulation and so-called "supply-side" economics, whereby the state provides benefits and exemptions to those who own the means of production rather than helping the consumer and promoting consumer demand. The second case in England took the form of sweeping privatizations and efforts (not always successful) to reduce spending and welfare benefits. The third case in France was even more spectacular. Socialism and the socialization of major sectors of the economy were abandoned by the French Socialist government in favor of a return, first, to indirect forms of privatization in socialized sectors of the economy and, later, to an outright acceptance of the free market.

In Eastern Europe and the former Soviet Union, the same phenomenon was very much in evidence. The state began to privatize by selling off nationalized sectors and firms, legalizing private property, and attempting to liberate the market from state subsidies and price controls. It has been a process that links the return to the free market and the profit motive with the restoration of political democracy.

POLITICAL PARTIES AND THE SHIFT TO CAPITALISM

Everywhere the move is in the direction of capitalism, and this is reflected in the shift of the platform and the ideologies of all political parties. From the Communist party, excepting some diehards, to the British and other Conservative parties—all have moved, some more assertively than others, from socialism, a mixed economy, and welfare spending to privatizations, a free market, and economic liberalism.

Communist Parties   Even before the fall of the Soviet Union, Communist parties throughout all industrialized democracies had undergone a significant transformation. They abandoned their rigid commitment to the socialization of the means of production and in some cases, as in Italy and Spain, began to favor privatizations of nationalized sectors. They also abandoned their commitment to class struggle and revolution. Instead, they accepted democracy and majority rule and periodic elections. For all practical purposes, they became reformist parties, with the Italian Communist party showing the way by renaming itself the Democratic Party of the Left.

Despite such efforts to redefine themselves, the Communist parties of Western Europe are struggling just to stay alive. When the bell tolled for the Communist parties of Eastern Europe, it may have sounded the death knell for their western counterparts as well. Or so the precipitous drop in the popular vote for the Communist parties in such countries as France and Spain seems to suggest.

Socialist Parties   Since the end of World War II, and more rapidly in the last decade, virtually all socialist parties abandoned their original tenets and have begun to endorse the free market. They continue to advocate state controls but only when the market cannot provide needed services. The British Labour party, the German Social Democrats, and the French Socialists have abandoned the major tenet of socialism—the nationalization of the economy. After the first nationalization was instituted by the Labour party (1945–1951), during which coal mines, railroads, electricity, gas, iron, and steel were nationalized, the emphasis was put on welfare legislation, an equitable incomes policy, and efforts to meet the demands of the trade unions and to arrest inflation. Reconstruction of the economy, in order to maintain Great Britain's competitive position in the world economy, became a primary goal. Today the Labour party is divided, but the moderate wing is gaining ground. It is beginning to appeal again to the middle classes as a reformist party that accepts the free market even though it continues to favor welfare policies.

In Germany, the Social Democrats abandoned their commitment to socialization as early as 1959 in the Bad Godesberg Congress with the slogan "the state whenever necessary, freedom whenever possible." In office, the German Social Democrats undertook no major structural reforms of the economy. However, they introduced welfare legislation and maintained a wage policy that favored the workers, something that was made possible by the remarkable strength and competitiveness of German industry. But they lost the election in both 1983 and 1987 and again in 1990.

Perhaps nothing better illustrates the predicament of socialism than the rise and fall of French socialism. The French Socialist party came to power in May 1981—with the election of a Socialist president and a Socialist majority in the National Assembly. It proceeded with speed and great ideological commitment to put into practice the Socialist blueprint: the nationalization of all banks and of most of the major industrial sectors and the strengthening of the welfare programs. Health, retirement, and unemployment benefits were increased; paid vacations for the workers were extended to five weeks; wages were raised and early retirement provisions were made. The intent of these reforms was to achieve what virtually all other European Socialist parties, including the British Labour party, had forsaken. However, by 1983, the French Socialists abandoned their plan in the face of growing unemployment, high budget deficits, a growing trade deficit, a high rate of inflation, and negative public opinion. They began to turn to the private sector and to gradually privatize the firms they had nationalized, many of which showed deficits. From public management they moved to private entrepreneurship. In the election of March 1986 it was the conservative and centrist parties that won a majority in the National Assembly and proceeded to privatize a number of firms— with assets of about 20 billion dollars. When the Socialist President, François Mitterrand was re-elected in 1988, he promised not to return to nationalizations, but also not to allow any further privatizations. Early in 1991, however, all major nationalized firms were allowed to raise capital in the private market by issuing stocks and bonds. The state would continue to own 51% of the assets, thus maintaining technically control. But in effect the French economy was becoming "mixed" and moving in the direction of the free market.

The Future of Socialism   It appears that socialism may have run its course as virtually all Socialist parties have come to terms with, even if with reservations, a free-market economy. Socialism bequeathed a legacy—a social ethic of equality, collective effort, and cooperation. It served well the working classes, the under-privileged, and society as a whole. But what about its future? Without a commit-ment to broad structural economic reforms and the socialization of the means of production, without a strong advocacy of economic planning, unable to suggest policies that can put an end to unemployment and rescue the underclass from its miseries, how can we distinguish socialism, even if it were to remain faithful to the welfare state, from other parties? The answer at this stage is that we cannot. What is next, then?

The prospects for socialism lie in the efforts of socialist leaders to build viable coalitions around certain issues that attract groups of voters, not in the projection of a new socialist philosophy, a new ideology about the state and the economy. A new coalition is possible, which could begin with many Communists who have lost their faith. It is in this spirit that the Italian Socialists revealed their pleasure at the proposal by the Italian Communist leadership to change its party name and to form a "broad reformist coalition." A second group that could embrace such a coalition might be the environmentalists, and thus the coalition could assume lead-ership for one of the potentially most powerful movements in the upcoming decade. A third group to reach out to would be the feminists and women voters and to project a vision of equality that would satisfy women's demands for the pro-vision of social services that deal with women's issues. Fourth, there is the prospect of attracting the faceless underclass that will need to be mobilized and made con-scious of its potential political strength by promising the services they need and hope for. There is also, finally, now that the Socialists have virtually forsaken the socialization of the means of production, the possibility of an alliance between them and progressive Catholic forces, many of them in Catholic and Christian democratic parties.

Christian Democratic Parties   Christian democratic parties founded in the nineteenth century reemerged with renewed strength after the liberation of Eu-rope in 1945: in Germany, France, Belgium, Austria, Holland, and Italy. In the 1970s, these parties have surfaced in Portugal, Spain, and Latin America with new vigor. Their renewed strength was due to the synthesis they provided between *so-cial Catholicism,* which was committed to social reform, and *liberal* or *democratic Catholicism,* which was committed to democracy.

Christian democratic movements had opposed fascism and participated in great number in the various resistance movements against the Nazi and Fascist regimes and the puppet regimes they established. The MRP in France ("Popular Republicans") became the largest single party in the year immediately following liberation. In the election of June 2, 1946, the MRP won 28.1 percent of the vote, and its leaders held key positions in the cabinets formed thereafter. In Italy, Chris-tian democracy emerged as the largest single party after the liberation and, despite losses, has held this position ever since. Christian Democrats in the Federal Republic of Germany—replacing the old Catholic "Center" party—have continued strong ever since the end of World War II, heading the governing coalition for twenty-eight out of the last forty-five years. In Switzerland, Norway, Austria, Holland, and Belgium, Christian democratic parties have continued to command the vote of 20 to 30 percent of the electorate. In the 1970s and 1980s, Catholic parties in Spain and Portugal reappeared and gained momentum. Beyond Europe, Christian democracy also developed, especially in Latin America. In Chile, Christian Democrats won the presidency in 1964 and commanded 31 percent of the vote in the election of 1973. They have opposed both military dictatorship and communism.

While they defend the interests and moral tenets of the church with regard to legislation concerning the subsidies, immunities, and freedoms for the church and the clergy, as well as legislation regarding primary education, divorce, and abortion, Christian democratic parties are no longer "confessional parties." They appeal to all citizens, irrespective of their religion, and they get the vote of many non-Catholics.

With the collapse of Communist regimes throughout Eastern Europe, after 1989 Christian Democratic parties resurfaced and showed strength in this part of the world; the Christian Democrats won as much as 46 percent of the vote in East Germany. Their vote ranged from 8 to 12 percent in Eastern Europe. And as it has been the case with Socialist and Social Democratic parties, Christian Democrats have veered increasingly in the direction of a market economy. This is clearly so with the Italian Christian Democrats and also with the German Christian Democratic party, which won a majority in the first elections in a united Germany on December 2, 1990. It is even more so with the resurging Christian Democratic parties throughout Eastern Europe where, as we noted, the anti-Communist movements were linked with demands for economic freedoms. Christian democracy today is generally allied with liberal parties and groups that favor a free-market economy, even when the conscience of many Catholics is with social services for the poor and the underprivileged.

Environmentalist Parties   The small environmentalist parties that have sprung up throughout Europe remain committed to state controls of the economy. Ironically enough, they are perhaps closer to genuine socialism than most of the Socialist parties. Their adherents advocate a plan to deal with industrial growth and environmental issues. Most of them consider capitalism to be the single major cause for the degradation of the quality of our lives and of the environment. But most of the environmentalist parties are in their infancy, and their political weight is small in England, Austria, Germany, Belgium, the Scandinavian countries, France, Eastern Europe, and the former Soviet Union. What is even more relevant, however, is that a number of their leaders are beginning to come to terms with the notion that capitalism can be tamed and reformed to become compatible with environmental protection and regulation.

Liberal and Conservative Parties   Liberal parties throughout Europe, as is the case with the Democratic and Republican parties (including conservatives) in the United States (see Chapter 4), are the most outspoken advocates of economic liberalism—of capitalism. Conservatives in Europe have traditionally favored a paternalistic economy and state controls and regulations, including even national- izations; now they have become advocates of deregulation and a free market. Both the British Conservatives under Margaret Thatcher (1979–1990) and the Gaullists in France, ever since the early seventies, have moved ever closer to the tenets of a free-market economy. They urged and brought about privatizations in the socialist sector of the economy, and they are committed to the reduction of taxes and gov- ernment spending.

The political spectrum in Europe, North America and throughout the world is changing; a great number of political parties everywhere have shifted to the "right," as they come to terms with the free market economy and as they move from socialism to the mixed economy. The welfare consensus is eroding and a new consensus appears to be evolving away from statism and in the direction of indi- vidual economic freedoms, competition and profit incentives in the direction of a free market. The trend has been reinforced in the last decade by the growth of an international economy and free trade, which obeys the logic of a global free mar- ket and calls for the reduction of tariffs and state subsidies and controls. Related to this growth is the remarkable performance of the economies of the so-called newly industrialized countries (NICs)—Taiwan, Singapore, South Korea, Hong Kong, and perhaps Thailand and Malaysia. Events in these countries have reinforced the arguments of economic liberals. The state—any state—is at bay, and the welfare ideology that combined the socialist ethic of equality and state service is on the defensive. The association of political freedoms with a free market, particularly so in Eastern Europe and the former Soviet Union, has strengthened capitalism as an ideology everywhere—at least for the time being.

CAPITALISM: PROBLEMS AND PROSPECTS

There are many critical problems with capitalism that should not be overlooked, especially now that it is being associated with the spread of democracy.

The Crisis of Rising Expectations

Everybody is familiar with the phrase "the revolution of rising expectations." It is common not only among poor nations, which have recently gained their indepen- dence and are underdeveloped, but also among peoples of the rich countries in Western Europe and the United States. The most characteristic manifestation of the "revolution" is that all people want *more of everything*— more wealth, a high- er standard of living, better education, greater security, better health care, more participation in decision making, more leisure, and greater equality. The speed with which these expectations have escalated and have converged has created seri- ous problems.

A crisis in modern democratic regimes is primarily caused by the disparity between ideology and institutional capabilities. Ideology conjures up a world of plenty and immediate fulfillment. It shapes the new moral imperatives of equality and of equal sharing in opportunities and benefits. However, institutions are slow to respond to the pressure, and as a result, democratic regimes are faced with the prospect of instability.

It is simply difficult to meet all the rising demands, not only because resources are limited, but because structural and institutional changes are needed in order to meet them. New services are required and new institutional mechanisms must be put in place. Even the most open and responsive systems experience a time lag between when demands are made and registered and when new mechanisms are developed to respond to them—let alone satisfy them.

The intensity and number of demands from minorities, professional organizations, trade unions, student groups, cultural associations, and so on (many couched in sharp ideological terms) threaten to overwhelm the existing democratic institutions. This is likely to cause upheavals in the institutional framework of democratic societies.

Social Costs

Private firms and industries whose major incentive is profitability often neglect basic social considerations and do not take proper steps to protect societal interests. For instance, virtually all industrial companies directly utilize goods that affect us all—the air we breathe, for instance, or the water we drink. Many of the activities of these corporations may adversely affect resources on which we depend for our very lives. Yet these industries do not assume a liability for the social predicaments they cause—leaving it to the state to do so. The public ultimately incurs the expenditure, while the companies pocket the gain. Similarly, industrial firms show little consideration for the community within which they operate; for example, they may sell themselves to another firm—domestic or foreign—for a profit. In all such cases the costs to the workers and the community are great. Capitalism appears, therefore, as an impersonal force, without social, human, or communal concerns.

Inequalities

Capitalist economies show a growing disparity between the wealthy and the poor.[13] We are beginning to refer to an "underclass"—the homeless, the unemployed, the unemployable, the mentally ill or handicapped, the drug addicted. Depending on the exact definition of the term—and there is none—the number is large and growing. In many Western European democracies, unemployment has become virtually chronic for as many as 10 percent of the workers. It has been rising in the United States between 1988 and 1990 and by 1992 it had reached 7.4 percent. By 1994 it declined to 6.1 percent.

Moreover, on a worldwide basis, the disparity between a few wealthy nations (not more than twenty-five or thirty, as measured in terms of resources, gross

---

[13]See Kevin Phillips, *The Politics of Rich and Poor.*

national income, and per capita income) and all others, especially those of the Third World, has been growing. Since the capitalist economy is becoming increasingly an international economy, we may speak, therefore, of a growing *worldwide underclass,* excluded from the benefits that capitalism promises.[14] The poor throughout the world are migrating in despair to the industrialized, rich countries, where they hope to find shelter and food. Misery and poverty breed resentment and may incite violence. If so, not only the global economy will be held responsible, but its capitalist foundations, favoring free trade in goods and services and the free movement of capital as well as individuals, will be seriously questioned. So will political democracy with which the resurgence of capitalism is linked.

Any economic upheaval, even if not as severe as the Great Depression of 1929, will shatter the democratic political order that is rising. It will snap the links between economic liberalism (capitalism) and democracy, and weaken both. The coming decade or two will decide their future and our fate!

BIBLIOGRAPHY

Socialism

Bernstein, Eduard. *Evolutionary Socialism.* New York: Scribner's 1961.

Brucan, Silviu. *World Socialism at the Crossroads: An Insider's View.* Westport, CT.: Greenwood Press, 1990.

Buber, Martin. *Paths in Utopia.* Boston: Beacon Press, 1958.

Cerny, Philip G., and Martin A. Schain (eds.). *Socialism, the State and Public Policy in France.* New York: Methuen, 1985.

Cole, G. D. H. *A History of the Labour Party Since 1914.* London: Routledge and Kegan Paul, 1948.

———. *A History of Socialist Thought,* 6 vols. London: Macmillan, 1953–1960.

——— and A. W. Filson. *Working Class Movements: Selected Documents.* New York: St. Martin's Press, 1965.

Crossman, R. H. S. (ed.). *The New Fabian Essays.* New York: Praeger, 1952.

———. *The Politics of Socialism.* New York: Atheneum, 1965.

Engels, Friedrich, "Socialism: Utopian and Scientific." In Robert C. Tucker, *The Marx–Engels Reader,* 2nd ed. New York: Norton, 1978, pp. 683–717.

Gay, Peter. *The Dilemma of Democratic Socialism.* New York: Columbia University Press, 1952.

Hancock, Donald M., and Gideon Sjoberg (eds.). *Politics in the Post-Welfare State.* New York: Columbia University Press, 1972.

Harrington, Michael. *Socialism: Past and Future.* New York: Little, Brown, 1989.

Joll, James. *The Second International, 1889–1914.* New York: Praeger, 1956.

---

[14]See Robert B. Reich: *The Work of Nations: Preparing Ourselves for 21st Century Capitalism.*

Manuel, Frank. *Utopian Thought in the Western World.* Cambridge, MA.: Harvard University Press, 1979.

Markovic, M. *Democratic Socialism: Theory and Practice.* New York: St. Martin's Press, 1982.

Shaw, George Bernard (ed.). *Fabian Essays in Socialism.* London: Allen and Unwin, 1958. (Reprint of 1889 edition.)

Wallace, Lillian Parket. *Leo XIII and the Rise of Socialism.* Durham, N.C.: Duke University Press, 1966.

Reforming Capitalism

Cyr, Arthur I. *Liberal Party Politics in Britain.* New Brunswick, N.J.: Transaction Books, 1977.

Berkowitz, Edward, and Kim McQuaid. *Creating the Welfare State: The Political Economy of Twentieth-Century Reform,* rev. ed., New York: Praeger, 1988.

Flora, Peter, ed. *Growth to Limits: The Western European Welfare States since World War II: Sweden, Norway, Finland, Denmark,* vol. 1, Berlin and New York: Walter de Gruyter, 1986.

———. *Growth to Limits: The Western European Welfare States since World War II: Germany, United Kingdom, Ireland, Italy,* vol. 2. Berlin and New York: Walter de Gruyter, 1986.

Galbraith, John Kenneth. *American Capitalism: The Concept of Countervailing Power,* rev. ed. Boston: Houghton Mifflin, 1956.

———. *The New Industrial State.* Boston: Houghton Mifflin, 1967.

Goldthorpe, John. *Order and Conflict in Contemporary Capitalism.* Oxford: Clarendon Press, 1984.

Halévy, Elie. *The Growth of Philosophic Radicalism.* Boston: Beacon Press, 1955.

Heilbroner, Robert L. *The Limits of American Capitalism.* New York: Harper & Row, 1967.

Huntington, Samuel, et al. *Crisis of Democracy.* New York: New York University Press, 1975.

Jallade, Jean-Pierre, ed. *The Crisis of Redistribution in European Welfare States.* Stoke-on-Trent: Trentham Books, 1988.

Jordan, Bill. *Freedom and the Welfare State.* London: Routledge and Kegan Paul, 1978.

Keynes, John Maynard, *Collected Writings of John Maynard Keynes,* New York: St. Martin's Press, 1971.

Maier, Charles S. *Changing Boundaries of the Political: Essays on the Evolving Balance Between the State and Society, Public and Private in Europe.* New York: Cambridge University Press, 1987.

Paterson, William E., and Alastair Thomas. *The Future of Social Democracy in Western Europe.* New York: Oxford University Press, 1986.

Phillips, Kevin. *The Politics of Rich and Poor.* New York: Random House, 1990.

Schlesinger, Arthur, Jr. *The Age of Roosevelt.* vols. 1 and 2. Boston: Houghton Mifflin, 1957.

Schumpeter, Joseph A. *Capitalism, Socialism and Democracy.* New York: Harper & Row, 1950.

Thomson, David. *Democracy in France Since 1870,* 5th ed. New York: Oxford University Press, 1969.

Capitalism Again?

Bell, Daniel, and Irving Kristol (eds.). *Capitalism Today.* New York: New American Library, 1971.

Friedman, Milton. *Capitalism and Freedom.* Chicago: Chicago University Press, 1962.

────── and Rose Friedman. *Free to Choose.* New York: Harcourt Brace Jovanovich, 1980.

Hayek, F. A. *Road to Serfdom.* Chicago: University of Chicago Press, 1944.

──────. *The Constitution of Liberty.* London: Routledge and Kegan Paul, 1960.

Kymlicka, Will. *Liberalism, Community, and Culture.* New York: Oxford University Press, 1989.

Lloyd-Thomas, David. *In Defense of Liberalism.* Cambridge, MA.: Basil Blackwell, 1988.

MacFarlane, Alan. *The Culture of Capitalism.* Cambridge, MA.: Basil Blackwell, 1989.

Novak, Michael. *The American Vision: An Essay on the Future of Democratic Capitalism.* Washington, D.C.: American Enterprise Institute for Public Policy Research, 1978.

──────. *Spirit of Democratic Capitalism.* New York: Basic Books, 1983.

Reich, Robert B. *The Work of Nations: Preparing for 21st Century Capitalism.* New York: Knopf, 1990.

Seldon, Arthur. *Capitalism.* Oxford: Basil Blackwell, 1990.

Zysman, John. *Governments, Markets and Growth.* Ithaca, N.Y.: Cornell University Press, 1983.

Chapter
4

The Conservative Tradition

The good citizen is a law-abiding traditionalist.

Russell Kirk *What Is Conservatism?*

*I*t could be said that conservatism is more a state of mind than a political ideology. In order to be conservative, one must have something to conserve—property, status, power, a way of life. Conservatives are therefore likely to be those who have power or wealth or status and who simply want to keep things the way they are. Also, a significant number of people—mostly among rural groups, those who live in small towns, the old, and the uneducated—cannot imagine something different, or are afraid of change. They too want to keep their way of life the way it is.

However, even if we were to define conservatism simply as the defense of the status quo and the rationalization and the legitimization of a given order of things—in other words as a "situational ideology"—we would find that conservative ideology has its own logic.[1] Conservative movements always and everywhere borrow from some of the same principles, irrespective of the particular situation they face at a particular time. They are the following:

1. Individual liberties are more important to conservatives than "equality."
2. Conservatives have a pronounced allergy for political power—and are against its concentration in the hands of anybody, especially the people.

---

[1]In a penetrating article, Samuel Huntington indicates that conservatism can be viewed as (1) an ideology that emanated from the aristocracy as it rationalized its position and interests against the French Revolution of 1789—*aristocratic conservatism;* (2) an ideology that contains substantive prescriptions about the organization of social and political life—*autonomous conservatism;* (3) an ideology arising from a given situation in which the status quo is threatened by the prophets and the activists of change—*a situational ideology.* Conservatism is "the articulate, systematic, theoretical resistance to change. It is primarily an ideology that defends the status quo." (In *American Political Science Review,* v. LI, June 1957, no. 2, pp. 454–473.)

3. They insist on an organic theory of society, involving a hierarchy of groups and classes and a cooperation among them—the community and its interests are always above the individual.
4. They have a respect for tradition and "inheritance"—that which is bequeathed to us from our ancestors.
5. Religion, with its reverence for authority, is dear to conservatives.
6. They distrust "reason" and the propriety of using it as a solution for social problems.
7. Almost all conservative ideologies are elitist. Some people are better equipped than others; some are superior, while some (generally the many) are inferior.

These principles were invoked throughout the nineteenth century as certain groups fought to maintain their position against the egalitarian and reformist principles of democracy, liberalism, and, later on, socialism and Marxism.

A final note: the terms "conservative" and "reactionary" should not be confused as they so often are. A conservative doesn't want change—but will acquiesce to it—at least to gradual change. A "reactionary," on the other hand, is often one who wants to change things radically in order to reestablish the past. A conservative is against rapid change; a reactionary is one who doesn't accept the change that has already taken place! Nor should conservatism be confused with authoritarianism. The latter favors a concentration of political power in the hands of a leader or a group, is against individual and political freedoms, rejects popular participation in almost any form, and accepts repression and the use of force.

CLASSIC CONSERVATISM: THE BRITISH MODEL

The best formulation of conservative ideology was given by Edmund Burke, in the latter part of the eighteenth century. The best implementation of it has been, through the nineteenth century and until today, that of the British Conservative party.[2] Variants of the British model could be found in Germany under Bismarck, in France during the so-called Orleanist period (1830–1848) and in some of its offshoots during the period of the Third French Republic (1871–1940), and in Gaullism. But almost nowhere on the Continent did an alliance of the aristocracy and the upper classes, the church, the monarchy, and the army lead to the "classic" form of conservatism tied to constitutional democracy that prevailed in England.

European conservatives often chose to reject constitutional democracy and representative government. In the United States there have been many variants of a conservative ideology, but the absence of a nobility and the success of the egalitarian ethic and liberalism account for the virtual absence of any genuine conservative movement or ideology that has had any impact.

---

[2]An excellent discussion of the evolution of conservative ideology can be found in Samuel H. Beer, *British Politics in the Collectivist Age.*

Classic conservatism is characterized by certain basic propositions that relate to political authority, to a conception of society and the nature of the individual, and to the relationship between the national economy and the state.

The Political Society

Society, according to early British conservative thought, is organic and hierarchical. Classes and social groups fit together in the same way as do the various organs of the human body. One is indispensable to the others; it cannot function without them. Relations between them must be harmonious and balanced, and each group and each class performs the functions that are necessary to the others for the good health of the whole. Society is not like a machine, say a clock, in which the motions are eternally identical and where each part has no idea of what the other parts are doing. Rather, it is a combination of many parts, each one of which understands its role and perceives society as a whole. Unlike the machine, society knows it has a purpose; unlike a clock it grows and changes. "The whole," wrote Edmund Burke, "is never old, middle-aged, or young." It "moves on through . . . perpetual decay, fall, renovation, and progression."[3]

Society thus consists of interdependent parts—and all the parts are equally conscious of the interdependence. Each one does its own work, but what it does makes sense only when the whole is understood and valued. Farmers grow crops; soldiers keep order and give protection; priests improve our minds and souls; the leaders govern and balance the various parts. The parts working together almost lose the sense of their separateness. Society is not a "mixture" of various roles, groups, qualities, and activities. It is, as Aristotle said, much more of a "compound" in which the parts blend with each other to become something different from what they are individually. They become a society.

Different functions and roles inevitably suggest a hierarchical organization and social inequality. Some of society's roles are more important than others, and some people do more important things than others. This means that there must be a subordination of some individuals to others. Persons endowed by nature with certain qualities that others do not have should play the most important roles. Equality and freedom, as abstract propositions, are not acceptable to the conservative ideology. Instead, it emphasizes *rights* and *liberties*. These derive not from rational principles or from natural law but from specific institutional and legal arrangements, and from history and tradition. They give to individuals and to groups specific benefits, protections, and claims that are commensurate with their functions and roles. Nor is the idea of material equality for all seriously entertained. Material benefits should correspond to the talent shown and the work done.

The "whole"—this society that consists of the harmonious interdependence of many parts—is formalized in the Constitution. This is not a written document, and in fact there is no way, according to conservative thinkers, a constitution can be set

---

[3]Edmund Burke, *Reflections on the Revolution in France,* p. 162.

Edmund Burke (1729–1797)

Edmund Burke was the most eloquent expounder of British conservative ideology. Originally, Burke appeared to be a liberal, arguing not only against the prerogatives of the crown and in favor of Parliament, but also for the autonomy of the colonies in North America. These views were expressed in *Thoughts on the Causes of the Present Discontents* (1770). It was the French Revolution and its excesses that accounted for his masterpiece, *Reflections on the Revolution in France* (1790), in which he presented arguments favoring tradition and prescription, and the sanctity of law and authority, while cautioning against anything but the most gradual expansion of popular participation in affairs of state.

down. The Constitution is a set of customs, understandings, rules, and especially traditions, that define political power and set limits upon its exercise. Power thus enshrined by habit, custom, and tradition becomes authority; that is, it is accepted and respected. In this way, it is the Constitution that binds the whole of the citizenry to its rulers, and the rulers to the citizenry within the nation. Conservatives, however, are not necessarily nationalists. To them the nation-state is a social and historical reality, the product of many centuries of common life and togetherness. But it is not a supreme moral value unless it has managed to embody justice and order. "To make us love our country, our country must be lovely" was the pithy comment of Burke.

Political Authority

In contrast to those who establish the foundations of political authority on contract and consent, conservatives find it in tradition, custom, and in what they call inheritance and prescription. Society as a living whole is the result of natural evolution. The Constitution of England and its various parts—the monarchy, the House of Lords and the nobility, the House of Commons, individual rights, the judiciary— are an "entailed inheritance." One accepts it, and lives on it, but cannot waste it. In a famous passage, Burke sees in the state something like a mystery: its parts and its majesty cannot be dissected, analyzed, and put back together in the same or in a different way. *The state cannot be made.* He wrote:

> The state ought . . . to be looked upon with . . . reverence. . . . It is a partnership in all science; a partnership in all art; a partnership in all perfection . . . between those who are living, those who are dead and those who are to be born. . . . Each contract is but a clause in the great primeval contract of eternal society, linking the lower with the higher natures, connecting the visible with the invisible world, according to a fixed compact sanctioned by the inviolable oath which holds all physical and all moral natures, each in their appointed place.[4]

Conservatives, therefore, have no use for the "contract" theory of the state propounded by the early liberals. The idea runs counter to the organic theory of society and to the role history and tradition play in the formation of a state. Burke insisted that even if there were a contract it was shaped by history and tradition, and once made "it attaches upon every individual of that society, without any formal action of his own." We are born into political society like our father and forefathers; we do not make it.

Change

Given the emphasis on tradition, conservative thought is generally opposed to change unless it is gradual. Our "partnership with the dead" should not be broken, for fear that this would undermine the living and those still to be born. Modifications become necessary, but on balance the past carries more weight than the present. As for the future, there are many would-be reformers and social engineers,

---

[4]Burke, pp. 139–140.

and conservatives distrust them. Innovation is suspect, and Burke claimed it was prompted by "selfish temper and confined views." As a result, the conservatives fall back upon the existing and widely shared values that have kept the society together. Religion is one of the most important; so is common law and even prejudices. As Edmund Burke put it, "wise prejudice," consecrated by long usage, is "better than thoughts untried and untested."

Religion, tradition, the common law, and prejudice—all give the individual shelter and solace; they provide stability that in the last analysis is a higher value than change. All these things, together with the state and its organs, must be strengthened with the proper pomp and ritual that appeal to the common people. The crown itself is a symbol that, through ritual, secures support and obedience. More than fifty years after Burke, another British Conservative, Walter Bagehot (1826–1877), spoke of the "symbolic" or "ceremonial" part of the Constitution— the monarch—providing for the attachment of the common people and unifying political society. The cabinet, the prime minister, and Parliament were the "efficient part"—the government—though this was understood only by the elite and hardly appreciated by the common people.[5]

If change is to come, however, it must be natural and slow—one and the same thing for conservatives. Conservatives may even favor change in order to preserve. Change must reflect new needs and be the result of cautious adjustment with past practices. The British Conservatives *allowed* for changes in the Constitution, which they venerated; thus came about the gradual extension of the franchise, the ascendancy of the popularly elected House of Commons over the hereditary House of Lords, and the development of a civil service based on merit, as well as economic and social reforms. But they did so often under pressure, and with the aim of preserving what they valued most. In their efforts to slow down reform, however, British Conservatives remained firmly attached to the basic democratic principles of representative government, elections, and the rule of law.

Leadership

The purpose of the state and its leaders is to balance the whole and to create unity and commonality of purpose out of diversity. Government leadership and decision making should be entrusted to "natural leaders"—men or women of talent, high birth, and property, who have a stake in the interests of the country and in its fortunes. As late as the middle of the nineteenth century, many argued in England that noblemen could own, outfit, and command whole regiments in the army, and the explanation given was simple—they cared more about England's welfare than did the common people. They had a greater stake in the defense of the country.

As a conservative put it recently, "Government is instituted to secure justice and order . . . and . . . the first principle of good government allows the more energetic natures among a people to fulfill their promise while ensuring that these per-

---

[5]Walter Bagehot, *The English Constitution.*

sons shall not tyrannize over the mass of men."[6] Quality and not election should therefore be the source of leadership. Conservatives fought against the rapid extension of the franchise, acquiescing to it reluctantly, and did not accept the full logic of majority rule until very recently. The principle of one man–one vote was unacceptable, and the notion that decisions could be made by simple arithmetic majority could be entertained only when that majority, by long habits of obedience, had become self-disciplined. That would be when the majority had accepted the restraints that law and tradition had inculcated so as to act in accordance with the fundamental rules of the past.

The natural leaders hold the interests of the country in trust. They act on behalf of the people and the society. The trust, however, is almost a complete and blanket grant of power—it is not a delegation. Another way of explaining the same conservative notion of trusteeship is to refer to it as the theory of *virtual representation*. Today we agree that representatives represent their constituency, those who elect them, and the country in general, but their capacity to make decisions for us stems directly from elections and from the *mandate* they receive from their constituency or the electorate at large. Virtual representation, on the other hand, is the capacity to represent and make decisions by virtue of qualities other than mere election. Conservative thinking returns to the idea of birth and wealth. Persons who have one or both can represent the people and the nation by virtue of their position better than elected representatives. They are what in medieval times were called the *valentior pars* (the better part) of the community. This again shows the reluctance by conservatives to extend the franchise and accept majoritarianism.

Thus, the natural leaders should govern and the many should follow. This reflects the typical British conservative attitude, which still is evident today. Many of the members and leaders of the Conservative party still think that they are endowed with capabilities with which they can govern better than any other party and leadership. They still believe that they can hold the interest of the country in trust better than all others. They also think that the government has autonomous and independent powers to govern and that, once elected, it is free to exercise them. It is a government that once elected cannot be given instructions or be delegated to do some things and not others. So, there is an element of authoritarianism and elitism still lurking in the hearts of all good conservatives, together with a certain distrust for the "common people" or the "masses."

Paternalism

While conservatives believe that the propertied classes and the landed aristocracy have special privileges, they also agree that such privileges and their exercise have corresponding social obligations. Here there is a strong element of paternalism, whereby the natural leaders have to cater to the well-being of the common people

---

[6]Russell Kirk, "Prescription, Authority and Ordered Freedom," in F. S. Meyer (ed.), *What Is Conservatism?* p. 33.

by providing them with relief when out of work and at other times improving their living conditions. Because of their organic theory of society, conservatives tended to subordinate economic interests to the overall interest of the collectivity. Social solidarity and social cooperation are given precedence over particular interests. Finally, the purpose of "the whole" goes beyond simple material considerations. The state is an all-encompassing agency for providing justice and order. It has a moral purpose to which particularisms and economic interests must yield.

For all these reasons, conservatives reject the utilitarian philosophy of economic liberalism. Self-interest, unrestrained competition, individualism, and the very notion that the society is held together by competing claims and antagonisms—such ideas are repugnant to them. They reject laissez-faire economics, or at best tolerate it on condition that individual effort and competition not be allowed to tear apart the fabric of the society. They accept economic individualism if it allows everybody to show his or her worth and capabilities; they reject it if it leads to sharp inequalities and social strife that would upset the balance of the whole. British conservatives have favored state intervention and welfare measures, unlike other conservative parties on the Continent and elsewhere.

Constitutional Government and Democracy

The British Conservatives and their Conservative party became strong advocates of constitutional and representative government. In contrast to the European conservatives, they did not waver in their support of democracy and parliamentary institutions. Authoritarian and totalitarian solutions appealed to only a negligible number of their leaders and followers. In this way conservatism, while representing the status quo groups, recognized the realities of social change and the necessity of guiding it and reducing its speed rather than arresting it altogether. Classic conservatives appear something like a well-controlled dam and not a bulwark against the forces of change.

After the nineteenth century, Conservatives not only accepted major economic changes, such as the establishment of Britain's welfare state and the nationalization of its industries, but they themselves also *introduced* social and economic reforms. In 1951, when the Conservatives replaced the Labour government, they assumed the direction and the management of the nationalized industries and the welfare system Labour had built. The Conservative party did not reject Labour's social economic and welfare legislation; it tried to slow their pace of reform until it judged society as a whole had time to adjust to it. Thus, British Conservatives reconciled themselves to a new social and economic order.

The Conservative party remains staunchly committed to democratic principles. While the authority of the leader of the party is given greater scope than in the case of other parties, notably Labour, the Conservative party developed into a mass party with 3 to 4 million members. It holds annual conferences, allows its various organs considerable autonomy, holds free debates in which policy resolutions come from the floor, and can be endorsed despite the opposition of the leadership. It now recruits its candidates for the House of Commons without consideration of their personal wealth and ability to contribute to their own campaign or to the party. In general, despite its affinities with the upper status groups and wealthier segments of the population, it has managed to appeal to and get support from many of the voters who belong to the working or lower middle classes. The marriage between the cottage and the throne that the great Tory leader of the Victorian period, Disraeli, had suggested, developed into strong ties between the people and the Conservative party leadership. As a result the party has survived as one of the two major political groups in England.

To sum up some of the basic characteristics of classic conservative thought: there is a belief that society is like an organism; that its parts are hierarchically arranged; that authority should be entrusted to natural leaders. There is a rejection of individualism and egalitarianism; a strong belief in custom and tradition and an aversion to change; emphasis on religious and ritualistic symbolisms to solidify the union of the whole. Yet at the same time there is a strong commitment to a government under law guaranteeing individual rights, an acceptance of representative government, and with it an acknowledgment of the increased participation of all the people, an implementation of the welfare state, and above all, a rejection of authoritarian solutions. Conservatism has thus legitimized itself as an ideology consistent with democracy.

People who like change and innovation, and find themselves at odds with the conservative ideology, should not be particularly hasty in rejecting it. Classic conservatism, as portrayed here, was and remains a brake to rapid change. But it channeled the well-to-do and, more important, millions of voters, into accepting gradual and peaceful change. Conservatives have been distrustful of human reason and majoritarianism. But they never attempted to control the first or to outlaw the second. They (like the British Socialists) presented their position and policies in the context of democracy. The conservative ideology—in a sense the creature of the British ruling groups—tamed the class that formulated it, disciplined its followers to act within the logic of individual and associational freedoms, and accepted free political competition without which democracy cannot exist. By creating an ideology that taught the British ruling classes how to bend in order not to break, they legitimized not only gradual change but all change, if and when the electorate demanded it, and they prepared their followers to accept change, if not always with grace, at least without countering it with force.

AMERICAN CONSERVATIVES AND THE BRITISH MODEL

As we saw in our discussion of British conservative ideology, conservatives admire and try to preserve the past; they are elitist in that they believe in natural leaders; they accept only gradual and incremental change; they admire a well-balanced and hierarchically structured society, and they emphasize the need for authority. "Civilized man lives by authority," according to a (British-born) American conservative.[7] Conservatives believe that societies develop norms—that is, enduring standards of behavior—and that we obey them because of habit and tradition. "The

---

[7]Kirk, p. 23.

sanction to norms," writes the same author, "must come from a source other than private advantage or rationality"—the two basic propositions used by liberals to explain our obedience to the state. The real source of authority and obedience "is tradition." For conservatives, "the good citizen is a law-abiding traditionalist."[8]

To most Americans these propositions are alien. "Man is created equal"; all of us are "endowed" with liberty. The American dream has been that change, through the manipulation of the environment in order to get more out of it, is equated with progress toward a better future, and a person's worth lies in achievement, not birth, inheritance, or status. As for society, it has no meaning and reality outside of the individuals who make it and can remake it. There is no hierarchy and no organic quality about it; there is no fixed subordination of some to others, and no structure of deference. The self-made person is still the symbol of Americanism, and of the constant restlessness, mobility, and change of Americans and American society. Law is but a convenient external standard that we set up and change to accommodate our domestic conflicts—hardly a norm maturing and gaining strength and respect with time until obedience to it becomes a tradition.

As noted earlier, economic liberalism became the dominant American political creed, and virtually all social thinkers called themselves liberals. Few dared call themselves conservatives until very recently. There was little to conserve and a lot to change and to conquer: more wealth to amass and greater material benefits to realize for all. Outside of individual effort and achievement neither norms nor "tradition" nor "wise prejudice," as Burke had put it, restrained the myth of material success and self-improvement that was the heart of the beliefs of Americans. When the labor leader Samuel Gompers was asked in the latter part of the nineteenth century what it was that American labor wanted, he gave the answer that all Americans understood: "More!" In a society holding such an ideal, genuine conservatives were likely to find themselves out of place or, what amounts to the same thing, with no place for them.

The American political tradition therefore has few conservative authors or leaders in any way comparable to the British ones: Henry Adams, John Calhoun, Herman Melville, Brooks Adams, Irving Babbitt, and Walter Lippmann are among the best known. Calhoun, without any doubt, had a profound influence in the years until the Civil War. But his impact has not been a more lasting one than that of the others. The real classic conservatives—the "humanistic value preservers"—who venerate tradition, order, and natural law, have been very few indeed. The reason is that the American system and American society were made in the name of human reason and individual rights, not tradition. Real conservatives in the United States must either go directly to the British sources for inspiration, which they often do, or try to find the particular institutions and ideas that best correspond to the conservative ideology in the American experience, which they have tried to do. The only conservative ideology they claim to find is in the Constitution and in the thinking of the framers that produced it and, of course, in the political philosophy of some of them as it was expounded in the Federalist Papers.

---

[8]Kirk, p. 31.

American conservatives have tried to draw their inspiration from the Constitution because of its limitations on direct democracy and because of its emphasis on law. The American republic is "a government of law and not men." It is a republic and not a democracy—a state in which separation and the balance of powers make it impossible for any single branch of government to gain enough power to endanger the rights of the people. It is a system carefully engineered to make it impossible for a numerical majority to control all branches of government, at one and the same time, and to establish a tyranny—one that is considered just as bad as the tyranny of a minority or a group of men or of one man. Restraints are built into the system not only against the governmental organs, federal and state, but against the peoples as well. It is in this that American conservatives find the "wisdom of the framers."

Similarly, in the Federalist Papers which provide for a defense of the Constitution and embody the philosophy of the framers, notably James Madison and Alexander Hamilton, references are made and institutions are defended in terms that are close to British conservative ideas and vocabulary. Thus, the "electoral college," that was supposed to be free, once chosen, to elect the president, is viewed and defended as a body of wise men who are considered more reliable to make the proper choice than the people directly. The early mode of election for the Senate, by the state legislatures, again provided for an indirect mode of election whose purpose was to filter the popular choice. It is significant, however, that the electoral college has ceased to play the independent role it was supposed to play, and that the Senate is now elected directly by the people of the various states. Emphasis on law—a government of law and not men—remains an important ingredient of a conservative ideology, yet only a careful examination of the jurisprudence of the Supreme Court, the ultimate custodian of the Constitution, can answer to what extent. Furthermore, it should be remembered that nowhere did the Constitution grant power to the Supreme Court to declare acts of Congress unconstitutional and to set them aside.

This interpretation of the Constitution and the intentions of its framers as being essentially conservative and a reflection of a conservative ideology must be considered seriously. The framers were afraid of "the people," the majority, and they looked for "natural leaders." Many had a profound respect for tradition, but this hardly makes them and the Constitution, as it developed, conservative. Conservatives in England believed in the wise exercise of power and extolled established authority; they put politics and political wisdom above everything else except religion and divine or natural law; they thought, as we have seen, that a political society was a living organism to which material and functional interests were subordinated. Wise leadership kept this organism together.

The framers of the U.S. Constitution, on the other hand, feared political power. It could be abused and might be abused by anybody and everybody—even by "wise rulers." They were skeptical about the possibility of legitimizing power and creating a strong political authority. Their solution was to weaken authority as much as possible by fragmenting it and dividing it. The solution was a mechanical one—it reflected no belief in tradition, custom, or in natural leaders. Like the Newtonian physics which influenced the framers, the intent was to establish an equilibrium of forces and governmental organs.

This philosophy was fully consistent with the climate of opinion of the times. By downgrading the powers of the government and by providing for checks and balances for each and all its organs, the framers hoped to liberate society (i.e., the individual, the economy, voluntary associations, the churches, and so on) from the state and from political domination. The best government was the one that governed the least and left individuals free to pursue their material interest in the best utilitarian manner, and to maximize their pleasure and avoid pain as they saw fit. The "do-it-yourself man" of Benjamin Franklin was to emerge not only unfettered by political power, free of tradition and prescription, but also free from the wisdom of political elites and their natural leaders. This was, and remains, the very opposite of classic conservatism.

THE AMERICAN CONSERVATIVE IDEOLOGY

The doctrine of economic liberalism—emphasizing the market economy and competition, exalting the profit motive and private entrepreneurship, and building on the premises of self-interest in its pursuit of a world of social harmony and progress—was constantly contested in England, where it originated, and on the continent of Europe, where it never managed to gain a firm foothold. It provoked a strong reaction from intellectuals, Socialists, Christian reformers, liberal and traditional Catholic intellectuals as well as the Catholic hierarchy and was looked upon with strong repugnance by monarchists and the aristocracy. Liberals, buffeted from their right and their left, had to qualify economic liberalism by allowing for restraints and regulation of the market economy.

Economic Issues

In contrast, economic liberalism, or rather capitalism, flourished in the United States. It began to reflect the remarkable industrial growth which the country enjoyed after the Civil War and which continued until the Great Depression of 1929.

Andrew Carnegie (1835–1919) considered the search for and accumulation of wealth to be the central goal of our civilization, and found in the market and competition the best arena to test the caliber of men—their abilities and industry. As with the earlier Protestant ethic, Carnegie believed that wealth was an indication of divine grace and that it was bestowed only on industrious and frugal individuals. But he also believed that, commensurate with their station in society, the wealthy had a special duty to help the less fortunate through charity and other humanitarian endeavors.

In contrast to Carnegie's paternalistic capitalism, William Graham Sumner (1840–1910) suggested a pure individualistic ethic. Competition was to be the rule and success or failure would be determined in the marketplace. It would provide a selective mechanism to sort out the industrious from the lazy, the virtuous from the wicked. He contended that the search for equality, espoused by the Socialists, would bring only disaster. For Sumner, equality meant that the "worst would become the standard" and that it would pull down the rest to the lowest common denominator of competence, work, production, and wealth. Only through conflict, competition, and struggle could the best impose themselves and thus attain wealth for themselves and the society as a whole. As with Carnegie, the market became the best instrumentality for the "survival of the most able," just as nature had been for the "survival of the fittest" in Charles Darwin's theory of evolution. So that capitalism was the precondition of human progress. Conservatives therefore ask that the federal government move out of the economy; that if and when welfare measures are needed they should be undertaken at the state and local levels and not the federal one; that the federal budget and federal expenditures be sharply reduced; that income taxes and many other federal and state taxes be sharply curtailed. In effect, conservatives ask for the dismantling of much of the New Deal legislation and the welfare state.

The Moral Issues

Conservatives in the United States, however, and increasingly so elsewhere, move beyond the "economic man" and "rugged individualism," reaching out for "moral" issues that affect our society: violence and crime, pornography, premarital sex, abortion, drugs, and secular education. They join hands with the "religious right," which we discuss in Chapter 11. They favor, when it comes to "moral" issues, restrictive legislative measures; they demand the death penalty; they ask for religious education in schools, for community controls against obscenity and pornography, and for strict antiabortion legislation. Moral issues are becoming just as important as economic ones. Alongside the emphasis on a free-market economy, these moral issues account for the strength of the conservative movement, and not only in the United States.

Box 4-1   **Capitalism—The American Version**

1. The major actor in society—indeed the primary actor—is the individual who, using reason, is best suited to satisfy his or her needs and interests. The maximization of individual well-being (material wealth and profit) is the driving force of the economy. Consumer demand determines the supply of goods and the inventive entrepreneur provides them.
2. The free market is the most reliable and flexible mechanism for regulating supply and demand through the price mechanism.
3. Change (often used synonymously with progress) can be brought about through the dynamics of individual effort, competition, and entrepreneurship.
4. The individual, however, is not only an "economic man" to be left free to act according to his interests; he is also a moral man with a conscience, volition, and reason. To curb the economic efforts of individuals would be to seriously undermine their other freedoms and, most important of all, to deprive them of their right to pursue their own lives according to their individual best judgment.
5. The state must remain out of the market.

Reaganism and the Conservatives   Conservatives, by and large, supported Ronald Reagan. Both as a candidate and as a president, Reagan endorsed most of the conservative propositions. He was a fundamentalist on most moral-social questions (abortion, pornography, school prayer, etc.); he disavowed a "permissive" society by advocating greater police powers against suspected criminals; he opposed the ERA; he appointed conservative justices on the federal courts; and he strengthened national defense against the Soviets—he was the president who called the Soviet Union an "Evil Empire." Reagan emerged as the champion of economic liberalism, favoring deregulation, reduction in taxes and welfare spending, and a return to the market and free-enterprise economy. It is difficult to imagine a president who could be closer to the conservative positions while at the same time appealing to the center.

The conservative support began to wane, however, as Reagan had to compromise with the center of his party and with many of the Democrats who held a majority in the House of Representatives and in both houses of Congress in the last two years of his term in office. He was unable to sustain an interventionist policy in Nicaragua, and he began to shift his position on the Soviet Union by considering and ultimately signing agreements on nuclear arms in December 1987. The Gorbachev visit to Washington that December, the signing of the treaty on missiles in Europe, and Reagan's visit to the Soviet Union in May 1988 were blows to the conservatives. Conservatives also became impatient with the lack of decisive measures for dismantling the welfare state and reducing government spending, and they fought for a constitutional amendment to set a limit on the federal deficit.

Subsequent events under the George Bush presidency—the meetings with Mikhail Gorbachev in 1990, the weakening of the Soviet Empire, the dissolution of the Warsaw Pact, which had brought Eastern Europe under the military control of the Soviet Union, the democratic revolutions in Eastern Europe, and the reunification of Germany—all spelled one and the same thing. Soviet communism appeared no longer to be a threat. These developments took the wind out of the sail of the anti-Communist and the anti-Soviet rhetoric of American conservatives. They continued to raise warning signals, but their followers began to lose interest.

Conservative intellectuals, however, are gaining prominence by addressing themselves to moral and economic issues. Speaking through the influential *National Review* and other journals, they are beginning to shape the country's political agenda. The outline for political action they present is familiar and finds many Americans in agreement: decentralization of the federal government in the direction of state and "community" control, lower taxes, dismantling of the welfare state, reduction of the federal bureaucracy, and, above all, emphasis on moral issues, including the restoration of religious education in schools to combat secularism.

Influential conservative research institutions and organizations expound the philosophy of conservatism, among them the American Heritage Foundation, the American Enterprise Institute, and the Bradley Foundation. Many organize political action and provide funding. There is the Conservative Caucus and the recently established Conservative Political Action Committee, under the direction of Newt Gingrich, who became the single most newsworthy Republican congressman after the landslide victory of his party in the congressional elections of 1994. They sponsor candidates for election, seek and provide funds, and attempt to maintain in many states an identity separate from the Republican party on which, however, they continue to put pressure. With the old idols gone—Barry Goldwater and Ronald Reagan—and with President Bush failing to satisfy many of their aspirations, lower taxes for instance, they are determined to bring their weight to bear in nominations of candidates for the presidency and Senate.

But there are two issues on which conservatives may divide. With the Soviet threat gone, conservatives may split into two camps: "globalists" and "isolationists." The first wish to assert American hegemony and to maintain it through a strong military establishment and military intervention if needed. They supported the U.S. policy vis-à-vis Iraq. The second are beginning to revert to the old Republican faith in isolationism: to maintain America strong at home, U.S. leadership must emphasize economic development and moral values and let our allies—Western Europe and Japan, for instance, and of course, a reunited Germany—assume the burden and responsibility for their own defense. For the same reason, there may be a split between free traders and protectionists—the latter returning to the theme of unfair competition from abroad and the imperative of buttressing our national economy. Having entered what many consider a "mild recession" at the end of 1990, it is a theme that may gain momentum if the American economy were to continue to stagnate.

Deep, even if muddy, remains the soil from which American conservatives continue to draw—economic liberalism and free enterprise, hostility to big government, government spending and high taxes, a growing demand for state and community control, in line with de Toqueville's interpretation of American democracy, and the full and firm reassertion of "moral" and even religious values and "law and order." Barring an economic depression or prolonged international conflict, these are the bread-and-butter issues for the American public as they are presented to them with renewed urgency by a growing number of conservative intellectuals.

BIBLIOGRAPHY

Bagehot, Walter. *The English Constitution.* New York: Oxford University Press, 1936.

Banfield, Edward C. *The Unheavenly City.* Boston: Little, Brown, 1970.

Beer, Samuel H. *British Politics in the Collectivist Age.* New York: Vintage, 1949.

Bellah, Robert N., Richard Madsen, et al. *Habits of the Heart: Individualism and Commitment in American Life.* Berkeley, CA: University of California Press, 1985.

Buckley, William F., and Charles R. Kesler (eds.). *Keeping The Tablets: Modern American Conservative Thought.* New York: Harper & Row, 1988.

Burke, Edmund. *Reflections on the Revolution in France.* New York: Bobbs-Merrill, Library of Liberal Arts, 1955.

Calhoun, John C. *A Disquisition on Government.* Indianapolis: Bobbs-Merrill, 1958.

Cecil, Lord Hugh Richard. *Conservatism.* London: Williams and Nurgate, 1912.

Diggins, John P. *Up From Communism: A Conservative's Odyssey in American Intellectual History*. New York: Harper & Row, 1976.

Filler's, Louis. *Dictionary of American Conservatism*. New York: Philosophical Library, 1986.

Hayek, F. A. *The Constitution of Liberty*. London: Routledge and Kegan Paul, 1960.

———. *The Road to Serfdom*. Chicago: University of Chicago Press, 1946.

Hearnshaw, F. J. C. *Conservatism in England*. London: Macmillan, 1933.

Holden, Mathew, Jr. *Varieties of Political Conservatism*. Beverly Hills, CA: Sage, 1974.

Huntington, Samuel. "The Conservative Ideology" *American Political Science Review*, Vol. LI, No. 2, June 1957, pp. 454–473.

Kirk, Russell. *The Conservative Mind*, rev. ed. Chicago: Henry Regnery, 1960.

———. (ed.). *The Portable Conservative Reader*. New York: Penguin, 1982.

Kristol, Irving. *Reflections of a Neo-Conservative*. New York: Basic Books, 1983.

———. *Two Cheers for Capitalism*. New York: Basic Books, 1978.

Meyer, Frank S. (ed.). *What Is Conservatism?* New York: Holt, 1964.

Nash, George H. *The Conservative Intellectual Movement in America*. New York: Basic Books, 1976.

Nisbet, Robert A. *The Quest for Community*. New York: Oxford University Press, 1953.

———. *Conservatism*. Minneapolis: University of Minnesota Press, 1986.

Podhoretz, Norman. *Breaking Ranks: A Political Memoir*. New York: Harper & Row, 1979.

Rogger, Hans, and Eugen Weber (eds.). *The European Right: A Historical Profile*. Berkeley, CA: University of California Press, 1981.

Rossiter, Clinton. *Conservatism in America*, 2nd rev. ed. New York: Knopf, 1966.

Schuettinger, R. L. (ed.). *The Conservative Tradition in European Thought*. New York: Capricorn Books, 1969.

Sigler, Jay A. *The Conservative Tradition in American Thought*. New York: Capricorn Books, 1969.

Steinfels, Peter. *The Neoconservatives: The Men Who Are Changing American Politics*. New York: Simon and Schuster, 1979.

Viereck, Peter. *Conservatism: From John Adams to Churchill*. Princeton, NJ: Van Nostrand, 1956.

Wills, Garry. In *Confessions of a Conservative*. New York: Doubleday, 1979.

PART Two

Two

COMMUNISM: THE VERSION AND THE REALITY

In place of the old bourgeois society . . . we shall have an association in which the free development of each is the condition for the free development of all.

Karl Marx and Friedrich Engels *Communist Manifesto*

*T*he Communist parties throughout the world that emerged after the Bolshevik Revolution of 1917 and the single-party totalitarian regimes they established were a harness to a vision—a vision of a free and egalitarian society and a peaceful world. This vision encompassed a world which need and poverty, which dwarfed human values and impeded the full development of our individual freedoms, would come to an end; it encompassed a world in which material abundance would at last follow the remarkable growth brought about by the capitalistic world, but only after capitalism and the capitalistic class had been destroyed and the means of production—the economy as a whole—had been socialized. Not only the workers, but all of us, would then gain our freedoms and shape our destiny instead of having it decided by the impersonal forces of a capitalistic market and the not so impersonal rule of those who control the means of production.

In this part, we first examine the vision—Marxism. Then, we turn to the reality—to the Communist regime as it was fashioned in the Soviet Union under Lenin and Stalin and copied elsewhere. We then take an overview of the collapse of communism as an ideology and of Communist regimes, except in some "last bastions"—in Cuba, North Korea, Albania, Vietnam, and, for the time being, China.

Chapter
5

The Theory and the Vision

Marxism

Marx was a genius; we others were at best talented. Without him the theory would not be by far what it is today. It, therefore, rightly bears his name.

Friedrich Engels

*C*ommunism is literally an economic and social system whereby all the means of production are concentrated in the hands of the community or the state, and in which the production and allocation of goods and services are decided upon by the community and the state. Generally, however, communism has meant much more. It has been "an ideal, a political movement, a method of analysis and a way of life."[1] As an ideal, it promises an egalitarian society with production geared to need—a society in which the dream of abundance will be realized. As a political movement it represents the organization of men and women striving to attain freedom; as a method of analysis it sets forth propositions that explain the past and point to the future development of our societies; finally, as a way of life it portrays a new type of citizen for whom the communitarian and social attributes of human nature will gain ascendancy over egotism and private interest.

Whether taken singly, or all together as they usually are, the trends represent what communism has been—one of the most powerful myths and ideologies in history. It takes the form of a moral imperative—how to create a collective and social ethic that will override self-interest and do away with the demons of profit and private property, which are seen as the cause of subjugation of the many to the few.

---

[1]Alfred G. Meyer, *Marxism: The Unity of Theory and Practice*, p. 1.

Ever since antiquity, the theme of the *moral* superiority of communal ownership, in contrast to private property, interest, and individualistic aspirations, has been kept alive. It is defended in Plato's *Republic,* where no private property is allowed the rulers, the Guardians, in order that they can give their full attention to communitarian values and govern in the interest of the whole. The myth of communism appears and reappears in many religious writings in which property is viewed as the result of "man's fall." It is part of secular law and does not exist by "divine" or "natural" law. The theme reemerges with particular force in the writings of many Utopian Socialists in the decades after the French Revolution and well into the nineteenth century. After the Industrial Revolution, the dream of collective ownership, which would eliminate income inequalities and poverty, has been particularly potent.

Not until the middle of the nineteenth century, however, was the vision spelled out in the form of a political movement, and not until the end of the century did the ideology take on shape with the formation of Communist political parties. In 1917, communism gained ascendancy in one country, Russia. It spread after World War II with renewed vigor over Eastern Europe and beyond.

Almost a century and a half ago, in 1848, Karl Marx and Friedrich Engels wrote their now-famous *Communist Manifesto;* with it, they transformed communism from only a theory into a strong political movement. In the opening sentence they spoke of "a specter" that haunted Europe—"the specter of communism." It did indeed become a reality for many throughout most of the twentieth century. Communism, either in the form of established political regimes or as a powerful political revolutionary movement, inspired, mobilized, and organized for political action a greater number of people than any other political ideology had to date.

As with other ideologies, communism can be viewed in two different ways. First, we can look at it as a body of theory and philosophy. This requires us to examine and analyze it with one question in mind: How valid is its theory and underlying philosophic assumptions? Second, we can look at communism as a political ideology and movement. This requires us to examine the way in which its basic philosophic and theoretical propositions have been translated into an action-oriented movement (i.e., a political ideology). While the first level of analysis is important, we emphasize communism here as a political ideology and a movement for political action.

THE LEGACY OF MARX

It was Karl Marx and his associate Friedrich Engels who provided us, through their writings and their political activities, with the foundations of contemporary communism. Of the two, Marx was the dominant intellectual figure. He published major theoretical works on economics and philosophy and produced a series of pamphlets on various aspects of political tactics. After his death in 1883, Engels synthesized, some might say simplified, some of his ideas. When we speak of Marxism, however, we are referring to the combined work of Marx and Engels.

The Sources That Inspired Marx

Four sources combined to produce the overall synthesis that constitutes Marxism. They are:

1. Hegel's philosophy, especially his philosophy of history.
2. The works of the British economists, notably Adam Smith, David Ricardo, Thomas Malthus, and others.
3. The French Utopian Socialists, even though they were sharply criticized by Marx and Engels.
4. The social and economic reality of the mid-nineteenth century, particularly in England.

First, Hegel gave to Marx a dynamic and evolutionary theory of history based on conflict; second, the British economists provided him with a new objective analysis of economic phenomena in which all economic factors were viewed in abstract terms as commodities, or variables, relating to each other on the basis of demonstrable and quantifiable laws; third, the Utopian Socialists provided hints on the construction of a future society. As for the reality of British industrial society in the middle of the nineteenth century, it had a profound impact on both Marx and Engels. Working conditions were dismal, hours of work long, children and women were employed at starvation wages for twelve, fourteen, and sometimes sixteen hours a day, living conditions were abominable, and life expectancy low. The miseries of the workers contrasted sharply with the well-being of those who had land, property, and money (i.e., capital), and could employ others. Conditions like these provoked not only moral indignation but also widespread protest. Workers rebelled and destroyed the new machines for fear they would deprive them of work; regimentation in the factory under the new industrial order was deeply resented; and workers attempted to use their numbers against the employers who, in turn, made use of the instruments of coercion available to them.

The Rejection of Capitalism

For Marx, the rejection of capitalism is *not* based on moral or humanitarian considerations. It derives from what he considered to be the empirical reality of the capitalist economy. It obeys certain laws. Understanding them and studying them leads to the unavoidable conclusion that capitalism is doomed. Marx's anatomy of capitalism is also its autopsy!

The key to understanding capitalism and its inevitable demise is the notion of value, surplus value, and profit. The student can easily follow the Marxist critique of the capitalist economy by following Marx's own steps.

1. Only labor creates value.
2. Machines, land, and all other factors of production create no new value. They pass on to the product a value equivalent to the portion of their value used as they depreciate during the process of production.
3. The capitalist (the entrepreneur) pays the worker only a subsistence wage.

Karl Marx (1818–1883)

Born in Germany, where he studied law, philosophy, and history, Karl Marx and his family settled in London when he was thirty years old. There he began a lifelong collaboration with Friedrich Engels to develop a communist ideology and to translate it into political action. In 1848 they produced the *Communist Manifesto,* urging the workers to rise and take over the means of production for the exploiting capitalist class. In 1864 he founded the First International, whose purpose was to unite workers everywhere in a revolutionary struggle. A prodigious worker, a committed man, and also one of the most learned and creative minds of the nineteenth century, Marx, like Freud half a century later, suggested a new way of looking at social life and history. Accordingly, he saw material and economic conditions as responsible for the shaping of our values, morality, attitudes, and political institutions. Marx singled out property relations to be the key element and the exploitation of "have-nots" by the "haves" to be at the heart of liberal capitalism. It was, at the same time, the reason for a working-class revolution, and the vindication of communism. He wrote voluminously, but his major work is an analysis of capitalist economy in *Capital,* the first volume of which was published in 1867 and the second and third posthumously, by Engels, in 1885 and 1894, respectively.

4. The worker produces a value that is twice as much (generally speaking) as what he or she gets in wages.

5. The difference between what the capitalist pays the worker and what the worker produces is the *surplus value* pocketed by the capitalist.

6. All profits derive from the surplus value, though the actual profit does not correspond to the amount of surplus value extracted by a given capitalist.

7. In the market there is a fierce competition among capitalists. Each tries to sell more; a large volume of goods sold, even at lower prices, will bring added income.

8. This incites the capitalist to modernize and mass-produce, to introduce better machines, and to increase the productivity of labor.

9. A modern firm manages with fewer workers to produce and hence sell more. As a result, more and more workers are laid off.

10. Thus the modern firm can reduce prices by lowering its profit *per unit.*

11. Many firms that fail to modernize are gradually driven out of business. They employ more workers, pay out more in wages, and thus cannot compete with the lower prices the modernized firms set.

12. As a result, many firms have to close down. Capital becomes increasingly concentrated into fewer and fewer hands and in larger and more modern firms, in which more machinery and modern technology are introduced.

13. Capitalism reaches a point at which a small number of highly modernized large firms can produce goods efficiently and cheaply. However, with a great number of people out of work, there are not enough buyers for the products, so firms can no longer make a profit. Production becomes restricted.

14. Profit and private property, the great incentives of the Industrial Revolution, now become obstacles to the plentiful production of goods.

15. The legal forms of capitalism (private profit and private property) come into conflict with the means of production (efficiency, high productivity, and potential abundance).

This is the Marxist critique in a nutshell. The heart of capitalism and capitalist production is to be found in private property and profit. The purpose of production is *profit*—how the capitalist can get from the market a value for the product that is higher than the cost of production. The difference between what the entrepreneurs spend to produce and what they receive for the product is the *profit*—one of the most dynamic incentives for capitalist production and growth.

Marx develops an ingenious theory to explain profit. It is *the theory of surplus value.* The worker is paid wages that are determined by the market through the law of supply and demand. The daily wage corresponds to the price of goods the worker and his family need and consume in one day. During the same day, however, the worker has produced goods that have a much higher value. The difference between value produced (owned and sold by the entrepreneur) and what is paid out in wages is the *surplus value.* Marx contends that generally wages tend to correspond to not more than half of the value the worker produces. So the other half goes to the entrepreneur—to the capitalist. This is Marx's argument.

The Laws of Capitalist Accumulation and Pauperization

The quest for profit accounts for modernization; the technologically advanced firms with the newest machines benefit at the expense of the backward ones. Many firms go bankrupt, but the survivors accumulate in their hands an ever greater part of the capital. Fewer and fewer capitalists own the means of production, while more and more small firms disappear. The whole social structure becomes lop-sided, with a tiny minority controlling production for the purpose of making prof-it; at the same time, the vast majority of the people have nothing but their labor to sell, precisely when it becomes all the more difficult to sell!

As more and more people are dispossessed of the means to produce, more and more fall into the class of the proletariat. Thus, as the firms develop more sophis-ticated machinery, a greater number of people find themselves living in a state of misery. Many cannot find work. Many become "marginals," moving from one place to another without a role, without skills, and in a state of constant deprivation and humiliation. They are the *lumpenproletariat*—the army of the unemployed and also the unemployable, the people from the countryside or those recently demot-ed from the middle or lower middle classes. They become a permanent fixture of capitalist societies.

The profit motive—a driving and dynamic motive in the early stages of capi-talism—becomes a drag and an impediment in its most advanced stage. It pushes the capitalists to modernize and to accumulate capital and industrial equipment; it indeed makes production easier and much more efficient; *objectively speaking*, it makes it possible for human beings in a society to supply all their wants and more. Capitalism thus achieves a most remarkable breakthrough by creating all the mate-rial conditions for the good life. Marx is full of praise for the bourgeoisie and for capitalism when he views their historical role.

> The bourgeoisie has through its exploitation of the world market given a cosmopolitan character to production and consumption in every country. In place of the old wants, satisfied by the production of the country, we find new wants, requiring for their satis-faction the products of distant lands and climes. In place of the old local and national seclusion and self-sufficiency, we have intercourse in every direction, universal inter-dependence of nations.
>
> The bourgeoisie, by the rapid improvement of all instruments of production, by the immensely facilitated means of communication, draws all, even the most barbarian, nations into civilization. . . .
>
> The bourgeoisie has created enormous cities, has greatly increased the urban pop-ulation as compared with rural, and has thus rescued a considerable part of the popu-lation from the idiocy of rural life.[2]

Yet it is precisely at this advanced stage that the capitalistic economy can no longer provide for profits. By pressing heavily upon the middle class, and by creat-ing a chronic state of unemployment among the independent artisans and small farmers, which reduces them gradually to the ranks of the poor and the dispos-

---

[2]Karl Marx, *The Communist Manifesto*, in Robert C. Tucker (ed.), *The Marx-Engels Reader*, pp. 469–500.

sessed, many are being deprived of the means to buy things and meet their needs. Demand goes down and with it comes lower profit. To keep the rate of profit, the capitalist is now forced to produce less, to control prices, to develop monopolies in order to avoid competition, and to form cartels to keep prices up. Whereas profit was a positive incentive to industrial growth and production, now it becomes a shackle. It is at this point that capitalism has outlived its purpose—it can produce plenty, but there is no incentive to do so. It is at this point that Marx pronounces its death sentence!

The student will note that thus far there has not been a single note of moral approbation or disapprobation. Marx gives us a "scientific" account—that is, a description of what he sees happening, a description which fits his basic laws of the capitalist economy. They account for its inevitable demise.

The analysis of the laws accounting for the demise of capitalism, however, does not amount to a "rejection" of capitalism. People must become aware of something, become dissatisfied with something, and move actively against something in order for there to be a rejection. Rejection is a subjective phenomenon associated with a collective desire and consciousness and with concerted action. *This is the revolutionary side of Marxism.*

THE DYNAMICS OF THE COMMUNIST REVOLUTION

In contrast to his economic analysis, in which Marx set up theories and hypotheses and sought their confirmation in the empirical world of the capitalist economy, his whole notion of a revolution is the culminating point of philosophic speculation and is not amenable to the same rules of scientific inquiry. It includes: (1) a philosophy of history, (2) a theory of class struggles, (3) a theory of the state, (4) the historical act of "revolution," and (5) the utopian world to follow. We discuss each of these briefly.

A Philosophy of History

History has been defined as a set of tricks that the living play upon the dead. For Marx, there are no such tricks! For him, the living constantly interact with the dead. Men and women are both the product of history, bound by the conditions it creates, and also the makers of history, in reacting to those conditions and changing them. But this is only within the limits that history itself allows. How does this unfold? Marx answers by using the works of the German philosopher Georg W. F. Hegel (1770–1831) to develop a theory of history and change.

According to Hegel, history moves through conflict—a conflict of ideas.[3] He believes that there is something like a divine will, an Absolute, destined to finally unfold itself fully in the universe, but the process of unfolding is not evolutionary. It takes place through struggle between opposing ideas. The idea of beauty has

---

[3]Georg W. F. Hegel, *The Philosophy of History*.

opposing it the idea of ugliness, the idea of truth that of falsehood, the idea of liberty that of slavery, and so on. Throughout history and its various stages, there is a constant and Homeric battle between opposing ideas, called by Hegel *dialectic idealism*. It goes something like this: each phase in history corresponds to the manifestation of certain ideas or an idea. It is called the *thesis*. However, it includes its opposite, its *antithesis*. Thesis and antithesis struggle with each other until the antithesis manages to absorb the thesis or to combine with it in one form or another. This combination is called a *synthesis*, representing a new stage in history. Every synthesis, in turn, becomes a thesis that suggests automatically its antithesis, which comes into conflict with it to lead to a new synthesis, and so forth. . . . A point comes *when history will have exhausted itself—the best possible synthesis will have occurred*. God or the Spirit will have fully unfolded itself in the universe!

Marx maintains the dialectic (the notion of conflicting opposites); he maintains the whole scheme of historical movement in terms of thesis–antithesis–synthesis. However, he is clearly not an idealist. Writing in his preface to *Capital*, Marx tells us himself how he changed the very foundations of Hegel's philosophy of history while maintaining the basic structure.

> My dialectic method is not only different from the Hegelian, but its direct opposite. To Hegel, the life-process of the brain, i.e., the process of thinking, which under the name of "the Idea," he even transforms into an independent subject, is the demiurgos (creator) of the real world, and the real world is only the external, phenomenal form of "the idea." With me on the contrary the idea is nothing else than the material world reflected by the human mind, and translated into forms of thought. . . . With Hegel (the dialectic) . . . is standing on its head. It must be turned rightside up again.[4]

Dialectic Materialism   Marx found in the material world, our senses, and our working conditions—not in our ideas—the source of conflict and change. This is what, in contrast to "dialectic idealism," has become known as *dialectic materialism*. The stages of historical development—the specific contents of a thesis, an antithesis, and a synthesis—are not to be found in the not-so-easily observable world of ideas but in the empirical world, in our society. It is a momentous shift. The Hegelian abstraction now becomes a theory leading to hypotheses about human and social life that can be observed and tested.

Class Conflict

The major source and type of conflict are those among individuals and groups. It is not an indiscriminate conflict, haphazardly pitting individual against individual; it is highly structured. The conflict is between classes; it is a *class struggle*. *A class is defined in terms of the relationship individuals have to the means of production.* Very simply put, there are two classes: those who own property and those who do not. This has been the reality of social life and the basic source of conflict and change. Class struggle is the engine of dialectic materialism.

---

[4]Karl Marx, Preface to the second edition, *Capital*, Modern Library, p. 25.

Each historical phase corresponds to new and different forms of private property. Landed property was the characteristic of the feudal period and the landed aristocracy; but within it money, gold, and commerce made their appearance. Artisans, small manufacturers, and merchants later emerged, with them commercial capital and finally manufacturing and industry. They were destined to become a new class, an antithesis, the *bourgeoisie*. The French Revolution of 1789 epitomized, in a way, the end of the landed aristocracy and the coming of the middle class to power, emphasizing new types of property and new productive forces. But the moment the capitalists and the various groups allied to them emerged, the antithesis was already present. It was *the working class*—a small cloud on the blue horizon of bourgeois capitalism. With no property of its own, with nothing to sell but its labor, and subject to the laws of capitalistic economy, the cloud of the working class grew bigger and bigger. The class struggle was on, presaging the storm and the inevitable revolutionary conflict between the workers and the bourgeoisie.

Infrastructure and Superstructure   In the constant interaction between society and environment, and in the constant class struggle that corresponds to various historical stages, human beings not only develop particular forms of property, they also change them. For each stage there is a particular set of ideas and norms, and these correspond to and are fashioned by the interests of the property-owning class. They rationalize and legitimize (i.e., make acceptable to all) the dominance of the ruling and property-owning class. This theory, which traces and attributes moral ideas and norms directly or indirectly to economic factors, is called *economic determinism:* it states that how and where we live and work fashion our ideas about the world. Capitalists have a set of ideas about society and the world that correspond to their interests and to their dominance. The workers begin to develop theirs to express their needs and interests.

In the Marxist vocabulary, the totality of factors that determine a person's relations to private property and work constitute the *infrastructure:* they are the material and objective social conditions. On the other hand, the way we look upon society—the ideas we have about it, in a word our ideology—is the *superstructure.* This superstructure includes religion, law, education, literature, even the state. It is an ideology fashioned by the dominant class, the one that owns property, and its view of society is forced upon all (including the workers) until a moment comes when they begin to question it.

Objective and Subjective Conditions   Each phase of the class struggle and each form of property relations differ in content from the preceding one. Bourgeois capitalism revolutionized the *objective economic conditions* of production. Division of labor, capital accumulation, technological progress—all these profit-inspired activities changed the world in the late eighteenth century and ever since. But by also creating a vast proletarian army, by divesting the lower classes of property, and by concentrating capital in a small number of firms, individuals, and banks, capitalism has ironically made it easier for society to replace the capitalist class. With this turn of events, a mass of people begin to demand the end of capitalist rule. These are the *subjective economic conditions.* A point thus comes when objective conditions (i.e., technology, concentration of capital, the capability of the economy to provide abundance) coincide with the subjective conditions (i.e., the will and the consciousness of the workers to take over the industrial apparatus created by the capitalist and to use it for the whole community). When subjective and objective conditions converge, it is the moment of revolution.

Note this carefully: the revolution was not, according to Marx, a matter of will, indignation, or even leadership. Conditions, both objective and subjective, must be ripe. The workers must gain full consciousness that they are a class and that they must demand a change in the existing property relations. Only then can revolution under the appropriate leadership be envisaged.

The Theory of the State

The state is viewed by Marx as part of the superstructure. It is used to keep the majority of the people, who do not own the means of production, under the control of the small minority who do. While many (including Hegel) see the state as the embodiment of noble purposes—rationality, an agency for social justice and protection, the equitable distribution of goods, an impartial umpire keeping and administering the rules and laws equitably—Marx sees it as the instrument of the capitalist class. It is a repressive agency—a policeman!

But the state is not the only agency of domination. The whole superstructure, as we have noted, is fashioned by the ruling class. Religion inculcates observance of bourgeois values and respect for property; the family and the laws of inheritance perpetuate the rule of property; the educational system socializes everybody to respect the capitalist ethic and, most important, private property; art and literature extol the same virtues. No matter where they turn, the workers and their children will confront the same values and principles, and many of them will be brainwashed into accepting them. The peculiar characteristic of the state, however, is that it is the only part of the superstructure that can use force. Hence it is necessary to use force against it.

The Revolution

Revolution, therefore, is necessary and unavoidable. "But what about democracy?" the student asks. "What about free and equal voting, freedom of association and of trade unions, of political parties and even of Socialist parties? What about the freedom of the majority to change the economy?

The answer is complex. First, when Marx wrote, trade unions were only beginning to emerge; second, there were no Socialist parties, although some were just making their appearance; third, political parties almost everywhere were just about to become national parties with national organizations and members; fourth, outside the United States, universal suffrage did not exist or could not be freely exercised. Most important of all, however, Marx did not really believe that a capitalist system and the capitalist state would ever allow Socialist parties to gain ascendancy, nor did he believe that a majority would ever be allowed to challenge private property directly or to control production and the allocation of goods and services.

If a majority did, the state would use force against it on behalf of the capitalists. Revolution, therefore, was necessary.

The Utopian Goal: The Communist Society

Marx gives us only a sketchy account of the Communist society to come after the working-class revolution. In fact, he provides us with what amounts to a two-stage program. The first corresponds to the transitional stage toward socialism, and the second is the ultimate one, the utopian level of communism.

In the first, the revolution is followed by the "dictatorship of the proletariat." The workers take over the state and all its instruments of coercion and use these instruments against the capitalist class. "The development towards communism," he writes, "proceeds through the dictatorship of the proletariat; it cannot do otherwise, for the resistance of the capitalist exploiters cannot be broken by anyone else or in any other way."[5] In contrast to all other dictatorships, however, this is one by the majority against the minority. Therefore, this is a dictatorship that corresponds to, and gradually becomes, a democracy of the people and the workers. The few—the capitalists—are excluded or suppressed by force.

As the state is now being used by the workers against the capitalists, its substance changes. It becomes the instrument of the many against the few. As the means of production become socialized, classes disappear, since there can be no classes without property. Without classes, there is no need for coercion. *The dictatorship paves the way toward its own disappearance and to the establishment of a classless and stateless society.* The state simply "withers away."

The second phase corresponds to communism. The economy, both production and distribution, is now in the hands of the community. Nobody can exploit anybody; "bourgeois rights" (individual rights) give their place to "common rights." The final and ultimate phase is reached with the collectivization of all the means of production, with the harnessing of production to common purposes, with the transformation of the state from a coercive power to a purely administrative one. The objective conditions of production bequeathed to the new society from capitalism can now be used to make the slogan *"From each according to his ability to each according to his needs"* possible.

This is the apocalyptic or utopian element. And although Marx did not go to the lengths some earlier Utopian Socialists did, he shared their general optimism and was influenced by it. Crime would disappear, the span of life would increase, brotherhood and cooperation would inculcate a new morality, scientific progress would grow by leaps and bounds. Above all, with socialism spreading around the world, war, the greatest blight of humankind, and its twin, nationalism, would have no place. International brotherhood would follow. Engels waxes enthusiastic over the prospects and goes so far as to declare that, with the socialist revolution, humanity will complete its "prehistoric" stage and enter for the first time into what

---

[5]Karl Marx, *The Communist Manifesto*, in D. McLellan, *Karl Marx: Selected Writings,* University Press, 1977 p. 237.

might be called its own history. Until the revolution, he claims, society submits to outside forces while the majority of humans within a society submit to a ruling class. After the revolution a united classless society will be able, for the first time, to decide which way to go and what to do with its resources and capabilities. For the first time we can make our own history! It was to be, in Engels words, "the ascent of man from the kingdom of necessity to the kingdom of freedom."[6]

The skeptics were now confronted with the anatomy of capitalism, a theory of history, a theory of revolution, a theory of state—all of them pointing in the same direction, toward a Communist society. With it, of course, the laws developed by Marx to explain the economy, the society, and history would come to an end, and individuals and the society would be free to make their own laws and shape their own future. It was this Marxist vision that provided the intellectual basis for the Bolshevik Revolution and that inspired Lenin to whom we now turn.

BIBLIOGRAPHY

Avineri, Shlomo. *The Social and Political Thought of Karl Marx.* New York: Cambridge University Press, 1968.

Berlin, Isaiah. *Karl Marx: His Life and Environment,* 3rd ed. New York: Oxford University Press, 1963.

Berstein, Eduard. *Evolutionary Socialism.* Translated by E. C. Harvey. New York: Schocken, 1961.

Bober, M. M. *Karl Marx's Interpretation of History.* New York: Norton, 1965.

Bottomore, Tom (ed.). *Modern Interpretations of Marx.* Oxford: Basil Blackwell, 1981.

Burns, Emile. *An Introduction to Marxism.* New York: International Publishers, 1966.

Cohen, G. A. *Karl Marx's Theory of History.* New York: Oxford University Press, 1978.

Cornforth, Maurice. *Communism and Philosophy: Contemporary Dogmas and Revisions of Marxism.* London: Lawrence and Wishart, 1980.

Fromm, Erich. *Marx's Concept of Man.* New York: Frederick Ungar, 1965.

Gottlieb, Roger S. (ed.). *An Anthology of Western Marxism: From Lukacs and Gramsci to Socialist-Feminism,* New York: Oxford University Press, 1989.

Gregor, James. *A Survey of Marxism.* New York: Random House, 1965.

Hegel, Georg W. F. *The Philosophy of History,* translated by J. Sibree. New York: The Colonial Press, 1900.

Heilbroner, Robert L. *Marxism: For and Against.* New York: Norton, 1980.

Kolakowski, Leszek. *Marxism and Beyond: On Historical Understanding and Individual Responsibility.* Translated by Jane Zielonko Peel. London: Pall Mall Press, 1969.

———. *Main Currents of Marxism,* 3 vols. Translanted by P. S. Falla. Oxford, England: Clarendon Press, 1978.

---

[6]Friedrich Engels, "Socialism: Utopian and Scientific" in Robert C. Tucker, *The Marx–Engels Reader,* p. 716.

Kolakowski, Leszek, and Stuart Hampshire (eds.). *The Socialist Idea: A Reappraisal.* London: Weidenfeld and Nicolson, 1974.

Lichtheim, George. *Marxism: An Historical and Critical Study,* 2nd ed. New York: Praeger, 1965.

Luxemburg, Rosa. *Selected Political Writings.* Edited by Dick Howard. New York: Monthly Review Press, 1971.

Marx, Karl. *Capital, A Critique of Political Economy.* Modern Library, 1925.

Marx, Karl, and Friedrich Engels. *Selected Works.* New York: International Publishers, 1968.

McLellan, David. *Karl Marx: His Life and Thought.* New York: Harper & Row, 1973.

———. *Karl Marx.* Baltimore: Penguin, 1976.

——— (ed.). *The Karl Marx Reader.* New York: Oxford University Press, 1977.

———. *Marxism after Marx.* Boston: Houghton Mifflin, 1981.

Meyer, Alfred G. *Marxism: The Unity of Theory and Practice.* Ann Arbor: University of Michigan Press, 1963.

Seliger, Martin. *The Marxist Conception of Ideology: A Critical Essay.* Cambridge, England: Cambridge University Press, 1977.

Tucker, Robert C. (ed.). *Philosophy and Myth in Karl Marx,* 2nd ed. New York: Cambridge University Press, 1972.

———. *The Marx–Engels Reader,* 2nd ed. New York: Norton, 1978.

Wolfe, Bertram, D. *Marxism: One Hundred Years in the Life of a Doctrine.* New York: Dial Press, 1965.

Chapter
6

The Reality

Leninism and Stalinism

The organization of the Party takes the place of the Party itself; the Central Committee takes the place of the organization; and, finally, the dictator takes the place of the Central Committee.

Leon Trotsky *Our Political Tasks*

W ith Lenin, Marxist ideology and revolutionary tactics were given a new sharpness and urgency. Lenin was able to take the theoretical Marxist blueprint and adapt it not only to a revolutionary movement in Russia in the early part of the twentieth century but also to the independence movements of the colonial world. The first successful revolution in the name of Marxism, the Bolshevik Revolution, was made under his leadership in Russia on November 7, 1917.

Joseph Stalin succeeded Lenin in 1924 and became in a true sense the builder of Soviet communism. He remained in power for almost thirty years until his death in 1953. Collectivization, economic planning, rapid industrialization, the expansion of Soviet power, and also a one-man authoritarian government are associated with his rule. During the same period of time, Communist regimes were established in many parts of the world. They were built upon the Leninist-Stalinist model.

LENINISM

Lenin faithfully accepted the body of Marxist thought and devoted a good part of his life to defending it against its many critics. His two most important contributions to communist thought can be found in two pamphlets—*What Is to Be Done?* (1903) and *Imperialism, the Highest Stage of Capitalism* (1917). In the first, Lenin developed a new theory for the organization of the proletariat through the Communist party; in the second, he attempted to show that the highest stage (and last stage) of capitalism was inextricably associated with colonial wars among capitalist nations. In a third long essay, *The State and Revolution* (1918), he elaborated on such key concepts as the revolutionary takeover of power, the period of the dictatorship of the proletariat, and the final stage of communism where the state was to disappear and material abundance become a reality. But his most important contribution, as the head of the Russian Bolshevik party, was to make a revolution and to preside over its consolidation.

Lenin's Revolutionary Doctrine

The greater part of Lenin's life was devoted to the development of a revolutionary doctrine. In *The State and Revolution* he summarized the Marxist theses: the state is the product of the irreconcilability of class antagonisms and the agency of the capitalist class; liberal democracy is another name for capitalism, ensuring domination of the workers; law and the state are instruments for the domination of the ruling class against the working classes; and, of course, revolution and the triumph of the working class are both desirable and inevitable.

The revolutionary stages Lenin envisages are the following:

1. The armed uprising of the proletariat, under proper leadership.
2. The seizure of political control by the workers, in the form of a temporary "dictatorship of the proletariat," against the remnants of the capitalist classes.

Lenin's concept of dictatorship was as succinct as it was brutal. "The scientific concept of dictatorship [of the proletariat] means neither more nor less than unlimited power, resting directly on force, not limited by anything, not restricted by any law or any absolute rules. Nothing else but that."[1]

3. The socialization of the means of production and the abolition of private property.
4. Finally, the slow "withering away of the state" as an instrument of coercion and class oppression, and the emergence of a classless, stateless society.

The Communist Party

What does Lenin mean by a revolution of the working class *under proper leadership?* Marx's position was that objective economic factors and the class consciousness of the workers world move in parallel. The maturing of capitalism would mean the maturing of the social (i.e., revolutionary) consciousness of the workers.

Lenin posits from the very beginning, however, the need for leadership and organization. The working class—and particularly the Russian working class— could never develop revolutionary consciousness by itself. An elite, organized into a Communist party, would have to educate the masses, infuse them with revolutionary spirit, and inculcate in them class consciousness. This would lead them toward the revolution and, ultimately, communism. *Dialectic materialism is*

---

[1]Lenin, quoted in Bertram Wolfe, "Leninism," in Milorad M. Drachkovitch (ed.), *Marxism in the Modern World,* p. 69.

Lenin (1870-1924)

Vladimir Ilyich Ulyanov ("Lenin" was originally a pseudonym, but became the better-known name) spent his childhood—a happy one according to all accounts—in the province of Kazan. After receiving his law degree, he was arrested for revolutionary activity and exiled to Siberia. In 1900 he was allowed to go abroad where, as a professed Marxist, he pursued his revolutionary activity with remarkable energy. He formulated, and imposed on his followers, a program for a highly centralized party consisting of trained revolutionaries.

The collapse of the czarist armies and the democratic revolution of February 1917 found Lenin in Switzerland. He managed to negotiate with the German government for a passage across the front line between the German and Russian armies; on the night of November 6–7, 1917, the Bolsheviks seized power and Lenin was made chairman of the new government. By 1918, Lenin had established what amounted to a dictatorship. He dissolved the Constituent Assembly after the Bolsheviks failed to get a majority in the elections, but his main attention was given to the war against the tsarist loyalists. Not until 1920 did the Russian Civil War come to an end with the victory of the communist forces.

brushed aside here to be replaced by a theory of voluntarism. The Communist party is based on the will and dedication of Marxists. They are the revolutionaries. They can make the revolution irrespective of the prevailing social conditions.

A number of consequences, both at the theoretical and tactical levels, follow these assumptions.

Elitism   The party is to be composed of gifted individuals who understand Marxism and therefore understand the direction of history better than the rest of the people. The leaders of the party are particularly endowed with scientific knowledge and foresight that the common people lack. Leadership is likely to come not from the ranks of the working class but from "outside"—from middle-class intellectuals who are able to comprehend the totality of the society's interests and hence promote socialism. They are trained in Marxist dialectics and can discern the historical pattern leading to socialism. This party is the *vanguard* of the proletariat. It speaks and acts on behalf of the proletariat.

Organization of the Party   The rank and file of the party is united with its leaders by bonds of allegiance and common action, but also obedience and discipline. They must be prepared for any kind of action, legal or illegal, at any time. "The one serious organizational principle for workers in our movement," Lenin wrote, "must be the strictest secrecy, strictest choice of members, training of professional revolutionaries."[2] The party has to be organized on the basis of *democratic centralism,* according to which:

1. All decisions are to be made in an open and free debate by the representative organ of the party, the congress.
2. Once a decision is thus made, it is binding upon all. No factions are to be allowed within the party and no minority within the party is permitted either to secede or to air its grievances in public.
3. All officers of the party—secretaries, the Central Committee, and other executive organs—are elected indirectly from the lowest membership upward.
4. All decisions and instructions of the party executive officials are binding upon all inferior organs and officers.

The organization of the Soviet Communist party thus became increasingly hierarchical. Orders for action flowed from top to bottom. Throughout his whole life Lenin was able, despite opposition, to hold the supreme decision-making power in his hands and to control the nomination of local party leaders. The party did not tolerate dissent and, under Lenin's leadership, indulged in purges in the years after the revolution. He invented the notion "enemies of the people." It was during this same period that thousands of so-called wreckers, saboteurs, petit bourgeois, and many others were jailed, and sentenced to death.

From Lenin's model of the party, it is obvious that he had no respect for democracy. "Lenin and his friends [insisted] upon the need of absolute authority

---

[2]Wolfe, p. 78.

by the revolutionary nucleus of the party." The revolution was to be "the supreme law." "If the revolution demanded it . . . everything—democracy, liberty, the rights of the individual—must be sacrificed to it."[3] Accordingly, Lenin had no scruples at all in dissolving democratically elected bodies when the Bolsheviks were in a minority. The party was to be the single guiding spirit and the governing body of the nation.

Colonies and World Revolution

In *Imperialism: the Highest Stage of Capitalism,* published in 1917, Lenin attempted to show that the highest and last stage of capitalism ("monopoly capitalism") corresponds to a period of control by the big banks and trusts that have investments in overseas colonies, the division of the world into colonial areas of domination and exploitation, and wars. The most important thesis of the book, however, was that capitalism had become a world phenomenon despite the uneven economic development of the various countries and the backwardness of the colonies.

If capitalism had indeed become a worldwide phenomenon, if the imperialist nations had divided the world among themselves, and if they had managed to blunt the revolutionary class consciousness of their workers by providing them with benefits and advantages that were being extracted from the colonial peoples, where would the revolution come from? For Lenin, as we have seen, it would have to come from trained revolutionaries, well organized and sharing a common will. But where would the revolution take place?

The answer given by Lenin, with the support of Leon Trotsky, was that one should not wait for the stages of capitalistic development to unfold themselves. It was tactically necessary to push for revolutionary seizures of power anywhere in the world rather than wait until each and every country had reached the level of maturity required by Marx and Engels. The capitalistic chain which bound the world had some weak links, particularly its colonies, where it was vulnerable because colonial peoples began to demand what many liberal bourgeois leaders had advocated for themselves—national independence, political rights, equality, and so on. One step in the fight against capitalism, therefore, was to try to snap the chain at any of its various weak links. Communists were asked, in the name of Marx, to promote revolutions in countries where the peasantry and not the workers represented the most numerous social group; they were to do this in the name of nationalism rather than internationalism. From a tactical point of view, every colonial independence movement that succeeded was a break in the capitalistic chain and hence a victory for Communist Russia.

It was a masterly tactical twist designed both to defend communism in a backward country like Russia against potential enemies (and in so doing defend Russia

---

[3]Isaiah Berlin, "Political Ideas in the Twentieth Century," in *Foreign Affairs,* vol. 98, April 1950.

as well) and to expand and export the Communist revolution made in Russia to virtually anywhere in the world.

Conclusion

Emphasis on political and revolutionary tactics, no matter what the objective conditions, are the hallmarks of Leninism: reliance on the human factors of will, leadership, and organization irrespective of their social contents; and the subordination of everything else to political organization, political will, and leadership to make the revolution. Very often this is referred to as the theory of *substitutism*. With Marx, the working class develops the consciousness to make the revolution and establish communism, thus substituting itself for the whole of society. With Lenin, the Communist party substitutes itself for the working class and speaks for the interests of the working class. It is then the executive and higher organs of the party, the Central Committee, that speak for the interests of the working class, which speaks for the interests of the whole. But since the same Central Committee controlled the world Communist movements, it also spoke for the interests of all the Communist parties, which spoke for their respective working classes, that spoke for the world community! It takes only one more step for the single leader to substitute for all the others in order to arrive at the logical outcome of such an organization—the subordination of *everything* to the leadership of *one* man. Such was the essence of Stalinism.

STALINISM

The name of Stalin is becoming as remote to many students as that of Napoleon. But still for many contemporary Communists, inside and outside the former Soviet Union, Stalin and Stalinism remain important and highly controversial. A member of the Russian Communist party and an associate of Lenin, Stalin succeeded him after his death in 1924. After five years, during which he managed to eliminate all opposition within the Communist party, he became its absolute ruler. While Lenin was backed by his enormous prestige and was respected for his intelligence and writings, Stalin relied on the organization he had built with the party as well as outright force. Stalin institutionalized in his own person the dictatorship of the proletariat: not bound by any law, indeed being above any law.

Stalin succeeded Lenin at a moment when the revolutionary spirit in Russia, and everywhere else, was at an ebb. Long years of strife, civil war, and economic hardships had disillusioned a number of revolutionary leaders and undermined the morale of the party's rank and file. A party organizer above all, Stalin wove within the Central Committee of the party and within the regional and district committees a web of personal and organizational contacts. He controlled the appointments of Communist party members to local and district administrative jobs; he was in charge of party admissions; he was asked to reorganize and purge the administrative apparatus of the state and assume control of the police. He used

Joseph Stalin (1879–1953)

Born in Georgia, Stalin became the head of the Communist party of the Soviet Union after Lenin's death in 1924. Though originally a lesser figure among the Communist leaders who made the revolution, and lacking the literary, oratory, or intellectual talents of many of them, Stalin neverthe-less assumed a controlling position within the organization of the party, becoming its Secretary General, and his rule prevailed. He launched what is generally called the Second Revolution, collectivizing agriculture and socializing all the means of production. His rule, which lasted until his death, saw the rapid increase of Soviet power, economically, interna-tionally, and militarily. But it was in substance a personal dictatorship based on the most ruthless application of force and terror, and it is char-acterized by many as a great betrayal of the original principles upon which the revolution was predicated.

these powers in order to consolidate and promote his own personal position within the party.

No Internal Democracy

Another indication of the demotion of the status of the party was the lack of any genuine free deliberation and criticism among its assembled delegates. Congresses, whenever they were convened, spent their time in giving their approbation without any debate to the resolutions of the leadership. After 1930, not a single protest was raised; not a single dissenting voice or vote expressed. The slate of candidates for the various exective organs was prepared in advance by Stalin and his immediate associates and was always approved unanimously.

The Police

The new organ, which in effect replaced the party, was the police, which operated directly under Stalin. It was the duty of the police to maintain communist legality. Lenin had used it to first operate against "deviationists" and "dissenters," but it was always understood that it was to be an adjunct of the party acting on its behalf. But by 1935, the secret police became the instrument of control and intimidation not only of the society as a whole but also vis-à-vis the party. Party members were totally at its mercy as were high-placed party officials. The secret police gradually became the most feared coercive and punitive force. It had its own private army (including tanks), a huge network of spies and informers, and was in command of the forced labor camps where the inmates—variously estimated to range from 3 to 4 million to as many as 10 million over the whole Stalinist period—were interned. Terror thus became an instrument of government.

The Organization of the Communist Party

The organization and functions of the Communist party under Stalin represent the ultimate development of what Lenin had started. The party remained an *elite* composed of loyal and energetic members. Its mission was to maintain and further the cause of Soviet socialism and to educate the masses into socialism. Its membership continued to be relatively small. Sometimes it was described as the "chief of staff of the proletariat," sometimes as "the teacher" of the Russian masses, and at other times the "vanguard of the working class and the masses." It grew into an exclusive organization which controlled every aspect of governmental and social life of Soviet society.

The Leninist conception of the hierarchical relationship between leadership and rank and file hardened into an institution. The role of the leader began to be expounded upon in a semireligious, semi-Byzantine manner: he was omniscient and omnipresent, he was the father of the people, his word was law. There was in Stalinism a marked similarity to the despotic paternalism of the czarist regime.

The development of this concept of leadership is also related to the internal development of the party organization. Decision-making powers became concen-

trated exclusively in the hands of the executive organs of the party, and any semblance of democractic centralism was abandoned in favor of rigid centralization
and control from the top. Nominations to party posts were made from above and
not by the rank and file. Criticism was allowed only when leaders would permit it,
and only on subjects selected in advance by them; periodic purges accounted for a
constant turnover of the rank and file and middle-echelon officers and organizers.

The Economy

In 1929, Stalin introduced what is often referred to as the "Second Revolution" or
the "Revolution from Above." All means of production and all private property
were socialized, and agriculture was collectivized. The Communist party became
the political instrument for controlling society and bending it to the task of rapid
industrialization. This entailed a rigorous centralization and bureaucratic control
of the national economy—what is often referred to as a *command economy.* Economic targets were formulated over five-year periods (the Five-Year Plans) with
priorities and specific quotas. Capital investment—the building of factories and
industrial equipment—and the training of the labor force took precedence over
consumption. Education became an indispensable part of industrialization,
because technicians, scientists, skilled workers, engineers, and service personnel
such as doctors, administrators, accountants, and so on, were vital to economic
growth.

Force and Incentives

The overall effort amounted to a radical overhaul of Russian society. In the name
of socialism, the task was to create what socialism should have inherited, an industrialized society. Three basic incentives could be used. The first was propaganda
and persuasion: to extol the myth of socialism and incite people to communal
efforts and sacrifices. But ideological exhortation has limits, and Stalin had to fall
back on the two classic means of encouraging compliance: the carrot and the stick.
The carrot was monetary incentive; the stick, force.

He who did not work would not eat. Income was to be proportionate to the
quality and quantity of work done; inequality of income was declared to be
unavoidable. Trade unions that favored equality of pay were put in their place—
their leaders arrested and eliminated; the right to bargain was abolished, and the
right to participate in the decisions of the plant manager were withdrawn.

The differences in pay created a salary structure that began to resemble that
of the capitalistic societies, with the right of certain individuals to save and get
interest, to pass on some of their gains to their heirs, to provide their children with
better education, and to enjoy special advantages for vacation, leisure, and travel.
There was even status—the recognition that they belonged to an elite class consisting of the top group of the *intelligentsia* (the Russian word denotes a very large
class of people, comprising all groups other than workers and farmers). In recognition of their services and as an added incentive, they were allowed membership

within the party—thus bestowing upon them political status as well. The percentage of workers and farmers within the party decreased correspondingly.

Force took a number of forms and served many purposes. It was used against those who did not work, or did not work regularly, and failed to live up to the quotas assigned to them. These people found their way to labor camps, and their disappearance was only a reminder to others of what they might have to face. Force was also used directly to create regiments of workers in labor camps who were responsible for tasks that nobody else would take (except for very high pay), such as mining of gold, lumber cutting, and road construction. In a more comprehensive sense, force was also a constant reminder, even to those who received a good pay for their work, that any relaxation or negligence would be followed by swift punishment.

SOVIET DOMINATION: THE COMINTERN

How would the Communist parties and the movements that sprang up almost everywhere after the Bolshevik Revolution be organized? The answer was the Third International—the Comintern—founded in 1919. The Communist parties that formed in many countries agreed to coordinate revolutionary strategy and tactics. There were thirty-five national parties in the Comintern when it was founded. By 1939—on the eve of World War II—the number had grown to about sixty.

The Twenty-One Conditions

What bound all these new Communist parties and movements together in the Third International were the famous twenty-one conditions set forth by Lenin. The same (or almost the same) characteristics of discipline, organization, and loyalty that Lenin imposed upon his Bolshevik party were required of all other national Communist parties. Some of the conditions for Communist parties everywhere were as follows:

- They must accept absolute ideological commitment to communism.
- They were to assume direct control over their communist press and publications.
- They accepted the principle and practice of democratic centralism (i.e., the compliance of the rank and file to the instructions of the higher authorities and the obligation not to allow any factions to exist within their party). Reformists, revisionists, trade unionists, were to be ruthlessly eliminated from their ranks.
- Underground and illegal organizations and activities were to be established, and party members should be ready for illegal work.
- A pledge was taken to make special efforts to undermine and disorganize the national armies.
- Pacifists and pacifism were not to be tolerated.
- All Communists undertook the obligation to give aid and support to revolutionary movements of colonial peoples.

- They were ordered to break with all trade unions affiliated with the Second International.
- Communist members in national parliaments were mere delegates of the party.
- All Communist parties in the world undertook to support the Soviet Union and "every Soviet republic."
- The Communist party program for every country had to be accepted by the executive committee of the Third International.

In this manner Lenin transformed the Communist movement into a worldwide organization to counter the worldwide grip that he claimed the capitalists had established. Any threats on the part of the capitalists against socialist Russia would meet with the resistance of this well-organized force everywhere outside of Russia.

With the offices of the Comintern in Moscow, the Soviet leadership under Stalin established its control over all other parties. Aside from ideology, many organizational and financial ties linked the individual Communist parties of various countries with the Soviet Union. Seven Congresses of the Third International were held and, in the beginning, there was freedom on the part of delegates from abroad to express their points of view and engage in dialogue. Soon the choice of these delegates became controlled by the Soviets, and the Congresses simply confirmed the "line" suggested by the Soviet leaders.

In 1943, the Third International was formally dissolved. The reasons given were that the various Communist parties in the world were "mature" enough to take care of their own programs and tactics and move about in their own way. The dissolution, however, was meant to placate the Western Allies (especially the United States) by showing that the Soviet Union was no longer bent on world revolution. But the Third International had played its role—it had coordinated tightly the Communist movements throughout the world according to Soviet designs and had solidly infused the belief that the defense and protection of the Soviet Union were the ultimate duties of all workers.

STALINISM: CONTRADICTIONS AND STAGNATION

For a long period of time, the Marxist vision sustained the communist reality, fashioned first by Lenin, and then worked out in its political and economic structures by Stalin, despite the disparity between the two. Such is the force of a grand ideology. Communist visionaries, ideologues, and intellectuals simply refused to examine the Stalinist reality because of the vision. Soviet leaders, on the other hand, exploited the vision to impose their rule and gain support both at home and abroad. Nonetheless, the disparities could not be accepted for too long. Some were noticeable even before Lenin's death—notably the imposition of a single-party rule by a party that allowed no free debate; the growing role of the police; the silencing of opposition by force; and the efforts to impose total communism upon a backward economy—in which 75 percent of the people were peasants. The disparities became more glaring, however, after the consolidation of the Stalinist regime. The party came under the complete domination of a single person—Stalin—who ruled by ruse and force like an Oriental despot.

With Stalin, revolutionary ideology and revolutionary movement became state and party orthodoxy. Speculation, argument, and debate gave place to imposition and dogma. Arguments, or even mere disagreements, were magnified to mean treason. Persuasion gave place to force, and the state and the police became the agencies to administer it, frequently against the party itself. Marxism was now presented in simple didactic terms to settle every dispute, especially when the presentation of the ideas was made by Stalin himself. Marxist ideology became a catechism repeated through all the socializing mechanisms available to the party—the party agitators, the press, the schools, the radio, the universities, the trade unions, and so on. The state and its bureaucracy, instead of withering away, grew and so did the totalitarian reach of the party; the use of force became, through the police, institutionalized into a permanent instrument of terror to exact compliance; all forms of public debate and argument were silenced—with all the media coming under the control of the appropriate party organs, just as it was the case under the authoritarian regimes that had sprung up in Germany and Italy. All societal groups and associations—professional, cultural, religious—were subordinated and came under the control of the party, including the family and the church. The state became the sole owner of property and the sole manager of the economy.

A despotism that was so reminiscent of the czars was but one of the developments that could not be reconciled with Marxism. But it was also the economy that failed to live up to the vision as well. The first decades of socialist buildup called for rapid mobilization of resources and was relatively successful. Under Stalin, Russia did indeed industrialize but only in the building of an industrial infrastructure that other countries had attained much earlier. Coal, cement, iron and steel, oil, rapid urbanization, and housing construction—the quantitative targets of the Five-Year Plans were impressive. Until well into the sixties, the authoritarian nature of the regimes, including even the police and the *gulags,* was ignored or even excused because of the vision of modernization and economic abundance promised by communism and by all those who believed that a planned and socialist economy was superior to capitalism; this was the conclusion of many Western European and American intellectuals as well. But the command economy, even in the days of Stalin, began to show inevitable weaknesses. First and foremost, it was unable to produce consumer goods—to meet the rising expectations of the Soviet citizens; second, and glaringly so, the collectivized agriculture could not produce enough food; third, inflexible mechanisms for the transport of goods were unable to move them from the producer to the consumer; and, even worse, planners were unable to manage so that materials needed in industrial firms could arrive in time and their products leave the factory on schedule. The socialist economy was unable to make the critical shift in the direction of diversification and experimentation and to introduce up-to-date technology.

With the economy stagnating, another of the Marxist visions began to fade away—that of equality. For a long time, a kind of ideological trade-off had been made between democracy (political freedoms) and equality (economic freedoms and satisfaction of economic needs, for all). The first was to be sacrificed to the second, *for a time.* The democracies of the West, it was claimed, gave the citizens equality of opportunities only; socialism provided them with real material equality. In the first there were formal rights; in the second substantive rights. Increasingly, however, it became apparent that this was not so. In a stagnating economy, the political oligarchy—notably the party members, the bureaucrats, the army officers, the police, and selected members of the intelligentsia— began to assume economic and social privileges that gave them a higher standard of living and access to special services. Political power became increasingly synonymous with privilege. Special food stores for shopping, vacation spots, and advantages for the education of their children were added to their higher benefits and salaries. Abuses and corruption inevitably followed. The vision appeared flawed as the communist ideology seemed to have become but a shield that protected a new political elite. It began to be looked upon with disdain by the rest of the population—including the populations of many nationalities whose standard of living was well below the level of the Russians. Joining the Communist party, and professing to be a Communist, was but a way for many to ensure their future and careers. The party gradually became a vast bureaucratic machine for maintaining the privileges accruing to its members. The ideology that sustained and nurtured it began to decline rapidly.

Waiting for . . . Gorbachev!

In 1956, after a short power struggle, Nikita Khrushchev, who replaced Stalin as General Secretary of the party and Chairman of the Council of Ministers of the Soviet Union, gave a "secret report" to the delegates of the Soviet Communist party at its Twentieth Congress. He criticized Stalin sharply for the many crimes committed during his long stay in office.

> Comrades!. . .
>
> After Stalin's death the Central Committee of the party began to implement a policy of explaining concisely and consistently that it is impermissible and foreign to the spirit of Marxism-Leninism to elevate one person, to transform him into a superman possessing supernatural characteristics akin to those of a god. Such a man supposedly knows everything, sees everything, thinks for everyone, can do anything, is infalliable in his behavior.

Only minor reforms were undertaken, however, in the economy, the society, and hardly any in the organization and rule of the party. Among them the most important were:

1. The control that the Soviet leadership once exercised over the other Communist parties in the world declined. References were now made to polycentrism, with multiple and independent centers of Communist rule, and to "national communism" in which Communist parties would follow a path dictated by specific national conditions and not by the Soviet leadership according to the Soviet model.
2. The "inevitability" of conflict between communism and liberal democracies gave place to "peaceful coexistence." In great part this was due of course to the development of nuclear weapons—and the "mutual assured destruction" they would bring upon all.

3. Stalin came under increasing criticism both with regard to the political practices he used and with reference to the kind of socialism that developed. His name was gradually removed from every corner of Soviet life. He was no longer regarded as one of "the founders" of communist ideology. Efforts to rehabilitate some of the Communist leaders who were put to death or "disappeared" during his reign have been successful. Many of the Communist leaders executed by Stalin were proclaimed innocent in 1988. Finally, but only in 1989, Gorbachev admitted that Stalin's "guilt is unforgiveable."

4. Stalin, as the leader—omniscient and omnipotent—was replaced by "collective leadership." The General Secretary of the Party, however, continued to maintain his ascendency. Yet the servile adulation and deference were gone. Through the party, Stalin's successors continued to exercise control, but it was no longer the direct and personal iron grip that Stalin held through the police and through outright intimidation and force.

5. The police and its arbitrary practices came under control, thanks to the development of some general rules and procedures to curb and subordinate it.

Little else was changed, however, until the mid-eighties. The official ideological orthodoxy of the party remained immune from criticism. The "dictatorship of the proletariat" continued to be proclaimed. The state in the hands of the Communist party maintained its coercive traits and Soviet military power dominated Eastern Europe, stifling by force national uprisings. Little was also changed in the economy. It continued to operate under the same bureaucratic and centralized controls, and the disparity between its progress (or rather lack of progress) and that of the Western world became manifest. The command economy was unable to provide for the consumer, and the standard of living of the Soviet citizen declined. The Soviets began to experience their own kind of "stagflation"—increased centralized controls by a burgeoning privileged Communist elite, with fewer and fewer goods for the population.

BIBLIOGRAPHY

Berlin, Isaiah. "Political Ideas in the Twentieth Century." *Foreign Affairs*, April 1950.

Bialer, Seweryn. *Stalin's Successors*. New York: Cambridge University Press, 1980.

Borkenau, F. *The Communist International*. London: Faber, 1938.

Braunthal, Julius. *History of the International 1914–1943*, 2 vols. New York: Praeger, 1967.

Conquest, Robert. *The Soviet Political System*. New York: Praeger, 1968.

Conquest, Robert. *The Great Terror: A Reassessment*. New York: Oxford University Press, 1990.

Deutscher, Isaac. *Stalin*. New York: Oxford University Press, 1949.

Djilas, Milovan. *The New Class: An Analysis of the Communist System*. New York: Praeger, 1957.

————. *The Unperfect Society: Beyond the New Class*. New York: Harcourt Brace Jovanovich, 1969.

Drachkovitch, Milorad M. (ed.). *Marxism in the Modern World*. Stanford, CA.: Stanford University Press, 1965.

Gorbachev, Mikhail. *Perestroika*. New York: Harper & Row, 1987.

Lacqueur, Walter. *Stalin: The Glasnost Revelations*. New York: Scribner's, 1990.

Lenin, V.I. *What Is To Be Done?* New York: International Publishers, 1969.

————. "Imperialism: The Highest Stage of Capitalism" and "The State and Revolution." In *Lenin: Selected Works in One Volume*. New York: International Publishers, 1971.

NcNeal, Robert H. *The Bolshevik Tradition*. Englewood Cliffs, NJ: Prentice-Hall, 1975.

Medvedev, Roy. *Let History Judge—The Origins and Consequences of Stalinism*. New York: Columbia University Press, 1990.

Meyer, Alfred G. *Leninism*. New York: Praeger, 1957.

————. *The Soviet Political System: An Interpretation*. New York: Random House, 1965.

Miliband, Ralph. *Marxism and Politics*. New York: Oxford University Press, 1977.

Plamenatz, John. *German Marxism and Russian Communism*. New York: Longmans, 1954.

Schapiro, Leonard. *The Communist Party of the Soviet Union*, rev. ed. New York: Vintage, 1978.

————. *The Government and Politics of the Soviet Union*. New York: Vintage Books, 1978.

Shub, David. *Lenin: A Biography*. New York: Penguin, 1976.

Simon, Gerhard. *Church, State, and Opposition in the USSR*. London: C. Hurst, 1974.

Solzhenitsyn, Aleksander. *The Gulag Archipelago*, 3 vols. New York: Harper & Row, 1974–1979.

Stalin, Joseph. *The Essential Stalin*. Edited by Bruce Franklin. New York: Anchor-Double-day, 1972.

Trotsky, Leon. *History of the Russian Revolution*. Ann Arbor: University of Michigan Press, 1952.

Tucker, Robert C. (ed.). *Stalinism: Essays in Historical Interpretation*. New York: Norton, 1977.

————. *Stalin in Power—The Revolution from Above*. New York: Norton, 1990.

Ulam, Adam B. *The Bolsheviks*. New York: Macmillan, 1968.

————. *Stalin: The Man and His Era*. New York: Viking, 1973.

Wolfe, Bertram D. *Three Who Made A Revolution*. New York: Delta/Dell, 1964.

Chapter 7

The Collapse of Communism

The Myth was transformed into Lie . . .; for Soviet Socialism as actually realized was a fraud in terms of the Myth's own standards. This Lie could be made to appear to be the truth, and the fraud concealed for a time . . . by the combination of terror and drumbeat indoctrination. . . . The collapse of the Lie under glasnost *is destroying acceptance of the system itself.*

"Z" (for Martin Melia) "To the Stalin Mausoleum"

*D*espite minor reforms undertaken after Stalin's death and as late as the 1970s, the contours of the Soviet regime changed little. It remained a single party controlling the society in the name of communism and imposing an ideology that was becoming increasingly irrelevant, with a centralized and bureaucratized command economy increasingly unable to provide for economic growth and satisfy the consumers' needs.

It was only in the 1980s, and more specifically after Mikhail Gorbachev became Secretary-General of the Communist party in March 1985, succeeding at fifty-four a line of old party stalwarts, that reforms began to affect the party, the regime, and the communist ideology. But it was not before the end of 1989 that radical reforms were undertaken, or made necessary, that affected the very citadel of communist orthodoxy—the rule of the single party and the command economy. By 1990, the very fabric of the Soviet polity had been torn apart. Dramatic change also took place in the Eastern European satellites—in Poland, East Germany, Czechoslovakia, Hungary, Bulgaria, and Romania, spreading even into isolated and small Albania. In each and every case, there was a profound crisis in communist ideology and communist institutions, which we survey in this chapter. It was a crisis that foreshadowed the worldwide collapse of communism.

To appreciate the magnitude of change, let us recall the essential features of the communist totalitarianism:

1. The ideology is official, that is, espoused by the leadership to the exclusion of all other ideologies. It is total and comprehensive and everything becomes subordinate to it. Society is to be restructured in terms of the posited ideological goals.
2. The purpose of the single party is to control, intimidate, and govern. It is the major vehicle of political mobilization and recruitment. No political competition is tolerated.
3. All associations, all groups, and all individuals are subordinate to the party, the state, and the leader. There is no cultural pluralism. Education, literature, art, music, architecture—all must yield and conform to the overriding objectives and goals of the political ideology. Groups and individuals, family life, social and recreational activities, the schools, and the economy must all be synchronized with the political regime. All must "march in step" with it.
4. The use of violence is institutionalized through the police and other specialized instruments of coercion and intimidation.
5. The party directly, or through the state, has a monopolistic control of mass communications and overall economic activities.

DECLINE OF THE COMMUNIST IDEOLOGY

Even before the period of stagnation (1964–1985), the official communist ideology, and with it the Communist party, had begun to weaken. It lost its mobilizing force as the disparity between its promise and reality became apparent; it became especially irrelevant to the young for whom Marxism and Stalinism appeared dogmatic and incapable of resolving new societal, domestic, and international problems, or for that matter, of explaining the successes of Western and American free-market economies whose doom had been clearly spelled out by all Marxists. Socialists, technicians, academics, and in general the growing professional class within the Soviet society became restive at first, disillusioned during the years of stagnation, and downright critical throughout the 1980s.

Yet no counterideology to confront communism emerged. This was the result of two reinforcing factors prevalent both in Russian and Soviet history. Until 1917, ideologies that had emerged in Russia had never taken hold by gaining popular support. Anarchism, conservatism, liberalism, democratic constitutionalism, or socialism never crystallized into political movements that gained widespread support. To be sure, the peasantry reclaimed the land. "We are yours but the land is ours," its leaders proclaimed to the Czar, but this was the substance of their demands, except for some utopian schemes involving collective village ownership proposed by some intellectuals. The church followed a servile attachment to the autocracy. The aristocracy did, by and large, the same, and the emerging bourgeoisie in the latter half of the nineteenth century was too weak to gain any representation. Group life, associational life, and intermediary institutions linking authority with participation and consent did not exist and, as a result, no ideology was formulated to confront the czarist despotism.

With the coming of the Soviet revolution, whatever group and political life existed—in the church, the trade unions, and nascent political parties and groups—was destroyed, as we have seen, in the name of a single all-encompassing ideology professed by an elite and enshrined in the Communist party. So when the Communist regime began to falter, there were no potential centers from which a new reformist anticommunist ideology could spring. As one intellectual close to Gorbachev put it in assessing the impact of communism on the Soviet society: "When you have destroyed all natural structures of life—in the family, the state, in religion—then how can you recreate them?"[1] Or more to the point: How can they reassert themselves?

The decline of communism in the late 1980s and early 1990s was associated, therefore, only with the reemergence of ideological fragments rooted in past history: anarchism, ethnic manifestations, workers' strikes, a return to religious attachment, nationalist anti-Soviet protests in virtually all fifteen republics of the former Soviet Union. Grass-roots citizens' groups have emerged representing a host of claims, ranging from demands for religious freedom to environmental movements and anti-Semitic protestations. Curiously enough, the peasantry did not seize the opportunity to reclaim the land that had been collectivized. The ruthless liquidation of private farmers by Stalin may well have stifled their secular aspirations to own their land. Communism—or the term increasingly used, "socialism"—remained the only ideology. If there was a "revolution," as Gorbachev dubbed *perestroika,* it had none of the characteristics of a genuine revolutionary movement involving a coherent set of principles.

It was the nonbirth of a new ideology, while the old one was dying, that amounted to a genuine crisis of authority and institutions. The communist institutions weakened, but the new ones in the process of being set up lacked legitimacy because of the lack of a coherent set of values to sustain them. The crisis in ideology became a crisis of institutions, and the continuing ineffectiveness of institutions intensified the crisis in ideology.

Many claim that Gorbachev and some of his associates were, from the very beginning, committed to the liquidation of Marxism as an ideology. They had to move slowly, however, first within the top leadership of the party, then in the Central Committee, and then among the party members before they reached out to seek popular support. It is uncertain Gorbachev had this in mind. Reforms undertaken at first in the name of *perestroika* and democratization were not the result of ideologic reflection but the children of necessity. The economy had come to a virtual standstill and the food supplies were dwindling; at the same time, burdens upon the Soviet system, because of military and international commitments, were growing heavier. All Gorbachev offered at first was a reformed Communist party. Reforming the party, weeding out inefficient and incompetent bureaucrats, and decentralizing the state and the command economy became necessary, but in all cases they were made in the name of communism.

---

[1]*New York Times,* April 1, 1990.

A New Ideology?

It was only in November 1989 that Gorbachev provided, in a major address on "Revolutionary Perestroika," what pretended to be a new ideology. There was a forceful declaration favoring privatizations and the liberalization of the market and a gradual democratization of the political process. Yet Gorbachev continued to cling to the Communist party and to its monopoly on political power. Whether to control the pace and direction of change or out of genuine belief, he insisted that he was a communist. "We are using the Leninist method," he proclaimed. "We must analyze how the future arises from reality." He explicitly rejected the Stalinist method that imposes "ready-made recipes on society and adjusts reality to these recipes."

It was the "Leninist method" that led Gorbachev to the conclusion that the political regime and the command economy should be drastically reformed in the direction of the free market and cultural and political pluralism. At the same time he propounded new humanitarian goals. The centerpiece of socialism is "Man," according to Marx, and despite Marx's shortcomings in predicting the course of capitalism and the dynamics of the capitalist economy, socialism remained for Gorbachev "the ideal." He promised a new revolution not from above but "from below." He suggested the growth of a grass-roots and participatory socialism to replace statism. "Perestroika," he claimed, "has shown that only the drawing of people into social and public affairs as a responsible field of activity will make it possible to overcome their alienation, close the gap between personal and common interest and change the activity of the individual in all spheres of life." After giving an outline of a variety of economic and social reforms that, in many cases, sounded like an endorsement of democratic socialism as practiced in the Scandinavian countries, Gorbachev returned time after time, whether for tactical reasons or out of conviction, to the Communist party. "Developing the independent activities of the masses and promoting democratization of all spheres of life under a one-party system is a noble but very difficult mission for the Party. . . . And a great deal depends on how we cope with it." Even after February 1990, when the monopoly of the Communist party was officially abandoned by revising the Constitution, Gorbachev was asking it "to elaborate and generate political and ideological platforms that are recommended to the society and the state."[2]

Speaking before the Central Committee on February 6, 1990 on the draft platform that was to be submitted to the Twenty-Eighth Party Congress, Gorbachev declared again his ideal of a "humane, democratic socialism" and called for the "restructuring of the party as a democratic force." "We remain committed to the choice made in October 1917," he said, "to the socialist idea."

No new doctrine emerged, no new vision dawned, no new comprehensive programs developed. Even the position of the Communist party remained uncertain. An end to its political monopoly was decided in February 1990, but Gorbachev remained its leader, exhorting it to new efforts, even if in the name of plu-

---

[2]Mikhail Gorbachev, "The Socialist Idea of Revolutionary Perestroika," *Pravda,* November 26, 1989, translated by the Soviet Embassy Information Services.

ralism and democracy! The collapse of communism, therefore, amounts to an internal collapse—some call it an "implosion." The fabric that Stalin had woven—the personality cult, the rule of the nomenklatura, the command economy and the huge bureaucracy that managed it, the party with its pivileges and benefits, the secret police that pervaded the lives of all, the conformity imposed by the party upon nationalities—was taken apart stitch by stitch. The old Bolshevism "withered away" but its demise did not signal the rise of a vigorous successor ideology.

THE "OPENING": *GLASNOST* AND *PERESTROIKA*

Perhaps Gorbachev tried so hard to stay within the Communist fold because he saw no other way to hold the Soviet Union together while rebuilding it top to bottom, bottom to top.

After becoming Secretary–General of the Communist party in March 1985, Mikhail Gorbachev consolidated his power in the Politbureau, the Central Committee, and within the party as a whole. By the middle of 1986, he was vigorously advocating a policy of "openness"—a liberalization of the political system (*glasnost*) and an economic restructuring (*perestroika*).

The aim of *perestroika* was to decentralize and ultimately dismantle the huge bureaucracy that planned, directed, and implemented industrial and agricultural production and trade. The central bureaucracy was to be replaced by smaller functional units at the regional and local levels, right down to the business firms and their managers. They would be free to plan production, secure labor and raw materials at the best possible prices, establish their own budget, and seek benefits from their products. "Profits" would be realized through both an increase in productivity and efficiency, which would reduce costs, and through creative marketing practices that would increase sales and income. Such moves would inject some flexibility into the system so that production could be increasingly geared to consumer demand, needs, and tastes. There could even be competition among firms; for example, differential profits and wages could be established and a special bonus for productivity could be granted. In other words, the Soviet economy would move in the direction of the "capitalistic" world in order to spur growth.

Glasnost is the term used to denote reforms undertaken to liberalize the political regime by allowing for greater public debate within and outside the political party, in the press, on radio, and on television. Moreover, *glasnost* sought to develop procedures through which public officials—mostly party members—could be scrutinized and held accountable. It was not originally interpreted as a move toward democracy; there was no pretense, as we have seen, of abandoning the monopoly of the single party, nor was there a desire to publicize the deliberations of the higher decision-making units of the party. Only some democratization at the grass-roots level and in local elections was envisaged and implemented. More important at this stage was Gorbachev's new policy of "openness," reflected in the photograph of the Soviet leader on this page. Dialogue, debate, reexamination of the roots and the destiny of the Soviet society and the Soviet Union, and the liberalization of societal forces, including the economy, were gradually introduced.

"We are for a diversity of public opinion," Gorbachev proclaimed, "for a richness of spiritual life. We need not fear openly raising and solving difficult problems of social development, criticizing and arguing. It is in such circumstances that the truth is born and that correct decisions take shape." Gorbachev further asserted that critical inquiry should also be directed to Soviet history and the reconsideration of the role of revolutionary leaders—including, above all, Stalin and many of his victims. In short, Gorbachev was urging the Russians, for so long treated as subjects, to become citizens—free to participate, equal before the law, and protected from personalistic and dictatorial regimes, such as the one shaped by Stalin. He also opened a wide window to the world. "Peaceful co-existence," he seemed to indicate, was no longer enough. The present and the future require "interrelatedness" and "interdependence," cooperation and solidarity. This outlook was necessary, he said, because of technological changes, the role of mass communications, world environmental and resource problems, the social and economic problems in the developing countries, and, above all, human survival from the dangers of nuclear weapons.[3]

Without doubt, the move toward economic freedoms (and efficiency) and political freedoms (and political responsibility) became one of the most exciting prospects for the Soviet society. The inertia of the past, the heavy hand of a bureaucracy that had institutionalized itself over so many years, the preferential treatment and privileges that went with the top decision-making jobs—among the politicians, the managers, the military, the bureaucrats, and the Soviet intelligentsia in general—seemed all to be in jeopardy if public officials were to be freely scrutinized and criticized (see Table 7.1).

The End of the Communist Party Monopoly and the Liberalization of the Economy

It was not until 1988, and particularly between 1989 and 1990, that change reached a critical point. It became radical; it questioned, at least indirectly, the communist ideology and its regime. In effect, it put an end to both, as Gorbachev and his associates initiated and began to implement genuine democratic and some liberal economic reforms. The "Soviet Bloc" split into its parts—with Eastern Europe, Latvia, Lithuania, and Estonia claiming independence. Within the Soviet Union itself, the federated political units (the republics) moved also to assert their will as independent entities.

The Single-Party Monopoly   Until the end of 1989, Gorbachev favored, as we noted, reforms within the party and by the party. Communism and the party,

---

[3]Quotes from excerpts of a speech printed in the *New York Times,* November 3, 1987.

Table 7.1   SIX YEARS OF CHANGE UNDER GORBACHEV, 1985–1991

March 1985	Gorbachev assumes power and promises to reform the economy.
April 1985	Before the Central Committee of the party, Gorbachev introduces *perestroika*—a policy aimed at reforming the Soviet bureaucracy and the rigidities of the command economy.
March 1986	Communist Party Congress approves Gorbachev's resolution favoring "true revolutionary changes in the economy" in the direction of liberalization.
November 1987	On the occasion of the seventieth anniversary of the Bolshevik Revolution, Gorbachev acknowledges Stalin's crimes, favoring reconsideration of the history of communism in Russia. Censorship is loosened; freedom to publish and criticize encouraged. But democratization provides the ethnic republics—Armenia and Lithuania, for example—the justification to reassert claims of independence.
March 1989	In freely held elections for the newly established Congress of People's Deputies, many Communist leaders are defeated, but the majority remains in the hands of the party.
November 1989	Gorbachev produces a long manifesto in which he endorses Marxism as the only force capable of reviving the system and reemphasizes the guiding role of the Communist party. He urges development of a communism "with a human face."
February 1990	The monopoly of the Communist party is formally abandoned by the Central Committee, and the Constitution is revised accordingly.
March 1990	Elections are held in the Soviet Socialist Republics and in many cities. In Russia, the Ukraine, and Byelorussia, the independent pro-democracy candidates make significant gains. In some major cities—Moscow, Leningrad, Kiev—they gain outright control.
March–June 1990	Constitutional changes—confirmed by the Central Committee—create a new all-powerful presidency, and Gorbachev is elected by the Congress of People's Deputies as the first president.

he asserted, had a vital role to play in the democratization of the society and in economic reforms. He urged the Communist party to lead the way. Yet in February 1990, by a virtual unanimous vote, the Central Committee put an end to the party monopoly. Article 6 of the Constitution, the very cornerstone of Leninism, which we discussed earlier, stated:

> The leading and guiding force of Soviet society and the nucleus of its political system and all state organizations and public organizations is the Communist Party of the Soviet Union. . . . Armed with Marxism–Leninism [it] determines the general perspectives and the development of society.

The abolition of Article 6 signaled an "opening" to other parties and groups—already tentatively organized—to compete in national and state (republic) elections. But it meant much more: it signified that the Communist party relinquished its role as the educator and the guide of society. The ideology

Table 7.1 (Continued)   SIX YEARS OF CHANGE UNDER GORBACHEV, 1985–1991

July 1990	The Twenty-Eighth Congress of the Communist party meets. Gorbachev maintains his leadership but is sharply criticized by both the conservatives and the democratic reformers. The latter blame him for not moving ahead rapidly with reforms in the economy.
December 1990	Congress of People's Deputies convenes to consider constitutional changes that give President Gorbachev additional powers and to debate a new Union Treaty. A proposal to change the Union of Soviet Socialist Republics to the Union of Soviet Sovereign Republics is defeated. A new post of vice president is created, and Gennadi I. Yanayev, a loyal and long-time official of the Communist party, is nominated for the post by Gorbachev and endorsed by the Congress. He declares himself to be a Communist to "the core of my soul." Many of the liberal democratic reformers withdraw. Major legislation regarding the economy, property rights, and the new Union Treaty has yet to be enacted.
March 17, 1991	A referendum on the "Union Treaty" is overwhelmingly endorsed, but both the wording of the referendum and the answers to specific questions included in the referendum in various Republics cloud the popular verdict.
March 31, 1991	Georgians participate massively in a referendum and favor overwhelmingly the independence of Georgia.
June 12, 1991	The wavering pro-democracy forces get a powerful boost when Boris Yeltsin is elected President of the Russian Republic, which accounts for over half of the Soviet Union's population, in a free and open election. He wins 60 percent of the vote, defeating all other candidates, including the Communist Party candidate, on the first ballot.
last week of August, 1991	The Communist Party stages a coup against Gorbachev. The attempted return to the old order fails and Yeltsin steps forward as the man of the hour.
September, 1991	Gorbachev is removed from office. End of the Soviet Union.

embodied in communism, therefore, was no longer deemed to embody the truth. Other emerging ideologies, speaking through newly founded associations, parties, and groups—including the church, nationalist and patriotic organizations, and, above all, ethnonational minorities—asserted their own claims. They could compete freely with the Communist party on a footing of equality. Political pluralism was in the air, and by the end of 1990 a great number of political organizations had mushroomed.

Side by side with the political reforms we outlined, comprehensive reforms of the economy were contemplated. They all pointed in the same direction—toward economic liberalism. In the last omnibus proposal introduced by President Gorbachev in November 1990, the following measures were outlined, to be implemented over a period of time:

1. Freedom of producers to produce for profit.
2. Competition among producers.
3. Gradual deregulation of prices.
4. Privatization of the land and farming.
5. Gradual incorporation of the Soviet economy into the international economy.
6. Finally, the dismantling of the huge bureaucracy in the economic plan and in the economic ministries.

These reforms are staunchly resisted in the name of ideology by the millions of bureaucrats (most of them party members). They struck also at the privileges of major segments of the society—workers, retirees, salaried personnel, and farmers. To many they were as revolutionary as the Bolshevik Revolution of 1917!

To add to the overall disarray, the Soviet Socialist Republics were in the process of developing their own economic reforms independently of the Soviet Union. They were beginning to enter into trade agreements with each other and even with foreign countries independently of the Soviet authorities; they have even threatened to print their own money and declare it as the only legal currency; they stated—and this was far more noticeable in the three Latvian republics, but also in Armenia—that their citizens would not be recruited into the Soviet army; and some set up their own police, defying, at times, the all-powerful Secret Police.

The Failure of Gorbachev's Final Gambit

In the midst of a profound ideological crisis, with the communist ideology dying without giving place to another, with relatively free elections in which oppositional groups asserted their strength, with rampant ethnic violence and movements in favor of the independence of a number of Republics against the central Soviet authority, we can begin to understand the frequent institutional changes introduced by Gorbachev to cope with the crisis and, even more, the constant tinkering with the institutional reforms he introduced.

In March 1990, Gorbachev mobilized the delegates to the Congress of People's Deputies to push through legislation favoring the creation of a powerful Soviet presidency. And he secured his own appointment as president for a five-year term, not through the party but through the Congress, without having to stand for popular election. The new president was to be commander-in-chief of the armed forces. He also was to appoint the leading members of the government, subject to confirmation by the Congress of People's Deputies and the Supreme Soviet. The most distinctive, and inherently controversial, powers granted to the president by the constitutional reforms of March 1990 were the ability to issue decrees that have the force of law for the entire territory of the USSR; the power to dissolve the Supreme Soviet in certain circumstances; and the power to impose martial law on areas of the Soviet Union.

A new "presidential council" was established, and a reorganization and redistribution of executive authority and functions allowed it to operate as a kind of cabinet-like advisory body to the president. Together with the plan to submit the presidency to direct popular election in the future, these changes have brought the

Soviet Union closer to the establishment of a strong "semi-presidential" system of government.[4] In this manner, Gorbachev tried to develop a basis of power outside the Communist party

Tocqueville once remarked that "the most perilous moment for a bad government is when it seeks to mend its ways." No one has ever had better reason than Gorbachev to appreciate Tocqueville's insight. To Bolsheviks of the old school Gorbachev was moving too fast toward reform; to Boris Yeltsin, President of the Russian Republic, he was moving too slowly. Throughout his reign it was said of Gorbachev that his was the unenviable task of struggling to rebuild an aircraft while it was in flight. Come August of 1991 the plane carrying Gorbachev crashed: hardline Bolsheviks, frightened to see their world slipping away, staged a coup against Gorbachev. Yeltsin, after helping to end the coup, blamed Gorbachev for failing to break definitively with the Communist party. Before the passing of the month of September Gorbachev was out of a job and the Soviet Union was no more. The various republics decided to go their own way.

THE COLLAPSE OF COMMUNISM IN EASTERN EUROPE

Communism fell earlier and with more dramatic consequences in Eastern Europe than in Russia and the former Soviet Union. The list of Communist regimes that disappeared during 1989 and 1990 includes Poland, East Germany, Czechoslovakia, Hungary, Estonia, Lithuania, and Latvia. The dismemberment of Yugoslavia and the outbreak of devastating civil war within its territories proves that the fall of Communism, far from automatically marking the advent of a new age of freedom, can mean the return to a regrettable and murderous nationalist past.

There are many reasons for the precipitous collapse of communism in the Eastern European countries. All these countries had one thing in common: the revolt against Communist regimes was profoundly nationalist and it sought independence from Soviet domination and from the indigenous Communist parties that had been imposed by the Soviet leadership. The weakening of the Soviet capabilities to maintain its control and the liberalization within the Soviet Communist party and the regime triggered the pent-up demands for national independence. Related to the Soviet Union's failure with its command economy, the Eastern European societies suffered the same economic stagnation as the Soviet Union. Experimentation with market economics and individual entrepreneurship had been carried out, but it ran against the common grain of communist orthodoxy and was looked upon with suspicion until the Soviets began to entertain thoughts about instituting the same reforms. When this happened, the revolt against both communism and Soviet domination became irresistible. The revolt affected all the mainstays of communist ideology and of their regimes.

---

[4]For a full discussion, see Roy Macridis and Steven Burg, *Introduction to Comparative Politics*, chap. 8.

The End of Communist Party Monopoly and Governance

The stranglehold of the party ended, for all practical purposes, first in Poland, where widespread dissatisfaction had produced repeated confrontations between the state and society in the past and led in 1979 to a grass-roots trade-union movement—Solidarity. After failing to silence resistance through repression, the near-collapse of the economy finally forced the Polish regime to permit, at least partially, democratic elections through which Solidarity finally broke the Communists' political monopoly. In June of 1989, Solidarity won an overwhelming victory in the first free parliamentary elections, in effect putting an end to Communist rule. In August 1989, a new government was formed, headed by Solidarity, but with Communist participation. After introducing radical economic reforms, this new government proceeded in July 1990 to oust all Communists from the Council of Ministers. Finally, in December 1990, the leader of Solidarity, Lech Walesa, was elected president.

In Hungary, declining economic performance led to conflict within the Communist political elite over the future course of reform, and this conflict soon spilled over into society. Under the pressure of increasingly frequent and growing demonstrations demanding democratization, the Communist leadership rapidly fragmented, and the party disintegrated. By spring 1989, it was clear that a new, more democratic, and more pluralistic order was emerging in Hungary, as opposition groups coalesced into parties. In an attempt to break with its own past, the Hungarian Communist party changed its name, abandoned any claim of political monopoly, and negotiated an agreement with opposition forces on the calling of free elections.

Growing impatience with authoritarianism in East Germany provoked popular demonstrations and uprisings that the police could not contain. Thousands of East Germans fled to West Germany in 1989, and mass demonstrations calling for democratization took place in Leipzig and other cities. A "new" Communist leadership attempted to win popular support by making concessions to the people's desire to travel, including the momentous opening of the Berlin Wall. But continuing demonstrations forced the ousting of the Communist party, clearing the way for the emergence of a non-Communist regime in East Germany and opening the door to reunification.

In Czechoslovakia, mass demonstrations beginning in mid-November 1989 toppled the Communist leadership by the end of December. And in Romania mass demonstrations overthrew the Ceausescu regime—in effect a personalistic tyranny—in the last days of 1989 (see Table 7.2).

After Communism: Democracy or Virulent Nationalism?

In the first free elections held in 1990 throughout virtually all Eastern European states that had been dominated by Communist parties, the verdict was overwhelmingly against them. In Czechoslovakia (June 8 and 9) the Communist party received only 14 percent of the vote; in East Germany (March 18), only 18 percent; in Hungary (March 25–April 8) two communist parties—one "reformed" and

Table 7.2   **TRANSITION IN EASTERN EUROPE: THE COLLAPSE OF COMMUNISM, 1989–1990**

January 1989	*Poland* Communist party agrees to negotiations with Solidarity opposition.
	Hungary Communist party leaders promise multiparty system.
April 1989	*Poland* Communist leader Wojciech Jaruzelski and Solidarity leader Lech Walesa reach agreement on partly democratic elections to parliament.
May 1989	*Hungary* Demolition of "iron curtain" begins with removal of barbed wire from Hungarian-Austrian border.
June 1989	*Poland* Solidarity wins overwhelming victory in first partly free parliamentary elections; gains control of strengthened parliament.
August 1989	*Poland* Solidarity-led government is elected by parliament, with Tadeusz Mazowiecki as prime minister. Non-Communists lead social and economic ministries, Communists head military and security ministries with non-Communist deputies, and Jaruzelski remains as president.
October 1989	*East Germany* Flow of refugees to West Germany, through Hungary and Czechoslovakia continues as internal demonstrations for change increase in size and frequency.
	Hungary Communist party reorients itself toward more liberal political program and renames itself Socialist party; parliament revises constitution to end Communist political monopoly, allowing multiparty system.
	Bulgaria Protest rally leads to promise of reform by Communist leadership.
November 1989	*East Germany* Shakeup of Communist party leadership fails to stem either flow of refugees to West or rise of internal unrest; politburo resigns; Berlin Wall is opened and free travel to West permitted; Communist leadership promises free elections.
	Czechoslovakia Opposition groups form "Civic Forum" alliance; despite efforts by Communists to retain power through concessions, opposition forces prevail; Communist party renounces monopoly of power and concedes need for free elections.
	Bulgaria Longtime Communist party leader, 78-year-old Todor Zhivkov, is ousted; replaced by 53-year-old Petar Mladenov, who begins to carry out a program of modest political liberalization.

the other unreformed—managed 11 percent; in Poland in the elections for the Senate held earlier (in June 1989), Solidarity won 92 of the 100 seats; while in the Presidential election of December 1990 there was no Communist candidate. The leader of the Solidarity, Lech Walesa, won. In Bulgaria (June 10 and 17), the ex-Communists, running under the label of a Bulgarian Socialist Party, received 47 percent of the vote and sought to form a coalition cabinet. Only in Romania (May 20) did the Communists, running under the label of National Salvation Front that included a number of political groups, win a majority.

With the ousting of the Communist party from power, new political institutions were introduced. They all copied Western European democratic

Table 7.2 (continued)   TRANSITION IN EASTERN EUROPE: THE COLLAPSE OF COMMUNISM, 1989–1990

December 1989	*Czechoslovakia* New government, with non-communist majority is formed; Vaclav Havel elected president of Czechoslovakia by parliament.
	Romania Local protest against harassment of ethnic Hungarians escalates, with support from ethnic Romanians, into mass demonstrations against Ceausescu tyranny; Ceausescu and wife are arrested and executed.
January 1990	*Yugoslavia* The League of Communists (Communist party) of Yugoslavia convenes an extraordinary Congress at which it renounces its constitutional monopoly of political power and endorses a multiparty political system.
	Poland Communist party (Polish United Workers Party) formally disbanded and reconstitutes itself as a non-Communist but Socialist-oriented party known as Social Democracy of the Republic of Poland.
March 1990	*Hungary* First free multiparty elections produce electoral victory for democratic opposition; the moderate-to-conservative "Democratic Forum" wins 24.7 percent of vote, the more radical Alliance of Free Democrats wins 21.4 percent, and the Independent Smallholders' party wins 11.8 percent.
	East Germany First free multiparty elections produce electoral victory for alliance of conservative democratic opposition.
April 1990	*East Germany* Conservative democratic coalition led by Christian Democrats forms government.
December 1990	*Poland* Lech Walesa, the former leader of Solidarity, is elected president, replacing General Jaruzelski, the only remaining representative of Communist rule; beginnings of "de-Stalinization". Albania liberalization in Albania, where an opposition Democratic party is formed.
June 15, 1991	*Yugoslavia* Slovenia and Croatia, inspired by the secession of the three Baltic republics from the USSR in 1990, seek autonomy. Serbia, the dominant republic, uses force, to prevent such a move.
June, 1993	*Czechoslovakia* Czechs and Slovaks choose in an election to form two separate republics, effective January 1, 1993

constitutions. Legislative assemblies were freely elected and were given the power to freely legislate and to control the government; the executive was vested either in a presidency or in a cabinet, elected by the legislatures or by the people and responsible to them; judicial review was instituted and the independence of the judges guaranteed. The Secret Police, the pillar of Communist regimes, was dismantled or purged and its powers now carefully circumscribed. Pluralism—political and cultural—was affirmed. On the surface, at least, Eastern Europe moved toward democracy in politics and toward the market in economics.

But the question remains whether democracy and a free-market economy will survive the difficult period of transition from Communist rule and a command economy to democracy and individual entrepreneurship. Grave economic difficulties afflict the countries of Eastern Europe, so grave that democracy may well seem too much a luxury. Making things all the worse has been the dramatic resurgence of nationalism and the pattern of intense ethnic conflict. The worst case, so far, has been the outbreak of bloody war in what was once Yugoslavia. In sharp contrast, the division of Czechoslovakia into two autonomous political units, a Czech republic and a Slovak republic, has occurred peacefully, by virtue of a general election held in June of 1992. The prospects for democracy in what was once Yugoslavia are dim, indeed; far more hopeful is the situation in the area known until recently as Czechoslovakia.

THE LAST BASTIONS

Communist regimes, together with the ideology that nurtured them, seem to be in the process of being swept away almost everywhere. There are some, however (we can call them the "Last Bastions"), that are resisting change and remain defiant in proclaiming their commitment to communism and in maintaining the rigid one-party authoritarian rule. They include North Korea, Albania, Cuba, Vietnam, and notably China. Among some African regimes that have paid lip service to communism as an ideology to rationalize military rule, Marxism is also rapidly waning—but not military rule!

In the remaining Communist regimes, the reaction to Gorbachev's "opening" was a defiant rejection of the changes made or contemplated and a reassertion of the true faith. In North Korea, where the military and political dictatorship of Kim Il Sung ruled the country for over three decades until his death in 1994, and where the "cult of personality" of the leader emulates the one Stalin enjoyed, the leadership reaffirmed its intention to "safeguard the principles of socialism—no matter what." Intimidation, repression, and indoctrination were reinforced, and the vigilant control of the police strengthened. So far there is no indication that the death of Kim Il Sung has led to a change in the nature of the political regime.

In Cuba, where communism was proclaimed as the official ideology in 1961, the reaction to the changes in the Soviet Union and Eastern Europe was swift. There would be no "Castroika"! Conceding that "difficult days are ahead," Fidel Castro proclaimed Cuba to be the "last bulwark of socialism" and had sharp words for revisionism and revisionists. There has been no relaxation of the single-party rule, of the role of the police, or a move in the direction of liberalizing the economy. Cuban socialism, with a strong dose of nationalism directed against "Yankee imperialism," remains firm. Similarly, in Vietnam, the Communist party and the command economy are organized along Stalinist lines. Here the Communist regime maintains its intransigent posture. In its "Platform for Building Socialism in the Transition Period," released on December 1, 1990, the Vietnamese Communist party asserted: "In certain countries the Communist parties have even lost their leadership role. Hostile forces are taking advantage of these errors and difficulties to launch a counter offensive with a view to abolishing socialism. . . . Socialism will regain its vitality and. . . . will prevail."[5]

China: Mao and Beyond

China is of course the most important of the countries that remains Communist. It presents a special case. "Maoism" was the label for the Communist movement and its ideology that developed in China under the leadership of Mao Tse-tung and continues now after his death. "Chairman Mao" was, for more than forty years, the undisputed leader of the Chinese Communist party and the head of the Communist government in China after the civil war (1946–1949) and until his death in 1977. But there has been a high degree of fluidity, and at times downright instability if not chaos, in the development of the Chinese Communist system, both during Mao's leadership and after his death. The following ideological and institutional stages of the Chinese Communist regime since its inception can be outlined:

1. A period of consolidation but also of education and mobilization in the principles of socialism (1949–1953).
2. The move in the direction of economic planning and socialism (1953–1956), followed by a period of liberalization, known as the "Hundred Flowers" campaign.
3. A massive effort to industrialize, known as the "Great Leap Forward" (1957–1960).
4. A subsequent period of retreat from the goals of rapid industrialization that lasted until 1965.
5. The "Cultural Revolution" (1966–1969), again followed by a period of consolidation until 1972.
6. The period since Mao's death when, after a brief conflict between "moderate" leaders and "revolutionaries" (who hailed from the period of the Cultural Revolution and claimed to be Mao's intellectual heirs), the moderates have gained the upper hand. Their emphasis has been on stability, industrialization, and modernization, with the help of capitalist countries in Western Europe, and even the United States itself.
7. In the 1980s we again witness a period of flux in which "capitalistic" incentives in the economy and especially in agriculture were being tried side by side with socialist modes of production.
8. The early 1990s present a struggle between the forces of democratization and economic liberalization and the forces of a wavering party oligarchy.

The constant flux between a democratic and participatory urge and Communist control and domination—continues, and events both in the Soviet Union and Eastern Europe have only sharpened it. In China, the democratic and participatory urge is directed against an aging party leadership, and yet the party maintains its political monopoly, has refused any genuine democratic reforms in allowing for

---

[5]Quoted in *The Economist*, December 8–14, 1990, p. 35.

political competition, and has denied freedoms to the press, the intellectuals, and the universities. The confrontation with students and intellectuals (and some workers) in Tiananmen Square in June 1989 only highlighted the tension between liberal and democratic forces and the party leadership. After wavering at first, the party leaders decided to take repressive measures against the advocates of democratization and asked the army to intervene. Hundreds apparently died, and many more were arrested or went into exile. The Communist party reasserted its role and political monopoly and accused the Soviet leadership of deviations from the socialist model.

Will the Last Bastions Fall?

With the fall of the Soviet Union, the remaining Communist regimes, including China, find themselves in a serious predicament. The Soviet Union had been for most of them, at one time or another, the source of ideological truth, the banker that provided them with needed resources, and the supplier of weapons and military technology. The protector is gone! All of the remaining Communist regimes therefore face the same ideological uncertainty—all may experience economic and political crisis. Several observations can be made about these last bastions.

1. The socialist command economies everywhere face the same crisis. Central controls and bureaucratization have led to blatant inefficiencies, corruption, low productivity, and a decline in the national and per capita product, in contrast with the free-market economies. The leadership in almost all of these regimes has been forced to tinker, in one way or another, with the economy by adopting some measures that allow for private incentives and by freeing the market, but within a strictly controlled command economy.

2. Now that the Soviet subsidies are gone, alternate sources of support must be sought in international trade. The more these regimes answer to the logic of the international economy, the less they can maintain their control over their economies.

3. Given the rapid expansion of worldwide communication networks, the people in all these regimes are beginning to become conscious of the disparities between their standard of living and that of the so-called capitalist world. This is clear for many Chinese, as they get signals and messages from Taiwan, Hong Kong, and Japan, to say nothing of the tens of thousands of Chinese students studying in the United States and Western Europe. The Cubans themselves listen to radio programs from the United States and elsewhere in South America and can watch TV programs, including news, sports, and commercials beamed from Key West in Florida. A sort of a black market in public opinion is growing that no regime can control.

4. In virtually all of these remaining Communist regimes—even in Cuba— the leadership is getting old. The heroic years of the revolution are over and the vision is beginning to wear off, especially among the young who know little of the past and assess their regime in terms of present performance. There is a genuine intergenerational conflict today that pits the majority of the population against its Communist leadership. The Marxist ideology, so

precious to those who fought for it, is becoming irrelevant to most. Nowhere is this phenomenon clearer than in China where very old men remained too long at the top in the Communist party.

The Communist leadership in all of the "last bastions" is desperately trying to cling to power, and the ways to do it are uncertain, to say the least. One is to reinforce repression with the help of the military; the second is to promise to undertake incremental reforms through the democratization of the party and the liberalization of the economy. Such reforms, however, inevitably whet the appetite for more. They may undermine and perhaps displace the political elite in power. Caught between two choices—repression or reform—the future of the Communist regimes still in power remains uncertain.

There is, finally, the critical question of "ideology." As is the case with the Soviet Union, there is no new ideology to replace communism.

EPILOGUE: A WORLD WITHOUT COMMUNISM?

The vision of a communist world, as formulated by Marx in terms of a new body of social and economic theory and sharpened by Lenin into a political weapon for the conquest and consolidation of political power by a single party, became a reality first in Russia. The vision and the Leninist party became vehicles for the establishment of an autocratic regime, fathered and nurtured by Stalin and his heirs, until a sharp disparity became evident between the Soviet "reality" and the Marxist vision. Yet, as we noted, until the late 1970s Soviet communism was considered by many loyalists and intellectuals in Russia and the West, but also where it had gained ascendancy in China, Eastern Europe, Cuba, Vietnam, and some other countries, as a progressive and liberating force.

Historians and theorists will argue for a long time about the cause of the Communist collapse. Some will claim that the reasons for the Stalinist autocracy lay deep in the Russian political culture and that the failure of the socialist command economy was due to the very backwardness of Russian society; other will argue the exact opposite—that Stalinism was but a necessary authoritarian device to bring about rapid industrialization. The ideological vision of abundance spurred many to work and accounted for their allegiance both during the heroic years of industrialization (1929–1940) and in the years of the war against Nazi Germany (1941–1945). With industrialization, the growth of new technological and managerial elites, and the spread of education, the ideology and the party could no longer harness the society into one single plan. Technology itself spawned new means of communication, new professional groups, and new demands. The monolithic and hierarchical structure began to crack and to fragment. Communism became the victim of its success! There are others who will hail the stamina and successes of democratic societies in the West and in the United States. "Containment," suggested by George Kennan in 1947, worked well and put pressure on the Soviet economy and society until the leadership itself and many of its supporters began to realize the weakness of their system. There will be, finally, sociologists and philosophers who will argue that a huge intellectual fraud was perpetrated upon us all in the name of Marxism. Marxists claimed that capitalism led to a growing alienation of the individual. It was a "false" ideology into which we were socialized. It distorted human nature and made us all slaves to things alien to our free nature. Many will now point out that perhaps the reverse was true—that it was communism that imposed a false ideology, contrary to human nature, and in the process caused alienation and misery. Therefore, the demise of communism and the collapse of the Communist regimes will be viewed by them as a reassertion of the true human nature—prone to selfish interests, needy of individual fulfillment, attached to property, as Aristotle and many others have argued, and in search of self-gratification. The alienated individuals have reclaimed their true selves, just as Marx had asked the workers to do, but in doing so have caused the collapse of communism.

Whatever the reasons and causes, the collapse of communism as an ideology and system of governance has created a set of unanticipated problems. It leaves the societies in which it was implemented in complete disarray. In contrast to all other authoritarian regimes—military, despotic, tyrannical, nationalist, including even German national socialism—communism destroyed the societal forces in the name of its revolutionary vision. Human motivation was altered; self-interest ground out; participatory mechanisms shaped in a way that secured the domination of a political elite. Conformity replaced consent and command replaced free initiative. Individuals even lost the ability to plan their own lives, since the all-powerful state determined the course for each individual by promising to care for it. With communism gone, the societies over which it ruled may well be compared to the land where a huge flood is receding. It is in shambles but the landmarks we take for granted—self-articulation, self-interest, entrepreneurship and initiative, the joys and poisons of private property, the ability to assume responsibility and to take risks, and, finally, the ability for sustained grass-roots action and associational life—have to be learned all over again.

Communism, therefore, left all the societies over which it reigned with no opportunities to reshape a new ideology. The challenge for democracy as an ideology and as a system of governance is to fill the vacuum created by the collapse of communism. Will democratic political institutions and liberal economic structures be able to meet the challenge? Perhaps so, but in Russia and Eastern Europe there is no native democratic tradition waiting to be restored. The old world which has resurfaced is one of militant nationalism (see Chapter 9).

BIBLIOGRAPHY

Brzezinski, Zbigniew. *The Grand Failure: The Birth and Death of Communism in the Twentieth Century.* New York: Scribner's, 1989.

Brown, F. J. *Eastern Europe and the Communist Rule,* Duke University Press, Durham and London, 1988.

———. *Surge to Freedom, The End of Communist Rule in Eastern Europe,* Duke University Press, Durham and London, 1991.

Gorbachev, Mikhail. *Perestroika.* New York: Harper & Row, 1987.

Hosking, Geoffrey. *The Awakening of the Soviet Union.* Cambridge, MA: Harvard University Press, 1990.

Kagarlitsky, Boris. *The Thinking Reed: Intellectuals and the Soviet Union from 1917 to the Present.* Translated by Brian Pearce. New York: Routledge, 1989.

Laqueur, Walter. *The Long Road to Freedom: Russia and Glasnost.* New York: Scribner's, 1989.

Macridis, Roy, and Steven Burg. *Introduction to Comparative Politics: Regime and Change.* New York: HarperCollins, 1990.

Melia, Martin ("Z"). "To the Stalin Mausoleum." *Daedalus,* Winter 1990.

Medvedev, Roy. *On Socialist Democracy.* New York: Knopf, 1975.

Schammell, Michael. *Russia's Other Writers: Selections from Samizdat Literature.* New York: Praeger, 1971.

Shlapentokh, Vladimir. *Soviet Ideologies in the Period of Glasnost: Responses to Brezhnev's Stagnation.* Westport, CT. Greenwood Press, 1990.

Other Reading

"Eastern Europe. . . . Central Europe. . . . Europe." *Daedalus,* Winter 1990.

"A Survey of Perestroika: Ready to Fly?" April 20, 1990 and A Survey of the Soviet Union— "Now What?" Two excellent surveys of the Soviet economy have appeared in *The Economist.* October 20, 1990.

PART Three

THE AUTHORITARIAN RIGHT

Preventing the sick from making the healthy sick . . . this ought to be our supreme object in this world. . . . But for this it is above all essential that the healthy should remain separate from the sick, that they should not even associate with the sick.

Nietzsche *The Genealogy of Morals*

*E*dmund Burke was a conservative and a strong proponent of constitutional government. The ideologies of the authoritarian right, by contrast, hold the notion of checks and balances, of limited government and of inviolable rights, in contempt.

Authoritarian governments of the right come in different varieties, all odious but some especially abhorrent from the standpoint of anyone committed to the belief that individual human personality is or should be sacrosanct. Spain under the rule of Franco and Portugal under Salazar were dominated politically by authoritarian Catholic regimes, which safeguarded the privileges of the traditional social elites. Far worse was Nazi Germany, where a totalitarian right wing government engaged in outright genocide.

Today the extreme right is showing signs of once again becoming a force to be reckoned with in Europe, and in America right-wing fanatics appear to be gaining in strength. In this part, we shall examine the ideologies of the radical right.

Chapter
8

The Intellectual Roots of Fascism

A socialism liberated from the democratic and cosmopolitan element fits nationalism as a well-made glove fits a beautiful hand.

Charles Maurras

*F*ascism may well be the most hideous phenomenon of the twentieth century. It is also one of the most paradoxical: bitterly opposed to democratic politics, the fascists[1] nevertheless utilized every means to sway public opinion and build a mass movement; supposedly members of a party of order, fascists roamed the streets and committed wanton acts of violence; authoritarian heart and soul, they compromised and discredited all the established authorities and ruling elites; yearning for the past, the arch-reactionary Nazis overturned tradition and erected a government and society entirely new; implacable detractors of the French Revolution, the National Socialists conducted a revolution of their own, and the Italian Fascists went so far as to mimic the Jacobins by introducing a new calendar wherein 1922, the year of the ascendancy of Mussolini, figured as Year One.[2]

For our purposes the most pertinent paradox is that the fascists, although cynical in their manipulation of ideas and notoriously contemptuous of effete intellectuals, were absolutely determined to make the world over in the image of their ideology. It is typical of fascism—and a gesture which distinguishes it from other doctrines of the European right—that after 1932 every person joining Mussolini's party was issued a copy of his *Dottrina del fascismo,* along with a membership card and a rifle. Unlike his Italian counterpart, Hitler did not wait until he had seized power before publishing his violently anti-Semitic, racist, imperialist diatribes: *Mein Kampf* ("My Struggle") appeared in 1925 and 1926, years in advance of the

---

[1]Fascism in the uppercase refers to Italy; in the lower case to both Italian Fascism and German National Socialism, the latter more popularly known as Nazism.
[2]The French revolutionaries (Jacobins) declared 1792 "Year One" of the new republican order.

Third Reich. From the outset to the last day, it was ideological fervor rather than old-fashioned power politics which was the hallmark of the Nazi movement.

What are the sources of fascist ideology? The first step in answering this question is to set aside the list of proper names Mussolini let drop in interviews with journalists. There is no evidence, for instance, that he read William James with any care, and every reason to suspect Mussolini grasped at the label of Pragmatism simply because he thought it might excuse his habit of acting first and deciding his meaning later. We learn nothing about his intellectual roots by taking him seriously in this regard, not to mention that poor William James suffers the defamation of guilt by association. A much more promising strategy is to examine the popular movements of thought and feeling which Hitler and Mussolini drew upon and molded to their ends. German romanticism and its talk about the *Volk;* Italian syndicalism; nationalism that is rabid, aggressive, and expansionary; conservative and reactionary ideologies dedicated to repealing the Enlightenment, the French Revolution, and liberalism, are among the currents of opinion that had a direct impact on the leaders of Italian Fascism and German National Socialism.

But before discussing these intellectual sources we shall initially turn our attention to the relationship between fascism and Marxism, because on this topic there has long existed an inordinate amount of confusion.

FASCISTS AND MARXISTS

No sooner is the issue of the relationship of fascism to Marxism posed than the investigator meets with diametrically opposed opinions. To true believers—the faithful of both parties—it is obvious that Marxism and fascism are polar opposites, the most deadly enemies, one party marking the extreme left wing of the ideological spectrum, the other the extreme right; one the champion of revolution, the other of counterrevolution. Yet in such countries as England and America it has long been fashionable to regard Mussolini, Hitler, and Stalin as interchangeable. Regimes that are dictatorial, expansionary, and that practice terror against their own people may wave different flags and hate one another even more than they despise the moderates, but to their victims the differences between one such government and another are negligible.

What shall we make of the foregoing claim that fascism and Marxism, despite the mutual animosity of their protagonists, amount to much the same thing? In one sense this conclusion is warranted, but in another it is both inaccurate and grossly unfair to many Marxists. Certainly Carl Friedrich, Zbigniew Brzezinski, and other social scientists who wrote about totalitarianism in the 1950s were correct, insofar as they focused on the political regimes of Hitler and Stalin, to conclude that "fascist and communist totalitarian dictatorships are basically alike."[3] In both cases a single party ruled uncontested and was dominated by a single person; in both countries one all-encompassing ideology was imposed upon everyone. In Germany and in Russia constant propaganda, censorship of the media, and the omnipres-

---

[3]Friedrich & Brzezinski, *Totalitarianism Dictatorship and Autocracy,* p. 5.

ence of official and secret police, were devices which not only silenced dissenting speech but were meant to prevent dissenting thoughts. Purges against enemies, real and imagined, became a fact of everyday life, and men and women lived in constant fear. Insofar as Hitler's Germany and Stalin's Russia were totalitarian regimes, the distinctions between fascism and Marxism do indeed fade into insignificance.

But here we must beware of falling into the trap of repeating ideological polemics while pretending to set forth a fair-minded account of various ideologies. For there is a definite danger that the argument about totalitarianism may degenerate into another version of the repeated efforts of liberals to discredit their Marxist competitors by blaming them for fascism. Which is not to suggest that the Marxists have been more fair to the liberals: they simply turn the tables by suggesting that fascism is an ideology produced by bourgeois, liberal society when it reaches the stage of monopolistic capitalism. To complete this exchange of insults we must add that fascists blame liberals for setting in motion the egalitarian-fostering and tradition-destroying forces that naturally evolve to a Bolshevik finale. Each of the three contending ideologies, liberalism, Marxism, and fascism, not only repudiates the other two but unfairly declares them intimately related and blames the lesser for producing the greater of the two evils.

It should be obvious that Stalinism and Marxism are not the same; the "critical" Marxists of the Frankfurt School,[4] to cite a noteworthy example, deliberately aimed to save the integrity of Marxism by repudiating Stalinism no less vigorously than they denounced capitalism. Not even Bolshevism may be equated with Stalinism: the Lenin who in *What is to be Done?* argued that the party could not survive unless organized along military lines was also the author of *State and Revolution,* a pamphlet written on the eve of the revolution in which the man who was to lead the Bolsheviks to victory rededicated himself to the most libertarian and utopian aspects of the vision of Marx, most notably the belief that the people—in Lenin's words—could learn to run the administration "within twenty-four hours after the overthrow of the capitalists and bureaucrats." True, a few months later he would complain that a capitalist who could make a railroad run was worth more than twenty resolutions passed at Communist meetings. But the vision of the people governing themselves set forth in *State and Revolution* remained one to which disaffected Marxists appealed time and again when they bemoaned the betrayal of the revolution (see Chapter 12).

Perhaps the most effective way to underscore the difference between Marxism and fascism is to contrast their attitudes toward the use of violence. Hitler proclaimed war "the most powerful and classic expression of life"; Mussolini's verdict was that there is "no life without shedding blood," for "man is a warlike animal." "He who says fecundation," added the Italian dictator, "says laceration." Both liberals and Marxists, in dramatic contrast, have historically aspired to a world without war: to the liberals the fall of the aristocracy, to the Marxists the demise of the

---

[4]Composed of members of the Institut für Sozialforschung who were forced into exile by Hitler. Named the Frankfurt School after their return to Germany in 1950. See Martin Jay, *The Dialectical Imagination.*

bourgeoisie, was to mark the happy day when war would become obsolescent. Fascists, however, glorify war, which they see as morally uplifting, an outlet for the heroic and grand passions stifled by humanitarianism. A life without war, to a fascist, is a life not worth living.

In Marxist thought violence is purely a means, and must be minimized throughout its duration and discarded at the earliest possible date. The revolution of which Marx spoke would be carried out by the overwhelming majority against a small minority; such violence as is necessary to remove the ruling class would therefore be minimal. Karl Kautsky, intellectual spokesperson for the Second International, denied that Marx could have supported the Bolshevik revolution, carried out in a backward country, hence inevitably a failure, and very likely to issue in a bloodbath inimical to the humanist ideals of Marxism. "A means which is in opposition to the end cannot be sanctified by that end," wrote Kautsky in *Terrorism and Communism* (1919). A year later Trotsky replied with a book bearing the same title. Even liberalism has resorted to violence to establish or save its reign, Trotsky argued, citing the American Civil War as an example; and on the basis of such reasoning he concluded, "who aims at the end cannot reject the means." Still, Trotsky never rejected the sanctity of human personality; he simply maintained that "to make the individual sacred we must destroy the social order which crucifies him"—and in the process some individuals, unfortunately, will die.

"Once humanism attempts to fulfill itself with any consistency it becomes transformed into its opposite, namely, into violence," wrote Maurice Merleau-Ponty, the French philosopher and Marxist theorist. This is the tragic fate of revolutionary Marxism: that in order to change humanistic ideals from theory to practice, warlike deeds are necessary, especially so after we recognize how wrong Marx was to think that impersonal forces will bloodlessly eliminate most of the obstacles to the coming of the new society. Hence a revolutionary Marxist is fated to struggle with the problem of "dirty hands"—with the question, that is, whether to use means in the short term that contradict the long-term end.[5]

Fascists, unlike Marxists, experience no dilemma of means and ends. Alfred Rosenberg, the Nazi ideologist, likened fascism to an army forever on the march but unconcerned about its destination or purpose. Violence to a fascist is means and end simultaneously. Where a Marxist revolutionary encounters tragedy in the conflict between violent means and peaceful end, a fascist finds in bloodletting heroic grandeur and sublime fulfillment.

Violence is always a problem for Marxists because they share with liberalism a respect for the heritage of the Enlightenment. The dissatisfaction of Marxists is not with the value liberalism places on the individual human being; it is with the failure of liberals to recognize that under capitalism, in Marx's words, "capital is independent and has individuality, while the living person is dependent and has no individuality." Marxism is a humanism; fascism is the vehement, strident denial of the Enlightenment and of all humanist ideals.

---

[5]See Trotsky, *Terrorism and Communism* (Ann Arbor: University of Michigan Press, 1961) and Maurice Merleau-Ponty *Humanism and Terror* (Boston: Beacon Press, 1969).

In one sense the confusion of Marxism with fascism is understandable, given that both German Nazism and Italian Fascism were supposedly amalgams of nationalism and socialism. But the socialistic element in Nazism had nothing to do with Marxism and everything to do with hatred of the Jews, who were blamed for all the dislocations created by a capitalist economy. To Hitler the point of the socialistic planks in the platform of his party was to reach the lower classes, a goal that might have eluded rabid nationalism left to itself. It must be remembered that long before seizing power the Nazis were combatting Communists in the streets of Berlin. Nothing impressed Hitler more in the record of Mussolini than the success of the Italian squadrons of armed thugs, assisted by the wealthy landowners of the Po Valley, in destroying Socialist party offices.

Perhaps it is a sign of the sometimes paranoid mentality of Cold War liberals that they obscured the distinction between fascists and Marxists despite the glee with which the former destroyed the Communists of Italy and Germany. It must be admitted, however, that the case of Italian Fascism does invite considerable confusion over what is Left, what is Right; especially so because Mussolini, shortly before assuming leadership of the Fascist movement, was known as a figure of the revolutionary Marxist left.

Once we have examined the ideological origins of Italian Fascism, it will be apparent that Mussolini was always a proto-fascist and never a Marxist in more than name. By and large it was from the French thinker Georges Sorel, a writer loosely associated with the syndicalist movement, that Italian Fascists learned to cite Marx even as they espoused the most radically nihilistic ideals imaginable.

FASCISTS AND SYNDICALISTS

It is not in syndicalism as such that Mussolini's thought is rooted; rather it was Sorel's abuse of the syndicalist movement for his own purposes of repealing the heritage of the Enlightenment that is relevant to the structure of Fascist belief. So much did Sorel hate liberalism, pacifism, secularism, and individualism that when the workers failed to destroy parliamentary government and the liberal ideology underpinning it, he and his followers decided to collaborate with the *Action française* of Charles Maurras, a rabidly nationalist, reactionary, and proto-fascist group. National syndicalism was the upshot, a movement that is a betrayal of the original revolutionary syndicalist doctrine. Unsuccessful in France, national syndicalism triumphed in Italy under the leadership of Mussolini who was well versed in the thought of the Sorelians on both sides of the Alps.

Before Sorel distorted its message, syndicalism was known as an anti-authoritarian version of socialism, Marxist in its vocabulary yet sympathetic to the anarchist cause Marx had fought against in the First International. When the Second International refused to seat anarchist delegates in 1896, socialists with a hankering for Proudhon and his anarchist themes of decentralization, federalism, and workers' self-rule found that they could stay in the movement and continue to espouse the old anarchist refusal of the state if they championed the syndicalist cause against parliamentary socialists. Roughly speaking, the syndicalists were heading toward the principle that later would be called workers' control of management. At the time of the Russian revolution they initially cheered the soviets of workers as a fulfillment of their aspirations, but soon decried Bolshevism as a form of authoritarian state socialism—a flat contradiction of their ideals. Nothing, surely, could be further removed from the authoritarian and totalitarian movement of fascism than the quasi-anarchist movement called syndicalism.

Alas, Sorel attained far more notoriety than Fernand Pelloutier or any other figure boasting syndicalist credentials. In his *Reflections on Violence* (1906) Sorel sounded all the themes that would later endear him to Maurras and finally to Mussolini, the dictator-to-be who vacillated but eventually went over not only to syndicalism but to its nationalist, proto-fascist, variant.

One way to grasp the significance of *Reflections on Violence* is to say that Sorel arrives at a conclusion directly opposite that drawn by Eduard Bernstein in 1899—this despite Sorel's entire agreement with the analysis of socialist prospects articulated in *Evolutionary Socialism,* Bernstein's classic statement of Marxist revisionism. It is undeniably true, as Bernstein held, that the economic situation of the worker is improving; Marx was wrong to hold that wages might never rise above subsistence level, wrong to predict that misery would forever be the lot of the proletariat under capitalism. Nor is there anything to be said in behalf of Marx's prediction that capitalism was headed toward a catastrophe. More and more the state was intervening in the economy to prevent the downturns of the economic cycle from getting out of hand. Under such circumstances, thought Bernstein, the best course of action was to drop revolutionary rhetoric and work for victory at the ballot box. With the rise of the welfare state it was possible for socialism to achieve democratically and peacefully all that Marx regarded as possible only through a revolutionary upheaval.

First Sorel concedes that Bernstein is right on the facts; then, shockingly, he issues a bold call for a violent confrontation of bourgeoisie and proletariat. Hatred is Sorel's motivation—hatred of the mediocrity of the middle class and contempt for its liberal humanitarian ideals. Marx blamed liberals for failing to live up to their humanitarian ideals; Sorel blamed them for allowing humanitarianism to stifle their will-to-power. Forever speaking of decadence and renaissance, cowardice and heroism, Sorel utters words foreign to the writings of Marx and Engels but strongly redolent of Machiavelli and Nietzsche. For what he regarded as the sickliness of modern culture, Sorel could think of no better therapy than violence on a grand and glorious scale.

"Proletarian violence," wrote Sorel, "seems to be the only means by which the European nations—at present stupefied by humanitarianism—can recover their former energy." Hence he advocated a bloody showdown of class against class, no matter that nothing socialist would come of it. Sorel admired the separatism of the syndicalists, their refusal to engage in parliamentary politics or to deal with other classes, because isolation, he hoped, would diminish their willingness to settle for material gains; "when conflicts are confined to disputes about material interests, there is no more opportunity for heroism." All that is best in humans, Sorel believed, comes to the fore when society is divided into two armed camps, each manned by dedicated warriors, ready for battle. The church of militant and warlike ancient Israel affords images of exactly what the modern world needs. "Conviction is founded on the competition of communions, each of which regards itself as the army of truth fighting the armies of evil. In such conditions it is possible to find sublimity."

It did not matter to Sorel that the syndicalist faith in the efficacy of a general strike was misplaced; it was irrelevant that the vision of such a strike bringing the bourgeoisie to its knees was only a dream, a "myth" in Sorel's terminology. So long as the workers believe, that is enough, since their faith will spur them to destructive action. In a larger sense one might suggest that Marxism itself was a "myth" to Sorel, a set of symbols to be used and abused at will, much as the workers meant nothing to him except insofar as they could be called upon to accomplish the one objective that unites all his writings, the desire to destroy modern culture, especially liberalism, reformist socialism, and parliamentary democracy.

Revulsion against the heritage of the Enlightenment, disgust with the supposed "decadence" of modern culture, was by no means peculiar to Sorel in the early twentieth century, nor was he isolated in his conviction that a cleansing violence could restore the vitality Europeans had lost. In France, Italy, and Germany the same doctrine was preached by ardent nationalists. Already in the *Reflections* Sorel commented in passing that "a great foreign war . . . might renew lost energies"—a hint of his willingness to turn to nationalism, should the proletariat disappoint him. If Sorel could spout Marxist expressions while contradicting everything Marx stood for, so could Enrico Corradini, leader of the extreme nationalists in Italy. It was Corradini, not a Marxist, who first made the celebrated distinction between "bourgeois" and "proletarian" nations—in order to proclaim that nationalism should henceforth be for all Italians what socialism had been for the proletariat.

By 1910 the unholy alliance of the Sorelians with the archreactionary *Action française* was well under way. With the approval of Sorel and Maurras the mainly literary *Cercle Proudhon* called its first meeting in December of 1911. There Édouard Berth, Sorel's favorite disciple, made the acquaintance of Georges Valois, then a follower of Maurras, later a founder of the Faisceau, which would be known as the first officially fascist movement outside Italy. In the judgment of Berth, the *Cercle Proudhon* was the birthplace of *fascisme avant la lettre*.

Why did the once revolutionary Berth evolve into a national syndicalist, which is to say, a proto-fascist? No doubt because he was excited, in his own words, about the "revival of heroic values that appears to be taking place among the younger bourgeoisie." His reference, of course, is to the growing popularity of the *Action française*, the political movement which Sorel himself found enticing from the moment that the proletariat yielded to the temptation presented by higher wages, unemployment insurance, and the like. To turn the question around, Why were Valois and Maurras willing to join forces with persons they had previously upbraided as despicable leftist militants? Undoubtedly because they were eager to incorporate the workers, whose absence prevented their organization from becoming a mass movement.

In any case the outlook of Sorel and Maurras was much the same, no matter that one was regarded as a figure of the extreme left, the other a leader of the radical right. For both men it was what they despised that mattered, and they were as one in vilifying the Enlightenment, liberalism, rights, and humanitarianism. Hence Maurras, having discovered his affinities with Sorel, could utter words that once would have been unthinkable: "a socialism liberated from the democratic and cosmopolitan element fits nationalism as a well-made glove fits a beautiful hand." And Sorel in 1912 could return the favor by declaring that "the defense of French culture is today in the hands of Charles Maurras."[6]

The closer Sorel moved to Maurras, the more unable he was to resist the temptation of anti-Semitism. Near the turn of the century the Dreyfus case showed how deeply France was split into two nations, one republican, democratic, anti-clerical, individualistic, and a second nation, conservative, Catholic, and given to fits of anti-Semitism. In the early going Sorel sided with Dreyfus, presumed a traitor by many simply because he was a Jew. Later, the Sorel of the *Reflections* expressed his disgust that socialists, to prove that Dreyfus was falsely accused, had joined forces with liberally and democratically minded republicans. Finally, after discovering his affinity with the *Action française,* Sorel proved his mettle by spewing forth hateful comments against the Jews.

Writing to an Italian friend a year before his death, Sorel admitted that "the Fascists [in Italy] are not entirely wrong to invoke my opinions." It is impossible to disagree with his assessment: their cult of glory and violence, their language of decay and rebirth, their national syndicalism links them to Sorel, as does the anti-Semitism to which they belatedly succumbed in the anti-Jewish legislation of 1938, much as Sorel had bided his time before joining the ranks of Jew-baiters.

There was a time when Mussolini refused to embrace Sorel. The man who would eventually be the leader of Fascist Italy initially took his Marxist phraseology seriously enough to sneer at the prewar merger of Maurras and Sorel in the *Cercle Proudhon.* But the lesson Mussolini drew from World War I was that the force of nationalism was as genuine as the fervor of the proletariat was specious. During 1922 Mussolini delivered a speech in which he chose to propagate nationalism as a Sorelian myth capable of arousing all Italians to great deeds.

> We have created our myth. The myth is a faith, it is passion. It is not necessary that it shall be a reality. It is a reality by the fact that it is a goad, a hope, a faith, that it is courage. Our myth is the nation, our myth is the greatness of the nation!

Switching from hostility to enthusiastic support of imperialism, Mussolini adopted Corradini's motto that Italy was ready to build a Third Roman Empire.[7]

Opportunism affords part of the explanation of Mussolini's conversion from revolutionary to nationalist syndicalism. It would be a mistake, however, to ignore the ideological motives that confer a unity upon his changing political positions. From his earliest days as a public figure Mussolini shared with Sorel an absolute contempt for evolutionary socialism: "our conception rejuvenates," Mussolini remarked; "reformism, on the other hand, the wise and duly evolutionary, positivist, and pacifist reformism, is henceforth condemned to decrepitude and decay."

---

[6]See Zeev Sternhell, *The Birth of Fascist Ideology* (Princeton: Princeton University Press, 1994).
[7]Ancient Rome was the first empire; the medieval papacy the second.

Sorelian to the core was Mussolini's wish to prepare the proletariat for "the day of the 'greatest bloodbath of all,' when the two hostile classes will clash in the supreme trial." Mussolini and Sorel were alike from the start in yet another way: both admired the concept of the will-to-power and were willing to transform it, in defiance of Nietzsche, into a political doctrine. Indeed, Mussolini went so far as to speak of reviving the writings of Max Stirner, which were in effect a diluted version of what Nietzsche would later commit to paper. How remarkable this suggestion was, coming from a reputed socialist, can only be recognized if we recall that Marx had devoted all the second part of *The German Ideology* to a savage rebuttal of Stirner.

After the Fascists took power, their movement quickly took a sharp turn to the political right. It is important, therefore, to observe that in the first instance Fascism was intellectually an avant-garde ideology, a repudiation of liberalism that was thoroughly modernist in form, unlike Nazism which, as we shall see, always spoke the language of reaction. The Nietzsche of *Il Duce* was not the Volkish, backward-looking thinker Elizabeth Förster-Nietzsche, the anti-Semitic sister of the great writer, made him out to be; he was, instead, Nietzsche the cultural radical and darling of the most "advanced" thinkers of Europe. It is no accident that in the early years Fascism enjoyed the support of the poet Filippo Tomasso Marinetti, who announced the end of the art of the past (*le Passéisme*) and the birth of the art of the future (*le Futurisme*). All things in the modern world move and change, he stated in a manifesto released in 1910; hence art must be energetic and dynamic, depicting speed and luxuriating in visions of powerful mechanical forces. Full of hate for the bourgeois world, convinced violence can be beautiful, fanatically nationalistic and eager for war, Marinetti and the Futurists were naturally attracted to emergent Fascism. The best and the brightest of Italy were well represented in the ranks of Fascism during its march to power.

Once in power Mussolini consolidated his position through concessions to the pillars of conservatism in Italian society, the papacy, monarchy, army, bureaucracy, and big business. It was only a matter of time before syndicalist aspirations to economic autonomy vis-à-vis the state degenerated into an excuse for the Party, which was the state in disguise, to control all aspects of production. Here, too, Sorelian rhetoric proved useful as Fascists learned to speak of "producers" rather than "proletarians," of "renovation" rather than "revolution." Along with everyone else, the workers found themselves following the dictates of the Single Party, the Grand Council of Fascism, and the Corporate State.

And yet, despite the rush of Fascism triumphant to the political right, Mussolini seems never to have forgotten his early years devoted to radicalism. Fascinating in this regard is the Salò Republic he set up with Nazi sponsorship following the coup of July 24, 1943, when he was removed from office. An unpopular puppet regime, the Salò or Italian Social Republic, as it was officially called, declared its intention to "return to the origins of Fascism"; which is to say, Mussolini shortly before his demise reaffirmed the socialist program of his beginnings.

Understandably scholars continue to debate whether Mussolini was on the Left or the Right. One may well ask, however, if they are posing a meaningful question. During the Salò Republic Mussolini glorified war and violence as he had throughout his career, from the beginning to the finale and including every intermediary stop. Like Sorel, Mussolini despised the liberal middle and cared little whether he stood to its left or right when he delivered blow after blow against constitutional government. Definitely he was a revolutionary, unlike Franco in Spain or Salazar in Portugal whose regimes were sometimes termed fascist but fit far better under the label of traditional Catholic authoritarianism. Always Mussolini was a revolutionary, but never was he an authentic Marxist revolutionary; never was he a humanist grappling with the problem of "dirty hands." Mussolini's was a "revolution of nihilism," to apply to Italy a phrase Hermann Rauschning coined to characterize Nazi Germany.

Compared to Hitler's regime, the incidence of political murders and terrorist acts in Fascist Italy was relatively low. But the road to power was soiled with the blood shed by the victims of the black-shirted thugs who roamed the streets and countryside. Fear was there from the start and did not disappear after the seizure of the state, as anyone familiar with the novels of Ignazio Silone knows all too well. It was Mussolini's proud boast that his was a "totalitarian"[8] regime, whose leaders were willing to issue a new catechism, a new set of ten commandments, a list of fascist martyrs, and to do whatever else it takes to create a *uomo nuovo*—a new man who in peace no less than in war would be a soldier, an automaton ready to follow orders, any orders. Nationalism, even the fanatical and expansionary nationalism of Corradini, is limited in its thrust; Fascism was unlimited. Repeatedly Mussolini and the ideologues of the Fascist regime proclaimed theirs a universal doctrine, and for ideological reasons they followed Hitler into battle even though the interests of Italy dictated otherwise.

Mussolini's spokesmen never tired of declaring Fascism a "total" and "permanent" revolution. Such indeed it was—a revolution of incomplete nihilism that would be surpassed by the complete nihilism of Nazi Germany.

FASCISTS AND THE VOLK

Like Italian Fascism, German National Socialism was in its origins a cultural revolt that later, with the help of favorable circumstances and determined leadership, would be transformed into a political revolution. Nazism shares with Fascism a profound hatred of the Enlightenment, liberalism, individualism, and parliamentary government. What makes Nazism doctrinally different from Fascism is that the purveyors of the "folkish" ideology, far from constituting an avant-garde, were backward looking in the extreme. There is no equivalent of the Futurists in the ranks of the Nazi ideologues; no artistic fascination with machines, speed, and modernity; no determination to create an art of the future that will mark a deliberate and total rupture with the past. Nazism was a traditionalist rebellion not just against liberalism but against modernity in general. In their original incarnations Nazism was as rear-guard as Fascism was avant-garde.

---

[8]Mussolini invented the word "totalitarian."

The thinkers of the nineteenth and twentieth centuries who were sources of Nazi ideology were revolutionary because they were hopelessly reactionary. To discuss them inevitably leads to a scrambling of our ideological vocabulary, as when historians refer to these figures as "radical conservatives" or, again, when they classify themselves as "conservative revolutionaries." Paul Lagarde, Julius Langbehn, Moeller van den Bruck, and other champions of the German Volk were conservatives who found little to conserve in the past and much to destroy.[9] Hegel and Bismarck, the prominent persons we frequently identify with German conservatism, the first with its theory, the second with its practice, were viewed as dangerous innovators by the proponents of the Volkish ideology. For the self-proclaimed defenders of the Volk, all the past had to be undone before it could be rejoined. "I live with every breath in a past that never was and which is the only future I crave," wrote Paul Lagarde. "I am an alien in all places." His kind of desperation was shared by many another German, and would eventually lead to a politics of revolutionary and nihilistic reaction.

Ironically, the very notion of the Volk which was to play so large a role in the thought of those Germans who repudiated the Enlightenment was itself born of the German Enlightenment (the *Aufklärung*). Johann Gottfried von Herder (1744–1803), the father of folkish writers, was in his own right a figure who advocated the humanitarian ideals of the Enlightenment. Come the nineteenth century, German romantic and nationalist intellectuals forced a choice between the *Volk* and *Humanität;* no such choice is necessary in Herder's estimation since an appreciation of the rich assortment of folkish cultures is an excellent way to substitute an embodied, colorful, and expressive humanity for the vapid abstractions (e.g., the "state of nature") and empty universalistic formulas (e.g., the "rights of Man") of French *philosophes.*[10] Nothing could be more alien to Herder than the narrow nationalism and aggressive imperialism so common among the thinkers of the next century who claimed his name.

From the start, talk about the Volk was aimed against the Enlightenment. But whereas Herder was a cosmopolitan whose criticisms were meant to improve the Enlightenment, the nineteenth-century romantics following him cited the Volk to repudiate the progressive ideals of the eighteenth century. It was the French Revolution that made all the difference. Typically the German romantic nationalists were men who as youngsters had admired Voltaire, Diderot, and the other major figures of the French Enlightenment; at the outbreak of the French Revolution these same Germans marvelled that the ideals of the Enlightenment were about to become reality. Understandably Fichte reversed his position when Napoleon invaded German territory and forcibly introduced the Code Napoléon. Not even the homegrown administrative reforms of Stein and Hardenberg were acceptable to the romantics, who in their day were as determined to turn back the clock as their descendants were much later, at the time of the Weimar Republic. Generally speaking, Fichte, Adam Müller, and the other early romantics despised doctrines of natural rights, opposed free trade and economic development, and

[9]The best study of these writers is by Fritz Stern, *The Politics of Cultural Despair.*
[10]Voltaire and other figures of the French Enlightenment were known as *philosophes.*

yearned for a hierarchical, feudal, corporate, organic society in which individualism would be a vicious deviation except in the case of the creative genius.

Throughout the nineteenth century, Herder's legacy was read in two mutually contradictory ways by the many German intellectuals struggling to find stability and roots in a modern world torn asunder first by the French and then by the Industrial Revolution. One group of thinkers who claimed the mantle of Herder rallied to the intellectually impressive banner of *Historismus* (historicism); the other group promulgated the racist ideology that, sadly, is one of the unique characteristics of modern times. Such scholars as Ranke, Mommsen, Dilthey, and Meinecke were responsible for the brilliant German historical studies of the nineteenth century and beyond. Their racist counterparts also used history but only to abuse it in a search for scapegoats; feeling dispossessed in the modern world, they blamed the Jews when their focus was on Germany, and levelled accusations against black and yellow peoples when they looked abroad. In only one respect was there overlap between the historicists and the racists: both groups turned to history to reunite the seemingly orphaned present to the beckoning warmth of the long lost paternal past.

Other than Herder, the historicists were indebted to Hegel for their method of understanding the human world. Not just the *Volk* but the *Geist* (spirit) was Hegel's concern, the spirit of an age (*Zeitgeist*) or of a people (*Volksgeist*). From Herder and Hegel the historians of Germany learned that the first rule of historical method is to understand an age in its own terms, as opposed to reading themselves and their nineteenth-century outlook into an earlier age. Beyond the natural world of animal instincts there is a second world of culture which testifies to human freedom and creativity, and results in art, literature, science, and philosophy. To understand an age or a people, the historian must enter mentally into its culture—its values, mores, social practices, and its way of interpreting human experience. This method is still alive today in the researches of cultural anthropologists and among political scientists who focus on the "political culture" of this or that country.

By no means were the German historians examining the past simply for the sake of the past. Hegel and his successors sought through their studies to reconnect the present to the past, undoing the rupture suffered at the time of the French Revolution, when the Jacobins decided to jettison all that had ever happened and to start over again at day one, to which end they constructed a new calendar. Historicists were intent on experiencing the present as part of a continuum with the past; theirs was an effort to admit the reality of change and yet to fulfill a program of conservation. They were conservatives, not reactionaries. Knowing it is impossible to turn back the clock, their modest but plausible strategy was, through their historical research, to connect the moments of time in a meaningful progression to their own present. To feel at home in history, not to be alienated, was their objective.

Studying the past had at least two other benefits, in the view of the historicists. Many historians in the German universities had lost their faith in the orthodox Christianity of their fathers, who frequently were ministers. For these loyal sons, wayward against their desires, unbelievers yearning for belief, it was comforting to know that in studying history they were in the presence of *Geist,* spirit. Thus they had succeeded in raising themselves above the philosophical materialism of the French intellectuals to a new, if this-worldly, idealism. Secondly, the devotees of the "historical school of law" found it within their power to affirm the rights of Germans at the same time that they defused the explosive doctrine of natural rights, which had been set loose upon the world by the French revolutionaries. It is the *Volksgeist,* they affirmed, that creates *Volksrecht* (people's rights). Against the universalistic French Declaration of the Rights of Man and Citizen, the German historians asserted the historically sanctioned rights of Germans, much as Edmund Burke has substituted the rights of Englishmen for the rights of mankind in his famous anti-revolutionary diatribe, the *Reflections on the Revolution in France* (1789–1790).

The historicists should not be confused with the Volkish ideologues who preached racism, reactionary and expansionary nationalism, and *Führer*-worship. It is from this latter group, not the former, that the Nazis took their ideas and propaganda. The ardent romantic nationalists born of the Napoleonic wars planted the first seeds of the "Germanic ideology"; Paul de Lagarde, among others, continued their work in the late nineteenth century, and he was duly honored by the Nazis when they issued an anthology of his works to German soldiers fighting in World War II. Another precursor of National Socialism was Moller van den Bruck, author of a book entitled *The Third Reich,* which was published during the early years of the ill-fated Weimar Republic.

Without question racism is the most vile component of the Germanic ideology. One of the many ironies of Volkish thought gone mad is that thinkers who regarded themselves as idealists were the driving force behind the crudely materialistic doctrine of race. As Jacques Barzun has remarked, the foundation of racist thought is "the conviction that mind is simply the correlate of physiological structure"; racist argumentation rests on the notion that "any spiritual or intellectual product may be explained genetically in terms of its physical origin."[11] Racists seek to account for all cultural achievements—or the lack thereof—in terms of skulls, noses, hair, blood, and skin color.

In every respect racism is a denial of the historicity of human existence. No longer was a Volk, as Herder held, created in time by persons sharing a territory and language and building a common culture. No longer was culture a collective spiritual inheritance passed on from one generation to another, with allowances made for revisions on the basis of new needs or desires. Instead, people were German because they were instances of a fixed, eternal German essence. The Germans act as they do because they are Germans, argued the folkish fanatics; the Germans are what they are because of the actions they have taken, replied the historicists, whose position permitted evolutionary change just as surely as the folkish thinkers ruled it out in advance. The only change admitted in folkish thought was a fall from primitive purity under the corroding influence of modern civilization,

---

[11] Jacques Barzun, *Race: a Study in Modern Superstition* (New York: Harcourt, Brace & Co., 1937), p. 60.

symbolized by the Jews. Unwilling to leave the past alone despite their refusal to approach it historically, the German ideologists projected their hatreds into previous periods. A purely mythological history in which liberals, cosmopolitans, and Jews had betrayed Germany was their specialty.

Unlike many other nationalists, the folkish ideologues who called out for a Third Reich had little use for Bismarck's Second Reich. Nationalists standing outside the folkish movement admired the policy of *Machtpolitik* (power-politics) Bismarck had ruthlessly pursued in his successful campaign to unify Germany: "not by speeches and votes," he commented, "are the great questions of the day decided— that was the great error of 1848 and 1849—but by blood and iron." Advocates of the Germanic, folkish ideology had no objections to this use of force, but their emphasis was on "blood and soil," not blood and iron. Crying out for roots, they complained that Bismarck's Reich, which lasted from 1871 to 1918, proved to be a devastating period of accelerating cultural decline. The movement of population from countryside to city, the increasing influence of "decadent" Berlin, the economic dislocations, the growing significance of international and "Jewish" finance, the rise of science and the waning of faith—all the evils, as they saw it, of the modern world—made enormous headway during the soulless Second Reich. Eager to insult Bismarck, the Germanists did not hesitate to brand him a liberal—this despite his authoritarianism and the fraudulence of the parliamentary institutions he permitted, which were a pure facade meant to soften the image of his semi-autocratic rule.

Americans are traditionally accommodating to populism but so hostile to the state that it barely figures as a topic in the history of American political thought. It may come as a shock, therefore, to learn that in German history it is the populist, folkish thinkers who were the sources of Nazi ideology and the worshipers of the state who afforded an alternative. Anything but a racist, Hegel held that a proper state has as one of its highest callings the task of facilitating the harmonious interaction of different ethnic and religious groups. On the Jews his position was similarly enlightened: "to exclude the Jews from civil rights would be to confirm the isolation with which they are reproached."

In his political philosophy Hegel recapitulates the strategy present in his interpretation of history: he strives to maintain the contact of Germans with their past while showing how their traditions may be updated to meet the challenges of the present. Accordingly he retains the time-honored monarchy and the civil service staffed by aristocrats, proud of their code of public service. To Hegel the state is the fulfillment of "ethical life" and as such should be administered by public servants who regard themselves as a "universal class," dutifully attending in an impartial manner to the highest concerns of the entire community. Corporate representation of the particular interests present in "civil society" is another feature of the Hegelian state. But for such notions as "public opinion" or representation of persons considered as collections of individuals, he has no use. High above the patriarchal family and an economically dynamic society pulsating with activity, Hegel visualizes a coordinating modern state dressed up in reassuringly traditional garb. For him organic imagery begins with the state, not the *Volk*, because the people are not a people unless there is a state to keep them such. Hegel fully accepted modernity in his *Philosophy of Right and Law* (1821) and sought a political structure which would permit his countrymen to do the same. Innovation linked to continuity is his theme, much as in his philosophy of history he saw each period as a totally new formulation of one and the same *Geist* marching across the ages.

The criticisms Hegel lodged against the democratic state were turned by the folkish thinkers against his finely wrought, painstakingly institutionalized, undemocratic state. Counting votes one by one or tabulating the latest whims of public opinion seemed to Hegel mechanical and artificial. Turning the tables on him, the Germanic polemicists condemned his impersonal *Rechtsstaat* (state of laws and rights)[12] on the grounds that it is a mechanical structure, incompatible with the vitality of the Volk. This is not, however, to say the people is unwilling to accept leadership; on the contrary, the Germanists insisted that etymologically Volk implies a need to follow. It was for a *Führer*, in the opinion of the folkish ideologues, that the people cried out; not for the cold impersonal rules of a *Rechtsstaat*.

Long before it conquered the state, the Germanic ideology made significant inroads into the schools. Whereas in France and England university students repeatedly ran to the barricades to fight for liberal, constitutional, republican regimes, their German counterparts supported the liberal cause on only one occasion, 1848. Throughout most of the nineteenth and well into the twentieth century German students usually gathered under the flag of the political right. At the time of the Napoleonic wars they rallied to the rancorous, venomous Father Jahn; a century later their fraternities were hotbeds of anti-Semitism. For a teacher to contribute to anti-Semitic journals was far from unusual, and nothing was more common in nineteenth-century textbooks than major doses of Volkish ideology fed to innocent, unsuspecting youngsters.

Well in advance of the Weimar Republic and throughout its duration, the Volkish ideology was a prominent force in Germany and one which grew stronger with each of a succession of reversals: the loss of World War I, the humiliating treaty of Versailles, the constant fear of a Communist uprising, and the runaway inflation of the 1920s. More and more frequently world-weary intellectuals succumbed to the temptation to follow the lead of earlier ideologues in declaring that Germany, with its incomparable culture, had never belonged to the Western world or shared its ideals. When Hegel spoke of the Germanic peoples his reference was not only to Germany proper but to other nations such as England and France. To folkish thinkers Germany alone was Germanic, with the partial exception of persons of Germanic heritage living in other nations and awaiting their incorporation, by whatever means, into the Fatherland.

In their desperate longing for a faith, Paul Lagarde and the other mouthpieces of the Folk could not be satisfied, as the Hegelians were, with contemplation of the *Geist*. Idealistic though he was, Lagarde found the "spirit" of the historicists too nebulous, too cerebral, too far removed from his conviction that the German

---

[12]*Recht* means both "law" and "right." Thus, although Hegel's *Philosophie des Rechts* is usually translated as the *Philosophy of Right*, his title could equally well be rendered into English as the *Philosophy of Law*.

nation has a "soul." He would settle for nothing less than a faith springing from the Folk, a Germanic religion under the banners of which his Fatherland would create havoc in Europe, especially in the lands to the east, throughout those vast eastern and southern territories he was certain Germany was destined to rule. All who followed in his footsteps repeated his demand that Germany should expand into Central and Eastern Europe, not for reasons of *Machtpolitik,* but in fulfillment of a divine dictate. It did not matter that their vision of Germany was a myth; war would unite Germans and transform myth into reality. One way or another Germany would be a *Volksgemeinschaft.*[13]

By now it is obvious that the ideology of National Socialism did not spring into being overnight; its arguments, its rhetoric and tone, and arguably its foreign policy may be traced back deep into the nineteenth century. Even the program of combining nationalism with socialism had been outlined decades in advance by the champions of the Volk. Sorel, we have seen, insisted on instigating an all-out war between bourgeoisie and proletariat. The sharp contrast of the Germanic ideology with the one that fed Italian Fascism may be seen in the words of Moller van den Bruck: "the antithesis of bourgeois and proletarian must vanish." "Socialism today must transform itself from a class socialism to a peoples' socialism."

Folkish socialism has nothing in common with Marxism. All Moller could see in Karl Marx was a rootless Jew who compensated for his lack of a fatherland by projecting internationalism upon the working class. Capitalism was evil because it, too, was Jewish: the social mobility and constant change that accompany a capitalist economy benefit the Jews and destroy the world of peasants and artisans, the true Germans. Ransacking the past, the Germanists recalled with approval Friedrich List's protectionist *National System of Political Economy* (1841) and Fichte's *The Closed Commercial State* (1800). In Germanist hands socialism means little beyond revival of the old notions of guilds and estates; it stands for an organic and corporatist order, paternalistic, hierarchical, and uncompromisingly hostile to individualism.

When at long last a liberal political regime came to Germany, it did so in the pitiful form of the Weimar Republic, a polity which in its weakness seemed to vindicate everything the Germanists had been saying for a century against liberalism. The Reichstag could do nothing: excessive pluralism, created by a scheme of proportional representation, divided the regime against itself at a time when the Republic needed every bit of support it could possibly muster against strong enemies arrayed both to the left and the right. Any government that had a policy did not have a majority in the legislature; any majority was predicated upon a makeshift coalition and the absence of a coherent policy. Finally the Nazis and Communists gained so many seats that no government with majority support could be formed.

To blame liberalism in general, as the Germanists did, for the disability of the Weimar Republic is manifestly unfair. Fairness, however, is forever the first victim

---

[13]Roughly translated as a "folkish community." No English expression, unfortunately, conveys the strong sense of warmth and community evoked by the German word.

of ideological fanatics. How obsessed the Germanists were may be seen in their incessant efforts to blame liberalism for everything that had gone wrong in modern German history, in spite of the blatant failure of liberalism to play a role of any significance in their country. Marx once remarked that the Germans had only thought what other nations had done. German liberalism is surely a case in point, for it was all theory and no practice.[14] Kant set the stage for the timid liberalism that was to follow when he admired the French Revolution as a tribute to human freedom, and yet adamantly refused to admit there were circumstances under which revolutionary action should be taken.

Such hope for liberalism as once existed ended definitively in the disruptions of 1848–1849, when authoritarian nationalism triumphed and liberalism faded into insignificance. In Germany as in no other society, feudal forces at the top stood juxtaposed to proletarian forces at the bottom; and the middling bourgeoisie, which elsewhere provided liberalism with a social anchor, was deliberately kept politically infantile by Bismarck. Parliamentarism was indeed a sham, as the Germanists claimed—a sham because Bismarck had made it such. The parliamentary institutions he permitted were all form and no substance. Lacking power and responsibility, parliamentarians were members of little more than a debating society.

Before the advent of the Weimar Republic, the Germans had been educated to disdain parliamentary government. When the German leaders established the Republic, they did so as part of a scheme to win a favorable peace settlement from Woodrow Wilson. But by the time the victorious Allies had finished claiming the spoils, the terms of the Versailles treaty were so harsh that Weimar was saddled from the beginning with the myth that liberals and Jews had stabbed Germany in the back.

Laboring under the burden of an unbroken historical record of impotence, the liberals of the nineteenth and early twentieth century settled for the objective of transforming Germany into a *Rechtsstaat*, a state ruled by impersonal laws. In this quest they could count on Hegel and his heirs who, though fundamentally conservative in outlook, would not allow Germany to retreat to the patriarchal politics advocated by K. L. von Haller, whose position was a throwback in the nineteenth century to the doctrine espoused by Robert Filmer in England two centuries earlier. A *Rechtsstaat* is not the same as a liberal, constitutional polity; its modest aim is the elimination of arbitrariness, as guaranteed by professional jurists and administrators.

Well in advance of Hitler's rise to power it was obvious that a government of laws and not of men is impossible in the absence of a loyal citizenry and professional elites committed to upholding constitutional norms and procedures. The final shipwreck of the *Rechtsstaat* took place during Hitler's reign, when the legal elites willingly dispensed Nazi "justice." But much earlier, during the early days of Weimar, the judiciary was already applying a conspicuous double standard in political cases. Offenders who stood on the political left received harsh punishment;

---

[14]This is the theme of Leonard Krieger, *The German Idea of Freedom.*

those on the right received little or none, with the consequence that the reactionary enemies of the Republic took their carte blanche to the streets as often as they pleased.

The breakdown of the *Rechtsstaat* symbolizes the overall fate of the Weimar republic. It could not count on the liberals to shore it up because the liberals were too weak to support themselves. Only the conservatives might have saved the Republic; they enjoyed a tradition of rule and responsibility; they could have remade themselves into a German version of Tory democrats, and if they had, the Republic might have prospered and they along with it. But the respectable conservatives chose in thought and in action to pursue a course that placed them at first in the camp of the reactionary Germanists, and later in the orbit of National Socialism.

"The German mind has always been conservative and will remain so forever," wrote the great novelist Thomas Mann in 1919. A mere three years later, faced with mounting evidence of the increasingly radical, revolutionary, and reactionary bent of the new conservatism, he defected from its ranks. One respectable conservative who stayed in the movement long enough to serve Hitler's regime for a few years before rejecting it was Hermann Rauschning. His book, *The Revolution of Nihilism* (1938), records the nausea of his awakening to the horror of National Socialism. Some of his pages evoke considerable pathos, such as the chapter on "The Suicide of the Old Order," which includes a section on "The Degeneration of Conservatism." Rauschning notes the "temptation into which the older conservatives fell—the temptation to capitulate to an unscrupulous use of power which was proving effective," namely, the Nazi Party. The younger conservatives went further than the elders: mesmerized by the Nazi ethos of power and domination, German youth cried out for a reactionary revolution. Under these circumstances, argues Rauschning, the Jacobins of Germany massed not on the left, as anticipated, but on the right.

In the largest sense Rauschning saw the capitulation of conservatism to the hoary tradition of folkish, Germanic, Jew-hating thinking as the key to the horror that had befallen the proud German nation. "German conservatism had been decaying and degenerating since the middle of the nineteenth century, and this is the chief explanation of the plunge into a nihilist revolution." With the disasters that beset Germany in the early decades of the twentieth century, the conditions were ripe for the Germanic ideology to advance from a cultural program to a devastating political force.

FASCIST IDEOLOGY: ITS SIGNIFICANCE AND CONSEQUENCES

How important was fascist ideology? Some scholars, citing the cynical manipulation of ideas by Maurras, Sorel, Mussolini, and Hitler, deny its significance. After all, it was Sorel's explicit claim that myths were valuable precisely because they were not subject to rational criteria and thus could not be falsified; to congeal and intensify emotion was their point and their worth. Similarly, Maurras and other leading figures in the *Action française* were atheists who nonetheless staunchly advocated Catholicism because of the power it wielded in rallying the French to reactionary causes. In much the same vein, Mussolini gave Giovanni Gentile a mere two months during 1929 to churn out a philosophical rationale for the Fascist doctrine, two months and no more because Mussolini was indifferent to the content of Gentile's statement and cared only that the document be in place by the time of an upcoming meeting of the National Congress.

But before rushing to the conclusion that ideology did not matter, we should stop for a moment and realize that it was because of their fervently held ideological beliefs, in particular because of their unreasoned conviction that the world is divided into elites and "masses," that the fascists reduced ideas to political weapons. Even Rauschning, as is evident in *The Conservative Revolution* (1940), accepted the view of the conservative ideologues that the "masses," left to themselves, will never amount to anything more than shapeless, amorphous matter—until the day comes when an elite imposes a form upon them, by force or by fraud. Fearful of Weimar democracy, fearful of democracy in general, and obsessed by the vision of democracy fostering a new Jacobinism, he placed his bets on a pact with the devil. Hitler did indeed provide a new elite that would lead the "masses" and provide them with a faith. Too late did Rauschning comprehend that the consequence would be, in his own words, a "revolution of nihilism."

Robert Michels is another person of stature who ended up in the fascist camp after deciding that "the masses experience a profound need to prostrate themselves, not simply before great ideals, but also before the individuals who in their eyes incorporate such ideals." Rauschning hails from the conservatives; Michels was a socialist and revolutionary syndicalist before he settled in Italy and became a national syndicalist, a fellow traveler of Fascism. In his classic study of *Political Parties* (1911), Michels came to the conclusion that the prevalence of oligarchy in the German Social Democratic Party proved the irrelevance of egalitarian ideals. Many of the reasons he cited to explain why organizations drift toward oligarchy are compelling. But his talk about the "perennial incompetence of the masses," his belief that the many would always live in "eternal tutelage," amounted to a purely gratuitous rehash of Filmer on the part of a thinker who professed to be a leftist.

In reality fascism is the cause, not the consequence, of an elite/mass dichotomy. Neither Rauschning nor Michels appreciated that fascism, far from providing a means to deal creatively with an unfortunate divide between elite and mass, was a regime that attempted to inflict this miserable social and political dualism upon Italy and Germany. The fascist elites did not encounter an undifferentiated "mass" when they assumed power, but with the state at their disposal they tried their best to reduce the Italians and Germans to a pliable mass. Ideology blinded Rauschning and Michels; they saw a world peopled with elites and masses, wherein ideas were no more than propaganda, because that is what their ideologies taught them to see. The same is true of the hard core fascists.

Of one thing we may be certain. Even if Hitler did not formulate a specific program of action until 1934, he always knew what and whom he hated: modernity in general, and especially those persons he regarded as its symbols, liberals and Jews. For tactical reasons he eventually came to terms with the social forces of modern industry, not because he forgot his anti-industrial ideology, but because his ideological program to reduce the world to a master race served by slave races could only be achieved through a vigorous warfare economy. Hitler made peace with the German industrialists so that he could make war on the non-German world.

Whether fascism was based, as in Italy, upon a modernist repudiation of the Enlightenment, liberal democracy, and all humanitarian ideals, or, as the *Action française* proposed and Nazism put into effect, upon a call to a reactionary revolution, initiated not just against humanitarianism but against all of modernity, the result was much the same. Where violence is regarded as manly and proof of prowess, and a program of extermination interpreted as proof of resolve, the threatened outcome is the transformation of nihilism from theory to practice, from literary text to everyday reality.

Fanatically pursuing their ideology, overriding in its name the national interests of Italy and Germany, overextending themselves and uniting everyone against them, the fascists forged their own demise. In their nihilistic fervor they added their own names to the list of their victims. After World War II Germans could not rejoin their past: the old elites had been permanently discredited, and the remainder of the old society no longer existed, having been eliminated as an unintended consequence of Hitler's need to modernize the economy so as to gain the wherewithal for a restoration of a Volkish past that never had existed.

A manifestly new Germany arose from the charred, irreparable remains. The Volkswagen, perhaps, is the symbol of the move from the old to the new Germany. Today it is a car available to the Volk in the democratic sense of "the people"; under Hitler, whose idea it was, the Volkswagen marked the confusion of the Nazi order: it was to be the vehicle driven by the preindustrial folk on their journey into the past, but was built by German heavy industry to compete with American autos.

BIBLIOGRAPHY

Adamson, Walter L. *Avant-Garde Florence: from Modernism to Fascism.* Cambridge, MA: Harvard University Press, 1993.

Barzun, Jacques. *Race: a Study in Modern Superstition.* New York: Harcourt, Brace & Co., 1937.

Benedict, Ruth. *Race: Science and Politics.* New York: Viking, 1947.

Germino, Dante. "Italian Fascism in the History of Political Thought," *Midwest Journal of Political Science,* May 1964, pp. 109–126.

von Klemperer, Klemens. *Germany's New Conservatism: Its History and Dilemma in the Twentieth Century.* Princeton: Princeton University Press, 1957.

Mann, Thomas. *Reflections of a Nonpolitical Man.* New York: F. Ungar, 1983.

———. *Doctor Faustus.* New York: Knopf, 1948.

Moravia, Alberto. *The Conformist.* New York: Farrar, Strauss and Young, 1951; movie version by Bernardo Bertolucci, 1970.

Mosse, George. *The Crisis of German Ideology: Intellectual Origins of the Third Reich.* New York: Grosset & Dunlap, 1964.

Muret, Charlotte Touzalin. *French Royalist Doctrines Since the Revolution.* New York: Columbia University Press, 1933.

Nolte, Ernst. *Three Faces of Fascism.* New York: Mentor, 1969.

Rauschning, Hermann. *The Revolution of Nihilism: Warning to the West.* New York: Alliance Book Corporation, 1939.

————. *The Conservative Revolution.* New York: G. P. Putnam, 1941.

Reiss, H. S. (ed.). *The Political Thought of the German Romantics.* Oxford: Basil Blackwell, 1955.

Silone, Ignazio. *Bread and Wine.* New York: Harper & Brothers, 1937.

Stern, Fritz. *The Politics of Cultural Despair: A Study in the Rise of the Germanic Ideology.* Berkeley: University of California Press, 1961.

Sternhell, Zeev. *Neither Right nor Left: Fascist Ideology in France.* Berkeley: University of California Press, 1986.

Sternhell, Zeev. *The Birth of Fascist Ideology: From Cultural Rebellion to Political Revolution.* Princeton: Princeton University Press, 1994.

Chapter
9

The Nazi Ideology and Political Order

For the Weltanshauung [the ideology] is intolerant . . . and peremptorily demands its own, exclusive, and complete recognition as well as the complete adaptation of public life to its ideas.

Adolf Hitler *Mein Kampf*

A historian of Germany entitles his chapter on German Nazism "Germany Goes Beserk."[1] It is only a mild comment on what occurred in one of the most advanced and civilized nations of the world. Nazism should be a constant reminder to all of us—no matter how special the conditions in Germany appear to have been—of how fragile the bonds of reason and law are and of how vulnerable we *all* may be to political fanaticism under certain circumstances.

German authoritarianism became a political reality when the leader of the Nazi party, Adolf Hitler, came to power in January 1933. Hitler immediately set about organizing the new system, the Third Reich,[2] implementing many of the promises he had made. Most notably, these included the abolition of the institutions of democracy, military preparations for worldwide domination, and the establishment of a single party. The Nazis managed to bring virtually all Germans and all elements of German society under their control. Germans were made to "march in step" to the tune of the Nazi party. This was the meaning of the famous term *gleichschaltung*—the "synchronization" of all aspects of social life with the political ideology and objectives of the Nazi party.

---

[1]K. S. Pinson, *Modern Germany,* p. 479.
[2]Third Reich was an expression intentionally used to indicate continuity with the German Empire (1871–1918) and the Holy Roman Empire.

THE ROAD TO POWER

The beginnings of the Hitler movement can be traced directly to the aftermath of World War I, and also to the rich background of German antidemocratic literature and right-wing political extremism.

Defeat in World War I caused a great disillusionment and eventually a desire for revenge. The discontent was focused on the Versailles Treaty, which had stripped Germany of its colonies and imposed a heavy burden of reparations, but there were also other factors. First, the galloping inflation of the early 1920s was unprecedented in the economic history of any nation. The inflation wiped out savings, pensions, and trust funds and made salaries and wages dwindle with the passage of every day, week, and month. It created a state of acute panic among the middle classes.

A second important factor was the reaction to Communist revolutionary movements. Revolutions actually took place right after World War I, and Communist regimes were installed temporarily in parts of Germany. Private groups and armies, led by officers and war veterans, took it upon themselves to stop the leftists. Often aided by the police and whatever remained of the German Army, they began to wage war against the Communists and their sympathizers. Many of these veterans and their organizations rallied to the Nazis and formed the hard core of the Nazi party.

The Nazi party was founded in 1921. Its original program included the usual nationalist and racist themes but also promised social and economic reforms that were downright socialist: land reform, nationalizations, and the "breaking of the shackles of capitalism." It also attacked the political and economic elites, and identified the "domestic" and "outside" enemies of Germany as the victorious powers—notably England and France, the Jews and "international Jewry." It was a small party at first. Few paid attention to its founding. After the economic Depression of 1929, however, the Nazis began to make rapid gains and soon emerged as the strongest party (see Table 9.1).

There were a number of reasons for the rapid growth of the Nazi party. Leadership was consolidated in the hands of Hitler—the Führer. Uniforms, a special salute, pomp and ritual, and, above all, discipline and activism appealed to many, especially the young. In 1931, some 35 percent of the party members were below the age of thirty. Party membership began to grow—especially after 1928–1929 when there were about 100,000 members, to 1.5 million by 1933, and up to about 4 million at the beginning of World War II.

Special shock formations were established. The SA (Brownshirts) and, after 1934, the SS (Black Guards) grew in numbers to almost equal the German army. At the slightest provocation they engaged in street fights or attacks against leftists and opposition leaders, whose headquarters they sacked and burned. Anti-Semitic demonstrations and acts of violence were common. All this was testing the will of the Nazis, preparing them for further action and intimidation.

A number of front organizations were created to strengthen the party's appeal and to recruit more members and sympathizers. In 1931, the Hitler Youth numbered only about 100,000. In 1933–1934, it was close to about 4 million members,

Table 9.1   ELECTIONS AND THE NAZI VOTE

Legislative elections		
1924 (May 4)	1,918,300 (32 deputies)	6.9%
1924 (Dec. 7)	907,300 (14 deputies)	3.0%
1928 (May 20)	810,000 (12 deputies)	2.6%
1930 (Sept. 14)	6,409,600 (107 deputies)	18.3%
1932 (July 31)	13,745,800 (230 deputies)	37.4%
1932 (Nov. 1)	11,737,000 (196 deputies)	33.1%
1933 (March 5) Nazis in power	17,277,200 (288 deputies)	43.9%
1933 (Nov. 12) Nazis in control	39,638,800 (661 deputies)	92.2%
Presidential election		
1932 (March)		
1 st ballot	11,339,288 (Hitler)	30.1%
2nd ballot	13,418,051 (Hitler)	36.8%

Source: Koppel S. Pinson, Modern Germany, 2nd ed. New York: Macmillan, 1966. Reprinted with permission of Macmillan Publishing Company, © 1986 by Macmillan Publishing Company.

and at the outbreak of the war in 1939–1940 it approached almost 9 million. In addition, there was a Hitler Student League, an Officers' League, a Women's League, a workers' Nazi organization (the Labor Front), and many others representing every academic, social, and professional group in the country. The party gradually became a state within a state with its private army, tribunals, police, and military formations all spreading the Nazi doctrine far and wide and creating within Germany a strong Nazi subculture. It had its own cult, slogans, and morality; they were antirepublican, racist, and nationalist.

With the economic depression, the Nazis made the breakthrough that led them to power in 1933. They became a mass party as the election results show, but they also attracted the attention and support of the conservative forces and the army. The business community and the financial elites opened up their purse, and the party's treasury was again full. The Nazis and their leader broadened their appeal to catch, if possible, every group, every section, and every occupation and profession.

Nazi Pledges

To the farmers, the Nazis promised "green democracy" and "soil-rooted" pure communitarian values as well as protection and subsidies. They pledged to uphold the rural values and traditions that were menaced by urbanization.

Adolf Hitler (1889–1945)

The Führer, ironically enough, was a non-German. Hitler was born in Austria in 1889. A poor student given to prolonged moods of melancholia and daydreaming, he found himself in the army, where he served with the rank of corporal with apparent diligence and courage. Defeat enraged him and he sought scapegoats in the "cowardice" of the civilians and the "conspiracy" of the Jews. Without any formal education—he wanted to be an architect and tried painting—he had read much of the nationalist literature.

After World War I he found himself in Munich, capital of Bavaria, where he founded the NDASP (the Nazi party) in 1921. After the abortive effort to seize power in 1923, he received a light sentence and spent the months of his imprisonment writing what became the political bible of Nazism, *Mein Kampf* (My Struggle). It was the Depression and the frustrations and political conflict associated with it that provided the climate for his ascent to power. On January 30, 1933, President Hindenburg asked him to become Chancellor of Germany, and he assumed full power until his "Thousand Year Reich" ended with his suicide in the ruins of Berlin on April 30, 1945.

To the workers, they promised jobs. Between 1929 and 1932, unemployment had shot up from 1 to 6 million. Many employed and unemployed workers began to join the party and to vote for it. The depression had weakened the trade unions, and left-wing workers were hopelessly divided between socialism and communism.

To the army, the Nazis promised rebuilding and an end to the Versailles Treaty.

To the middle classes, they promised special measures to arrest the decline of their income and give them security; above all, they promised to do away with the dangers from the left by eliminating communism. These promises appealed especially to the lower middle classes—merchants, artisans, shopkeepers, civil service personnel, clerical personnel, and so on.

The Nazi party promised a special place to the young. The future was theirs. "Make room for us, you old ones," was one of their battle cries.

Propaganda was developed into a fine political art along clear-cut lines suggested by Hitler: repetition of the same simple slogans and themes; appeal to the emotions; propositions that clearly distinguished the negative from the positive—"this *is* the truth, *they* lie," "*we* can, *they* cannot"; simple answers to complex problems—"*we* shall solve unemployment by giving jobs to all"; emphasis on nationalism and national togetherness—"*we*" (Germans) against "*they*" (Jews, plutocrats, capitalists, communists, and so on). These propaganda themes were to be strengthened by direct action taken against opponents. Truth lay not in demonstration but in belief *and* in action. A Nazi was someone who believed and strengthened his belief by acting. Force became the best vindication of belief.

In the 1932 presidential election the Nazi candidate, none other than Hitler himself, received 36.8 percent of the vote. More than one-third of German voters wanted him as their president!

THE NAZI IDEOLOGY

Nazism as an ideology and a political movement began as a gesture of negation, but there was also the formulation of a number of "positive" themes and propositions on the basis of which the new society would be constructed. Some of them were addressed to the immediate situation, others to long-range social, economic, and political problems created by liberalism and the threat of communism.

Negative Themes

The negative themes of Nazism were many:

1. *Against class struggle* The notion of class, developed by Marx and endorsed by all Communist parties, was inconsistent with national unity. As such, it was only an extension of the idea of conflict and competition developed by liberals and Marxists. The Nazis claimed that the notion of class was incompatible with the communitarian values of the German people and the German nation. Germany was "one"!

2. *Against parliamentary government* According to the Nazis, parliamentary government leads to the fragmentation of the body politic into parties and groups jockeying for position, compromising their particular interests, and forming unstable governmental coalitions. The "real" national interest was neglected. A common purpose could not develop from such a fragmentation of the national will. "There is no principle which . . . is as false as that of parliamentarianism," wrote Hitler in *Mein Kampf.*

3. *Antitrade union* Unions express the sectarian and class interests of the working class. However, the workers were also Germans and citizens. They had to be integrated into the community like all others instead of pitting themselves against other Germans.

4. *Against political parties* Like representative government, political parties expressed special ideological or interest particularisms, splitting the nation. The national purpose called not for parties but for one movement embodying it. Such a movement, even if it were called a party, should be given monopoly of representation. Hence all other political parties should be outlawed, and a one-party system instituted.

5. *Against the Treaty of Versailles* The Versailles Treaty, imposing an inferior status upon Germany that deprived it of its army and required it to pay reparations, had to be eliminated. But more than that, the existing international system that perpetuated the supremacy of some nations—notably England and France—should be drastically altered to give freedom and space to Germany.

   There were a number of other comprehensive negative themes that inevitably blend with some of the "positive " formulations of the Nazis.

6. *Anti-Semitism and racialism* Anti-Semitism had been a common phenomenon in many countries of Europe stemming from religious prejudices, cultural differences, and economic rivalries. The Jews were blamed as responsible for both liberal capitalism *and* for communism. There were extravagant myths attempting to show that the Jews were plotting the domination of the world. This was the case with a document (fabricated by nineteenth-century anti-Semites) called *The Protocols of the Elders of Zion,* in which the Jews were said to set forth their plans to conquer the world. This was widely used by the Nazis. They added a new twist, however—that Jews were biologically inferior. They were therefore not only dangerous because of their ideas, their beliefs, and their plans to conquer the world (how inferior people could do it was never explained), but because their very presence within Germany endangered the purity of the German "race." There were only half a million Jews in Germany at the time Hitler assumed power and over 65 million Germans—that is less than 0.7 percent. More than 200,000 Jews managed to escape the country by 1938. Those who remained were viewed as a germ just as virulent as botulism. It had to be isolated first and then exterminated.

   As soon as the Nazis came to power, they began to reduce the German Jews to the status of nonpersons. They could not keep their businesses; they could not receive any social benefits. They were relegated to special neighborhoods; they were constantly harassed and intimidated by the members of the Nazi party, the SA, and its various front organizations; they were arbitrarily arrested, could not engage in any gainful occupation, had their belongings confiscated, and were forced to pay special levies to the state authorities that invariably went to the Nazi party members. Intermarriage was prohibited, and existing intermarriages annulled. The Nazis developed the long-range policy of exterminating all Jews that led actually to the destruction of European Jewry wherever the Nazi armies gained a foothold.

Given its basis, German anti-Semitism left no room for compromise. But the same biological discrimination also threatened other groups and nations that the Nazis found dangerous or "impure"—Slavs, blacks, and so on.

7. *Anticommunism* If anti-Semitism derived from racist allegations, anticommunism stemmed primarily from political and international considerations. It was aimed not only against Communists at home, but against the "fatherland of communism," the Soviet Union. It called not only for the elimination of the German Communist party, but also for the elimination of international communism as spearheaded by the Soviet Union. The ideological crusade against communism would thus serve the secular strategic, economic, and geopolitical goals of Germany. It was part and parcel of the *Drag Nach Osten*—the German drive eastward.

"Positive" Themes

Every negation advanced by the Nazis (what they planned to do away with) naturally called for an affirmation (what they planned to do instead). It is therefore only in this sense that I am using the term "positive."

Anti-Semitism suggests racialism and the purity of the race; antiindividualism, a communitarian ethic transcending the individual; antiliberalism, a new political organization; and the anti-Versailles posture, the erection of some new kind of international order. It is the combination of the reasoning behind many of the negations that resulted in the new and dynamic synthesis of social and national life. No matter how morally repugnant, it must be analyzed and discussed if we are to grasp the full and ominous implications of the Nazi movement and regime.

1. *Nationalism and racialism* To understand the character of Nazi German nationalism, we must distinguish it from other nationalist movements. There were liberal nationalist movements in the wake of the French Revolution of 1789 identifying with the principle of nationality and demanding that people sharing the same national background—a common history, culture, language, religion—live within a given territory, the nation–state. This is basically the principle of self-determination, allowing peoples to form their own state. There have also been conservative nationalist movements which have extolled national virtues and asserted their superiority over others; they stress national integration and unity at the expense of particularisms, regionalisms, and even individual freedoms. But such nationalist

movements are content to see the values they assert cultivated and strengthened within the nation–state. They are not expansionist.

Nazi nationalism was both racialist and expansionist. While insisting on the superiority of Germanic values, it also proclaimed the superiority of the German race and the desirability of imposing its superiority upon others. Aryans were superior not only to Jews buy also to Slavs, Turks, Greeks, French, and so on. And among the Aryans, the Germans were the superior race because they had managed and, thanks to the Nazis, forever intended to keep their race "pure." They would not allow for a "mongrelization" similar to what they claimed had occurred in the United States. They were the *master race* destined to dominate all others. This racialist doctrine, coupled with extreme nationalism, led to the inevitability of war.

2. *Expansionism* The valor of the race could not be proven by assertion only. It had to be demonstrated on the proving ground of war and conquest. The master race was to be a race of warriors subduing lesser races. Germany was to conquer, and Berlin would become the capital of the world. But in addition to racism there were ideological, economic, and strategic reasons to justify an expansionist and warlike policy. A totalitarian system is "total" at home because it tries to subordinate everything to its ideology and control. It cannot allow competing units to exist. But the same is true in international terms. The logic of totalitarianism calls for the elimination of competing centers of power everywhere.

Economic reasons were also advanced. One was the notion of "proletarian" nations; another that of "living space." According to the former, World War I had allowed some nations to control the world's wealth—for example, England, the United States, France—while other nations like Germany, Italy, and even Japan were poor, "proletarian," without colonies, raw materials, and resources. Similarly, some nations had ample space at their disposal: the French, British, and Dutch had their colonial empires. The Soviet Union and United States had immense land at their disposal. Others nations did not, however, and Germany, without colonies, was squeezed into the center of Europe, while it population was growing and its needs increasing. Land would therefore have to be reapportioned to meet the German needs. To this argument yet another one was added—the distinction between "young" and "old" nations, suggesting growth against decay. In historical terms, Germany was "young" compared to England or France and needed "living space" and land into which to grow.

Thus the conquest of territory and the destruction of neighboring nation–states became an essential element of the Nazi ideology, and a long-range policy goal. It could not be attained overnight. The elimination of Soviet Russia (an old bulwark against German expansion to the east and also an ideological foe) and France (the spearhead of the "plutocracies," especially England and the United States) would have to come first. The Japanese and the Italians were offered only tactical alliances in the expansionist German ambitions. Their position in the international order that the Nazis would build would have to be settled later.

3. *Communitarianism* The elimination of all freedoms and their replacement by a single "freedom"—that of obeying the party that represented the German community and the leader of that party—was the essence of German totalitarianism. It was central to the building of a new political system that would replace liberalism and capitalism. All parties, all organizations, all associations, all religious groups, and churches would become subordinated to the communitarian will. After the Nazis came to power, freedom of press, of association, and of speech ceased to exist. All parties were abolished. The individual—alone, free, independent, thinking his or her own thoughts—would give place to the "new individual" imbued with communitarian and nationalist beliefs as dictated by the leader and the party. The individual and the community would become one. Dissenters were, of course, not to be tolerated; they were executed or sent to concentration camps. But individuals who tried to remain aloof and distant from the national community were declared to be "asocial." They had failed to respond to the demands of the party and the community; they were not fully mobilized; they were not one with the nation.

Communitarianism called for constant participation; it aimed to inculcate a spirit of individual attachment to the whole and a readiness not only to obey but also to sacrifice everything for the general interest as defined by the Nazis. Communitarianism also suggested the need to subordinate private interest in the economic sphere to general social goals and, thereby, the subordination of the market economy to the party and the leader. The early Nazi ideology was distinctly anticapitalist, and it advocated the supremacy of national goals over all economic interests.

4. *Leadership ("Führerprinzip") and the party* In what ways do communitarian values manifest themselves? One way is the direct participation of all in decision making—claimed to be the practice of the early Germanic tribes. A second way is for the community to select its representatives. This notion of representation was given a particular twist by the Nazis. They accepted it but they rejected free elections. The Nazi party "represented" the German people because it was in tune with the people and expressed directly the desires of the nation. Within the party, its leader instinctively and intuitively acted for the whole. It is the leader, therefore, who best expresses the communitarian values.

Within six months after it came to power, the "monopoly" of the Nazi party was legalized. The National Socialist Workers' party constituted the *only* political party in German. Whoever undertook to maintain the organizational structure of another political party or to form another political party was to be punished with penal servitude up to three years.

Communitarian aspirations gave a populist trait to nazism. It claimed to embody values and principles that stemmed directly from the people—the *volk*. It was the "people's spirit"—the *volksgeist*—that was tapped by the party and was represented by it. Hence the party, in the name of this unique representative quality, claimed to be the only vehicle of representation and the very essence of direct democracy. But because of this, it also claimed to be an entity above the state and to control the state while acting on behalf of the community. In the last analysis, the state was nothing but an agency, an instrumentality of the party, and all its offices and officials were subordinate to the party.

The leadership principle is the cornerstone of nazism and the institution that best combines authority and control with "representation." It is a principle that cannot be easily defined since it can be only "understood" by those who experience it. The leader decides everything and everybody must obey. He can delegate his authority to others but can never give it up. He is the law and hence above the law. He can legislate and then change that legislation overnight. His will is arbitrary, absolute, and superior. He can set procedures and change them at will. He is free to appoint his successor, just as a Roman emperor could make his horse a consul, or send him to the slaughterhouse!

But why do people obey? The link is the mystical and intuitive link between leader and followers. He speaks for the people and the people agree with him because he speaks for them! And where his authority does not quite prevail, the leader has at his disposal formidable instruments of coercion, intimidation, and downright terror to elicit obedience.

The Subordination of the Society

The vast majority of Germans acquiesced in the Nazi takeover, often with enthusiasm. They showed remarkable loyalty throughout Hitler's stay in power. Many did so out of self-interest; how many submitted out of fear is difficult to tell. Let us see how the various "social groups" reacted to the coming to power of the Nazis and their regime.

The Army   Diminished in status, reduced in numbers, bearing the brunt of defeat, and hostile to communism and left-wing movements, army officers saw, in the coming of the Nazis, the prospects of their rehabilitation. Never at ease with republican institutions, the army's position was that it either should be a dominant force in the society or a separate and distinct entity for training soldiers, maintaining order, and making war. It would not play a subordinate role. After World War I, many of its officers joined right-wing vigilante organizations against Communists and leftists. Throughout Hitler's rise to power, prominent officers cooperated with him or gave him a helping hand. He promised the rehabilitation of the nation and saw war as an answer for past failures. As General Blomberg testified at the Nuremburg trials: "Before 1938–1939 the German generals were not opposed to Hitler. There was no ground for opposition since he brought them the success they desired."[3] It was only when the fortunes of the war began to turn against Germany that a number of generals became impatient with Hitler and some even conspired to assassinate him.

---

[3]Cited in Pinson, p. 508.

Civil Service   German civil servants, federal and state, responded with satisfaction to Hitler's program and supported his regime. The Nazis seemed to represent the basic values of order, centralized authority, and national integrity to which they were accustomed. Once it became clear that party members would not replace them, the support of the bureaucracy was overwhelming. It was strengthened by generous promotions and increases in salaries.

Yet bureaucracies are accustomed to an orderly way of doing things. They accept hierarchical relationships and a careful structuring of inferior—superior lines of command. They are committed to a rational detached, and impartial way of reaching decisions and implementing them; they are concerned with efficiency. The Prussian, and later on German, bureaucracy was always considered to be both well-organized and efficient. As a result, the frequent intrusions into it of the Nazi leaders, and the ultimate power they had to intervene and make decisions themselves, alienated some civil servants, forced the resignation of others, and often created confusion. However, at no time during the Hitler regime was there an open defiance on the part of the civil service.

The Church   Religious groups tried to maintain a certain distance from the Nazis, but an effort was made to eliminate some and to bring the two major churches, Catholic and Lutheran, under control. Jews were quickly isolated and their synagogues burned; Jehovah's Witnesses were persecuted. A Concordat was signed with the Vatican giving the Catholic church some autonomy—the right to hold services, raise funds, and distribute pastoral letters to the faithful. But the Concordat also legitimized the Nazi state in the eyes of many Catholics. They were particularly receptive to Nazi anticommunist pledges and, during the war, considered it their patriotic duty to support the fatherland, especially when it was against the Soviet Union.

The Lutheran church maintained a distance from the state, distinguishing political from spiritual matters. Political obedience was one thing, and the worship of God another, but the Lutherans gave their support to the Nazis as citizens, whatever their innermost thoughts might have been. Even to those for whom Hitler was a tyrant, obedience to the state was an obligation and prayer the only answer.

Individual Catholic prelates and Lutheran pastors occasionally raised their voices against the Nazi regime and its atrocities, but they were the exceptions to the general passivity of the churches.

Business Groups   As for business groups, they gave their full support and cooperation once the "socialist" pledges that were in the original platform of the party were abandoned. Neither private property nor business profits were tampered with, and the antilabor and antitrade union measures satisfied them fully. Business elites cooperated closely with the Nazi leaders, trading favors and benefits with them.

The Middle Class, Farmers, and Workers   Germany had never experienced a genuine middle-class liberal movement as had England, France, and the United States. Rapid industrialization was grafted upon semifeudal and authoritarian social structures. Paternalistic and hierarchical relationships were the rule. The middle classes *fitted* themselves into these structures instead of creating their own kind of political and social relationships—egalitarian and participatory. They felt more at home with authoritarian solutions and hierarchical relationships, and hence they were inclined to accept nazism and the authoritarian and nationalist philosophy it represented. Furthermore, the Nazi anticommunist ideology and its intention of doing away with trade unions reflected the middle-class fear of the working class and their political parties. The overwhelming majority of middle-class voters elected the Nazis and supported them throughout their stay in power. The lower middle classes, the petit bourgeoisie—insecure, patriotic, and antisocialist—gave them their full support as they sought a niche in the Nazi order.

Similarly, the farmers gave the Nazis overwhelming support. The rustic virtues the Nazis extolled were also theirs: protection in the form of higher tariffs provided them with added revenue; anticommunism appealed to their traditional nationalism and conservatism. Small towns and rural communities voted overwhelmingly Nazi.

It was only the workers, then, who seemed to demur. But even among them it was only the politically and ideologically organized and committed, those who belonged to trade unions or were in the Communist and Socialist parties, who provided the opposition. The unemployed, as we pointed out, tended to join the party in return for promises of employment. With the coming of World War II in 1939, full employment was attained and the labor force was by and large materially better off than it had been at any time since before World War I. There was no organized opposition.

The Economy

The Nazis failed to implement their original economic program. They did not nationalize the monopolies—on the contrary, every effort was made to encourage concentration and cartelization; they did not confiscate war profits or unearned income; they did not undertake land reform and did not take over uncultivated lands and transform them into peasant cooperatives. Populist and socialist promises were forgotten when they came to power. Some of the Nazi party's leaders, many of whom had taken these promises seriously, were massacred in 1934.

Nazi economic policy consisted of a series of improvisations to meet the political objectives of rearmament and war. There is no doubt that the economy was subordinated not only to political and ideological exigencies, but also to the necessity of planning or waging war. From the very start, controls were put on foreign exchange. Special efforts were made to promote investment and direct it to key areas of economic activity; to secure raw materials and, when it became necessary, to produce them at home (as, for instance, with synthetic gas and rubber). In general, the emphasis was put on reducing imports and promoting self-sufficiency. Property, however, both individual and corporate, was respected.

Political and ideological imperatives prevailed. But the economy was not absorbed by the state; it was not nationalized. It became subordinate to the state and the party—a subordination that most other countries had experienced in time of war. Similarly, the churches, even if they remained submissive, maintained their autonomy under Nazi surveillance. And although various associations—business, legal, professional, and academic—were infiltrated by the Nazis and made to march to the tune of Nazi ideology, they, too, retained their identities.

All and all, the economy and the civil society even if subdued, subordinated, and infiltrated were never destroyed—they maintained their distinctiveness. This is one of the major differences between Nazi authoritarianism and communism. After the defeat of Germany and the collapse of the Nazis in 1945, the societal forces managed to reassert themselves. With the collapse of communism, on the other hand, as indicated, what followed was a societal vacuum.

AUTHORITARIANISM: INTERPRETATIONS AND PROSPECTS

What are the prospects for authoritarianism? Is right-wing authoritarianism dead? With the reunification of Germany in 1990, many ask the same question: "Will it happen in Germany again?" Before we answer, let us survey the major theories— the major explanations for right-wing authoritarianism.

The Marxist Theory   A classic interpretation widely used by many authors is the Marxist one, formally endorsed by the Communist Third International. According to it, nazism corresponds to the "last stage of monopolistic capitalism." It is spearheaded by the most extreme and expansionist elements of the capitalist class in an effort to maintain its rule at home and subjugate other peoples and their economies. Expansionism and war are two of the remaining means available to the capitalists faced with economic depression and the growing contradictions of their system that Marx had anticipated. The evidence was considered clear: both nazism and fascism geared the economy to war, distracting the people from their economic problems by appealing to their nationalism and by preparing them for war. They maintained private property and profits and destroyed the trade unions and working-class parties.

The Modernization Theory   Another theory views authoritarianism in terms of economic modernization. As the industrial and nonagricultural sectors gradually gain, there is a shift of power from the traditional landed and commercial elites to industrial and banking groups. Industrialization accounts for an influx of farmers into the cities and for urbanization and rapid growth in the numbers of industrial workers. These shifts bring about a new type of political mobilization and new political parties that attempt to recruit the workers, the urban masses, and also the disgruntled peasants. Invariably, such a mobilization frightens the middle classes and the industrial elite groups who begin to favor repressive and integrative solutions.

Psychological Interpretations   Authoritarianism has been viewed by many authors as a psychological phenomenon. People react to a "threat" or to "alienation," both of which occur during the development of industrialization and the concomitant creation of a "mass society." A mass society corresponds to the breakup of most intermediate social structures—village, family, neighborhoods—and many traditional institutions that structure and shape individual values, attitudes, and life. The ultimate result is the "atomization" of society. As the old groups disintegrate, the individuals find themselves alone and lonely. A reaction sets in in favor of communal and integrative ideologies.

The perception of threat strengthens authoritarian appeals when the threatened individuals belong to groups that are comfortable, relatively well-off, and satisfied with their lot. Such is the case with the middle classes, which enjoy a higher income and a better status than farmers or workers or lower middle-class individuals. They are, according to some authors, the key to the door to power for right-wing leaders. There is hardly any doubt that the middle classes, both in Germany and Italy, gave their full support to the Nazis and the Fascists in order to protect themselves against threats to their income and status. They sought protection against trade unions and workers, and found it.

As with the previous theories, this psychological interpretation fails to provide a satisfactory and general explanation. If Germany was a mass society in 1933, so were the United States and England. Why did right-wing extremism gain the upper hand in one country but not in the others? Similarly, if the middle classes were "threatened" in Germany, so were they threatened in other industrialized systems, including the United States, during the Great Depression. Why did they seek defense in a totalitarian system in Germany but not elsewhere? Why were antidemocratic solutions sought in some countries and not in others? A theory that does not provide us with the explanation of as many occurrences as possible is not satisfactory.

Managerial Revolution?   Totalitarianism and totalitarian regimes have been viewed by some as representing a "managerial revolution" to replace the inept political leadership of democratic regimes. The economic structure of capitalism, they argue, changes. Property is not in the hands of only a few; it is widely dispersed among stockholders. Property owners cannot and do not make decisions: their managers do. Decision making is therefore increasingly concentrated in the hands of a managerial elite that enters into close contact with other elites, not only in the economy but also in the army and the civil service; it even enters into close cooperation with labor leaders. In other words, it is a coalition of persons with technical skills in production, management, administration, and group organization.

It is this new managerial elite, then, that makes the major decisions in the economy (often through planning): production levels, the establishment of economic priorities, the utilization of resources, the supply of money, income distribution, wage policy, and so on. Gradually, the democratic institutions become an obstacle to this *de facto* government of experts and managers who control the heights of the economy and society.[4] Authoritarianism in the form of fascism or

---

[4]James Burnham, *The Managerial Revolution.*

nazism has been viewed accordingly as the triumph of the technocrat and the expert—of a power elite which finally does away with democracy for the sake of efficiency and organization.

The difficulty with this interpretation is that is assigns a role to rationality, knowledge, and technical expertise that neither the Fascists nor the Nazis valued. On the contrary, in both systems there was a constant struggle between the political ideological propositions, utopian or downright irrational, and the imperatives of rational management. There were constant conflicts between the economic managers and the party or the state, between the army officers and the party, and between the economic planners and the party leaders. In fact, fascism and nazism amounted to the predominance of politics over technical roles and considerations such as competence, organization, management, and efficiency.

Personality Theory   Considerable ingenuity has gone into efforts to show that authoritarianism appeals to and receives widespread support from individuals with a particular type of personality—the "authoritarian" or "potentially authoritarian." A number of attitudinal traits combined constitutes a "syndrome" or a "pattern" of the authoritarian personality: anti-Semitism, nationalism, fear of outsiders or aliens, conservative political outlook, strict family upbringing. Persons showing this syndrome are likely to be found among the lower middle classes, the workers, and the uneducated. Similarly, persons suffering from various types of anxiety, even paranoia, who are unable to make decisions and choices and often are afraid of the outside world, divest themselves easily of their freedoms in favor of authoritarian leadership which provides some degree of fixity and stability in their lives.

But there is no adequate evidence to attribute fascism or nazism and membership in and support for authoritarian movements to particular personality types. To begin with, both Nazi and Fascist movements received strong support from the middle classes, to say nothing of university students—persons, that is, with relatively comfortable backgrounds and higher education. Support was lowest from the working classes, where many of the traits associated with an authoritarian personality would be found. Second, even if we concede that there is an authoritarian upbringing in German families, a random distribution of political attitudes, ranging from authoritarian to democratic, would show only marginal differences for various countries of Europe and elsewhere.

Is There One Interpretation?   All the interpretations given of authoritarian movements provide us with only parts of an explanation. In some cases, it may well be that levels of modernization provided a setting; in other cases, the lonely uprooted individual may have sought shelter in unity and communitarian effort; in others, authoritarian solutions were sought by business and financial groups to defend the economic system that provided them with profits; in still others, the middle classes and the lower middle classes, confronted with loss of income and status, revolted against democracy and liberal in stitutions. No single interpretation will do; and even if all of them are put together, they do not point to the set of conditions that will inevitably lead to authoritarianism.

Prospects

As we have noted, ideologies often go through a process of ebb and flow. Right-wing extremism and authoritarianism have deep roots, and it is not at all unlikely that, given certain conditions, they may surface again. Many of the conditions for the rise of authoritarian movements and regimes continue to be present. The mass society has become even more impersonal and atomized because of rapid modernization and technological development. Individuals are very much "alone," and their discontents and frustrations may lead them to espouse unifying and communitarian themes. The liberal ethic that continues to emphasize individual effort and to promise material well-being has raised high expectations for abundance. But it has also undermined some of the basic intermediary "control mechanisms" of society—like the church, the school, trade unions—and in so doing, weakened the structures of deference, mutuality, and obligation. The political parties seem unable to hold people together around common programs and to pattern and regulate their expectations accordingly. The democratic society has been reduced to a myriad of competing and conflicting groups (some refer to them as molecular groups), each one of which tries to maximize its benefits and advantages. It is not unlikely, therefore, that new authoritarian parties may try to capture the frustrations and discontents of the many who are not satisfied with their position and material well-being. All that may be needed for virulent extremist movements to emerge is a severe international crisis or another serious economic crisis. Such a crisis could cause a resurgence of revolutionary leftist parties, of one denomination or another, that would put the elites and the middle classes on the defensive. It could bring forth a movement or a regime that would attempt to control group particularisms, to replace representative institutions, to set aside political competition, and to manipulate public opinion around nationalist and communitarian themes. Force would replace consent, even if only to a degree, and propaganda would replace persuasion. In other words, the prospects for extremist antidemocratic movements remain very much alive. So does the rich ideological background from which they can draw.

What About a United Germany?   Now we are ready for the questions we raised: "How likely is the return of nazism in Germany? After its reunification in 1990,[5] will Germany assume the same nationalist, antidemocratic, and racialist posture?" There are Germans and German territories still outside of Germany; there is the memory of defeat and humiliation in 1945; there are internal problems that may cause a resurgence of racism, namely, more than 4 million foreign workers in Germany today, among them Turks and North Africans; there is also the realization dawning upon the Germans that with unification Germany has once more attained the rank of a major power in the world, with a worldwide role to play. National strength requires unity that may lead to national exaltation and

---

[5]After World War II, Germany was divided into two: West Germany (German Federal Republic, with a democratic constitution) and East Germany (German People's Republic, with Communist domination).

reassertiveness. There are some who believe, therefore, that right-wing authoritarianism is likely to return.

There are developments, however, that point in the opposite direction. First, German unification has been attained by democratic means with an emphasis on new economic arrangements in the direction of the free market for East Germany. Second, ever since 1945, West Germany (the German Federal Republic) prospered and a new middle class has grown—liberal in outlook, with democratic parties and a democratic constitution. Third, the old elites that cooperated with Hitler—the Junkers, the army, and big business—no longer hold the power and influence they did; in fact, the old elites were destroyed by the Nazis and the new ones grew under a democratic regime that lasted for more than 45 years and that has now been extended to East Germany. Fourth, Germany—a united Germany—remains part of the European Community and has fully accepted the jurisdiction of the European Parliament, the European Commission, and the European Court. It is difficult to see it launch on nationalist and expansionist ventures.

Finally, in the last forty years a more egalitarian and participatory political society has emerged to replace the previous structures of deference and obedience. It had been often said that German revolutionaries who attempted to commandeer trains to transport their militants sought to buy a ticket first! Obedience had been ingrained into the German culture. It is no longer so, and it is more difficult to envisage a return to the political conformism that the Nazis imposed and exploited. However, in light of the interpretations of authoritarian extremism that we discussed and also of the special circumstances that may recur, notably an economic depression, there is no reason to exclude the possibilities of authoritarianism. No society—even less the German society—is immune!

THE RETURN OF THE EXTREME RIGHT IN EUROPE

Almost half a century after the defeat of the Nazis and Fascists in Europe, right-wing extremism is surfacing again. The ideology revolves around the same old staples: racism, xenophobia, and nationalism. Its springboard is also what it was in the early 1930s: the insecurities and anxieties that arise from an economic crisis, unemployment, and international tensions. Its political manifestations, tame for the time being, may well become increasingly intransigent.

The spearhead of the extreme right today is in France—it is the National Front, a party organized and led by Jean-Marie Le Pen. It is dedicated to the preservation of the purity of the French nation and its culture, and is directed against the immigrant workers (and their families) in France. There are more than 4.5 million immigrants in France today and at least half of them are Muslims from North Africa or from the African colonies of France. Le Pen's movement seeks to deny them citizenship, education, and employment and to repatriate them. Muslims speak a different tongue; they have a different religion (mosques have sometimes been built close to the French medieval cathedrals), different laws and customs (some practice polygamy), and they produce children at a much higher rate than French citizens or Europeans. They refuse to assimilate; they want to maintain their cultural, religious, and linguistic identity as well as their attachment to the countries they came from. However, since they also want to and do work in France, they are accused of depriving French citizens of jobs at a time when unemployment remains high.

In the elections for the European Parliament in 1984 and again in the legislative election of 1986, the French National Front received almost 10 percent of the vote; and finally to the surprise of all Jean-Marie Le Pen received 14.4 percent of the vote in the presidential election held on April 24, 1988. Le Pen also fared well in the presidential election of April 23, 1995, when 14.9 percent of the votes were cast for him. In many opinion polls more than one-third of the French "agree" or "agree more or less" with the positions taken by Jean-Marie Le Pen. For a time, the National Front was considered as a transient reaction to special circumstances—the rapid increase of immigrant workers from North Africa and unemployment. It seems, however, to have stabilized. Its hard core may represent less than 10 percent of the French public, but it operates within a favorable climate of opinion that may increase its strength. The major political parties have been unable to settle the status of foreigners and immigrant workers—especially North Africans—and to establish clear criteria for them on how to become citizens or face repatriation. Islamic fundamentalist movements are spreading throughout North Africa—especially in Algeria and Tunisia—and may create domestic and international problems that will provoke a backlash to swell the ranks of Le Pen's movement.

Right-wing parties like the French National Front have mushroomed in England, Belgium, and Holland, while similar movements are developing in Denmark and the Federal Republic of Germany. They have all taken up the same slogans of nationalism, xenophobia, and racism, although they have not yet challenged democracy and the democratic institutions of the countries where they have surfaced. A severe economic or foreign policy crisis could propel them into action against the "aliens" and the "undesirables" in the name of national unity and national independence. Once in power, they could jettison the protections that constitutional government and democracy provide.

In the legislative election held in Denmark on May 9, 1988 the right-wing Progress party received 9 percent of the vote; however, the election of September 21, 1994 showed a decline to 6.4 percent. In the parliamentary elections held in Austria on October 7, 1990, the extreme right-wing party—the Freedom party—doubled its popular vote to 18 percent from a little over 9 percent in 1986. The vote of the freedom party swelled to 23 percent in the election of October 1994. It stands for full Austrian sovereignty by putting an end to its status of neutrality, favors restrictions on immigration and the flow of immigrants from outside, notably Eastern Europe, and a return to "law and order." Its members are young—under forty—and many of its slogans are reminiscent of those used by pro-Nazi sympathizers in the 1930s.

Right-wing authoritarian movements, which may be joined by disgruntled Communists, are spreading to Russia and Eastern Europe. They are all nationalist, xenophobic, and anti-Semitic. In some instances, such movements have assumed many of the characteristics associated with nazism or with pre-World War II Fascists—uniforms, emblems, martial outlook, and paramilitary organizations. They all threaten the new and fragile democracies as they did in the years between World War I and World War II. Extremists are active everywhere—even in the United States—to which we now turn.

THE EXTREME RIGHT IN THE UNITED STATES

"Extremism," writes Seymour Martin Lipset with particular reference to American political history, "describes the violation, through action or advocacy, of the democratic political process." Despite sporadic flareups from what has come to be called the American "extreme" or "radical" right, the democratic process in the United States has held remarkably well. Extremist movements hardly ever succeeded in synthesizing their various negations into a program or an ideology or in transforming them into some kind of positive political formula in order to seek, let alone gain, broad national support and political power.

The strains and stresses of American society, however, have spawned extremist movements. Most but not all of these have come from the right. They have been movements of disaffection appearing in "periods of incipient change"; they are addressed to groups that "feel deprived" or feel "that they have been deprived of something they consider important" and also to particular groups whose "rising aspirations lead them to realize that they have always been deprived of something they now want."[6] Under such circumstances, and unless there is a deep commitment to democracy, the growth of authoritarian movements becomes a distinct possibility. Underlying economic factors have always played a crucial role in the rise of extremist movements, but in the American experience ethnic, racial, and religious factors have been more important. Only since World War II have economic as well as international and genuinely ideological political factors begun to gain prominence.

The Know-Nothings

One of the earliest extremist movements was the Know-Nothing party that developed in New England, with particular strength in Massachusetts, in the 1820s. It was primarily composed of workers and artisans who feared that the influx of immigrants would depress their wages and drive them out of work. They advocated the exclusion of immigrants and wanted to prevent their participation in politics. Direct action was often taken against foreigners: members were supposed to "know nothing" about such action. Even if wages appeared to be the central issue, psychological factors played an important role. In an expanding economy, there could be work both for immigrant workers and also for the indigenous Anglo-Saxons. But the very fact that "foreigners" would attain the income of the native work-

---

[6]Seymour Martin Lipset and Earl Raab, *The Politics of Unreason,* p. 428.

ers appeared to the latter an affront to their position and status within the community.

The Ku Klux Klan

The Ku Klux Klan (KKK) emerged in the South right after the Civil War, to intimidate blacks and thwart the federal measures taken to give them citizenship and extend constitutional rights after they had been freed. It was a regional movement based on community and vigilante organizations and gangs, designed to keep blacks out of politics and the economy, to deprive them of access to property, and to keep them at the level of farmhands and unskilled workers. It also kept a tight control on all whites suspected of showing tolerance and sympathy to blacks. In the years following World War I, the Klan had a particularly strong revival, emerging not only as the advocate of white supremacy but also as the champion of "Protestant" and native superiority over all immigrant and non-Protestant religious groups. It became the proponent of the purity of Americans—against Italians, Jews, Mexicans, Japanese, and so on. At one point in the 1920s, it numbered more than 4 million members and extended beyond the South into the Southwest and California. It exerted a strong influence over the Southern state legislatures.

The Klan did not directly challenge the Constitution. It gave it, however, a special interpretation favoring state rights and state autonomy. It was unwilling to see individual protection and civil rights extended to the groups and the minorities it had singled out. It favored restrictive and repressive legislation, and when it was not forthcoming, resorted to direct violence with burnings, intimidation, evictions, and not infrequently lynchings.

Like the Know-Nothings, the Ku Klux Klan's membership consisted of low-income and low-status groups: artisans, shopkeepers, unskilled workers, and farmers who had moved from the farm to small towns. Their leadership came from petty officials—police officers, small-town businessmen, realtors, and an assortment of veterans. Local ministers of various Protestant denominations played an important role and added biblical zest and justification to the movement, especially in the campaign against Catholics and Jews. In general, the movement preached religious orthodoxy and conformity, the simple values of rural life and the small town against the big city, and was against American entanglements abroad. It was fearful of industrialization and modernization because they were changing American society and shifting the weight of population and economic and political power into the cities and away from the countryside. The movement against the immigrants was a desperate effort to vindicate the position of white, small-town, low- and middle-class Protestant America, and to maintain its economic, social, and political status in a changing world.

Father Coughlin

The first genuine ideological and national extremist right-wing movement was spearheaded by Father Charles E. Coughlin, a Catholic priest, between 1928 and

1940—the years of the Great Depression. Unemployment peaked at a level of about 9 to 10 million until 1939, despite the New Deal measures. Not only did blue-collar and white-collar workers suffer, but also the farmers, the middle classes, and many of the manufacturing and trading groups. Fascism had triumphed in Italy, and the Hitler movement had begun its upward climb in Germany. Democracy, as we have seen, was on the defensive, and socioeconomic conditions in the United States were ripe for a strong movement against it. Father Coughlin tried to exploit all this.

His movement had many of the characteristics of an authoritarian right-wing movement similar to those in Italy and Germany. First, it purported to be a mass movement. According to surveys conducted at the time, almost one-third of the American people "approved" of what Father Coughlin said. What he said was not addressed to native Americans. It did not pit them against immigrants: it almost did the reverse. It struck at the major American institutions and the elites, pitting the "small man" against the "establishment."

A second important feature of the movement was its anti-Semitism. It endorsed the racist doctrines of the Nazis and described Jews in the same racist terms. But there were other special factors—one of them manifestly religious, exploiting the Catholic bias against the Jewish faith. It viewed the Jews as an "internationalist element," distinct from the American melting pot. The infamous and malicious *Protocols of the Elders of Zion,* which, as we have seen, Hitler had publicized, were frequently broadcast and printed in the various pamphlets of the movement.

Its third feature was anticommunism. Communism was a threat both because of its antireligious appeal and also because of its emphasis on class. This was in opposition to the national and communitarian philosophy Father Coughlin wished to impart.

Although a staunch nationalist and an isolationist, Father Coughlin began to lean increasingly in the direction of the Nazi and the Italian models, favoring support of both countries. Just before the demise of his movement in 1940 (by this time its popularity had waned, and at the beginning of the war it was outlawed) he identified fully with the cause of the Nazis to the point of declaring himself to be a "Fascist."

His program had all the familiar "antis": it was anti-elite, anti-Semitic, anti-internationalist (except, as noted above, his support for Hitler and Mussolini), anti-democratic, anti-liberal, anti-capitalist, and against the Constitution. It was one of the first movements to advocate directly the overhaul of the Constitution of the United States. It also suggested a new social order against *both* big capital and big labor. The name of the movement, characteristically enough, was The Union Party for Social Justice, and it merged with other extremist groups to form the National Union. It preached unifying and communitarian themes.

The social configuration of its support was not dissimilar from the one found in the early stage of nazism and fascism. It came from lower middle-class groups and from rural areas and small towns; there was considerable support among the middle classes, and higher support among Catholics and the unemployed in the urban and industrial centers.

Joseph McCarthy

It was a convergence of many factors that both sharpened and deepened the content and the thrust of the American extreme right in the 1950s. The major ones were similar to those that accounted for the emergence of fascism in Italy after World War I: profound discontent with the settlement that followed World War II. Many in the United States felt that the Russians had strengthened their position and began to search for scapegoats. Senator Joseph McCarthy found one in "international communism" and its agents in the United States. Single-handedly, he began to mount a campaign against not only Communists but also their sympathizers—left-wingers and liberals—the so-called "fellow travelers." The term included intellectuals, university professors, members of the "Northeastern establishment," bankers, and supporters of the United Nations. Not only Democrats but also Republican leaders—even President Eisenhower—were accused. McCarthy, in many highly publicized appearances and through investigations conducted by his Senate Committee, discovered "hundreds," of card-carrying Communists in the State Department. He claimed that agreements at Yalta and Potsdam during and after World War II were engineered by the fellow travelers to give undue benefits and advantages to the Soviet Union and to deprive the United States of its victory.

Senator Joseph McCarthy, whipping up anti-communist hysteria in New York in 1954.

While McCarthy never managed to organize a national movement, national response was widespread and positive. This was the period of "The Great Fear,"[7] when wholesale purges of "crypto-Communists" occurred in the federal government, universities, the army, and the trade unions. It was also a movement which began to show clearly the impact that the media of communication, especially TV, can have in creating a "national" state of mind. McCarthy and his activities were widely publicized.

Conspiracy theories are common in extremist movements. With Hitler, it was the conspiracy of the Jews and the failure of the civilians to support their soldiers in war that played an important role. The conspiracy of the Communists against the United States was a notion that satisfied many conservatives and appealed to others who felt that the international position of the United States was slipping. In a peculiar way the McCarthy crusade also appealed to the forces of nativism that we found in the Know-Nothings and the Klan. There were the "ins," the good Americans; and the "outs," the Communists, fellow travelers, crypto-Communists, immigrants, left-wing liberals, and so on.

The John Birch Society

Founded in 1958 by a candy manufacturer, Robert H. W. Welch, Jr. (who died in 1985), the John Birch Society has maintained that it exists to educate the public on the threat of communism. Its official ideology can be found in the John Birch Society Blue Book, and it should be noted that in contrast to other extremist organizations it does not espouse political violence.

The movement, named after a captain in World War II killed by the Chinese and seen as the first "hero" of the Cold War, opposes social and welfare legislation. Its followers consider social security as socialism and they call for the elimination of a graduated income tax. They claimed that Presidents Roosevelt, Truman, and Eisenhower were Communists and conspired with Russia to deplete U.S. power. The John Birch Society disapproved of all efforts leading to an arms treaty with the Soviet Union and wanted the United States to withdraw its recognition of the USSR. In addition, they opposed the United Nations. Welch said that he wanted the country to move toward "a militant form of Americanism."

During its heyday in the 1960s, the Society had 100,000 members, an annual budget of $8 million, and 400 bookstores nationwide carrying its message.

Fringe Movements

Minuscule groups of extremists keep mushrooming throughout the land. They constantly question political compromise and political tolerance, sometimes through the pulpit and the ballot, often with overt acts of defiance and violence. By and large, they preach white supremacy and many trace their origins to the KKK; many are overtly anti-Semitic and some are against Catholics and the new immi-

---

[7]David Caute, *The Great Fear: The Anti-Communist Purge Under Truman and Eisenhower.*

grants from Asiatic and Latin American countries. They all share a common anti-communist and anti-Soviet posture, drawing from the literature of the John Birch Society and the legacy of McCarthyism. In line with the evangelicals, they actively preach a return to traditional and moral values, but they do not shy away from violence. They appeal to poor farmers and the marginal groups in small towns in Middle America—those most threatened by economic changes. It appears that each group acts independently of the others and that the seeds of intolerance and militancy they sow have not found fertile soil. What are some of these movements? And what is their overall impact, if any?

1. "Minutemen" was the label for an extremist vigilante organization founded in 1960 by Robert DePugh, a Missouri businessman, with the purpose of training Americans in guerrilla warfare. They would be used to fight the Communists after they had taken over the United States (an event the Minutemen saw as highly probable) either through internal subversion or invasion. Membership estimates ranged from DePugh's claim of a high of 25,000 to a low of 500. Several groups of Minutemen were seized with illegal arms caches that included rifles, submachine guns, explosives, mortars, and antitank weapons. DePugh himself was arrested in July 1969 and sentenced to a ten-year prison term. Little has been heard of the Minutemen since then.

2. The Populist party, founded in 1984 as an arm of the Liberty Lobby, is intensely nationalistic and racist. Their motto is "America First." Claiming to be a revival of the nineteenth-century Populists, the party managed to receive 66,000 votes in the 1984 presidential race (they were on the ballot in not more than twelve states).

   The agenda of the Populist party is quite clear. "[It] will not permit any racial minority, through control of the media, culture distortion or revolutionary political activity, to divide or fractionalize the majority of the society in which the minority lives." Its weekly newsletter, *The Spotlight*, claimed a subscription list of "over" 50,000 in October 1984.

3. Lyndon LaRouche has formed a group within the Democratic party with some notable success in party primaries. He claims that there is an international conspiracy against the United States that includes Pope John Paul and Queen Elizabeth of England and has accused many prominent American statesmen of conspiring with Soviet leaders to impair U.S. power.

   In 1980, LaRouche received 177,784 votes in Democratic presidential primaries, representing 0.09 percent of the total votes cast. In 1982, a LaRouche candidate opposing Maryland Congresswoman Barbara Mikulski, Debra Freeman, won 19 percent of the Democratic primary votes.[8]

4. Some of the smaller groups include (a) The Liberty Lobby, founded in 1955 in Washington, D.C., which claims a membership of some 200,000 who subscribe to the *Liberty Ledger* and the monthly *Liberty Letters;* (b)

---

[8]"The LaRouche Democrats," Steven Strasser and Ann McDaniel, *Newsweek,* April 16, 1984, p. 31.

the Nationalist Socialist White People's Party, under the leadership of Lincoln Rockwell, with a handful of members; (c) the National Socialist Party of America, based in Chicago; (d) the National Association for the Advancement of White People, with about 6000 members; (e) the National Socialist Movement, founded in 1975 with chapters in twenty-two states; (f) the White Aryan Resistance, based in California with about 5000 members; and (g) the Invisible Empire of the Knights of the Ku Klux Klan, committed to the protection and maintenance of distinctive institutions, rights, privileges, principles and ideals of pure Americanism and to the defense and preservation of the Constitution as originally written and intended.

In the last decade extremist groups have remained active. In times of discontent, depression, and violence in the big cities, the gospel of Christian white supremacy finds support and votes. In the Louisiana election for the U.S. Senate held on October 7, 1990, David Duke, identified with the KKK, received 44 percent of the vote. In great part it was of course a protest vote, an expression of dissatisfaction with economic conditions, especially by the lower middle class rather than a vote for the philosophy of the KKK. But all extremist parties thrive on protest and dissatisfaction. Similarly, violence in the cities—especially in New York City—accounts for the growth of the Klan membership and the emergence of other extremist groups. To date, the most dramatic act of right-wing violence has been the blowing up of the Oklahoma City Federal building, in mid-April, 1995, resulting in some 170 deaths. It was a relatively new group of extremists, the so-called militia groups, that were responsible.

Among the white supremacist groups, the Aryan Nation and some of its offshoots—such as the Anti-Tax Vigilante Group, the White Patriot Party, and the Christian Identity—continue to agitate. Some of their spokespersons claim that blacks are "God's mistake" and that Jews are "Satan's offspring." These extremist groups are scattered through the Midwest and the far West but seem to have lost some ground in the South.

There are also a number of minuscule "hate groups," which according to the U.S. Attorney General totaled about 200 in 1989. They are responsible for numerous incidents of racial violence in schools, churches, and synagogues. The most extremist group among them are the "skinheads," consisting mostly of 13- to 25-year-olds. They indulge in indiscriminate acts of violence, almost for the sake of violence. Without central organization, leadership, or ideology, they simply defy and reject the norms and substance of civilized life. But there are also some 3000 or so neo-Nazi skinheads, predominantly in the Pacific Northwest, responsible for many acts of violence.

A feeling of frustration, resentment, and impotence has always provided the best climate for the growth of extremist movements, which invariably come up with simple answers to complex problems and nationalist solutions to endemic social and economic difficulties. Currently, they are dispersed, but in a turbulent political landscape, the voices of violence and "unreason" could grow loud, and coalesce under one leader. Under certain circumstances—economic depression or military setbacks—they could unite to challenge the foundation of constitutional government and democracy.

BIBLIOGRAPHY

Abel. Theodore. *The Nazi Movement: Why Hitler Came to Power.* New York: Atheneum, 1965.

Allen, William Sheridan. *The Nazi Seizure of Power: The Experience of a Single German Town.* New York: New Viewpoint, 1973.

Aycoberry, Pierre. *The Nazi Question.* New York: Pantheon Books, 1981.

Bracher, K. Dietrich. *The German Dictatorship.* New York: Praeger, 1970.

Bruce, Steve. *The Rise and Fall of the New Christian Right: Conservative Protestant Politics in America, 1978–1988.* New York: Oxford University Press, 1990.

Bullock, Alan. *Hitler: A Study in Tyranny.* New York: Harper & Row, 1971.

Burnham, James. *The Managerial Revolution.* Bloomington: Indiana University Press, 1973.

Carsten, F. F. *The Rise of Fascism.* Berkeley: University of California Press, 1980.

Dalton, Russell, and Manfred Kuechler (eds.). *Challenging the Political Order: New Social and Political Movements in Western Democracies.* New York: Oxford University Press, 1990.

———. *Interpretations of Facism.* Cambridge, MA: Harvard University Press, 1977.

DeFelice, Renzo. *Fascism: An Informal Introduction to Its Theory and Practice.* New Brunswick, NJ: Transaction Books, 1976.

Fried, Richard M. *Nightmare in Red: The McCarthy Era in Perspective.* New York: Oxford University Press, 1990.

Gallo, Max. *Mussolini's Italy.* New York: Macmillan, 1973.

Germani, Gino, *Authoritarianism, Fascism, and National Populism.* Transaction Books, New Brunswick, NJ 1978.

Gregor, A. James. *Interpretations of Fascism.* Morristown, NJ: General Learning Press, 1975.

Heiden, Konrad, *Der Fuehrer.* Boston: Beacon Press, 1969.

Hitler, Adolf. *Mein Kampf.* Boston: Houghton Mifflin, 1962.

Joes, Anthony James. *Fascism in the Comtemporary World.* Boulder, CO: Westview Press, 1978.

Karsten, F. L. *Rise of Fascism.* Berkeley, University of California Press, 1980.

Kater, Michael. *The Nazi Party.* Cambridge, MA: Harvard University Press, 1983.

Langer, Walter C. *The Mind of Adolf Hitler.* New York: New American Library, 1978.

Laqueur, Walter. *Fascism: A Reader's Guide.* Berkeley: University of California Press, 1976.

———, and George Mosse. *International Fascism.* New York: Harper, 1966.

Lee, Stephen J. *The European Dictatorships, 1918–1945.* New York: Routledge, 1987.

———. *The Making of a Stormtrooper.* Princeton, NJ: Princeton University Press, 1979.

Merkl, Peter H. *Political Violence Under the Swastika,* Princeton, NJ: Princeton University Press, 1975.

Mussolini, Benito. *My Autobiography.* New York: Scribner's, 1928.

Neumann, Franz. *Behemoth: The Structure and Practice of National Socialism,* 2nd ed. New York: Oxford University Press, 1944.

Pinson, K. S. *Modern Germany,* 2nd ed. New York: Macmillan, 1966.

Reich, Wilhelm. *The Mass Psychology of Fascism.* New York: Farrar, Straus & Giroux, 1970.

Smith, Dennis Mack. *Mussolini's Roman Empire.* New York: Viking, 1976.

Tannenbaum, Edward R. *The Fascist Experience.* New York: Basic Books, 1972.

The American Right

Barnhart, Joe Edward. *The Southern Baptist Holy War.* Texas Monthly Press, 1988.

Bell, Daniel (ed.). *The Radical Right.* New York: Doubleday, 1964.

Bozell, L. Brent. *Dialogues in Americanism.* Chicago: H. Regnery Co., 1964.

Caute, David. *The Great Fear: The Anti-Communist Purge Under Truman and Eisenhower.* New York: Simon and Schuster, 1978.

Crawford, Alan. *Thunder on the Right: The "New Right" and the Politics of Resentment.* New York: Pantheon Books, 1980.

Epstein, Benjamin, and Arnold Forster. *The Radical Right.* New York: Vintage, 1967.

Fachre, Gabriel J. *Religious Right and Christian Faith.* Erdmans, 1982.

King, Desmond S. *The New Right: Politics, Markets and Citizenship.* Chicago: Dorsey Press, 1987.

Kymlicka, B. B., and Jean V. Mathews. *The Reagan Revolution?* Chicago: Dorsey Press, 1988.

Lipset, Seymour Martin, and Earl Raab. *The Politics of Unreason: Right Wing Extremism in America, 1790–1970.* Chicago: University of Chicago Press, 1978.

Macedo, Stephen. *The New Right v. the Constitution.* Cato Institute, 1986.

Roelfs, H. Mark. *Ideology and Myth in American Politics: A Critique of a National Political Mind.* Boston: Little, Brown, 1976.

Shapsmeir, Edward. *Political Parties and Civic Action Groups.* Westport, CT.: Greenwood Press, 1981.

Viguerie, Richard A. *Establishment vs. the People: Is a New Populist Revolt on the Way?* Chicago: Regnery Gateway, Inc., 1984.

PART
Four

OLD VOICES AND NEW

What is truth? asked jesting Pilate, and would not stay for an answer.

Francis Bacon "Of Truth"

T his part deals with several significant movements and ideologies now being voiced throughout the world. All of them borrow a great deal from past ideologies—nationalism, anarchism, early Christian thought, utopian socialism, Marxism and Leninism, and even early liberal and democratic thought. The wine seems to be the same old heady wine, but one will find it mixed with many recent vintages. All of these ideologies demand the realization of long-unfulfilled imperatives: they all seek redemption "now and here." "This is our world" and "we must set it right," they all seem to affirm. They all share a profound, almost religious, sense of righteousness, of what is morally right and must be done, and of what is morally unacceptable and has to be destroyed. Some put great emphasis on human will—on our freedom to change and improve radically the circumstances that surround us. Others, however, notably nationalism and religious fundamentalism, invoke traditional values. With the collapse of communism and the resurgence of democracy, some threaten democratic institutions, as we point out in our concluding chapter.

Chapter 10

Nationalisms

This happy breed of men, this little world,
This precious stone set in the silver sea. . . .
This blessed plot, this earth, this realm, this England

Shakespeare Richard II

Without a country . . . you are the bastards of humanity. Soldiers
without banner . . . you will find neither faith nor protection.

Mazinni to the Italians, c. 1850

*P*eople who once every four years watch the Olympics or who occasionally turn their TV to U.N. debates cannot help but marvel at the number of nation–states with their delegates, flags, athletes, diplomats, and national anthems stressing the same themes—pride and strength, unity and loyalty to the fatherland or the motherland, military glory, a call to action and sacrifice, an assertion of superiority, and a demand for utter devotion. "Our fight for our land will never cease; it was ours and it will be ours forever and ever" (Uganda); "Fatherland, fatherland. . . . thy sons swear to breathe their last on thine alter" (Mexico); "Onward *enfants de la patrie*. . . . The day of glory is before you" (France); "Germany, Germany above all others" (Germany); "Sweet land of liberty . . . " and so on. Ours continues to be a world of nation–states. Today there are more than one hundred and seventy. Within nation–states there are also ethnic groups and "nationalities"—Basques, Bretons, Tamils, Catalans, Corsicans, Kurds, Ibos, Azeris, Welsh and Scots, Native Americans, and so forth—each with their own identity.

Nationalism has proved to be one of the most tenacious ideological bonds binding human beings together into separate political communities. Its values may vary, the particular content of the citizen's attachments may change, but fundamentally the nationalism is identified in terms of a common feeling of togetherness that separates the "we" and the "they." Nations are invariably defined in terms of a *community* and in terms of the *loyalty* of the individual to the community. It is a common mind, with common habits—moral, social, cultural, and political—common ancestors, common character, common race, common symbols, common language, a corporate will, and a common soul. Loyalty is invariably described in terms of dedication, sacrifice, subordination, love, and affection. Nations are either a "motherland" or a "fatherland," evoking the obedience and affection that children supposedly owe to their parents.

Even if we take it for granted, nationalism is something relatively recent. It is primarily a political ideology that developed in Europe in the latter part of the eighteenth century and throughout the nineteenth century. After the end of World War II, in 1945, it spread to the so-called Third World (the then colonies in Africa, Asia, and the Middle East) and also to Latin America. Like all political ideologies, nationalism is an instrument for the acquisition of political power by certain groups and the organization of political power on the basis of new principles—notably popular participation. Hugh Seton-Watson defines nationalism as "a policy of creating national consciousness within a politically unconscious population,"[1] and he notes that its purpose was precisely the mobilization of a population behind new leaders and social forces. Nationalism was, and remains, a unifying ideology aimed at manufacturing consent on the basis of a strong appeal and symbols of identification. Its aim is to generate emotional supports, create a state of exaltation and sacrifice, and provide for loyalty.

NATIONALITY, NATION–STATES, STATES, AND NATIONALISM

Some clarifications are needed in order to better understand the dynamics of nationalism.

Nationality denotes an ethnic and cultural identity, based on common values. A *state,* on the other hand, is a political organization holding and exercising supreme power through its various agencies over a given people within a given territory. A state may include a number of "nationalities." The most illustrious example of such a state was the Austro-Hungarian Empire that until 1918 was a political administrative organization governing Slavs, Slovenes, Croatians, Italians, Montenegrins, Hungarians, Poles, Austrians, Czechs, and quite a few others. A state, in other words, may be "multinational." The best recent examples are the now defunct Soviet Union and Yugoslavia, both dissolved as their various nationalities reasserted their separate autonomous claims to the point of demanding political independence. Multinational "states" seem to be in the process of being devoured by their "ethnic" and "nationality" parts!

A *nation–state,* in contrast to a nationality (which is not a state) and to a state (which is not necessarily based upon a common nationality), is supposed to be *both a state and a nationality.*[2]

---

[1]Hugh Seton-Watson, *Nations and States,* p. 449.

[2]Curiously enough, the most succinct definition of a nation was given by Joseph Stalin: "A nation is an historically evolved, stable community of language, territory, economic life and psychological makeup manifested in a community of culture." Add "common political authority," and you have a nation–state. Joseph Stalin, *Marxism and the National Question,* Foreign Languages Publishing House, Moscow 1954, p. 8.

Nationality and Nationalism: Objective and Subjective Factors

The terms *nation* and *nationality* began to appear only in the seventeenth century, to denote the emergence of a consciousness of a common identity of people in a given territory. People in a given location began to gain awareness of something they had in common as distinguished from others. There was a common sharing and a common predisposition for sharing. A people's feelings and a common predisposition accounts for the nation. The nation–state may be viewed, to put it very simply, as the creation of the individuals who comprise it; it exists and derives its existence from the support and the consent the individuals give to it. As a French publicist put it, *it is the result of a contract or of a "daily referendum."*[3]

The nation may also be viewed as having a separate reality outside and beyond the consent of the individuals who make it up. It is an objective and historical reality that overwhelms the individuals. Historical and other reasons give it a transcendental quality and a moral superiority that impose themselves upon the individuals. According to this view, individual freedom and morality cannot be attained except within the nation and in terms of the national values and beliefs. The nation, in other words, is "real"; the individual is not.

Objective Factors   The most common traits with which nationality is associated remain: (1) language; (2) religion; (3) a consciousness of common traditions and history and a will to maintain them; and (4) a common territory. When no common territory exists, as was the case with the Jews and the Greeks and the Poles, it was the memory of the common territory they occupied in the past that kindled their desire to regain it or to reclaim it. The same is true today for Kurds and many other nationalities.

Scholars who study nationalism have stressed at different times one or another of these objective factors.

- *Religion* was particularly important in the period of the formation of national consciousness. Religious wars were fought to both emancipate the state from the Papacy and to create internal unity, which was endangered both by papal control and by the existence of religious minorities.
- *Language* was an important criterion used by a number of authors, especially German. It was a common and distinct vehicle that bound people together, creating a special bond among its users. But, as the case of Switzerland shows conclusively, it is not a necessary condition.
- *Race* was used primarily, as we have seen, in the twentieth century by the Nazis to show the unique traits of the German nation. It is supposed to refer to specific biological traits which are not always clearly perceived or agreed upon.
- *Ethnicity* is a broader term that may or may not include race but usually refers to a number of the common cultural attributes. Both race and ethnicity are terms indiscriminately used in Europe as well as in Asia and Africa.

---

[3]Ernest Renan, "What Is a Nation?" in Hans Kohn, *Nationalism: Its Meaning and History,* pp. 135–140.

Some groups perceive themselves or are perceived by others as a "race" or as an "ethnic group" and often as both.

- The *common past* has been constantly invoked, and when it could not be easily found, every effort was made to manufacture it by rewriting history.
- *Geography*—a common territorial basis—is invariably invoked. Nations like an individual had to have "a home," a space under the sun.

Subjective Factors All the objective traits we outlined—religion, language, common history, and so on—may exist and may be commonly shared by a given "nationality." Nationalism, however, becomes an ideology and a movement only when it translates this self-consciousness into a demand to form a state. The subjective element is an element of will and purpose. Nationalism asserts the validity of the objective factors of nationality for *certain* political purposes; it affirms their uniqueness and often their exclusiveness. It is not only the will to live together but to have a government. It is the assertion that such a purpose has an inherent claim to be heard and to realize itself; it is a purpose that is presumed to be morally just. In this sense nationalism is, as Elie Kedourie writes in one of the most penetrating studies on the subject, "a doctrine *invented* in Europe at the beginning of the nineteenth century. . . . [It] holds that humanity is naturally divided into nations, that nations are known by their characteristics . . . and that the only legitimate type of government is *national* self-government."[4]

Nothing better exemplifies the differences between those who stress objective factors from those who rely on subjective ones in defining a nation—the first relying on history, language, religion, and tradition and the second on subjective factors—than the conflict between Germany and France over the provinces of Alsace and Lorraine occupied and annexed by the Germans in 1871. Ernest Renan, the French publicist, in his famous essay *What Is a Nation?* (1882), was willing to accept the verdict of the people given through a referendum. The Germans, on the other hand, asserted their claims in terms of historical right. "These provinces are ours by the right of the sword," wrote a German nationalist, "and we shall rule them by the virtue of a higher right. . . . *We desire, even against their will, to restore them to themselves*" [emphasis added].[5]

Self-determination is the demand made by a nationality to become a state. It became a doctrine when it was expressly stipulated in the famous Fourteen Points that President Woodrow Wilson issued as the guidelines for building a new political order in Europe after World War I.

"Self-determination," Wilson declared, "is an imperative principle of action, which statesmen will . . . ignore at their peril." World War I, he claimed, "had its roots in the disregard of the rights of small nations and of nationalities which lacked the union and the force to make good their claim to determine their own allegiance and their own form of political life." He suggested among other things, in the form of guidelines for the Peace Conference that was to follow the hostilities that ended in 1918, "a readjustment of the frontiers of Italy . . . along clearly

---

[4]Elie Kedourie, *Nationalism,* p. 77.
[5]Kohn, *Nationalism,* p. 61.

recognizable lines"; "the freest opportunity of autonomous development" for the peoples of Austria-Hungary; the redrawing of some of the frontiers in the Balkans "along historically established lines of *allegiance* and *nationality*"; "an absolutely unmolested opportunity of autonomous development" for the national minorities within Turkey; "an independent Polish state . . . inhabited by indisputably Polish populations."[6]

It is in the name of nationalism and self-determination that old multinational political organizations and empires gradually broke down until by the end of World War I most European nationalities became nation–states. The Austro-Hungarian and the Ottoman empires broke up under the force of nationalist movements. The czarist Russian Empire showed signs of disintegration and the Bolsheviks stepped in to consolidate their control; but now that control, too, has begun to unravel.

The French Revolution

It was the French Revolution of 1789 that asserted the sovereignty of the people *and* the nation. The revolution began as an assertion of individual freedoms and popular sovereignty. It finished with an absolutist ruler—Napoleon—and an expansionist nationalism that changed the map of Europe.

With the overthrow of the monarchy in 1792, the French Revolution quickly established patriotism, the unqualified attachment to the nation–state, as the highest ideal and as the most intimate bond among the people. Rituals, national festivals, symbolisms, national songs were all used to create a solidarity among the French. A system of national education was instituted to propagate patriotic values. Every attempt was made to wipe out regional and linguistic particularisms in favor of cultural unity, territorial integration, and centralization. The republic was to be "one and indivisible." Compliance with the revolution and its policies was promoted everywhere, requiring coercive measures that gradually were transformed into an outright tyranny. A revolutionary leader spoke of "the *tyranny of liberty* against despotism."

The last phase of the revolution produced an expansionist fervor and a desire to liberate other peoples by overthrowing their governments. French men and women were made to "march in step" with the republican and civic ideology, not only on the battlefield but also at home. "The citizen is born, lives and dies for the fatherland" was the inscription that all French could read in every municipality where they lived. "Oh sublime people! Accept the sacrifices of my whole being. Happy is the man who is born in your midst; happier is he who can die for your happiness," exclaimed Robespierre. The citizen-patriot gradually became transformed into the citizen-soldier, willing to die for his country. General Charles de Gaulle—the most eminent French political leader of the twentieth century—wrote in the same vein: "France is not really herself unless in the front rank France. . . . cannot be France without greatness."[7]

---

[6]Presented on February 11, 1918. Cited in Alan P. Grimes and Robert H. Horowitz, *Modern Political Ideologies*, pp. 501–503.

[7]Charles de Gaulle, *The War Memoirs*, vol. 1, *The Call to Honor* 1940–42 (Transl. by Jonathan Griffin). New York: Simon and Schuster, 1955, p. 3.

Thus we find in the manifestation of French nationalism the traits that appear again and again in many national independence movements throughout Europe: a revolutionary fervor associated with the destruction of the aristocracy and the economic and social order it represented; an effort to devise slogans to unify the country and to break down all internal barriers; the creation of new national symbols to mobilize the people and inculcate in them common values, and thus elicit their support; and, finally, the assertion of national virtue and right over individual citizens, and over other peoples as well.

Throughout Europe, nationalism played the same important role in forging tightly integrated communities. It was strongly related to the rise of the middle classes and the destruction of the feudal structures. Politically speaking, it was a vehicle for the acquisition of power by the middle classes by mobilizing the masses as they had never been mobilized before. Controlling "their minds and souls" was a source of far greater power than any ruler or class appealing to status, tradition, authority, or divine right had ever claimed or possessed before.

Traditional Nationalism

The French nationalism that came with and after the French Revolution was an intensely ideological phenomenon that broke from tradition and the past. It attempted to restructure society and formulate a new way of life, a new nation. This was not the case with traditional nationalisms as they grew in response to the French nationalism, especially in Germany. French nationalism was a matter of will and was future oriented. Traditional nationalism, on the other hand, sought its source in the past and was portrayed as a natural phenomenon, not an act of political will.

German nationalists set forth their ardently reactionary beliefs by misappropriating the writings of Johann von Herder (1744–1803). Although a figure of the Enlightenment, Herder was strongly critical of the universal and abstract statements of the French *philosophes,* as in their talk about the "rights of man." Herder sought to vindicate the culture of the people, the *Volk*—that is, the language, folkways, and mores that constitute national identity. But while Herder was a cosmopolitan seeking to reach out to as many cultures and peoples as possible, the German romantics who invoked his name in the nineteenth century were narrow nationalists who proclaimed their country superior to all others. In its worst incarnations this Volkish ideology served as an early intimation of the thought of National Socialists.

Reactionary nationalism was reinforced not only by biological and racial arguments but also by cultural ones. A German writer, Johann Fichte (1762–1814), called upon Germany to assert its "cultural" supremacy. Some asked that all those speaking the German language be united into one fatherland. Others, long before the Nazis, asserted the racial purity of the Germans. Unification of Germany was achieved by Bismarck in 1871 who was statist and traditionalist in outlook. The reactionary thinkers who championed a racially identified Volk were as hostile to Bismarck as to the Jewish people. They awaited the day when a Volkish leader would come to the fore (see Chapter 8, on the intellectual roots of fascism).

What characterized German nationalism, therefore, was its conservative emphasis. It looked to the past; it appealed to the establishment groups; it was part of the political tradition and culture, not "made" as in the case of French nationalism during the revolution. The same was true with many Eastern European nationalisms, notably the Russian one, which stressed religion as one of its primary forces and only indirectly race and language.

GERMAN NATIONALISM: THE 1990 VERSION

When Germany became a nation–state in 1870 after defeating France and annexing Alsace and Lorraine (two French provinces), the architect of unification, Chancellor Otto van Bismarck, called it "a victory . . . a divine judgement such as has never been seen, inscribed in letters of fire upon the tablets of history." In these words, he was expressing the traditional and transcendental point of view of German nationalism. On October 3, 1990, Germany (after being divided into two after World War II) was reunited. Nobody invoked divine intervention. Unification was accomplished in very much the same way two companies agree to merge. It was accomplished when the peoples of East Germany agreed by open vote to unite with West Germany and accepted its democratic constitution. It was a liberal and democratic unification accomplished by the consent of all parties involved.

In the very heart of Europe where it burned for so long, the fiery vision of German national unity was now inscribed upon the common tablets of economic and social cooperation—a common currency, common social security benefits, the need for investments, and the prospects of employment for all. Chancellor Helmut Kohl, the architect of the unification of 1990, emphasized democracy, pledged to respect the frontiers of the new Germany, and expressed on numerous occasions Germany's responsibility for the atrocities committed by Hitler's regime against other nations and peoples, especially the Jews. He firmly committed the new Germany to membership in the European Common Market. The fatherland was to become a part of Europe instead of striving to dominate Europe. Traditional nationalism appeared to be giving place to a democratic and liberal vision.

British and American Nationalism

Mazzini (1805–1872) outlined a theory of liberal internationalism which Woodrow Wilson attempted, with mixed results, to put into practice at the end of World War I. Both men believed that the self-determination of peoples would lead to governments liberal and democratic in internal politics and peace loving in foreign affairs. This *liberal internationalism* proved to be a mirage, but *national liberalism* has long been a reality in England and America. In both English-speaking countries there is a reverence for limited government, tolerance, and rights based upon an accumulation of historical experience.

In the United States, the main assertion of nationalism lay in the creation of a republic best exemplified in the Constitution. The country remained wide open to immigration, and as succeeding waves of immigrants came from England, Scandinavia, Germany, Ireland, Italy, Poland, and elsewhere, it lost whatever distinctive ethnic, cultural, or religious characteristics it might have claimed. As for its history—the Boston Tea Party, Lexington, Concord, Bunker Hill, and so on—it was repeated in the schools and in literature. It strengthened and maintained the political symbolism of individual freedoms and constitutional government. American "nationalism" remained political in character: it meant an attachment to the Constitution and to the individual rights spelled out. It was *civic* loyalty that counted.

Both in England and in the United States, of course, the assertions that the fatherland is above the individual were made, but not as often and not as convincingly as in Europe. No nationalist ethic developed that subordinated the individual to the collectivity; no religious, historical, or cultural bonds were imposed upon the individuals in the name of the nation; no uniformities of thought and action were shaped in the name of an overriding national reality and goals.

Of course, such views about American and British nationalism must be taken with a grain of salt. It is true that the two countries have remained relatively far more open and tolerant than others and that nationalism never managed to mobilize the people in one overriding conformist ethic as other nationalisms did in Europe. But there were frequent assertions of national supremacy in both countries. In England, Rudyard Kipling and many others spoke of the "white man's burden"—the self-appointed duty of the British to civilize and educate the masses of the colonial peoples, which were under their control. Both cultural and racist considerations entered into the formulation of English nationalism. By the end of the nineteenth century in the United States as well, there was a strong nationalist ideology with a revealing vocabulary. It claimed a "manifest destiny" for the Anglo-Saxon nations, like the United States, and an important role in world affairs for these nations as they assumed their share of domination and tutelage of "lesser" peoples. Considerations that were religious, political, economic, and not infrequently racist entered into this American form of nationalism. And the effort to exact civic conformity and loyalty around national symbols was and remains ever present. Deviations from the national and political ethos of American liberalism have been often branded as "un-American," and at times was viewed as synonymous with treason.

NATIONALISM IN ACTION: A HISTORICAL OVERVIEW

Three major waves of "nationalism" have swept over the globe ever since the French Revolution, and we are now witnessing a fourth wave. With the exception of the German nationalist movement of the nineteenth century, each and all of them are associated in general with the breakdown of multiethnic or colonial empires—the Austro-Hungarian Empire in Central Europe, the Ottoman Empire in the Balkans and the Near East, the colonial empires of Britain, France, and others, and more recently, the fall of the Soviet Union. Most, beginning with the French Revolution, are also linked with the spread of democratic and liberal ideas, even though Marxism, at its height, provided some ideological tools for the uprisings of the colonial peoples after World War II. We are witnessing, at present, a fourth and last wave—we can call it *ethnonationalism*. It is, as an ideology, an extension and a continuation of past nationalist movements, borrowing from the same vocabulary and, by and large, articulating the demands of distinct ethnic groups living within a state to emancipate themselves by asserting their identity and attempting to translate it into political autonomy or political sovereignty. They all attempt to translate *nationality* into some form of *statehood*.

The first wave solidified France as a nation–state and planted powerful seeds throughout Europe. The seeds grew throughout the nineteenth century into movements for national independence and statehood among many of the European nationalities—Czechs, Slovenes, Hungarians, Serbs, Greeks, Italians, Catalonians, Bulgars, Romanians, and Poles. In the name of nationalism, they stormed the citadels of centralized power and began to nibble at the periphery. Hungary carved its autonomy in what became the Austro-Hungarian Empire in 1867; in the name of antiquity and after centuries of struggle, Greece gained its independence from the Ottoman Empire in 1827; agitation in Italy confronted the last papal states and led, when the Papacy withdrew, to its national unification in 1870. Powerful messages for independence reached out to the Serbians, Czechs, Slovaks, and Croatians. As empires were tottering, new ones were born—in the name of nationalism. Germany became one in 1870, when Prussia was able to unify the various independent principalities, confederations, and kingdoms into one German nation–state. At about the same time, the United States, too, asserted its national unity after a bitter Civil War.

The second wave comes after the end of World War I in 1918. The Austro-Hungarian Empire was definitively dismantled, disgorging a number of national states—Hungary, Czechoslovakia, Austria, Yugoslavia—and bringing Serbs, Croates, Slovenes, and others together; Romania and Bulgaria emerged as independent states; Greece liberated most of its nationals from Turkey. Poland, at long last, became an independent state, accommodating within its borders most of the Poles. Finland, Latvia, Estonia, and Lithuania rid themselves of the czarist yoke without falling into the centralizing vortex that the Bolsheviks fashioned. By and large, the Wilsonian idea linking national self-determination, democracy, and statehood was realized—even though democracy did not survive for long! It was impossible, however, to accommodate all ethnic minorities and to create political borders that corresponded fully to ethnicity and nationality. Some newly founded and some old states continued to include ethnic groups that longed to join their brothers and sisters across their political borders or to change the borders of their states and bring them in.

The third wave swells after the end of World War II and follows the logic of previous nationalist movements. In virtually the whole of the colonial world, the "lower breeds"—the arrogant term of the British nationalist poet Kipling—began to demand independence. The colonial empires—England, France, Belgium, and Holland—began to crumble as the Austro-Hungarian and Ottoman empires did. The British and the French moved out of the Middle East to be replaced by new states reflecting nationalist political movements—Iran, Egypt, Syria, Israel, Tunisia, Morocco—and, in some cases, by artificial ones as in Iraq, Algeria, Libya,

Kuwait, the Arab Emirates, Oman, and Jordan.[8] In the whole of Sub-Saharan Africa, movements of national liberation led to the formation of new states. Between 1945—the end of World War II—and today, at least sixty new states emerged in Africa, the Middle East, the Caribbean, and Asia, most of them basing their right to be so on the principles of nationality. The logic linking statehood and nationhood—real or alleged—seemed irresistible.

The New Wave in Communist States

The fourth—but not necessarily the last—wave of nationalism is associated with the breakup of the Soviet Union and Yugoslavia. Nationalist independence movements rose against the Communist regimes that kept them under control for some seventy years in the Soviet Union and for almost half a century in Yugoslavia. They clearly show that communism was unable to tame nationalisms and that nationalisms frequently fail to tame themselves.

Marx, Lenin, Stalin, and Nationalities   Marxist ideology and theory underestimated the force and tenacity of nationalism. It was summed up in the pithy statement we find in *The Communist Manifesto:* "The working men have no country." Nationalism, Marxists claimed, was but one of the many ideological devices used by the capitalist class to distract the workers and to detract them from their revolutionary mission. Nationalism belonged to the superstructure. If religion was the opium of the people, nationalism (and the inevitable wars to which it led) was an equally powerful opiate. It gives the workers a false ideology and a false sense of identity that is contrary to their interests: to eliminate capitalism and to establish a proletarian international socialist world.

Lenin shared the same conviction. But as a great tactician, he had realized, as we noted, that nationalist movements could be used against the imperialist powers—in India, Iran, Egypt, and elsewhere in the colonial world—in order to weaken the capitalist countries and pave the way to their downfall and the collapse of capitalism as a worldwide system. It was a deviation from Marxist theory, but a necessary one to bring about the downfall of capitalism.

Stalin also discussed the concept of nationality and nationalism. "Self-determination" had been used by the Bolsheviks to promote nationalist uprisings against the Czar. The right of nationalities to secede was formally granted by the Soviet constitution. However, Stalin never departed from the Marxist notion that nationalism was a bourgeois ideology and that the moment communism had been established—through the expropriation of the means of production and the development of a classless society—the workers, not only in the Soviet Union but throughout the world, would abandon their nationalist attachments. With the

---

[8]For instance, in the 1930 Faisal, the king of Iraq wrote: "I say in my heart full of sadness that there is not yet an Iraq in the Iraqi people." In the 1950s, before the Algerian rebellion began, Ferhat Abbas, who became one of its leaders, proclaimed that he had looked in vain everywhere, including in the cemeteries, to find traces of Algerian nationality.

development of socialism in the USSR, it was expected that national particularisms would gradually wither away.

Stalin's remarks on nationalities in the Soviet Union are of special interest, especially since they embodied the official Soviet ideology until 1985 and have only been qualified but not quite abandoned yet. (For today's nationalities, see Table 10.1.) Speaking in 1921 to the Tenth Congress of the Communist party of the Soviet Union, he said:

> Whereas private property and capital inevitably disunite people, inflame national enmity and intensify national oppression, collective property and labour just as inevitably bring people closer and undermine national oppression. . . . The establishment of a Soviet system in Russia and the declaration of the right of nations to political secession have brought about a complete change in the relations between the toiling masses of the nationalities of Russia; they have undermined the old national enmity, deprived national oppression of its foundation, won for the Russian workers the confidence of their brothers of other nationalities, not only in Russia, but also in Europe and Asia, and have raised this confidence to a pitch of enthusiasm and readiness to fight for the common cause. The creation of Soviet republics in Azerbaijan and Armenia has been productive of similar results and has put an end to national collisions and the "age-old" enmity between the Turkish and Armenian toiling masses and between the Armenian

Table 10.1   MAJOR NATIONALITIES IN THE FORMER SOVIET UNION

	In thousands	Percentage
Russians	143,500	51.73
Ukrainians	43,500	15.68
Uzbeks	14,800	5.34
Byelorussians	9,760	3.52
Kazakhs	7,470	2.69
Tatars	6,600	2.38
Azerbaijanis	6,270	2.26
Armenians	4,580	1.65
Georgians	3,800	1.37
Tajiks	3,450	1.24
Moldavians	3,165	1.14
Lithuanians	2,985	1.08
Turkmenians	2,400	0.87
Kirghiz	2,240	0.81
Germans	2,000	0.72
Chuvash	1,790	0.65
Jews	1,750	0.63
Bashkirs	1,470	0.53
Latvians	1,445	0.52
Mordvinians	1,140	0.41
Poles	1,140	0.41
Estonians	1,030	0.37
Other peoples	11,115	4.00

Source: Peoples of the World: A Historical and Ethnographic Reference Book. Moscow: Nauka, 1988, p. 543.

and Azerbaijanian toiling masses. The same must be said of the temporary success of the Soviets in Hungary, Bavaria, Finland and Latvia. The consolidation of the Soviet republics and the abolition of national oppression are two aspects of one and the same process of emancipation of the toilers from imperialist bondage.[9]

In the same vein, Krushchev declared in 1959:

> With the victory of Communism on a world-wide scale, state borders will disappear, as Marxism-Leninism teaches. In all likelihood only ethnic borders will survive for a time and even these will probably exist only as a convention. Naturally these frontiers, if they can be called frontiers at all, will have no border guards, customs officials or incidents. . . .[10]

A Soviet policy on nationalities was based accordingly on the assumption that

1. Soviet socialism would gradually supersede nationalism and nationalities.
2. Soviet socialism would create a new fraternal union.
3. The various forms of national expression—language, culture, historic traditions, literature, religion, and so forth—would give way to the unifying trends of the new socialist culture.
4. The Communist party, the vanguard of the proletariat, would lead the way to the creation of the new fraternal union—and beyond, to internationalism.
5. Finally, the Communist party would gradually grind out nationalist predispositions and particularisms by weeding them out—by force, if necessary, just as we weed the beautiful garden we are growing.

Nationalist Movements in the Waning Years of the Soviet Union

Before its demise the Soviet Union sought to control four types of nationalities and nationalist movements. First, there were the nations of Eastern Europe dominated after 1945 by direct Soviet economic and military controls and through the Communist parties the Soviets had managed to impose—Poland, Czechoslovakia, Hungary, East Germany, Romania, and Bulgaria. All of these countries were established nation–states before World War II and have now managed to reclaim their national independence. Second, there were the Baltic republics annexed by the Soviets during World War II—the once-independent states, Estonia, Lithuania, and Latvia and also a part of Romania (Moldavia). Third, and most important, there were the "republics" *within* the Soviet Union. They had been a part of the Czarist Empire and of the Soviet Federal Union ever since 1920—the Ukraine, Georgia, Armenia, Byelorussia, Azerbaijan, and others—fifteen of them.

Finally, there were smaller ethnic and nationalist movements within the individual republics; they were what we call *ethnonationalisms*. They demanded

---

[9]Joseph Stalin, "Theses on the immediate Task of the Party in Connection with the National Problem," address delivered at the 10th Congress of the Communist Party of the Soviet Union in 1921.

[10]Quoted in Zbigniew K. Brzezinski, *The Soviet Bloc. Unity and Discord.* Rev. Ed., Harvard University Press, 1967, pp. 451–452.

autonomy, border changes, and, at times, even outright independence. For instance, the Crimean Tatars wished to move from Uzbekistan back to the fertile lands of the Crimea; the Armenians in Nagorno-Karabakh desired autonomy from Azerbaijan and hoped to join their brothers in the Armenian republic, which in turn wished to be independent; the Ossets in Georgia wanted to move into the Russian Republic; the Volga Tatars wished to form a new republic with the Bashkir Muslims.

Ethnic groups within the various Republics of the Soviet Union reasserted themselves. Some demanded autonomy from the Republics within which they were located; others sought to separate from the Republic in which they were situated and to join their ethnic brothers and sisters who lived in a different Republic—with ethnic identities being defined mostly in terms of religion, language, common traditions, and historical experiences. The move towards ethnic autonomy stretched across the vast Soviet land from Kaliningrad (the former German Konisberg) in the west, where the citizens wanted to create an autonomous political unit to be known as "people of Konisberg," all the way to Vadlivostok, where Ukrainian settlers wanted to establish an autonomous Ukrainian Republic in the southeastern corner of the country. In between there were the Poles in Byelorussia wanting their autonomy; Moldavians, near the Black Sea, pressing for union with Romania; and Crimean Tatars forced into Uzbekistan near Tashkent by Stalin who wished to return to the Crimean peninsula by the Black Sea. In Kazakhstan, there were more than one hundred ethnic groups in conflict with each other. But this gives only a sketchy account of the complexity, intensity and extent of ethnic conflicts. The Volga Tatars, the Mongols, the Uzbek Muslims, and ethnic Germans demanded autonomy while in Turkmenia the Persian speaking majority was at odds with the Turks each claiming the land of the other.

Despite Stalinist repression, during which, in the name of Marxism, nationalities saw their national heroes vilified, their national traditions shelved, their written scripts and printed books gone in the vaults of public libraries, their languages gradually cede ground to the Russian official language, and their deep-rooted religious feelings and practices scorned and outlawed, nationalities have remained defiant and alive. After 1985, with the coming of Gorbachev and *perestroika,* they reasserted themselves. With the fall of Gorbachev in 1991 nationalism triumphed everywhere in the former Soviet bloc—sometimes for better, too often for worse.

Nationalism Unchained

With the collapse of Soviet power and the Communist regimes, ethnonationalisms asserted themselves throughout Central and Southeastern Europe. Czechs against Slovaks, Ethnic Hungarians in Romania against Romania, ethnic Turks in Bulgaria, and so on. Ethnic strife everywhere may undermine many of the newly founded democratic regimes.

Without question Yugoslavia presents the worst case scenario. No sooner did Communism fall than what was once a nation degenerated into a series of warring nationalisms with the Serbs, in particular, practicing what amounts to genocide. The economically advanced Yugoslav republics of Slovenia and Croatia, encouraged by the secession of the Baltic republics from the USSR in 1990, decided to go their own way rather than find themselves paying the bills for the poorer republics. On June 25, 1991, Slovenia and Croatia declared their independence. In retaliation, economically weak but militarily mighty Serbia set out to squelch the defections by force. While Serbia was relatively restrained in its acts against Slovenia, the same cannot be said of the Serbian offensive against Croatia, where a sizeable Serbian minority cheered Belgrade's efforts to end the defection.

Serbia became especially violent when the republic of Bosnia-Herzegovina, mostly Muslim in compostion but with significant Serbian and Croatian minorities, declared its independence in April of 1992. Supported by Belgrade, the Bosnian Serbs proclaimed their independence from Bosnia and initiated a horrendous policy of "ethnic-cleansing" against the Muslim population. The Croatian minority sided at first with the Muslims, but when it became clear that the partitioning of Bosnia was inevitable, the Croats grabbed what land they could in those territories of northern Bosnia where they were in the majority. Under such circumstances the civil war spun completely out of control, each newscast featuring a report on the latest in a never-ending series of atrocities.

Of course, ethnonationalist movements are not confined to Eastern Europe and the former Soviet Union; we are witnessing their presence throughout the world. The Basques in Spain are on the move; in Quebec, which claims to be a "distinct society" within the Canadian federation, the Mohawk Indians assert their independence; and in Sri Lanka, the Tamils are waging war to preserve their autonomy while the Kurds face extinction.

In all parts of the world, ethnonationalist movements—some seeking autonomy, others agreeing to live within a loose federation, and still others seeking separation and sovereignty—are tearing apart some newly founded states. In Ethiopia, Sudan, Kashmir, Morocco, and India, ethnonational (often religious) minorities daily confront each other and the state within which they live. One should also be extremely alert to potential ethnonationalist movements by Muslim fundamentalists (Chapter 11) everywhere in North Africa, the Middle East, Indonesia, and possibly in some countries of the European community, where immigrant workers, many of them Muslims, amount to as much as 5 to 8 percent of the population. In the whole of the African Sub-Saharan continent, tribalisms that have many of the characteristics of ethnonationalisms are also on the rise.

Ethnonationalist movements are in the process of becoming the most virulent ideology today. They derive, by and large, from the same old ideology of nineteenth-century nationalism. The bottles are the same old bottles, but the wine appears at times headier. It is nurtured and ripened by the many discontents that our industrial society has spawned—impersonality, uncertainty about employment as technology requires a higher level of education among workers, a feeling of deprivation that rising expectations for economic growth and prosperity have heightened, ignorance and poverty. Like religious fundamentalism, with which many ethnonationalist movements are linked, they aim to provide a safe and secure home, a common center of loyalty and attachment, a feeling of togetherness in the reassertion of old values and traditions shared and cherished for so long. The call of ethnonationalism resembles the call for the revival of old neighborhoods that we heard about or dreamed of. It is part and parcel of a movement for small and manageable social units that we believe we can control, instead of the distant and impersonal forces that seem to rule our lives. Ethnonationalist emotions and attachments are so powerful that at the least sign of actual and perceived discrimination, the ethnonationalist temperature rises to the boiling point.

BLACK SEPARATISM IN THE UNITED STATES

Nothing displays more clearly the importance of ideology than the lack of African-American ethnonationalist separatism in the United States. A little more than 10 percent of the people in the United States are black. Brought to American until 1808 as slaves or born and raised in slave plantations until 1863, they were people without rights under the law, without property, deprived of skills and education. In some states, slaves were not allowed to learn to read or write. They were at the mercy of their white owners. The Civil War led to their emancipation and their political enfranchisement. But soon thereafter, discriminating practices developed. The blacks were for all practical purposes disenfranchised in the majority of states and remained without protection of the law, the right to vote, or the opportunity to learn the skills that would provide for a better life and income. They were excluded from the American liberal mainstream. Yet in contrast to most all other ethnic minorities in so many other parts of the world, the prevalent ideology among blacks in the United States has been to join, rather than to reject, the mainstream of American liberal values, to become part of it and to be integrated within it. Louis Hartz's *The Liberal Tradition in America* provides perhaps the best answer for the lack of black separatism. The overwhelming liberal ethos in America—stressing equality of opportunity and individual effort—could not be arbitrarily interpreted to exclude men and women because of their color. At the same time, it exercised an overwhelming attraction for blacks—it promised them the equality that they wanted and of which they were deprived.

There were many other reasons, however, for the lack of a black separatist movement. One reason was *the lack of education among blacks*. They were deprived of education for a long time, which made it difficult for them to gain a consciousness of their position and to translate it into a distinct and organized political movement. Second, they lacked a clearly identified territorial base—a territory in which they lived—distinguishing them from the Basques in France, the French in Quebec, the Croatians in Yugoslavia, or even the Scots and the Welsh in the United Kingdom and the Corsicans in France. To be sure, a preponderant percentage of blacks lived in the South, but after World War I, and even more so since World War II, the blacks who moved in search of employment to the urban centers of the North and the West began to outnumber those who remained in the South. The black population dispersed throughout the United States. Their predicament, economic or social, remains a national phenomenon; it is not associated with a given region, area, or state to which national resources have not been properly allocated, as it is with Soviet Georgia. The arguments of "internal colonialism" and "regional deprivation" could not be advanced in order to reinforce territorial separatist claims. Third, in contrast to most separatist movements, no common and different language existed for the blacks. They all spoke and wrote—when they were allowed to learn how—English. Finally, as the economy developed and the most overt forms of discrimination ended, blacks appeared less and less a homogeneous social force. They became increasingly differentiated on the basis of income, status, skills, and lifestyles. Some had fully entered the "mainstream" and became its supporters; to many, the mainstream continued to beckon. Even if most blacks remained out of the mainstream, the hope had been kindled that they too would "overcome," and become a part of it.

Without a clearly identified territorial base, without a commonly shared consciousness of their traditions and past, without a common and separate language, without a common social and economic identity or even a commonly shared sense of exploitation—which goes with "class"—the blacks, excluded and invisible to all others for so long, became increasingly visible to each other and to all as Americans.

Separatist Movements

The most spectacular phenomenon of American society remains the lack of black separatism and the lack of ideologies to promote it. There are only a few ideologies that can be mentioned. Black "nationalism" is associated with Marcus Garvey (1887–1940) and his movement, the Universal Negro Improvement Association, founded in 1914 in Jamaica and transferred to Harlem in 1920. Its platform advocated Negro nationhood, Negro race consciousness, inculcation of "ideals of manhood and womanhood" in every Negro, self-determination, and racial self-help and self-respect.

As stated in the platform, Africa was to be "territory" for the blacks in the same way that Israel was to be a home for the Jews, according to the Zionists. This meant that the liberation of Africa, virtually all of which was under colonial rule at the time, had to be undertaken. In the meantime, race consciousness would enhance the unity and cultural identity of all blacks—and Garvey was a segregationist. Racial self-help required the development of black capitalism and a black economy, and again Garvey was particularly instrumental in the building of black businesses and cooperatives. The founding of the African Orthodox Church just about completed all the elements of "nationality" to be imparted, namely economic autonomy, cultural autonomy, religious autonomy, and racial separateness. Self-determination would follow with a plea for the political independence of all blacks in Africa and of those who went to Africa and for the political independence of Africa from the colonial yoke.

It is interesting to note that at no time did Garvey assert or claim any territory of the United States as a "home" for the blacks. It was only in the years after World War I that a small group, under communist inspiration, asked for a "Negro republic" in the "Black Belt" of the South, a proposal that was not seriously considered by any of the black leaders. Instead, Garvey's dreams died with him, and until almost 1965 black activism focused instead on ending all discriminatory practices and attaining integration in education, jobs, law and political representation, and social life. This theme was strengthened by the massive move of blacks from the South to the booming industrial centers in the North, the Midwest, and the West, and also by some critical decisions of the Supreme Court in favor of integration. It was also strengthened by the assertion of the blacks themselves in favor of integration under the leadership of Martin Luther King, Jr., and others and in cooperation with liberal groups among the whites and a number of white political leaders—

Martin Luther King, Jr. (1929–1968)

Martin Luther King, Jr. was without a doubt one of the most prominent American political figures of the twentieth century—though he never held public office. Deeply influenced by Gandhi and his philosophy of "passive resistance," King was well versed in religion and philosophy before turning to social and racial relations and becoming the leader of the "nonviolent revolution" which swept the country in the fifties and sixties. Through preaching, demonstrations, and marches and the organization of the Southern Christian Leadership Conference, he mobilized blacks and whites and became the most inspired moral voice on civil rights. Rejecting the demands for "black power" and "black separatism," which other black leaders advanced, King argued for the full entitlement of blacks in American society. And progress was made: First, in 1964, with the Civil Rights Act, which abolished segregation in all public places, and then in 1965, with the Voting Rights Act, which abolished all discriminatory voting practices that had been widely followed in the south and elsewhere. King's "dream" was that of a society of equals in which the distinctions of color would be done away with. He was assassinated on April 4, 1968.

notably John F. Kennedy and Lyndon B. Johnson. Boycotts, marches, and demonstrations gradually brought down segregation.

Malcolm X

Yet it was at this juncture that a strong black nationalist movement emerged in the late 1960s first under Malcolm X (1925–1965) and the black Muslims and the Organization of Afro-American Unity, and later under the Black Panthers, among other groups, including white radical organizations like the Students for Democratic Society. Malcolm X gradually began to view the situation of the American blacks in the broader contexts of American capitalism. It was American exploitive capitalism, he argued, that accounted for their inferior status, and it was the destruction of capitalism that would liberate the blacks. It was not, therefore, a matter of appealing to black nationalism. Nationalism in itself could become, Malcolm X argued, a reactionary force and, even after emancipation, could keep black people under subjection. Black nationalism should become simply a component in the struggle against class oppression and exploitation everywhere in the world. Only a *revolutionary* nationalist movement could attain this. Only a movement such as socialism, which promised profound and radical change in the structure of the economy and the society, could liberate the blacks and the downtrodden.

The Black Panthers

The Black Panthers moved a step closer to this revolutionary position. Inspired in part by the revolution in Algeria against the French, the victory of Castro in Cuba, and the independence of almost all colonies in Africa during the 1960s, they saw the situation of the blacks as a phenomenon of "internal colonialism" and hence saw the redemption of the blacks only in terms of a revolutionary struggle against colonial masters in the United States and everywhere. The Black Panthers asked for "independence" at home; they set up their own cabinet with various ministers and organized paramilitary groups for self-defense. But they viewed the success of their movement in the context of a worldwide revolutionary struggle in which nation–states would give place to ethnic and cultural groupings cooperating with each other in a socialist world. This is what was meant by *intercommunalism*. No other specifics were given and no demands were made for any form of black autonomy or "territorial" autonomy within the United States. If the class structure in America was altered and if capitalism were superseded by a socialist commonwealth, only then would the position of blacks become safe and their lot equal with those of whites. Black nationalism was viewed as almost identical with the colonial emancipation movements. Its vision, however, remained far more difficult to realize for lack of a territorial base or "home." For Garvey it was Africa; for the Panthers, the world—a socialist world.

Garvey, Malcolm X, the Black Panthers, and other small black organizations that advocated positions ranging from separateness and autonomy to revolutionary struggle and socialism, never captured the following of even a minority of the blacks in the United States. In the last thirty years only a handful attempted to reject completely their "Americanism," stressing their roots and their past with

Malcolm X

Malcolm X was the preeminent figure among African Americans who rejected the goal of integration. Born Malcolm Little, he replaced his "slave name" with an X, a symbol of his unknown African ancestry. Malcolm argued that blacks had no need to prove themselves to whites who had kept them subservient throughout American history, and should not seek participation within a society fundamentally based on racism.

Malcolm X believed that Islam is the historical and appropriate religion for African Americans, and that Christianity is a religion borrowed from whites. He became a charismatic spokesman for Elijah Muhammed and his Black Muslim movement, but split away after a pilgrimage to Mecca convinced him that the movement shared many racist and materialistic traits with Christianity. After this split, Malcolm X founded the Muslim Mosque and the Organization of Afro-American Unity.

John Henrik Clark, (*Malcolm X: The Man and His Times.* Toronto: MacMillan Co., 1969) writes that Malcolm X expressed "black pride, black redemption, black reaffirmation." He was assassinated in 1965.

Africa or Islam. Some have reached out to their black-Hispanic origins, stressing their ties with Cuba and the Caribbean; some converted to Islam; some even tried to familiarize themselves with African dialects. Only tiny minorities began to seek identities outside of the American world to which their ancestors had been forcefully transplanted and which was the only world they had known.

In 1984 and again in 1988, the political symbol and leader of the blacks became Jesse Jackson, who ran for the presidential nomination of the Democratic party within the "system." Throughout his candidacy, Jackson asked for the support of all people (even if particular emphasis was put on the so-called Rainbow Coalition of blacks, women, Hispanics, and other minority groups) and sought equal representation in the electoral process and within the Democratic party for all minorities and blacks. He also reached out to solicit the support of whites. Jackson identified the blacks in political terms—as a political force that could be organized within the context of democracy and had to be counted, just as other ethnic groups and movements were, including labor, in the past. In this sense, he remained solidly in the tradition of Martin Luther King—the tradition favoring the full integration of the blacks as citizens within the United States on the basis of equality of opportunities for all and equal treatment to all. Today the only true separatist movement is represented by a religious leader, Reverend Farrakahn, but he has a very small number of followers.

But the American myth—the American ideology of equality and individual freedom—cannot be sustained unless they are both realized. Freedom—political and individual freedoms—may have been attained and with them go immense opportunities for all. But if adequate material means and services are lacking, those deprived over a long period of time will reject the validity of the myth. The message of Malcolm X continues to blur the vision of Martin Luther King.

There is every indication that poverty afflicts African-Americans' far more severely than any other group of the population. Over 30 percent of blacks live below the line of poverty (with an income of about $13,000 a year for a family of four) as compared to 10 percent of the whites. At least 40 percent of all black children live in families (usually headed by women) that are below the poverty line. Unemployment among blacks runs twice as high as for whites. Despite affirmative action and massive welfare spending, education and training and the opportunities for employment have not improved among blacks ever since the vision of the Great Society was outlined by Lyndon Johnson in the early sixties, despite the notable successes of blacks in securing elective office. Even more ominous is the return of what amounts to a *de facto* segregation: the whites live in the suburbs and their children are educated in virtually all-white schools; the blacks live in the inner city where schools are inadequate, poverty rampant, and crime and drugs a daily fare. The two communities—black and white—are drifting apart—culturally, educationally, economically, and in terms of lifestyles and expectations. Neither the army, nor the political leadership, nor sports or the churches provide adequate linkages between blacks and whites. The ghetto, many claim, is becoming a national phenomenon, dividing the American society in two.

Advocacy of black separatism, many point out, would be a prescription that is worse than the disease: it will divide the society even more and affect all of us adversely. But ideological fervor and protest, we have pointed out in this book, do not always stem from a rational calculation of benefits and losses. They often spring from powerful emotional impulses that human degradation produces. Black rejection and separatism may yet challenge the complacency of the American liberal myth.

BEYOND NATIONALISM—INTERNATIONALISM?

Are the nationalist and ethnonationalist impulses we surveyed unavoidable and inevitable? Is the ideology of nationalism to remain so powerful and pervasive as to splinter our political world to a myriad of exclusive and conflicting units? For unless we find a way to reconcile the needs of nationalisms and the imperative of political unity and order, nationalist and ethnonationalist ideologies may lead to what Thomas Hobbes called "a war of all against all." Is there a new ideology emerging to counter and accommodate nationalisms—big and small? This is the question we address in this second part of the chapter.

Cosmopolitanism

Cosmopolitanism as an ideology is the exact opposite of nationalism. According to it we are all citizens of the world. Literally, "cosmopolis" means a world–city or a world–state—from *cosmos* (the world) and *polis* (a city). Cosmopolitanism is based on an ideology of universal values deriving from our human nature, but does not exclude separate nationalities or even nations. They can exist side by side under fixed and common standards and rules that apply to all individuals and nations to guide their relations on the basis of equality. A common law, for example, an international law that is binding upon all, or a common political authority, or an international organization something like a United Nations, provides for order and the swift settlement of disputes and the protection of the rights of all, irrespective of individual, racial, cultural, or national differences. Cosmopolitanism allows for many cultures and many nationalities to live side by side, but in the last and ultimate sense there is but one law, one polis, one state.

The Stoics   The first genuine movement toward cosmopolitanism was a reaction against the Greek city–states (the small sovereign states into which ancient Greece was divided, just as our own world today is divided into nations). It came during the second and third centuries before Christ and was expressed by the Stoic philosophers. They preached simple human virtues, argued in favor of equality for all, and insisted that there were common and universal principles for all people that derived from human nature. They were against the artificial distinctions and exclusive loyalties the city–states had created. Their belief was that, since all people are part of a divine will or God (*Logos*), they are all alike and should be treated as brothers and sisters. They called for the city–state to give way to the imperative of equality and brotherhood. It was a universalistic ethic.

The Stoic philosophy was followed by Christianity. It, too, was based on the broadest universalistic assumptions; it preached equality and brotherhood and focused on the spiritual quality of life that would bind people together and give only minimal powers to the state. The world would be one for all—Greeks and barbarians, Phoenicians and Romans, Corinthians and Carthegenians. All the faithful constituted one community—universal and peaceful. The Vicar of Christ (later the Pope) would be the spiritual leader.

The Roman Empire

Yet it was not Christianity nor the Papacy, but the Roman Empire (31 B.C.–476 A.D.), that became the first and truly cosmopolitan arrangement that we know. The Roman Empire included virtually all the peoples and "nationalities" of Europe and parts of Africa and the Middle East; it established common measures, standards, and currency; it abolished all boundaries; and it developed an efficient communication system and a centralized administration that gave protection to all. Above all, it established a system of law for all and the proper judicial organization to administer it.

While the Roman armies and administration maintained the integrity of the empire, it was the Roman law that united the various peoples within it. During the early days of the empire, Roman civil law applied exclusively to Roman citizens and to any conflicts arising among them. Gradually, however, a new kind of law emerged that applied to disputes among all individuals—Roman and non-Roman alike. Similar to the common law that developed much later in England, Roman law was developed by special judges, case by case, first throughout all the provinces in Italy and later throughout the entire Roman Empire. It became known as the *ius gentium*—something like international law. It was simple, avoided formal procedures, allowed for rules of equity, treated all equally, and constantly adjusted itself to the changing nature of economic and social relations. All citizens of the empire—Scythians and Egyptians and Greeks and Romans—had access to it. Gradually, as the *ius gentium* evolved and developed general rules and principles, many began to confuse it with "natural law," a law consonant with human nature and therefore valid for all. It was a universal law—truly cosmopolitan.

What made the Roman Empire the first truly universal political organization, however, was citizenship. Citizenship in Rome was originally granted only to those born of Romans. But gradually many people began to be assimilated even though they were not "Romans." In 212 A.D., a famous edict was issued by Emperor Caracalla proclaiming all those living within the empire and, of course, the children to be born, to be Roman citizens. Thus every person became a citizen of the then known world, recognizing (or submitting to) one authority, with access to a common law and a common judge, free to move from one place to another, and assured of equal protection. This was the farthest ever that the institutionalization of cosmopolitanism ever went! The Roman Empire was not a "nation"; it had no "spiritual" entity and no "soul"; it had no common language and no common culture or "race." It was an administrative, judicial, and military organization that included many ethnic and religious groups. It did not impose uniform values, except when some emperors tried to outlaw or to impose Christianity. It was, as we would say today, a multiethnic, multiracial, multireligious, multilingual system in which all peoples could work, trade, and live. It provided for order and peace.

There were some other manifestations of cosmopolitanism after the fall of the Roman Empire. One was the Papacy—the spiritual head of the universal community of believers representing Christendom. The "Holy Roman Empire" represented the legacy of the Roman Empire and remained more of an assertion than a reality. After the fifteenth century, the Papacy was unable to impose its spiritual rule over the faithful. Schisms developed and national churches appeared with king rather than pope as their head. The king became "Pope and Emperor in his own kingdom" defying all the universalistic claims of the church. All aspirations to keep the Holy Roman Empire began to fade and they eventually died with the end of the seventeenth century.

Liberalism, Marxism, and Cosmopolitanism

Both liberalism and Marxism are internationalist and cosmopolitan ideologies. This is implicit in liberalism and quite explicit, as we saw, in Marxism. In fact, liberalism represents the essence of individualism—of men and women preoccupied and devoted to the satisfaction of their wants and pleasures, of a government that governs the least, of freedom of trade and movement. Nation–states, both large and small, should not interfere in economic life; should not engage upon destructive wars; should not try to impose heavy tariffs that would disrupt the free flow of goods and undermine a division of labor that would spread gradually throughout the world. Order, security, and peace were the conditions for economic prosperity, and governments in nation–states were to be responsible for little more maintaining them. Thus the middle classes would gain ascendancy and create a vast commercial brotherhood among nations in which individual and economic freedoms would keep governments limited and under control.

When applied to the international community, liberalism remained individualistic. It rejected mass appeals, mass movements, and unifying communitarian themes. It portrayed nations and the international community in terms of myriads of individuals interacting with each other; a society of "economic" men and women attached to professions, jobs, wealth, and profit recognizing no superior moral or political authority other than their own conscience and their own interests. Wherever they could set up a business and make profit was their fatherland, Rousseau hinted scornfully. In addition to economic individualism and commitment to profit, early liberals also shared what we described earlier as a "common moral core," which had cosmopolitan and universalistic aspirations. All men and women were free; all of them were endowed with rights; all of them should be secure in their person and property; all of them should be free to speak, think, and worship as they pleased; and ultimately all of them should be free to participate in forming a government and controlling its conduct. Human nature in this sense was not determined by national characteristics—it transcended them. Irrespective of their nationality and despite differences in language and habit, human beings had more in common with each other than their apparent national differences would indicate. It was not *human* for a German to be only a German or for a Frenchman to be only French. Their humanity was stronger than their nationalities. A stranger was a fellow human being. It followed that the spread of liberalism would reinforce the spirit of cosmopolitanism and internationalism and bring the civilized peoples of the nations of the world closer together.

Marxism, like liberalism and curiously enough for almost identical reasons, aspired to a cosmopolitan order. The working class was to be the genuine and liberating force that would overcome the prejudices and emotions of bourgeoisie nationalisms. The workers from Budapest, Paris, Berlin, and London would join hands in asserting common interests and universal human values. It did not come to pass!

With the demise of Marxism as an ideology almost everywhere, is it possible that the renewed emphasis on democracy and liberalism will provide a new cosmopolitan ideology? Economic interdependence and free trade, for instance, require an international order to safeguard them from nationalist movements. There is no ideology as yet to sustain interdependence, globalism, and an international order. There are no widely accepted international institutions and organizations to implement such an ideology. Heartfelt worldwide needs to protect the environment, regulate world resources, avert wars, and protect human rights may gradually bring them about. But if a liberal international order is in sight, we are only dimly aware of it.

INTERNATIONALISM AND INTERNATIONALIST ARRANGEMENTS

Ever since the ancient Greeks tried to group their small city–states into a confederation, innumerable efforts have been made by states and nations to establish regional arrangements. The most spectacular effort to date has been the European Common Market, established in 1956 by the Treaty of Rome to include initially the Benelux countries (Belgium, the Netherlands, and Luxembourg), France, the German Federal Republic, and Italy. In 1972, England, Denmark, and Ireland became members and were joined by Greece, Spain, and Portugal in the 1980s. Committed first to economic unity and economic integration, its ultimate goal was to bring about "political union." Similar efforts have been made (and often unmade) by Arab states, sometimes in the name of Islam or pan-Arabism, and among the Latin American and African states with the Organization of American States and the Organization of African Unity, respectively.

Regionalism

We think of a region as a given geographic area comprising a number of states where common beliefs and practices exist and within which various forms of communication—both economic and personal—are strong. We assume and expect that within a given region, defined in this manner, regional values and attachments will promote cooperation and inhibit conflicts among individual nation–states. In fact, we tend to assume that regional values and regional institutional arrangements may supersede national entities to lead ultimately to regional institutions and regional loyalties. This has not come about. If we limit ourselves to the period since World War II, individual nation–states have mushroomed while all efforts to build regional organizations, institutions, and genuine regional loyalties and ideologies have failed. No regional ideology has developed to supplant nationalisms. Neither liberalism nor Marxism has produced one. We talk about "French" liberalism or "British" liberalism and, until recently, about "Chinese Marxism" as opposed to the "Soviet" or the "Yugoslav" one. In the European Common Market that brought together nations with strong affinities, few of the citizens of the member states put the regional organization they have established above their nation–states. First and foremost are their loyalties to their own countries. There have been some efforts spearheaded by intellectuals—"Europeanists" and "Federalists"—to promote a supranational idea and doctrine, but they are only a handful and have been unsuccessful thus far. Even Islamic religious leaders have failed as yet to bring any semblance of unity to the "Arab nation."

CONCLUSION

No matter where we turn, we continue to be faced by the same stubborn reality—nationalisms, nations, and nation-states. A noted English author writing several decades ago (when World War II had come to an end and with it, many had thought, the dawn of a new era of internationalism) pinpointed all the defects of nationalism. "What has to be challenged and rejected," he wrote, "is the claim of nationalism to make the nation the sole rightful repository of political power and the ultimate constituent unit of world organization."[11] The claim has not been rejected yet!

Large or small, nationalism continues to shape the minds and the attachments of all of us—whether it is about Panama for the United States; New Caledonia for the French; the Palestinians in the search for a homeland; the Irish in their efforts to dislodge the British from Northern Ireland; the Czechs, the Slovaks, the Slovenes, the Croatians, the Armenians, and all the other nationalities in their efforts to establish a sovereignty. It provided a moment of exaltation to the Argentines when in 1982 they sent their navy and army into the Falkland Islands, miscalculating the immediate and profound nationalist response on the part of the British. A bitter war went on for three months over these remote and inhospitable islands in which both British and Argentines became emotionally involved. Nothing could show more aptly how seductive the old-time religion of nationalism remains. Like Rupert Brooke, a young British poet buried on a small Greek Island after dying in combat in World War I, many of the British soldiers buried in the Falklands will continue to whisper to the generations to come the same gospel that Shakespeare put in Richard II's famous lines:

> Think only this of me:
> That there is a corner of a foreign field
> That is forever England . . .
> A dust whom England bore, shaped, made aware.

If nationalism is, as it has been alleged, "the last refuge of scoundrels," most of us continue to remain scoundrels in our hearts and minds!

BIBLIOGRAPHY

Alter, Peter. *Nationalism.* New York: Routledge, 1989.

Bracey, John H., et al., eds. *Black Nationalism in America,* Indianapolis, 1970.

Bruilly, John. *Nationalism and the State.* Chicago: University of Chicago Press, 1985.

Carr, Edward Hallet. *Nationalism and After.* London: Macmillan, 1945.

Deutsch, Karl W. *Nationalism and Its Alternatives.* New York: Knopf, 1969.

———. *Nationalism and Social Communication,* 3rd ed. Cambridge, MA: The MIT Press, 1981.

——— et al. *Political Community in the North Atlantic Area.* Princeton, NJ: Princeton University Press, 1957.

Forsyth, Murray (ed.). *Federalism and Nationalism.* New York: St. Martin's Press, 1989.

Franklin, John H., and Alfred Moss, Jr. *From Slavery to Freedom,* 6th ed. New York: Alfred Knopf, 1988.

---

[11]Carr, Edward Hallet. *Nationalism and After.*

Gellner, Ernest. *Nations and Nationalism*. Cambridge, MA.: Basil Blackwell, 1987.

Gerassi, John. *The Coming the New International*. New York: World Publishing, 1971.

Grimes, Alan P., and Robert H. Horowitz. *Modern Political Ideologies*. New York: Oxford University Press, 1959.

Hayes, Carlton T.H. *Essays on Nationalism*. London: Macmillan, 1937.

Hinsley, F.H. *Nationalism and the International System*. London: Hodder and Stoughton, 1973.

Hobson, John A. *Imperialism*. Ann Arbor: University of Michigan Press, 1965.

Horowitz, Donald L. *Ethnic Groups in Conflict*. Berkeley: University of California Press, 1985.

Kedourie, Elie. *Nationalism*, rev. ed. London: Hutchinson, 1961.

Keohane, R.O., and Joseph Nye. *Transnational Politics*. Cambridge, MA: Harvard University Press, 1972.

King, Martin Luther, Jr. *Stride Toward Freedom: The Montgomery Story*. New York, 1962.

———. *Why We Can't Wait*. New York, 1964.

Kohn, Hans. *Nationalism: Its Meaning and History*, rev. ed. New York: Van Nostrand, 1965.

———. *The Idea of Nationalism*. New York: Collier, 1967.

Malcolm X. *Autobiography of Malcolm X*. New York: Ballantine, 1965.

Mayall, James. *Nationalism and International Society*. New York: Cambridge University Press, 1990.

McNeil, W.H. *The Rise of the West*. Chicago: University of Chicago Press, 1963.

Meinecke, Friedrich. *Cosmopolitanism and the National State*. Princeton, NJ: Princeton University Press, 1970.

Ronen, D. *The Quest for Self-Determination*. New Haven, CT.: Yale University Press, 1979.

Rothschild, Joseph. *Ethnopolitics—A Conceptual Framework*. New York: Columbia University Press, 1981.

Seton-Watson, Hugh. *Nations and States*. Boulder, CO: Westview Press, 1977.

Smith, Anthony. *Theories of Nationalism*. London: Duckworth, 1971.

———. *Nationalism in the Twentieth Century*. New York: New York University Press, 1979.

———. *The Ethnic Origins of Nations*. Cambridge, MA: Basil Blackwell, 1988.

Snyder, Louis L. *Global Mini Nationalism: Autonomy and Independence*. Westport, CT: Greenwood Press, 1982.

Stalin, Joseph. *Marxism and the National Question*. Moscow: International Publishers, 1934.

Tilly, Charles (ed.). *The Formation of the National States in Western Europe*. Princeton, NJ: Princeton University Press, 1975.

Walker, Connor. *The National Question in Marxist Leninist Theory and Strategies*. Princeton, NJ: Princeton University Press, 1984.

Waltz, Kenneth. *Man, the State and War: A Theoretical Analysis*. New York: Columbia University Press, 1954.

Watson, Michael. *Contemporary Minority Nationalism*. New York: Routledge, 1990.

Chapter
11

The Religious Impulse

Liberation Theology and Religious Fundamentalism

Render to Caesar the things that are Caesar's and to God the things that are God's.

St. Mark 12:17

Most all great religions ordain our temporal lives in terms of transcendental values. When we think of religion, we think of contemplation, inwardness, and a preparation for the life hereafter. "My kingdom is not of this world," Jesus Christ proclaimed. The kingdom of God is separate and very different from earthly kingdoms. The "church" does not pretend to assume or exercise temporal powers. The "secular sword"—politics—is in the hands of kings, monarchs, peoples, and governments. The "spiritual sword" is less visible. It is addressed to matters of sin and salvation and binds the faithful in an intricate web of faith, ritual, and sacraments. Within the civil society, it is the mission of the church to "evangelize"—to spread the "good tidings" and to convert pagans, agnostics, and "heretics." The mission of all religious orders has been to save us *from* the world in which we find ourselves temporarily.

Again, all great religions have developed a set of principles derived from revered sources in terms of which the faithful must behave. Whether it is the Bible or the Koran or the Torah—it is always the "Book" that spells out divine guidance. Churches, synagogues, mosques, and shrines where the faithful congregate to worship become the centers of religious activity; they set the standards of religious behavior and often can impose sanctions that, even when not supported directly by the law, are just as painful as legal sanctions: to be deprived of Holy Communion may be far more painful for a devout Catholic than a jail sentence.

Despite their transcendental emphasis, religions, all religions, therefore, directly influence behavior. They influence our perceptions about civil obligations, about our relationships with each other, about our family lives, and about the education of our children. Religion has spurred protest, revolution, even the assassi-

223

nation of a "bad king"—a tyrant—or, as the occasion called, counselled submission and obedience. No matter where, we find religious beliefs to make up a good part of the political fabric we wear—of our political attitudes. Whether a "superstructure" or not, to use the Marxist vocabulary, religion is a far more potent source of ideology and morality than class or state. And it is with religion as an ideology that we are concerned in this chapter, and only with reference to two most important and relevant political manifestations: liberation theology and religious fundamentalism, particularly Islamic fundamentalism and the fundamentalist movement in the United States—the Evangelicals.[1]

In our discussion we do not attempt any theological analysis or evaluation. We treat the religious origins only as ingredients that shape political ideology. Our question is always the same: How does the religious ingredient influence politics?

LIBERATION THEOLOGY

Liberation theology, as it has developed in the last thirty years, is a call for action, headed by bishops, many clergy, and laypersons, especially in the Catholic church, addressed to all but especially to the poor and the downtrodden of the Third World in order to redress, in the name of Christ, the social wrongs inflicted upon them— abject poverty, illiteracy, exploitation, and powerlessness. Liberation theology has spawned new forms of religious organizations that question the hierarchical organization of the church—especially the Catholic church. It has gained roots among populations where poverty has been endemic, where illiteracy is widespread, and where the law provides no security or protection. It claims to be a new religious movement addressed and applicable to the underdeveloped societies of the world, and it has been particularly in evidence in Latin America—in Colombia, Brazil, Peru, Nicaragua, Chile, El Salvador, and Guatemala. Though many of its leaders received training in European religious institutes, it is a truly indigenous intellectual and ideological movement addressed by native theologians and intellectuals to the social ills plaguing the Third World. Its major inspiration, however, came from the Second Vatican Council (1962–1965) and from a number of papal encyclicals that called upon the church and Catholics to spearhead social and political action.

Background

Ever since World War II, churchgoers, Catholic or not, began to experience a growing sense of dismay and indignation at the poverty, misery, and helplessness of the mass of people in many of the underdeveloped areas of the world. In most Latin American countries, daily income, social assistance, educational facilities, and health services are dismally low or nonexistent. Redress is impossible among the societies still ruled by dictators and military regimes—characteristics of underdevelopment, that often shield the ruling class. From a political standpoint, the

---

[1]It should be noted that not all Evangelicals are fundamentalists, as we point out later.

Gustavo Gutierrez

Gustavo Gutierrez was born in Lima, Peru, in 1928. He began his higher education at the National University in Lima, studying medicine. During the time that he attended the National University, Gutierrez was active in a number of political groups. After five years Gutierrez discontinued his medical studies and enrolled in a course in philosophical and theological studies and sought to enter the priesthood. These studies began in Chile but soon Gutierrez traveled to Europe, where between 1951 and 1955 he studied at the University of Louvain. He is a professor of theology at the Catholic University in Lima, Peru, and a national advisor for the National Union of Catholic students.

Gutierrez's *A Theology of Liberation* is considered by many scholars to be the definitive statement on the theology of liberation. Gutierrez's emphasis is on the theoretical rather than on the ideological movement associated with liberation theology itself. Gutierrez traces the origins of theological reflection since the early days of Christianity to a new and evolving orientation which stresses social *praxis,* a commitment to critical reflection, and a renewed commitment on the part of the church to the disenfranchised, the poor, and the destitute.

---

poor are powerless. They are unable to organize and articulate their demands, unable to participate in any decision, constantly at the mercy of a minority that abuses its power instead of promoting a degree of sharing that would raise the level of consciousness and participation of the masses. How does a society raise the people from their poverty and ignorance and give them a place consistent with their humanity?

One answer has been economic modernization, and many regimes, including military ones, have espoused it. But modernization in Latin America has involved an imitation of Western methods: a growth of investment (by borrowing from abroad) and a reliance upon free enterprise and the market. It has been advocated by intellectuals and economists and by some theologians, too. It was to be a modernization decreed from above, consistent with the social, political, and economic structures that prevailed; it was to be gradual and incremental.

This type of modernization as an answer to problems of poverty was disavowed by others. The reasons given were briefly the following: the Latin American economic structures were so closely tied to the world economy, or rather the U.S.

Leonardo Boff

 Leonardo Boff was born in the town of Concordia, Brazil, in 1938. He pursued his studies in Brazil (Petropolis, Curitiba) and Europe (Ludwig-Maximilian Universitat in Munich, Wurzburg, Louvain, and Oxford). He is a Franciscan. Boff has been a professor for over a decade at the Petropolis Institute for Theology and Philosophy, where he teaches courses in systematic theology. He has written a number of books and numerous articles on theology and liberation. He is perhaps best known for his summons to Rome in September 1984 to explain his views on liberation theology before the pope and the Congregation for the Doctrine of the Faith, headed by Joseph Cardinal Ratzinger. One of his more recent books, *The Church: Charisma and Power,* was formally criticized in March 1985 by the Congregation.

economy, that they were in a state of "dependency." They could not develop the autonomy and freedoms and the means to modernize in order to serve their own needs and purposes. They were but an adjunct of American capitalism. There was no way to break the cycle of dependency except by undertaking major structural reforms of the economy and the society, some in the direction of socialism.

The church doctrine especially in the Catholic Church began to change accordingly. The pope himself had pointedly referred to the uneven distribution of goods among nations, and in a number of his pronouncements had sharply criticized both the abuse of power and the abuse of wealth and property; he had expressed his particular concerns for the poor. On three occasions—at Medellin in 1969, in the *Letter Addressed to the People of the Third World* (1976), and in the Council of Latin American Bishops at Puebla in 1979—the contours of a liberation theology were outlined. They were fleshed out by many theologians—many from the Third World.

THE PHILOSOPHY OF LIBERATION THEOLOGY

A new body of thought developed before and ever since Vatican II that raises fundamental questions on the historical role both of Christ and the church and even more searching questions about the role and position of the church in society. Let us try to outline the philosophic assumptions of the theory of liberation theology and then discuss it as a political movement.

The Theory

Traditionally, the church viewed history as a temporary stage in our lives as compared to eternal life. The objective historical circumstances were not a matter of concern to the church when viewed with reference to the splendor of life hereafter. Orthodoxy, the maintenance of the true faith regardless of historical circumstances, was the church's central concern. In contrast, liberation theologians consider the church to be a vital agency of history, molding historical conditions and reflecting on these historical conditions. The gospel itself, and especially the role of Christ, is viewed as a historical basis for reform and change. Liberation theology therefore places its major emphasis on action—on the correct praxis or orthopraxis (*ortho* meaning correct and *praxis* meaning action) as opposed to orthodoxy (*ortho* meaning correct and *doxia* meaning belief). Indeed, the true faith can be found only in the proper action in line with Christ's life and teachings. Praxis—*action*—therefore becomes the essence of faith.

Critical Reflection   Not only does the concept of orthopraxis signal the significance of service and action, but it also requires that theology become a form of critical reflection, not just in a doctrinal sense but with regard to economic, political, and social issues. If praxis is to be advocated, guidance must be provided as to when and how to act. Critical reflection, derived from secular theories and the reading of the "signs of the times," serves to guide praxis. Present realities are confronted, and through the proper reflection, the seeds of future praxis are implanted. Praxis situates the church within historical realities and demands of it specific commitments and service. This means that the theologian should become engaged where domination and oppression run rampant, and where the poor clamor for their own salvation here on earth. But what is the truth behind the needed action—behind the correct ("ortho") action?

In analyzing society, liberation theologians use new tools to evaluate the present social, political, and economic realities. The analytical tools that help in critical reflection are derived from the social sciences: sociology, economics, politics, anthropology, and the behavioral sciences. Many also moved in the direction of Marxism.

The Marxist Option

The urgent task before Christians is to change society in order to improve the lot of the poor—indeed in order to eradicate poverty. But poverty arises because of faulty societal and economic structures, both national and international. Poverty can be alleviated by radical economic reforms in the direction of socialism. As liberation theologians put it, the preferential option for the poor is a socialist option.

The socialist option stems from an *analysis* of the society that—and here is the major source of controversy—borrows from Marxism. As we have seen, Marxism assumes the confrontation of two classes: those who own the means of production and those who do not—the workers for Marx, or the "poor" for the liberation theologians. In the same manner in which Marx assumed the workers would gain consciousness of their predicament and would rise to replace the property holders and socialize the means of production, the liberation theologians want to impart a reformist and even revolutionary consciousness to the poor to undertake the same task. The poor must improve their position by their own action and their own organization as the level of their awareness and consciousness improves. Self-reliance, community action, and spontaneous movements for reform and rectification of social evils are the means available to the poor, for the poor, and by the poor. In the process, local, community, regional, or national movements of the poor in their respective societies must keep their distance from international capitalism, which is blamed for the dependency of so many Third World countries and the concomitant subjugation of the poor to a local capitalist or bourgeois class. Liberation movements have to confront both their local oppressors and the international capitalist forces. When it comes to Latin America, this means "Yankee Imperialism."

In the eyes of liberation theologians, then, the church assumes the task of leading a revolutionary movement by one class, the poor, against the local and international forces of capitalism that account for their plight. It becomes, in the name of an inevitable class struggle, an agency of revolution and reform to bring about socialism and social justice. According to Gutierrez, class struggle is an "objective reality" and "the liberation" of the poor is "not an act of generosity or charity or Christian brotherhood"—though it may include them. It is, in his words, "a demand for the construction of a new social order."[2] Class struggle pitting the poor against the capitalist class appears to be inevitable and perhaps desirable if the poor are to regain their position as human beings by their own efforts. In this sense, commitment on the part of the clergy for the poor and their liberation appears to be, even in the name of class struggle, the epitome of religious commitment.

In choosing to associate its theology with secular theories, which explicitly or implicitly adopted Marxist analysis and terminology, Latin American liberation theology became associated, at least in the eyes of Western observers and some Vatican officials, with Marxism. In fact, the terms used (i.e., class struggle, alienation, dialectic, imperialism, proletariat, and so on) were directly borrowed from the Marxist vocabulary.

Collective Sin

Liberation theologians, particularly Leonardo Boff, went so far as to suggest the notion of institutionalized violence and sin. This notion derives from and is embedded in the social structure; it relates directly to groups and classes; it says that the owners of the means of production or wealth (the landowners, for instance) who oppose and exploit the poor are—by virtue of belonging to the same group or class—all sinners; they collectively represent a regime bent upon violence, which is sinful.

According to this notion, the redemption of the poor and the exploited lies in their collective struggle against the class that commits the sin. Violence must be

---

[2]Gustavo Gutierrez, *The Power of the Poor in History,* especially ch. 6.

met by counterviolence—by revolution. That is the only way to achieve liberation. This analysis comes close to the Marxist theory of class struggle and the ultimate liberation of the proletariat by revolution. The Marxist categories are used, even if couched in terms of theology. The individual is viewed with regard to his or her position in a given group rather than by his or her own volition, his or her own acts, and his or her own morality and reason. "When Christians take cognizance of the link between the personal and structural levels," writes Boff, "they can no longer rest content with conversions of the heart and personal holiness at the individual level. They realize that if they are to be graced personally, they must also fight to change the societal structure and open it up to God's grace."[3] Injustice is embedded in a given structure that must be changed or destroyed, if necessary. God's grace should extend beyond the individual to the structures—to groups, to classes, to political regimes. The church, therefore, has an obligation to act here in our world to change the socioeconomic structures that account for injustice.

The Voice of the Poor and Political Action (Praxis)

In Latin America, and in the Third World in general, the poor constitute the vast majority of the citizenry—peasants, a good percentage of Indians, the landless migrant farmhands, migrant workers, marginals, the urban poor. They remain separate from the centers of power and decision making, uneducated and unorganized. The church provided them with inadequate help and services in the past, and its emphasis on evangelization was not consistent with everyday needs and expectations. The last rites were still administered, but on a social scale it was far more urgent to see to it that infants did not die at birth and that life expectancy increased. Love your neighbor—yes; but what if your neighbor is the police officer who put your son in jail? There was also another problem, closely associated with the role of the church to help the poor. There were not enough priests even for religious services, let alone societal education and reorganization.

It soon became necessary to dispense with the formal education of priests and to establish seminars and workshops in which priests could be quickly trained (and some ordained). A Theological Education by Extension (TEE) program was developed, comprising study centers, lay training centers for missions, clinical pastoral education centers, community-based educational centers, pastoral education cells, groups for study and mutual care, centers of reflection on liberation movements, and a number of ad hoc centers to discuss immediate community problems.

Evangelization (the teaching and the bearing witness of the gospel) soon became superseded by the notion of social service. What would a priest—a lay or ordained "priest," a "missioner," or a "delegate"—be expected to teach the peasantry or the poor? The word of God, to be sure. But in various discussion groups, meetings, and seminars, social questions—about the lack of water, the lack of schools and health clinics, the heavy taxes, the exactions of those in a position of political or military power, the lack of food and housing—questions of everyday

---

[3]Leonardo Boff, *The Church: Charisma and Power*, p. 85.

life, and the need to satisfy urgent wants began to be raised. Religious and moral questions inevitably became related to everyday needs and predicaments. How can we all be brothers, according to the Bible and Christ's teaching, when we live under such unequal conditions? Where is mercy and kindness when only few have access to a clinic but the many do not? Where is the "humanity" of the many, without access to a school or even a church? A theological seminary that discusses these questions inevitably becomes transformed into a social sciences or social services seminar!

The Second Vatican Council's call for social reform and political participation could only strengthen the missionary zeal of the many clergy—and also the urgency shared by lay Catholics (as well as other Christians)—to reach out to the masses and help improve their lives. What developed was literally an explosion of new community ecclesiastic organizations, not only to educate and evangelize, but also to organize and make the poor conscious of their predicament but also of their potential power. To put it simply, new parallel "churches" were established under the name of "base Christian communities"—*communidades eclesiales de base*. There are over 4 million Brazilians who participate in the more than 50,000 Christian "base ecclesiastical communities." The church followers who comprise these base communities represent such societal segments as "labor unions," "Indian groups," "slum organizations," "activist feminist groups," and "peasant movements." They discuss the Bible and apply its religious teachings to everyday political life. In this sense the meaning of praxis appears clearer. It is action within historical circumstances, informed by history *and* the gospel, in order to transform them.

The base ecclesiastical communities today consist of a large network of communities comprising millions, headed by ordained or newly trained priests or lay surrogates, providing and giving awareness to many, not only of the Word but of the need of social and political action. They are the new ministers of God whose function, however, is to make the many and the poor conscious of their predicament and their power. Their function is no longer to proselytize and evangelize but to "conscientize": to make conscious, educate, and create a new dimension of personal and social awareness and, of course, political action.

Conclusion

To the ever-shifting winds of change so much in evidence throughout the Third World, a new ideology—liberation theology—has been added. Many of the Latin American bishops are uncertain about its scope and its Christian credentials; others espouse it. The Vatican itself seems deeply concerned about the adoption of Marxist analysis by its clergy. The erosion of Marxist ideology, however, may also take the wind from the sails of liberation theology as a potentially revolutionary movement. Movements spurred by liberation theology may begin to merge with Christian democracy and seek action through political means, notably the political parties and the ballot. The Vatican would favor such a course, and many progressive Catholics, especially in Latin America, would prefer it. But whatever develops, one thing is clear: by arousing and educating the heretofore excluded and by mak-

Reverend Jean-Bertrand Aristide

On December 16, 1990, Reverend Jean-Bertrand Aristide, a firm adherent of liberation theology, was elected President of Haiti with 70 percent of the ballots cast in what appeared to be the first open and free election in this country. In line with Vatican policy, he had to withdraw from the priesthood to devote himself to his office as advocate "for the poor." Sworn into office on February 7, 1991, he was ousted on September 30 of that year by the 7,000-man army led by Raoul Cedras. Under threat of an American invasion, Cedras permitted the restoration of Aristide to office in 1994.

ing them conscious of their power, liberation theology may have paved the way to what it sought to accomplish—to make the wretched of the earth here and now conscious of their miseries and incite them into political action to improve their lot.

RELIGIOUS FUNDAMENTALISM

The term *fundamentalism* is relatively new.[4] Even though it was used first in the United States for some Protestant sects, it applies to a variety of religious sects and movements among Muslims, Protestants, Hindus, Jews, Greek Orthodox Catholics, and Roman Catholics. They all share a hostility to the changing social mores of modern society—its emphasis on material values and gratification, the emancipation of women, divorce, the loosening of the family bonds, and the predominant emphasis on secular values to the detriment of religious and moral education in schools. Fundamentalist movements become overtly political in order to maintain the hard core of religious beliefs and traditional practices that are being threatened by the changing social environment. They reach out to preempt social change that undermines their values.

---

[4]For the discussion in this section, I am indebted to two papers: "Contemporary Fundamentalism" by Lazarus-Yafeh, Hava, *The Jerusalem Quarterly*, No. 47, Summer 1988, pp. 27–39, and the unpublished paper of Yaakov Ariel, "Fundamentalism in Christianity, Islam and Judaism." Dr. Ariel is with the Department of Religious Studies, The Hebrew University of Jerusalem.

Common Characteristics

All religious fundamentalist sects share common orientations and values.

Dogmatism   Most all religions, organized in churches, synagogues, mosques, and temples, are inherently dogmatic and authoritarian. Each and every one propound the truth and show the greatest intolerance for the beliefs of others. Foremost among them, for a long time, was the Catholic church, which refused, until the latter part of the nineteenth century, to accept democracy, freedom of conscience, majority rule, and the right to vote. Protestant sects displayed rigidity as well and imposed conformity. John Calvin (1509–1564) imposed, in the name of a reformed church, a rigid moral and religious code upon his congregation in Geneva. Various Protestant sects in New England imposed an iron spiritual rule of obedience on their members. Those who could not stand it left with their followers to adjacent areas, only to impose upon their members the same orthodoxy they had defied. Religious fundamentalism carries the same characteristics of rigidity, disciplinarianism, and conformity to the extreme, seeking to impose its views to the exclusion of all others.

Otherworldliness and Messianic Spirit   Fundamentalists do not care about the outside world. Their beliefs and their message are not addressed to secular matters. They are concerned with the sacred. The secular society and nation–states are, strictly speaking, irrelevant. This is true for the "Arab nation," for Israel, and for the United States. Ours is only a temporary life on earth, and we will all return to God. Hence the only activities to which we should devote our energy are those consonant with the word of God.

Subordination of Political Power   Political power should be subordinate to religious power. The Bishop, the Rabbi, or the Ayatollah should have the last word on societal issues. Whenever possible—as in Iran—they should govern. Compromises are inevitably made with the secular authorities, but the intrusion of "religious men" is becoming increasingly obvious as they try to influence political leaders and voters. Fundamentalist rabbis have tried to impose their religious preferences in a number of instances (sometimes with success) on Israel's political leaders—even from outside Israel; American fundamentalists are beginning to rewrite the agenda of American politics; the spread of Islamic fundamentalism is changing the political order everywhere in the Middle East and North Africa. Not unlike Calvin in Geneva many centuries ago, holy men wish to reestablish divine rule wherever they can and to the maximum degree possible when they cannot!

The Inerrancy of the "Written Word"   All fundamentalists believe in a literal reading of the holy script and in the "inerrancy" of the Bible or the Koran. It represents the word of God or Allah—it is the truth. And it is ultimately the Scriptures that should take the place of political constitutions.

Belief in the Supernatural   All fundamentalists believe in what we might call supernatural explanations and events. God is sending us messages that we should take into account. Similarly, "Satan" is ever-present and must be combatted. Explanation, therefore, moves from the logical canons of induction, deduction, inference, generalization, and proof into a world of divine intervention and revelation. Many, especially among the American fundamentalists, believe in individual mystic "experiences"—in specific events that show God's grace. To quote from the Bible, "Angels came and ministered into . . . [them]." Even some American presidents have experienced such visitations!

Against Science   Fundamentalists reject science when science differs from their beliefs—which is quite often. They reject any critical interpretation of the Bible and any historical or archaeological evidence that may be at odds with it. They reject Darwin's evolutionary theory, arguing for the fixity of the species, and believe that the universe was created in a few days—it was not a matter of gradual evolution and change.

Charismatic Leadership   Many of the fundamentalists believe in charismatic leadership. There is one version of the truth and one "leader" who embodies it and will implement it. In this sense, they are at odds with democratic thought. Throughout Islam, there is an ongoing effort on the part of a leader to gain ascendancy by invoking some relationship with the lost Prophet. In the Catholic faith, the pope remains the Vicar of Christ and he is "infallible."

Subordination of Women   A common trait in all fundamentalists is their perception of the role of women. While accorded "high respect" as mothers in the family, they are deemed clearly inferior in all other societal roles. A strict separation of the sexes is prescribed by fundamentalists—and this is notably so among Muslim (and some Jewish) fundamentalist sects, but not among the Evangelicals, at least not to the same degree.

Moralism   When it comes to "moral values," the fundamentalists everywhere are in agreement. The family is indissoluble; sexual promiscuity is condemned; the use of alcohol and, naturally, drugs must be severely punished. In Iran, as it was in Calvin's Geneva, special "police units" supervise the implementation of these prescriptions. Fundamentalists believe in censorship to eliminate pornography and to avoid violence on TV. In short, they want to have the media conform to a moral code. They also believe that religious education is necessary in schools where it is not provided—as in the United States.

A "New" Society   All these traits give us the common "profile" of fundamentalists. It is an ideological profile that amounts to a political vision of the world. It is a political ideology that promises to fashion a new society. But what kind?

1. It is a simple uncomplicated world with fundamental values imposed by a select group of "holy men."
2. It is one in which truth is there, ready-made like a water fountain. It is in the "Book."
3. It is a masculine society; women are subordinate to men.

4. It is a static society—the word of the Bible is "inerrant." No new ideas are to be allowed if they cast any shadow upon the literal interpretation of the Bible.

5. It is an authoritarian society—in which all must follow the religious doctrine and practice enunciated by the highest religious authority.

6. It is an ascetic society in which every effort is made to subordinate many pleasures and joys, in art, literature, entertainment, and other forms of individual expression, to the imperatives of a moral code and religious worship.

7. It projects a world in which all sects are intolerant of each other. They surround themselves with religious walls that invite constant conflict among them.

Muslim Fundamentalism: Iran and Beyond

In no other country has Muslim fundamentalist ideology been more fully realized than in Iran. The founder—Ayatollah Ruhollah Khomeini, a theologian, who was elevated to the stature of an Ayatollah (a "reflection of Allah") and subsequently became Grand Ayatollah—had one and only one overriding purpose: to establish an Islamic republic, supervised, if not controlled, by the Ayatollahs, to cleanse the Iranian society of Western and secular influence that became obvious during the years of the Shah's rule (1954–1979).

Khomeini promised to return the society to its Islamic traditions and to liberate the Muslim masses throughout the world. He waged a political war against the Shah for destroying the Iranian culture, persecuting the clergy, establishing a dictatorship, and allowing foreigners to control the state and the society. "God has formed the Islamic republic. Obey God and his Prophet and those among you who have authority [i.e., the clergy]. It is the only government accepted by God on Resurrection Day." "We do not say," he added, "that the government must be composed of the clergy but that the government must be directed and organized according to the divine law, and this is only possible with the supervision of the clergy."[5] This, in a nutshell, is pure Islamic fundamentalism.

But Khomeini appealed also to nationalism, national independence, and democracy. His plea against the Shah's dictatorship appealed both to the poor and downtrodden, who, in an industrializing society, continued to be deprived of the benefits of economic growth, and also to Iranian students and intellectuals who favored democracy. In fact, the Ayatollah found great support among the university students of Teheran and elsewhere. But his major appeal was to the *mullahs* (the clergy) and the mosques. They acted as revolutionary transmission belts, linking him with the masses at a time when all media were censored and controlled by the official government. When the Ayatollah returned to Iran from exile in Paris in 1979, he was hailed by the mobs, and within a few short weeks, he took power. He

---

[5]The citations come from the excellent article by Raymond H. Anderson: "Ayatollah Ruhollah Khomeini, 89, Relentless Founder of the Islamic Republic" (*New York Times*, p. B11, June 5, 1989).

was vested with lifelong supreme authority as the religious leader—a charismatic leader.

Secure in power, he proceeded to impose Islamic fundamentalist ideology upon the society: thousands were executed for dissent, including students, intellectuals, and leaders of Communist Party; foreign workers were dismissed in favor of Iranian workers; the university was purged; women were forced to retreat to their traditional positions and roles, and made to wear veils and full-length gowns; drug addicts and drug peddlers were summarily executed. Homosexuals and prostitutes met the same fate. ("If your finger has gangrene," the Ayatollah opined, "you cut it before gangrene spreads to your body."[6]) Alcohol was prohibited, and all religious Islamic practices were strictly enforced. The press and the media came under tight control; music was banned from radio and the state-controlled TV; and, of course, the masses came under the control of the Hezbullah (the Party of God) whose leadership was in the hands of the *mullahs*. Ayatollah's rule was a splendid demonstration of *jihad*— a "holy war" against the evils and vices of a society that had strayed away from the word of the Koran, but also against the forces outside that were inimical to it, including Muslim secular regimes like those of Iraq, Syria, and Egypt. This messianic spirit—a trait of all fundamentalist movements—may well have accounted for the eight-year war with Iraq, a secular, self-styled, socialist, modernizing society.

Thus Iran, in the name of religious fundamentalism, nationalism, and anti-Westernism, has become an authoritarian regime. It is a regime that constantly evokes traditional values and is addressed to the vindication of past values. It is a regime the eschews the concepts of enlightenment, rationality, science, and the institutions and practices of liberalism, where power is legitimized in religious terms. It is a regime that is dedicated to the elimination of all infidels, especially the state of Israel. It is also a regime that, after unifying the society around the basic myths it proposes, now wants to impose its ideology and political practices abroad—particularly among the Shiite Muslims who are spread throughout the region. It is dedicated to Islam. In terms of leadership, the organization of the single party, the conformity the regime has attempted to exact, the religious mythology that it has elevated into an official ideology, and the mobilization and use of force, the Iranian regime is truly totalitarian.

The clergy has recruited and organized a paramilitary force, the Revolutionary Guards, about 150,000 strong. They are the eyes and ears of the clergy, the dogs that sniff out treason and silence opposition. Whenever the spiritual arm of the clergy cannot assure conformity, the secular arm they forged is called upon to enforce it through intimidation and assassination. The party and the Revolutionary Guards permeate the society. They control family life, impose religious conformity, appeal to the young to join the army for both material and heavenly rewards, and punish those who fail to volunteer. They also deal out swift justice to anyone who violates religious taboos.

Over and above the party, the mosques, the Revolutionary Guards, and the Parliament, there are three institutions that stand supreme. The first is the

---

[6]NYT *Ibid.*

Supreme Religious Guide. The second is the Assembly of Experts (eighty-three clergymen), which was established in 1983 to decide Khomeini's succession. The third is the Council of Guardians, a very small group of clerics (with scholarly reputations) who go over legislation, government decrees, and orders to check their conformity with the religious faith. They are, in a sense, the highest court. Finally, there is the army. Purged of all pro-American or pro-Western elements, it is now manned with converts and new recruits and serves faithfully the religious–political leadership. Unable to win the war against Iraq, the army maintains nonetheless its position and prestige. It is and probably will remain an obedient instrument of the Islamic revolution that it hopes will extend beyond the borders of Iran. In the meantime, dissenters and critics have been eliminated at home, and those who live abroad have been the victims of terrorist attacks and threats. Salmon Rushdie is in hiding somewhere in England, sentenced to death for blasphemy contained in his book *The Satanic Verses,* which parodied some religious observances.

Beyond Iran   Muslim fundamentalism is spreading. In Sudan, the National Islamic Front (an outgrowth of Egypt's Muslim Brotherhood) has gained control in alliance with a military junta. The secular constitution was set aside to be replaced by Islamic religious law—the *charia.* In the local elections held in Algeria on June 12, 1990, the Islamic Salvation Front, advocating the establishment of an Islamic republic (as in Iran), won and carried a majority even in the big cities. The platform on which it ran was "Islam Is the Solution"! Many Muslim fundamentalist religious practices are returning, and the Salvation Front may win the legislative election. Echoes were felt in Tunisia and Morocco, and powerful Islamic fundamentalist groups are to be found in Jordan, Egypt, Syria, and among the Palestinians. Indonesia, the fifth most populous state with 155 million, has the largest Muslim population of any country. Muslim fundamentalists are in control in Mauritania; some are flexing their spiritual muscles in Albania and Yugoslavia and far into China. Muslim workers throughout Western Europe are beginning, too, to form enclaves. There are five Muslim republics in the Soviet Union on the southeastern rim of Russia. They are in revolt against the secular Marxist orthodoxy, imposed upon them for so long.

Muslim fundamentalism has been felt as far as Trinidad. A militant group rose in the summer of 1990 and took over the government, occupied the prime minister's office, and captured him. The coup failed, but it showed that Islamic fundamentalism was spreading far and wide.

Fundamentalism and Nationalism   A major source of strength for religious fundamentalism, not only Islamic, lies in its linkage with nationalisms or ethnonationalisms, which we discussed in Chapter 10. Nationalism is a secular ideology inconsistent, on its face, with the religious and transcendental aspirations of fundamentalism. Yet in a number of countries, and notably where there are strong fundamentalists, they have supported nationalist and separatist aspirations. Afghan fundamentalists represent the backbone of the resistance movement against a Soviet-imposed regime. The case was much clearer in Iran, where the fundamentalists claimed liberation and national independence from the Shah *and*

Far into China the Muslim fundamentalists are active. In the provinces of Xinjiang and Ningxia, new mosques are being built and Islamic study centers are well attended. Many Muslims are branded as separatists.

American and Western influence. Secular nationalist regimes like those of Iraq, Egypt, or Syria have come increasingly under the influence of fundamentalists and may align themselves on common themes. Throughout the Middle East, the ideology of Muslim fundamentalism—rigid, demanding, mobilizing, anti-Western—is seeking a reconciliation with the secular Arab states as the two most powerful forces in the Middle East—nationalism and fundamentalism—seek an answer to the search for a common identity among Muslims.

Yet while there is every indication that muslim fundamentalism is spreading and that it affects directly the lives and thoughts of hundreds of millions throughout the world, there are also some signs that its political weight may have peaked. Iran, for instance, has begun to reconsider its relations with the West and even the United States in an effort to improve its domestic economy. The grip of the clergy over the government and the people has been loosened. Despite the rhetoric, the muslim masses failed to rise during the Gulf War against the United States and the West. The mosques and the bazaars throughout the moslem world remained remarkably quiet and acts of terrorism were few. The religious zealots are as many and as active as before, but immediate problems of political power and economic survival and even more so, the prospect of military confrontations may have quieted their ardor. For the time being, the Prophet may have to wait until the faithful satisfy their urgent material needs.

The Evangelicals

American Evangelicals—as the fundamentalists are generally referred to in the United States—display the same traits that all fundamentalists do: emphasis on the word of God and the inerrancy of the Bible.[7] They show the same attachment to traditional values and religious practices and the same aversion to modernity. Besieged by a "modern" and liberal society, Evangelicals stand on a solid fortress, occasionally undertaking powerful thrusts at those that besiege them. They revolt against changing mores and societal trends —crime and violence, pornography, drugs, homosexuality, prostitution, teen pregnancies, premarital sex—and the dangers they seem to pose to the fabric of the society, to the family and stable family relations, to the school, and to the church.

In the last two decades, the Evangelicals have been gaining. In the United States, the most dynamic and mobile society in the world, where the only truth accepted is the freedom to question it, fundamentalists attempt to find a permanent shelter—an anchor that will hold us back from critical inquiry and experimentation. And the greater and faster the changes in a society, the greater becomes the longing for stability and certainty. As a result, both the depth and pace of change have forced many fundamentalists to come out and fight in order to protect what they feel is being threatened. They have become activists not only to preserve the values they cherish, but also to restore them. They have entered politics and their theology has been transformed into a political movement designed to

---

[7]They also are referred to as the Christian right, the religious right, or the Moral Majority.

enact or change legislation to promote their conservative views. They have moved "from the Pew to the Precinct," in the words of Jerry Falwell, one of their leaders.

It is not easy to clearly distinguish the theology of the various sects that comprise the religious conservative movement; Baptists and Southern Baptist, Pentecostals, and Southern Lutherans are among the most prominent. The greatest number of believers are situated in the so-called Bible Belt and beyond: Tennessee, Virginia, Georgia, Florida, Arkansas, Louisiana, Mississippi, Texas, North and South Carolina, and Alabama. (A Gallup Poll indicated that 50 percent of all evangelicals are from the South.) But they are also strong in Michigan, Missouri, Ohio, and in a number of western states. Tens of millions throughout the country have been mobilized by fundamentalists. In fact, one-third of the American population proclaims itself as "Born-Again Christians," according to a Gallup Poll.

While religious themes continue to prevail, it is the way they have been shaped into a political program and the way believers have been organized into political action that count. A common political philosophy emerges even when there are theological disputes among sects, as there are, particularly between fundamentalists and evangelicals. This common political ideology has been shaped by a number of prominent religious leaders—Rousas J. Rashdoony, Tim Lattaye, Gary North, Jerry Falwell, George Marsden, Pat Robertson, and others. Through newly established theological seminaries, foundations and universities, newspapers and journals, radio and television, the themes that organize the political battle lines, often in close cooperation with conservative organizations like the Conservative Caucus, the National Conservative Political Action Committee, and others, have become clear.

The shortest distance between the pew and the precinct, one might add, is radio and television. Through the Christian Broadcasting Network (CBN), the third largest cable network in the country, more than 30 million people are reached daily. If one were to add various affiliated stations, the figure is close to 50 million. The evangelicals have become increasingly "tele-evangelicals."

Both general and specific themes have been developed by ministers and theologians and espoused by others for political purposes. The "political ministers" have tried to create a mass movement that cuts across religious lines to include Protestants, Catholics, Jews, blacks, whites, farmers, businessmen, and housewives. This is the Moral Majority, which was formed "to combat the legalization of immorality." The movement directly confronts some of the critical issues that concern Americans, but it lumps together abortion, pornography, the use of drugs, the breakdown of the family, homosexuality, and other "moral cancers" to which AIDS has most recently been added.

Political Action and Organization   The fundamentalists who spearheaded the Moral Majority movement pride themselves on their strong organization, which is defined and described in terms appropriate to a paramilitary organization: commitment of the individual and readiness to sacrifice "even life itself" for the sake of the "company of the faithful"; absolute discipline in the willingness of all to obey the commands of the leadership; evangelical zeal—to spread the gospel and convert people; absolutism—the acceptance of God's word as the absolute truth; and, finally, fanaticism.

Fundamentalists have little patience with dialogue, argument, and self-criticism. But in building the Moral Majority, efforts have been made to allow for internal debate and pluralism, and present a common political front on those basic moral and political positions that unite the greatest number possible. The battles against pornography, drugs, and abortion are likely to receive the most widespread support. So is national defense, though there are differences as to how much defense is needed. A blanket anti-Communist stance is also widely supported by nationalists and those who fear atheism. School prayer is also overwhelmingly endorsed.

The scope of the movement's political activities has been comprehensive and multifaceted. Voters have been so well mobilized to register that millions of previously indifferent citizens have now joined the voting public. Large amounts of money have been raised to support candidates, but each candidate is carefully screened to determine his or her stand on the critical moral issues. Pamphlets, letters, and radio and television messages have been used to support or reject candidates. Lobbyists have also approached members of Congress in Washington and in state legislatures as well as federal and state officials. Above all, a constant stream of educational and political materials keep coming out of religious study and research centers to reach out to the believers.

In the 1988 presidential race, the Reverend Marion "Pat" Robertson surprised political experts, pollsters, members of the media, and the American electorate. Robertson, a television Evangelist and founder of the Christian Broadcasting Network and the daily "700 Club" program, finished third for the Republican nomination, placing ahead of political veterans, including former Congressman Jack Kemp, former Delaware Governor Pierre DuPont, and General Alexander Haig. Robertson's successes were not only in the deep South, the base of Evangelicalism and fundamentalism; they were spread throughout the country. While Robertson lost the nomination, President George Bush sounded some of Robertson's themes at the Republic National Convention in 1992.

The Convention of Southern Baptists   The strongest and most numerous group among the Evangelicals are the Southern Baptists—stretching from Georgia to California through Texas, Virginia, Oklahoma, Alabama, Florida, Mississippi, and South Carolina, with offshoots in Michigan, southern Illinois, Ohio, and Nebraska. There are over 15 million Southern Baptists, and a number of Evangelical churches have close links with them. In July 1990, their delegates—"messengers," as they are called—held their convention in New Orleans to select their president, and Mr. Morris H. Chapin was reelected with 58 percent of the votes. The president represented the conservative hard core of the fundamentalist doctrine. He stressed the inerrancy of the Bible. "The Bible," he pointed out, "is not negotiable." It represents the "inspired, infallible, inerrant word of God." The moderate candidate for the election, who lost, agreed. In addition to the inerrancy of the Bible, the platform included, among other things:

1. A demand for laws against pornography.
2. Strong laws against abortion. Abortion was the subject of two resolutions, and the Evangelicals seemed to agree with the Catholic church. They stressed the sanctity of human life and opposed abortion, except to save the life of the mother. They opposed the use of abortion drugs and also proposed a boycott against all businesses that contribute to pro-abortion organizations.
3. Renewed demands for religious education in schools.
4. The need to convert and evangelize; in fact, Evangelicals have been particularly successful in converting Hispanics from Catholicism—both in the United States and in Latin America.

In contrast to other fundamentalist movements, women attended the conference and voted. But they seemed to accept their special role in the society: "Father, let us be the mothers you want us to be" was one of their prayers.[8]

How lasting will the influence of the Evangelicals be? It is difficult to answer, but one thing is clear: the embattled ministers of God have entered politics in earnest. In their emphasis on traditionalism, their rejection of critical inquiry, and their goal of propounding their own moral and religious values, they are beginning to weigh heavily on the political agenda of the country. " Moral-social" issues dominate the political debate and increasingly affect the position of candidates. In other words, the fundamentalists and evangelicals are reshaping the political horizon.

The Soldiers of God

Everywhere religious beliefs are translated into political militancy. In Ulster, Catholics have been virtually at war with the Protestants; in Belgium, they hold each other at arm's length; in Jerusalem, Muslims, Greek Orthodox and Jews are fighting about their holy temples; the Hindus and the Muslims are at war over a mosque near Nepal, reputed to be on the burial site of the Hindu God Raman; in Yugoslavia, Roman Catholics, Greek Orthodox Catholics, and Muslims are ready to confront each other. Religious fundamentalist movements are spreading as an increasing number of people join their ranks. They all claim their truth to be superior to that held by all others, and they are ready to defend it by force and to impose it by force. At a time when communism and socialism are waning and democracy remains uncertain, religious fundamentalism (often linked with nationalist movements) marshals the hearts and souls of hundreds of millions seeking their own way of life against all others. "Will religion become the main force that sets one group of mankind against another," It may![9]

---

[8]Quotes from press releases on the 1990 Southern Baptist Convention, June 12–14, 1990.
[9]*The Economist,* "Soldiers of God," November 17, 1990, pp. 15–16.

BIBLIOGRAPHY

Liberation Theology

Abbot, Walter M. *The Documents of Vatican II*. New York: Herder & Herder, 1966.

Arias, Ester and Mortimer. *The Cry of My People: Out of Captivity in Latin America*. New York: Friendship Press, 1980.

Berryman, Philip. *Liberation Theology*. New York: Pantheon, 1987.

Boff, Leonardo. *Liberating Grace*. Maryknoll, NY: Orbis Books, 1981.

———. "Theological Characteristics of a Grassroots Church," in Sergio Torres and John Eagleson (eds.), *Theology in the Americas*. Maryknoll, NY: Orbis Books, 1976, pp. 124–144.

———. *Jesus Christ Liberator*. Maryknoll, NY: Orbis Books, 1978. (Originally published as *Jesus Christo liberador: Ensaio de Cristologia critica para o nosso tempo*. Petropolis: Vozes, 1972.)

———. "Christ's Liberation via Oppression: An Attempt at Theological Construction from the Standpoint of Latin America," in Rosino Gibellini (ed.), *Frontiers in Theology in Latin America*. Maryknoll, NY: Orbis Books, 1979a, pp. 100–132.

———. *The Church: Charisma and Power*. New York: Crossroads, 1985.

Cardoso, F. H.,and E. Faletto. *Dependency and Development in Latin America*. Berkeley: University of California Press, 1975.

Dussel, Enrique. *History and the Theology of Liberation: A Latin American Perspective*. Translated by John Drury. Maryknoll, NY: Orbis Books, 1976.

Gibellini, Rosino (ed.). *Frontiers of Theology in Latin America*. Translated by John Drury. Maryknoll, NY: Orbis Books, 1975.

Goulet, Denis. *A New Moral Order: Studies in Development Ethics and Liberation Theology*. Maryknoll, NY: Orbis Books, 1979.

Gutierrez, Gustavo. *A History of Liberation: History, Politics and Salvation*. Maryknoll, NY: Orbis Books, 1971.

———. *A Theology of Liberation: History, Politics and Salvation*. Maryknoll, NY: Orbis Books, 1973. (Originally published as *Teología de la liberacíon*. Lima: Perspectives by CEP, 1971.)

———. *The Power of the Poor in History*. Maryknoll, NY: Orbis Books, 1983.

Hanson, Eric. *The Catholic Church in World Politics*. Princeton, NJ: Princeton University Press, 1987.

Hennelly, Alfred T. *Theologies in Conflict: The Challenge of Juan Luis Segundo*. Maryknoll, NY: Orbis Books, 1979.

Medellin Conference Final Documents. *The Church in the Present-day Transformation of Latin America in the Light of the Council*, vol. II. Bogota, Colombia: CELAM, 1968.

———. *Freedom with Justice: Catholic Social Thought and Liberal Institutions*. New York: Harper & Row, 1984.

O'Brien, David J. *The Renewal of American Catholicism*. New York: Oxford University Press, 1972.

Rynne, Xavier. *Vatican Council II*. New York: Farrar, Straus and Giroux, 1964.

Sacred Congregation for the Doctrine of the Faith. "Instruction on Certain Aspects of the 'Theology of Liberation.'" Boston: Daughters of St. Paul, 1984 and 1986.

———. "Instruction on Christian Freedom and Liberation." Boston: Daughters of St. Paul, 1986.

Sigmund, Paul E. *Liberation Theology at the Crossroads.* New York: Oxford University Press, 1990.

Segundo, Juan Luis. *The Hidden Motives of Pastoral Action: Latin American Reflections.* Maryknoll, NY: Orbis Books, 1972.

Smith, Donald E. *Religion, Politics and Social Change in the Third World.* New York: Free Press, 1971.

Islamic Fundamentalism

Chehabi, Houchang E. *Iranian Politics and Religious Modernism: The Liberation Movement of Iran under the Shah and Khomeini.* London: Cornell University Press & I. B. Tauris, 1990.

Esposito, John. *Islam: The Straight Path,* expanded ed. New York: Oxford University Press, 1991.

Hiro Dilip. *Iran under the Ayatollahs.* New York: Routledge, 1987.

———. *Holy Wars: The Rise of Islamic Fundamentalism,* New York: Routledge, 1989.

Landau, Jacob M. *The Politics of Pan-Islam: Ideology and Organization.* New York: Oxford University Press, 1990.

Lazarus-Yafeh, Hava. "Contemporary Fundamentalism." *The Jerusalem Quarterly,* No. 47, Summer 1988, pp. 27–39.

Sivan, Emmanuel. *Radical Islam.* New Haven, CT: Yale University Press, 1985.

Watt, W. Montgomery. *Islamic Fundamentalism and Modernity.* New York: Routledge, 1988.

Evangelicals

Cole, Steward Grant. *History of Fundamentalism.* Hamden, CT: Archon Books, 1963.

Conway, Flo, and Jim Siegelman. *Holy Terror.* Garden City, NY: Doubleday, 1982.

Fackre, Gabriel. *The Religious Right and Christian Faith.* Grand Rapids, MI: William B. Eerdmans, 1982.

Falwell, Jerry. *The Fundamentalist Phenomenon.* Garden City, NY: Doubleday, 1981.

Gasper, Louis. *The Fundamentalist Movement.* Paris TN: Mouton & Co., 1963.

Hadden, Jeffrey, and Anson Shupe. *Televangelism, Power and Politics.* Boston: Beacon Press, 1988.

Jorsted Erlig. *Politics of Doomsday.* Nashville, TN: Abington Press, 1970.

Kater, John. *Christians on the Right: The Moral Majority in Perspective.* New York: Seabury Press, 1982.

Marsden, George M. *Fundamentalism and American Culture.* New York: Oxford University Press, 1980.

Wills, Garry. *Under God: Religion and American Politics.* New York: Simon and Schuster, 1990.

Chapter
12

Red Flags/Black Flags: Marxists against Anarchists

The errors committed by a truly revolutionary movement are infinitely more fruitful than the infallibility of the cleverest Central Committee.

Rosa Luxemburg

*E*veryone knows Karl Marx mercilessly upbraided liberals because they supported a capitalist economy which, in his judgment, made a mockery of their high-sounding commitment to freedom and equality. Few persons realize that the amount of time, energy, and passion Marx spent fighting the liberals amounts to nothing compared to the never-ending and ferocious battles, both ideological and organizational, he waged against fellow leftists, most of all the anarchists. And what was true of Marx was no less true of Marxists. The entire history of Marxism is a record of struggles with anarchists or with various heirs of the anarchists who call themselves the true Marxists. As for anarchism, it is a movement that might well have died considerably sooner than it did, were it not for the recurring need to challenge a Marxist, Leninist, or Stalinist political organization. Anarchism began as a movement in its own right but it evolved into a doctrine which more often than not lived parasitically off the body of the very Marxism it despised.

The last time the black flag of anarchy was raised in defiance of the red flag[1] of Marxism was during the events of May 1968 in France, when a student rebellion spread into a general contagion of strikes and demands for self-management. Previous landmarks included the battle between Marx and the anarchists for control

---

[1]In earlier French history the red and the black referred not to Marxism and anarchism but to the two Frances, one anticlerical and universalist, the other Catholic and nationalist. Stendal's *Le Rouge et le Noir* (1831) is the outstanding literary landmark of the earlier meaning.

of the International Working Men's Association founded in 1864, followed by the struggle to claim the glorious legacy of the heroes of the Paris Commune who suffered martyrdom in 1871. No less significant was the brutal Bolshevik suppression of the anarchists in the years immediately following the revolution of 1917.

All in all, the anarchists fared poorly in their combats with Marxists. When it came to theory, thinkers such as Stirner, Proudhon, and Bakunin were no match for Marx, whose intellectual superiority Bakunin was sufficiently magnanimous to admit. Politically, the anarchists fared even worse. Insisting with pride that their disorganization proved their commitment to the principle of personal autonomy, the anarchists suffered one crushing political defeat after another at the hands of disciplined Marxists.

Two arguments may, however, be entertained in favor of the anarchists. One is that, whatever was wanting in their philosophical credentials was more than compensated for in artistic splendor: Montmartre in the early 1890s was a haven for artists, anarchists, and artist-anarchists; Surrealism, some decades later, was a movement of avant-garde artists who were anarcho-Marxists committed to revolution but hostile to Stalin: their art and showmanship were as outrageous and exciting as the Stalinist art of "socialist realism" was dreary. The second plea to be entered in behalf of anarchism is that it served time and again, whether under the guise of left communism or some other anarcho-Marxist hybrid, as a significant critique of Stalinism from within the ranks of the revolutionaries. It was left-wing communists—that is, Marxists responsive to the libertarian message of the anarchists—who periodically issued calls urging the regime to return to its anti-authoritarian beginnings.

ORGANIZATION: WHAT IS TO BE DONE?

Polemics between Marxists and anarchists on the subject of organization have always taken the same form. The Marxist takes the position that the hostility of the anarchists to leadership and organization makes collective action impossible, defeat inevitable, and leads frustrated anarchists to commit random acts of violence which do nothing to advance and everything to discredit the revolutionary cause. Anarchists respond with the claim that an authoritarian revolutionary movement cannot possibly give birth to a libertarian society; the revolutionary organization must prefigure the world which will exist after the decisive uprising—otherwise the revolution will fail.

At the time of the founding of the International Working Men's Association (the First International, 1864–1876), Michael Bakunin (1814–1876) made all the arguments against Marxist political organization which were destined to be endlessly repeated throughout the long struggle between Marxists and anarchists. The French delegation, consisting of followers of the late Pierre-Joseph Proudhon, the father of anarchism in France, was very receptive to Bakunin's message, especially because as early as the 1840s Proudhon had warned Marx to avoid authoritarianism. "Do not let us fall into your compatriot Martin Luther's inconsistency," Proudhon wrote to Marx in a letter dated May 17, 1846.

> As soon as he had overthrown Catholic theology he immediately, with constant re-
> course to excommunications and anathemas, set about founding a Protestant theology
> . . . Let us set the world an example of wise and farsighted tolerance . . . Let us not set
> ourselves up as apostles of a new religion.[2]

Hating Germany as an authoritarian nation, both Proudhon and Bakunin did their best to use Marx's nationality against him, Proudhon by likening him to Luther, Bakunin by comparing him to Bismarck. It did not matter to Bakunin that it was Ferdinand Lassalle (1825–1864) who wanted to institute socialism through the Prussian state and Marx who vigorously attacked Lassalle for cozying up to Bismarck.

"How can you expect an egalitarian and a free society to emerge from an authoritarian organization?", asked Bakunin. "The International, embryo of future human society, must be from this moment the faithful image of our principles of liberty and federation." Opposed to leadership emanating from the General Council where Marx was influential, Bakunin sought to dissolve the International into autonomous sections, loosely federated. Like most anarchists, Bakunin believed organizations should be voluntary, temporary, set up to accomplish a particular objective, and then disbanded. Only in an extremely circumscribed sense does he admit that discipline is necessary.

> At the moment of action . . . there is a natural division of roles according to the apti-
> tude of each. . . : some direct and command, others execute orders. But no function
> must be allowed to petrify or become fixed, and it will not remain irrevocably attached
> to one person. Hierarchical order and promotion do not exist, so that the commander
> of yesterday can become a subordinate tomorrow. No one rises above the others, or if
> he does rise, it is only to fall back again a moment later, like the waves of the sea for-
> ever returning to the salutary level of equality.

Bakunin also gave classic expression to the anarchist point of view when he asserted that "the organization of the forces of the proletariat . . . must be the task of the proletariat itself." All subsequent anarchists locked in mortal combat with Russian communism had good reason to quote Bakunin against the Leninist notion of the party conceived as the "vanguard of the proletariat."

Marx, however, was not Lenin, and Bakunin's description of the danger emanating from the leadership of the First International was as misleading as the same words of warning would later prove accurate in the case of the Third International. Whatever resemblance to Lenin one might rightfully discern in the author of the *Communist Manifesto* had peaked during March of 1850, when Marx delivered a rousing speech calling for a seizure of power by the German proletariat despite its small numbers and the economically underdeveloped state of Germany; but by September 15 of that same year Marx had decisively reversed his position, saying that not for many years would the working class be in a position to transform society. The Marx who rose to deliver the inaugural address of the First International in 1864 was as willing to wait for historical conditions to ripen, and as eager to

---

[2]Stewart Edwards ed., *Selected Writings of Pierre-Joseph Proudhon* (New York: Anchor, 1969), pp. 150–151.

please moderate English trade unions representatives, as he had briefly been a hot-blooded revolutionary fourteen years earlier. Iron-fisted domination of the International was not Marx's objective; assuring its status as a working class organization was his concern, and to that end he worked to exclude French and Italian republicans, Jacobins in the former case, disciples of Mazzini in the latter.

Marx's inaugural address shows the most important reason why he was bound, sooner or later, to become embroiled in controversy with the anarchist members of the International. Nothing was more obvious to Marx than the need of the working classes to form trade unions and to alter their condition by political means. The French delegates, by the time the International saw the light of day, were evolving away from Proudhon's absolute rejection of unions; but anarchists of all stripes remained faithful to Proudhon's rejection of political action. To the anarchists the working class way of life is all good and the state all evil, whence it follows that the way to protect the producers from contamination is to have them abstain completely from politics. No anarchist could agree with one of the sentences Marx placed in his inaugural address: "To conquer political power has become the great duty of the working classes."

By the late 1860s Bakunin and Marx were deadly enemies, each bent on discrediting the other and preventing him from taking over the International. Repeatedly Bakunin charged that Marx and his followers, in advocating a transitional revolutionary government to replace a fallen bourgeois regime, were in reality the champions of authoritarianism. "Whoever in the name of the revolution wants to establish a state—even a provisional state—establishes reaction and works for despotism," Bakunin wrote in 1870. Three years later he complained that "the leaders of the Communist party will concentrate all administrative power in their own strong hands." Even if recruited from the laborers, the new rulers "will cease to be workers and will look down at the plain working masses." The Marxists, he added, "say that a yoke-dictatorship is a transitional step towards achieving full freedom for the people: anarchism or freedom is the aim, while state and dictatorship is the means . . . We reply that . . . freedom can only be created by freedom, by a total rebellion of the people."

Marx and Engels, turning the tables on Bakunin, noted that although anarchism in the sense of the abolition of the state is the end, it cannot possibly be the means.

> What all [Marxist] socialists understand by anarchy is this: once the aim of the proletarian movement, the abolition of all classes, has been attained, the power of the state . . . disappears. [Bakunin, however,] . . . demands of the International, at the very moment when the old world is seeking to crush it, that it should replace its organization by anarchy.

Did not Bakunin's revolutionary misadventures in France disprove the worth of his prescriptions? In Lyon, Engels noted, Bakunin simply declared the abolition of the state and in consequence managed to hold power for less than an hour before being booted out of the city hall. Even worse was the record of the Spanish anarchists who, to alleviate their fear of centralism, chose a Bakunian federalist organization which—in the words of Engels—"consisted precisely in the fact that each town acted on its own. They declared that the important thing was not cooperation with other towns but separation from them." The predictable upshot of their principled disorganization was that the government troops smashed one revolt after another.

On the question of authoritarianism Marx and Engels found that Proudhon and Bakunin, once again, had provided them with all they needed to launch a devastating counterattack. Proudhon's obsessive fear of disorder, his extravagantly patriarchal attitudes toward women, his anti-Semitism, and his support of the slave-owners of the American South on the grounds of their opposition to "centralization," explain why he was destined to be as much the darling of the French far right as of the left. For his part Bakunin was forever contradicting himself through association with one or another conspiratorial revolutionary elite, real or imaginary, or he was discrediting himself through his intimate relationship with the murderous Russian nihilist, Nechaev.[3] Marx and Engels delighted in portraying Bakunin's supremely authoritarian anarchism:

> What a beautiful model of barrack-room communism! Here you have it all: communal eating, communal sleeping, assessors and offices regulating education, production, consumption. . . . This same man who in 1870 preaches to the Russians passive, blind obedience to orders coming from above and from an anonymous committee, . . . this same man, in 1871, weaves a separatist and disorganizing movement into the International under the pretext of combating the authoritarianism and centralization of the German communists, . . . and of making of the International what it should be: the image of the future society. If the society of the future were modelled on [Bakunin's] Alliance, . . . it would far surpass the Paraguay of the Reverend Jesuit Fathers, so dear to Bakunin's heart.

By the time the First International met, Marx had long since repudiated all secretive and conspiratorial organization as a relic from a bygone era, when the working class was "not yet ripe for an independent historical movement." Now that capitalism and the working class had matured, revolutionary sects had become "essentially reactionary." "There is only one way of combating all these intrigues, but it will prove astonishingly effective; this means is complete publicity." Clearly Marx had the better of the argument with Bakunin, but the day would come when anarchists or anarcho-Marxists would have excellent reasons to repeat the most vital of Bakunin's objections to the "dictatorship of the proletariat."[4]

One unforgettable anarcho-Marxist who challenged Lenin's hierarchical and centralized party, organized in imitation of the army, and staffed with professional revolutionaries, was the firebrand Rosa Luxemburg (1870–1919). When Rosa questioned Lenin, first in 1904 and then shortly after the Russian revolution, the revolutionaries had to admit that she was ideally qualified to confront the leader of the Bolsheviks. Like Lenin, Luxemburg came to reject Karl Kautsky, the symbol of

[3]The infamous deeds of Nechaev were immortalized by Dostoevsky in *The Possessed*.
[4]Most of the attacks by Marx and Engels on Bakunin may be found in the First Section of *Anarchism & Anarcho-Syndicalism*. For Bakunin's ideas and his side of the debate, see Sam Dolgoff, ed., *Bakunin on Anarchism*.

the Second International (1889–1914), because his politics was hopelessly incrementalist. Her disdain for "parliamentary cretinism" and for the reformism of trade unions and German Social Democrats were equalled only by Lenin's. And yet she was as supportive of the anarchist themes of "spontaneity" and the need of the workers to free themselves as Lenin was hostile to the same in *What is to be Done?* (1902) and *One Step Forward, Two Steps Back* (1904).

Spontaneity, as Lenin understood it, meant the foolish bomb-throwing of the anarchists or the habit of following rather than leading the proletariat. He therefore insisted upon the priority of "consciousness" over "spontaneity," which is to say, he advocated acting solely on the basis of cool calculation, never on impulse. In direct contrast, the anarchists always placed spontaneity first. Proudhon, for instance, held that "all revolutions . . . have been brought about spontaneously by the people." Similarly, Bakunin repeatedly announced that, with the abolition of the state, there would be a "tremendous awakening of spontaneous life everywhere"; "the spontaneous self-organization of popular life, for centuries paralyzed and absorbed by the omnipotent power of the state, will revert to the communes." Rosa Luxemburg thought localism and federalism self-defeating in the age of centralizing capitalism, but her Marxism shared with the anarchists a confidence in the ability of the workers to free themselves. Writing against Lenin in 1904, she argued that "the errors committed by a truly revolutionary movement are infinitely more fruitful than the infallibility of the cleverest Central Committee." All the great Russian events of the last ten years—the general strikes of 1896 and 1903, the street demonstrations of 1901—were, she added, "the spontaneous product of the movement in ferment." No anarchist could have said it better.

Rosa Luxemburg attacked Lenin again after his emergence in late 1917 as the leader of a revolutionary government. She begins with several gestures intended to underscore her own credentials as an arch-radical, most notably by denouncing Kautsky's Second International while simultaneously crediting the November revolution with salvaging the honor of international socialism. Then she proceeds to express her disappointment that the Bolshevik version of the "dictatorship of the proletariat" was not in the least a regime run by the workers; rather, it was "the dictatorship of a handful of politicians, . . . a dictatorship in the bourgeois sense, in the sense of the rule of the Jacobins."

Our proper objective, she insists, is

> to create a socialist democracy to replace bourgeois democracy—not to eliminate democracy altogether. But socialist democracy is not something which begins only in the promised land after the foundations of the socialist economy are created. . . . It begins at the very moment of the seizure of power by the socialist party. It is the same thing as the dictatorship of the proletariat.

Much was wrong with parliamentary democracy, yet "the remedy which Trotsky and Lenin have found, the elimination of democracy, is worse than the disease it is supposed to cure." Rosa calls for freedom of the press, freedom of association, and—in words similar to those of John Stuart Mill—she proclaims that "freedom is always and exclusively freedom for the one who thinks differently." In lucid and emotionally charged language she indicts the Bolsheviks for "their suppression of public life" at a time when the masses must learn to govern themselves.[5]

Luxemburg was opposed to Lenin's proposal for a Third International (1919–1943) under Bolshevik leadership. When she was executed by the German military in January 1919, Lenin breathed a sigh of relief in private while in public he falsely claimed her heritage for his cause. But even with Rosa Luxemburg out of the way, Lenin continued to be bedeviled by other left (or anarcho-Marxist) communists whose position was uncomfortably close to the one outlined in *State and Revolution,* the tract he had written on the eve of the revolution and which he regarded as so important that he took steps to ensure its publication in the event of his untimely death.

Lenin's *"Left-Wing" Communism: an Infantile Disorder* was not only an attack on European leftists who wanted communism now, on the morrow of the revolution; it was also an attempt to bury his own *State and Revolution,* written just three years earlier. In the spring of 1917 he had held that "it is perfectly possible, immediately, within twenty-four hours after the overthrow of the capitalists and bureaucrats, to replace them . . . by the armed workers." Faced in 1920 with the burden of sustaining the revolution in a backward country racked by civil war, Lenin reversed his position and maintained that "only after very many years" would the people be able directly to control their affairs. Hostile in 1920 to left-wing communism, Lenin laments that little can be accomplished so long as he is forced to deal with the human material bequeathed the Bolsheviks by the capitalists. Conveniently forgotten are his words in *State and Revolution:* "we want the Socialist revolution with human nature as it is now"—that is, with the Old Adam. Now, immediately, the day after the revolution, the workers can begin to take turns as managers until they "soon become accustomed to the idea of no managers at all"; or so one reads in *State and Revolution.* If the left-wing communists were "infantile" in 1920, then Lenin himself had been a mere child in 1917. The first left communist Lenin had to suppress in 1920 was the Lenin of 1917.

By the early 1920s Trotsky's Red Army had succeeded in destroying the Russian anarchists on the battlefield. As for the "soviets" or workers' committees, so dear to the hearts of left communists, syndicalists, and anarcho-Marxists, and so vital to anyone who believed in self-management for the workers, they had been reduced to the status of tools of the party. Anarchism in Russia was dead and left-communists were living on borrowed time. Yet anarchism found a way to rise from the grave, thanks in part to a special dispensation granted by one of its formerly most deadly enemies.

Trotsky's career consists of an elaborately woven texture of ironies revolving around the theme of the relationship between Marxism and anarchism. The man who served Lenin by killing the anarchists in the years immediately following the revolution had issued a stern warning in 1904 against the Bolshevik leader:

---

[5]Rosa Luxemburg, *The Russian Revolution* and *Leninism or Marxism* (Ann Arbor: University of Michigan Press, 1961).

Lenin's methods lead to this: the party organization at first substitutes itself for the party as a whole; then the Central Committee substitutes itself for the organization; and finally a single dictator substitutes himself for the Central Committee.[6]

Stalin, of course, was the fulfillment of Trotsky's prophecy. One element in the exiled Trotsky's relentless efforts throughout the 1930s to save the revolution was the warm reception he accorded the leaders of Surrealism, despite the heavy dosage of anarchism they injected into their Marxism. Another element was his constant critique of the bureaucratic party and state machine constructed by Stalin, a critique so close to the traditional anarchist critique of Marxist organization that for decades many so-called Trotskyites were in reality closet anarchists.

THE PARIS COMMUNE: WHAT IS TO BE REMEMBERED?

Looking back at the Paris Commune (March 18–May 28, 1871) a decade later, Marx observed that "the Commune was merely the rising of a town under exceptional conditions; the majority of the Commune was in no sense socialist, nor could it be. With a small amount of common sense, they could have reached a compromise with Versailles." It is difficult to disagree with his assessment. Fundamentally the Communards were Jacobins and artisans, not socialists and proletarians. And the circumstances were indeed exceptional from Marx's standpoint, since they had nothing to do with economics or class struggle: Prussia had defeated France, Louis Napoleon had fallen, and the new republican government at Versailles was willing, the Communards unwilling, to accept the humiliating terms of peace dictated by Bismarck. By the time the French government finished squelching the Parisian revolt, the National Assembly had arrested 38,000, massacred 20,000, and deported another 7,500.

It is not especially surprising that Versailles, blinded by fear and hatred, should blame the Commune on the International, despite the meager number of its members in Paris and the minor role they played in the dramatic events which lasted for two months. What truly is surprising is that Marx and Bakunin accepted the false claim that the International was at the bottom of things, and chose to transform the Commune—through selective recall and inspired polemics—into one of the great myths of the political left. Marxists and anarchists were ever afterwards to fight many of their battles through wielding their contrasting interpretations of the Commune, each side using its ideologically filtered memory to prove the worth of its version of the proper way to conduct revolutionary politics.

Shortly before the event, Marx shared with the Central Committee in a public address, and with Engels in a private letter, his worry that a Paris Commune might be declared. Much discredit would befall the International, and the workers would

---

[6]Irving Howe, ed., *The Basic Writings of Trotsky*, (New York: Ramdom House, 1963), p. 9–10.

lose the opportunity to build up their movement within the framework of "Republican liberty." No sooner, however, was the Commune declared than Marx prepared to turn the inevitable debacle to the advantage of his brand of socialism. "On May 28," Engels recalled many years later, "the last fighters of the Commune succumbed. . . ; only two days later, on May 30, Marx read to the Central Committee the work in which the historical significance of the Paris Commune is delineated in short, powerful strokes."[7] The contest to claim the legacy was on, and Marx, with *The Civil War in France,* placed himself first in line.

At mid-century Marx had proven himself an excellent historian in his pamphlets treating the French revolution of 1848. Twenty years later he proved himself an equally skillful historical myth-maker in *The Civil War in France.* Only one of the leaders of the Commune was by any stretch of the imagination a Marxist; many were followers of Proudhon, whom Marx despised because of his reactionary efforts to cling to the pre-industrial past; still others were the disciples of Blanqui whose preference for conspiratorial, chauvinistic, and dictatorial politics earned him the animosity of Marx. From such recalcitrant materials Marx nevertheless fashioned, by audacious invention and legerdemain, an image of the Commune to which subsequent Marxists would repeatedly return for guidance and inspiration. Against all odds Marx succeeded in convincing many revolutionaries both that the Commune represented the first example of the proletariat in power and also that its government provided a model of how to handle the transition from the old world to the new.

In Marx's pamphlet the uprising of the Communards was a "proletarian revolution" that resulted in the establishment of what was "essentially a working-class government." Having, by a stroke of the pen, transformed artisans into proletarians, Marx went on to portray the Communards as cosmopolitans fighting to advance the cause of all European workers. Nothing could be more false than Marx's claim that the Communards were "emphatically international"; nothing, except his statement that they were "conscious of initiating" a "new era of history." Exactly the opposite is true: the Communards were engaged in a nostalgic and chauvinistic effort to repeat the experience of the first Commune of Paris, 1792. Just as their ancestors, under siege from foreign powers, had in 1792 organized from Paris the mass armies which successfully ejected the invaders and marched across Europe on a divine mission to carry French civilization everywhere, so now the Parisians of 1871 were trying to ignite the explosion that would blow the Germans back to Prussia. Opposed in September of 1870 to the creation of a new commune, Marx had told the International how deeply he feared that the French workers might be "deluded by the national memories of 1792." On May 30, 1871, Marx pretended his fears had not been vindicated.

Marx could afford to be somewhat less disingenuous when he examined the governance of the Commune. Passing in review the French revolutions of 1789, 1830, 1848, and their aftermath, Marx discerned a pattern of constantly intensify-

---

[7]Engels wrote these words on March 18, 1891, the twentieth anniversary of the Commune. His comments were published as an introduction to a 1891 edition of Marx's *The Civil War in France.*

ing class struggle met by an ever more desperately repressive state power. The year 1871, to his mind, marked a turning point: the direct democracy practiced by the Communards made possible what the French most needed, the "reabsorption of the state power by society as its own living forces instead of as forces controlling and subduing it." What better way to begin phasing out the state than for the workers to practice self-government in the literal sense?

All public functionaries, during the Commune, were elected by universal suffrage, held office for short terms, and were removable. Even the judiciary, Marx noted, was divested of its "sham independence." Moreover, "Public service had to be done at workmen's wages," so that bureaucratic privilege would become a thing of the past. A militia replaced the standing army, the church was disestablished and disendowed, and free education was made available to everyone. "Science was freed from the fetters which class prejudice and governmental force had imposed upon it." For two months the Parisians showed the world that the state is unnecessary, and taught a lesson that would live on after their defeat. Or so Marx chose to believe when he presented the Commune to his readers, not as a dismal failure but as "the glorious harbinger of a new society."

Barely had the ink dried on Marx's papers than Bakunin stepped forth with his version of the Commune's message. Unlike the "authoritarian communists" who sought political revolution and dictatorship, the Communards of Bakunin's imagination encouraged "the spontaneous and continued action of the masses." Consequently the Commune became noteworthy, "above all, because it was a bold, clearly formulated negation of the state"—this in France, which "had been hitherto the land of political centralization par excellence." In direct contrast to Marx, Bakunin spends no time delineating the disturbing growth of bureaucracy in the French state; rather, the anarchist leader devotes his attention to the pattern of centralization which, prior to the Commune, had characterized French revolutionary movements. The Jacobinism of many would-be leaders of the Commune, unmentioned in Marx's pamphlet, is discussed at length by Bakunin, who delighted in telling the story of how these bourgeois and authoritarian radicals, in order to have a revolution, "ended up becoming [libertarian] socialists in spite of themselves." "Since there is no revolution without the masses, and since the masses nowadays reveal an instinct for socialism," the Jacobins were forced to be free by the very persons over whom they initially wished to lord their superiority.

Alas, the Jacobinism which was kicked out the front door during the early days of the Commune returned through the back door at a later date and destroyed the revolutionary impulse.

> [The Communards] had to set up a revolutionary government and army against the government and army of Versailles; in order to fight the monarchist and clerical reaction they were compelled to organize themselves in a Jacobin manner, forgetting or sacrificing the first conditions of revolutionary socialism.[8]

---

[8]Bakunin, "The Paris Commune and the Idea of the State," in Dolgoff, ed., *Bakunin on Anarchism*, pp. 259–273.

Nevertheless, the Commune showed the way to the revolutionary future. The radicals of the Latin countries, Bakunin believed, would take its lessons to heart; the same could not be said of the German socialists.

Years later Peter Kropotkin (1842–1921), a Russian prince and steadfast anarchist, noted that the example provided by the Paris Commune had already been copied in Spanish uprisings, and he predicted that the 1871 model of a free federation of communes would inspire future anarchist revolts in the "Latin countries, in France, in Spain, in the French-speaking part of Switzerland, and the Wallonic part of Belgium." Predictably, Kropotkin argued that the revolution of 1871 "was made by the people themselves; it sprang spontaneously from the midst of the mass." To his mind, as to Bakunin's, it was a proof of the spontaneous nature of the Commune that its members acted first and "only afterward" set out to offer theoretical explanations of their behavior—to which one must contrast Lenin's view, stated in *What is to be Done?*, that "consciousness" must precede, guide, or even suppress "spontaneity." The undoing of the Commune, in Kropotkin's view, was that its external policy of calling for the proliferation of free communes was not matched by a decisive internal policy of freeing itself from institutions of political control. Specifically, the Communards gave themselves a council whose rulers, separated from the people, "paralyzed the popular initiative."[9]

In the largest sense the reason why the promise of the Commune went unfulfilled, Kropotkin believed, was that although the socialists of 1871 had learned to repudiate the "authoritarian communism" of 1848, the admirable alternative of "free communism, anarchist communism, was only beginning to dawn upon the minds of the workers." Proudhon's heirs, well represented among the Communards, still believed in private property and in outdated one-on-one economic exchanges; Bakunin, trying to adapt to the modern economy, advocated collective ownership combined with individual remuneration for items produced. Kropotkin, going one step further, favored the provision of common storehouses from which persons could take whatever they needed. His motto was, "from each according to his ability, to each according to his needs." The great mistake of the Communards, in his opinion, was that they did not collectivize private property. "They tried to consolidate the Commune first and defer the social revolution until afterward, whereas the only way to go about it was *to consolidate the Commune by means of the social revolution.*"

As late as 1968 the libertarian French student rebels of anarcho-Marxist persuasion, in their efforts to distinguish themselves from the authoritarian members of the French Communist party, appealed to the example set by the Commune. The greatest moment, however, in the struggle among twentieth-century leftists over the heritage of the Commune came in the years immediately following the Bolshevik revolution. Karl Kautsky, the leading theoretician of gradualist German Social Democracy, challenged the "proletarian dictatorship" instituted by Lenin and Trotsky. When Kautsky published *The Dictator-*

---

[9]Kropotkin, "The Commune of Paris," in Kropotkin, *Selected Writings on Anarchism and Revolution* (Cambridge, MA: M.I.T. Press, 1970), pp. 118–132.

ship of the Proletariat in 1918, Lenin quickly responded with *The Proletarian Revolution and the Renegade Kautsky.* A year later Kautsky renewed his criticism of the Bolsheviks in *Terrorism and Communism,* to which Trotsky replied in 1920 with a book bearing the identical title. The Paris Commune was repeatedly addressed in these works written by the most conspicuous representative of the defunct Second International and the leading personages of the upstart Third International.

Forever stressing the need for the preconditions of revolution to ripen through the slow maturation of capitalism, Kautsky (1854–1938) offers an accurate historical account of the premature Commune in order to deflate its revolutionary mystique. Paris in 1871 had no factories; its workers were petty bourgeois craftsmen, not proletarians; the majority of the politically assertive Communards were Jacobins, not socialists; and the International, to the extent that it participated, was represented by Proudhonists rather than Marxists. Because it was in his interest, Kautsky also gave a generally reliable, if incomplete, account of Marx's position on revolution. He notes with satisfaction Marx's opposition in September 1870 to the creation of a Commune, and reminds the reader that the youthful and rash Marx who called in 1848 for an immediate push in Germany from a bourgeois to a proletarian revolution was replaced as early as September of 1850 by a chastened and mature Marx who would never again endorse the premature seizure of power. In effect Kautsky was saying that Lenin and Trotsky, who were trying to leapfrog to the proletarian revolution a mere several months after the triumph of the Russian bourgeoisie, were reverting to a position decisively repudiated by Marx.

Perhaps best of all, Kautsky in *Terrorism and Communism* could subtly invite his comrades to hurl the epithet "anarchist" at Lenin, who had so often used the same pejorative word against fellow Marxists with whom he disagreed. In particular, Lenin had for many years accused Marxists of de facto anarchism, of succumbing to "spontaneity," whenever they waited on the masses before acting or supported the workers in their quest for reforms. Now, in 1919, Kautsky announced that the Bolsheviks and their leader, in their attempt to accomplish revolutionary change overnight, resembled "the Bakuninists of Spain in the year 1873."

Kautsky knew that to Lenin revolution was an act of "will"—the will of a self-selected "vanguard" acting in the name of the masses. Explicitly, Kautsky refuted Lenin by quoting the words Marx uttered in September 1850, when he bid adieu to his former hopes for a shortcut to the socialist future and indicated that not "will" but "conditions" would henceforth be "the driving force of the revolution." Implicitly, Kautsky encouraged good Marxists to draw a second conclusion: he invited them, in effect, to remember that it was Bakunin, and anarchists more generally, who had held that revolution is an act of will to be undertaken at any moment, in open defiance of social, economic, and political conditions, even in the most economically backward countries, the ones lagging far behind Germany. Kautsky's Lenin is a doubly vile socialist: a bad Marxist and an unwitting anarchist.

Kautsky called upon the Paris Commune to denounce, Lenin and Trotsky called upon it to laud, the Russian revolution. According to Kautsky the Bolshevik takeover, in marked contrast to the popular Commune, was a coup d'état followed by the establishment of a Jacobin dictatorship. Not 1871 but 1793, argued Kautsky, is the suitable French parallel to Russia in 1917 and thereafter. "The fall of Bolshevism will not be accepted by the masses of Russia in the same way as the fall of the second Paris Commune was received by the whole of the socialist proletariat at that time; but rather as the fall of Robespierre . . . was received by the whole of France, namely as salvation from a heavy load." In the unlikely event that Lenin's regime stays in power, Bolshevism will win but socialism will surely lose; for the Russian dictatorship, mislabeled as Marxist, should be termed "Asiatic" or "Tartar socialism."

Above all, continued Kautsky, the Commune was democratic, open to all shades of socialism, and refrained from acts of violence. By contrast, "the socialist party which governs Russia today . . . exercises its authority while excluding other socialist parties from the executive." Moreover, the Bolsheviks disbanded the Constituent Assembly, whereas the Communards held free elections with universal suffrage. Kautsky also reminds the reader of the emphasis Marx placed on the refusal of the Communards to carry out executions. It was the bourgeois who were violent in 1871, just as their predecessors had been in 1848.

Lenin's response was to point out that Kautsky had dutifully retained "everything in Marxism except revolutionary methods of struggle." On close examination, the Marx of the famous German social democrat turned out to be nothing more than "an ordinary liberal." Lenin accurately observed that although Marx entertained the possibility of a nonviolent triumph in England and America, he never wavered in his conviction that for countries such as Germany and France, where there existed massive bureaucratic and military establishments, revolution was the sole path to success. Marx was ever a revolutionary, and would have added America and England to his list of countries whose governments required violent overthrow, had he lived long enough to witness the advent of their bureaucracies.

What's more, continued Lenin, Marx from 1872 to 1875 repeatedly made references to the need for a "dictatorship of the proletariat" as a bridge from the bourgeois state to the stateless society of a future free humanity. Sometimes he and Engels specifically referred to the Paris Commune as a model showing what such a transitional regime would entail, and neither of the two founders of Marxism uttered a word to vindicate Kautsky's portrayal of the Commune as a form of parliamentary democracy. How, inquired Lenin, could Kautsky pretend that the elections held by the Communards gave everyone a vote when "it is well known that . . . the upper strata of the bourgeoisie had fled Paris to Versailles?" All states, in fact, are class dictatorships; so is the state run for and by the proletariat—but this would be a state to end states, a government seeking its own abolition through inviting the workers to administer and manage the country.

Throughout the course of the Kautsky/Lenin debate in 1918, Kautsky chided the German left communists for their Bolshevik-inspired impatience, and dismissed Russian workers' councils as signs of economic backwardness, to be cast aside the moment the trade union movement came to maturity. Soon Lenin would decry "infantile" left communism; but in 1918, when revolution in Western Europe seemed plausible, when the German left communists therefore had to be talked up and the "renegade" Kautsky shouted down, Lenin repeatedly mentioned *State and Revolution,* the pamphlet in which he cited the Paris Commune to advocate what amounted to a left communist or anarcho-Marxist position. The words Lenin had written in the spring of 1917 had not yet come back to haunt him: "to break up at once the old bureaucratic machine and to start immediately the construction of a new one which will enable us gradually to reduce all officialdom to naught—this is no utopia, it is the experience of the Commune, it is the direct and urgent task of the revolutionary proletariat."

It was in 1920 that Trotsky launched his salvo against Kautsky. Two years of civil war had passed since Lenin's attack on the "renegade" Kautsky, time enough for Trotsky to draw the conclusion that only a Red Army could save the revolution. So it is not surprising that when Trotsky conjures up images of the Paris Commune, it is to vindicate his resort to violent means. His intent is always lucid; his argument less so. Trotsky, the enemy of vacillation, himself vacillates between two positions in *Terrorism and Communism.* Sometimes he asserts that the Commune was dictatorial but not dictatorial enough; at other times his argument is that the government of the Commune would have become a dictatorship, if it had stayed in power longer than two months.

Trotsky was wrong to refer to the Commune as the "dictatorship of working class Paris over the peasant country." No doubt the Jacobins did want Paris to dominate France, but the best they could do, under the circumstances, was to endorse the anarchist hope that the Parisian example would spark a proliferation of autonomous communes across the nation. Even Marx had accepted the federalist position in the *Civil War in France,* to the great annoyance of the anarchists who believed, probably rightly, that he was dishonestly stealing their programme.

Far more plausible was Trotsky's claim that the Communards escaped the necessity of initiating a Red Terror solely because they suffered early defeat. Counter-revolutionary violence can only be met by the revolutionary violence toward which the working class Parisians were slowing inching at the time of their defeat. An incipient vanguard elite, in Trotsky's reading of events, had begun to take charge of affairs in the later stages of the Commune. Given enough time, they would have eliminated the indecisiveness and weakness of the early days which Kautsky interpreted as evidence of elevated moral feeling.

Trotsky's conclusion could not have been more Bolshevik: "The Commune was weak. To complete its work we have become strong. The Commune was crushed. . . . We are taking vengeance for the Commune, and we shall avenge it."

From 1917 to 1919 the proponents of the two leading schools of Marxism discussed the Commune at great length. The word "anarchist," insofar as it figured in these debates, was a smear term, a means of suggesting guilt by association; evidently the only matter on which German social democrats and Bolsheviks continued to agree was in their mutual antipathy to anarchism. After 1919 Marxists more or less ignored the Commune, Soviet Russia having assumed the status of the sole historical example pertinent to Marxian revolutionaries. Anarchists, however, never forgot what had happened in Paris in 1871, with the consequence that when the anarchist and anarcho-Marxist French students rebelled in 1968, they wasted no time before issuing an appeal to the memory of the heroic Communards.

THEORY: WHAT IS TO BE CONCEPTUALIZED?

Although many Marxists have been anti-Leninist, very few if any would disagree with Lenin's statement in *What is to be Done?*: "Without a revolutionary theory there can be no revolutionary movement." In part Lenin was taking aim against the British trade union movement, splendidly organized yet devoid of a revolutionary vision because of its lack of concern for socialist theory. Anarchists were Lenin's second target: revolutionaries they were, unlike the workers in England, but never would a revolution succeed when championed by a movement that substituted "spontaneity" for "consciousness," momentary impulse for considered reflection, mindless for mindful action.

One way to underscore the difference between Marxists and anarchists is to spell out their respective positions on the question of the proper relationship of theory with practice. Marx's theme being that of the unity of theory and practice, he was opposed both to all philosophies which were purely contemplative and also to all intellectual movements which praised action at the expense of theory. Early in his career Marx denounced German thinkers who were all theory and no practice; later, with perfect consistency, he would attack Bakunin on the grounds that he was all action and no theory.

When Marx in 1845 accused the supposedly radical Young Hegelians of mere "theoretical bubble-blowing," of deep-seated conservatism in their substitution of criticism for action, he was not speaking against theory. Rather, his point was that theory is nothing unless united with practice. Such is the meaning of his famous statement, "the philosophers have only interpreted the world in various ways; the point, however, is to change it." Two decades later he would complain that Bakunin was a "Mahomet without a Koran," a man who could never get an argument straight and yet deemed himself fit to lead the working class movement. Doing without thinking (Bakunin) is no improvement over thinking without doing (the Young Hegelians).

On occasion, admittedly, Bakunin did try to think philosophically, and he sometimes expressed interest in the promise science held out to socialism. But these comments in which he took theory seriously were no sooner uttered than abandoned, because he had neither the ability nor, more significantly, the desire to think rigorously. Rebellion and revolt in the name of freeing "life," destruction in the name of liberating repressed instincts, are Bakunin's recurring themes. Like many other writers of the romantic age, he frequently derided science as a force hostile to creativity: "What I preach is a revolt of life against science." As for philosophy, he twisted it into conformity with his irrationalist outlook. From Hegel he borrowed the notion of "antithesis" while ignoring "synthesis"; and whenever he had recourse to the Hegelian vocabulary of "negation," it was transparently for the sake of rationalizing his fascination with destruction. In a sentence typical of the man, Bakunin poetically asserted that "Revolution requires extensive and widespread destruction, a fecund and renovating destruction, since in this way and only this way are new worlds born." Marx's triumph over Bakunin in matters theoretical during the 1860s and 1870s was a victory by default.

Proudhon (1809–1865) in the 1840s was a famous figure, Marx was still relatively unknown. But when the two brandished their pens as swords against one another, it was the younger and less well established Marx who walked away the winner in a contest that proved to be a mismatch. For years Proudhon had been acclaimed in France for his familiarity with Hegelian thought, and in Germany for his acumen in economics. Marx was highly successful in his effort to show that Proudhon knew neither economics nor philosophy, and owed his fame to German ignorance of French economics and French ignorance of German philosophy. Proudhon fares so poorly in his philosophical showdown with Marx that Bakunin's refusal at a later date to engage his German rival in a clash of theories would seem to be the discretion which is the better part of valor.

Barely had Proudhon published *The Philosophy of Poverty* (1846) than Marx responded with a devastating rebuttal in *The Poverty of Philosophy* (1847). Throughout his career Proudhon justified poverty, sang its praises, and maintained that abundance for all is both an impossible and an unworthy goal. "Poverty has its own joys, its innocent festivities, and homely luxuries," he lyrically affirmed. "It would be misplaced to dream of escaping from the inevitable poverty that is the law of our nature and of society. Poverty is good, and we must think of it as being the source of all our joys." Not without reason did Marx regard Proudhon, and French anarchism more generally, as reactionary rather than progressive. There is much to be said in behalf of Marx's view that Proudhon was foolishly trying to prevent history, especially economic history, from happening; much to be said, also, for Marx's contention that Proudhon gave voice to that portion of the workers, the artisans and craftsmen, who reacted not simply against the dehumanizing aspects of industrialization, but who wanted to turn back the clock, to break up the machines and tear down the factories, so that they, with their small scale output, could once again be the proud producers of quality goods. These preindustrial artisans and craftsmen Marx terms the "petty bourgeoisie."

If there is one social type, to a Marxist, that is worse than the "bourgeois," it is the "petty bourgeois." However exploitative the bourgeoisie, it has created an expansionary economy pointing the way to a future society wherein poverty will be unknown and the individual will neither need nor desire to choose between self-interest and the good of society. In the meantime the market economy is simplifying the class structure, dividing it into two categories, the owners of the means of production and those forced to sell their labor at the marketplace, the bourgeoisie and proletariat, respectively. Both aristocracy and peasantry are doomed by capitalism, as is the petty bourgeoisie which cannot compete in the new world of mass production and international political economy. Proudhon sounds like Marx when he writes that the capitalists "want to squeeze out small industries, kill small business and thereby transform the majority of the bourgeoisie into wage-earners." The difference is that Proudhon abhors the demise of the petty bourgeoisie, whereas Marx applauds the same and abhors Proudhon's efforts to derail the progressive development of the modern economy.

Quoted without attribution, Proudhon's statement that "political economy . . . is a network of contradictions" could readily be misidentified as an example of

Marx applying Hegelian terminology ("contradictions") to classical political economy. In fact, however, Proudhon lacks Hegel's vision of history as a forward movement, spurred onward by cultural contradictions; and he lacks, more significantly, Marx's economic restatement of Hegel, according to which history is saved from incoherence, is given structure and significance, by the "simple reality that every succeeding generation finds itself in possession of the productive forces acquired by the previous generation." Marx postulated that the contradictions of capitalism, for instance the conflict between social production in the factory and individual appropriation by the owner, would eventually yield a socialist outcome; and he criticized the economists for treating the economic laws of a passing historical period as unchanging laws of nature. Proudhon repeated the mistake of the bourgeois economists, albeit on an appropriately petty bourgeois scale, when he postulated that France must never advance, economically, beyond a "natural state" consisting of agrarianism, modest-sized property holdings, and an ethos of thrift and frugality.

Classical political economists, though blind to the future, did at least set forth concepts grounded in the present reality of capitalism. Proudhon, by contrast, offers a dance of abstractions, none having any empirical referents. When he discusses a concept such as competition, the reader is referred to a second concept, such as monopoly—this as opposed to what Marx demands, an examination of the actual social forms of competition and monopoly. Even worse, argues Marx, is Proudhon's habit of substituting moralistic outrage for economic insight, as when he fumes against modern competition and nostalgically yearns for the good old days of simple exchanges between two producers; or, again, when he refuses to admit that labor has become a commodity. Also missing from Proudhon's thought is the realization that under modern conditions production incessantly creates new needs and wants; his is a society ever the same, with a few unchanging needs, miserly and austere.

Proudhon adumbrated a "philosophy of misery" because he was a miserable philosopher. Knowing neither history nor economics, and dedicating his life to arresting the forward march of economic history, Proudhon represented the unity of impoverished theory and reactionary practice. Not from him would anarchism receive the theoretical sophistication it needed to challenge Marxism.

It may well be that the most theoretically gifted of Marx's many anarchist opponents was his first, Max Stirner (1806–1856). In 1845, two years prior to his refutation of Proudhon, Marx devoted the entire second part of *The German Ideology* to an attack on Stirner's *The Ego and Its Own*. Both combatants were German by birth and Young Hegelians by training, with the vital difference that *The German Ideology* marked Marx's break with philosophy and the beginning of the historical, sociological, and economic researches of his maturity. Anarchism, strictly speaking, did not exist in the mid-1840s, but at a later date both the anarchist Kropotkin and the Marxist Plekhanov would regard Stirner as a pioneer of anarchist thought. Those who waive red flags agree with the representatives of the black that the conflict between Marx and Stirner was a struggle between Marxism and anarchism.

We have it on Kropotkin's authority that *The Ego and Its Own* was "spoken of in anarchist circles as a sort of manifesto of the individualist anarchists"—deservedly so, because Stirner's theme was that the individual person should answer to nothing and no one. Although a self-professed radical and an advocate of revolt, Stirner was vociferously anti-revolutionary and especially hostile to communism; his constantly reiterated argument was that leftist politics is incompatible with the autonomy of the individual human being. Obviously Marx could not afford to ignore Stirner, the man Plekhanov would later call the "father of anarchism."

The trouble with revolutionaries, Stirner believed, is that they want us to rise above ourselves. The person they ask me to be is not the concrete human I am but the empty exemplar of an abstraction I will become, provided I dutifully live in accordance with a "higher" ideal. In their view "I go toward myself"; in Stirner's "I start from myself." "In the former I long for myself; in the latter I have myself." Robespierre and St. Just, the better to serve *Man*, cut off the heads of *men* during the French Revolution. This same cheating of the flesh and blood person in the name of an abstraction called *Man* may be found, Stirner shrewdly observed, in the writings of his contemporary, the radical Young Hegelian author Ludwig Feuerbach. In his book on Christianity, Feuerbach rightly rids us of God by demonstrating that love, intelligence, and all the admirable traits attributed to the deity are in reality projections of human characteristics upon an abstraction. Then, unfortunately, Feuerbach turns around and demands that individual persons bow down before a new deity, the vapid abstraction called *Man*. Feuerbach was only half an atheist; after destroying the Christian deity he replaced it with a religion of humanity. It is for myself that I should live, argues Stirner; never for a revolutionary ideal, however high-sounding.

Stirner encouraged the workers to rebel but opposed the organizational structure necessary for victory. "The laborers have the most enormous power in their hands," he wrote, "and if they once became thoroughly conscious of it and used it, nothing could withstand them." Were the workers to end the slavery of labor, he adds, the state and all its hateful institutions of oppression would fall. Yet he denounces a workers' party because it would be a "dead union, an idea that has become fixed," a denial of individual sovereignty. The only laudable organization is a "Union of Egoists," which would be a voluntary association to which the individual belongs only so long as it suits his (or her?) interest. Each day this organization would have to be remade since it is based on an act of will, and the will of yesterday must never be permitted to bind the will of today.

If he rejected the organizational *means* advocated by Marx, Stirner was also outspokenly hostile to the *ends* of communists. "Every state is a despot, be the despot one or many," he insisted; consequently, "I am as badly off in one as in the other." Not even a constitutional state is an exception, nor is its communist counterpart, which would stand out from the others only insofar as it might well prove to be the most tyrannical of all. Where the state owns everything, the individual owns nothing, not even himself. Under communism, Stirner predicted, all persons will be overwhelmed with duties and swallowed by the collectivity.

In Marx's judgment Stirner was a Young Hegelian author who had deleted the best of Hegel and retained the worst. Gone is Hegel's invaluable insight that the self is not there, whole and complete from the start, but rather comes to be. Nowhere in Stirner's book does the reader meet with Hegel's demonstration that the transition from consciousness to self-consciousness, the acquisition of one's "I," occurs through interaction with others. Though *The German Ideology* marks his break with German philosophy, Marx never forgot Hegel's lesson that *the self is social*.

Nor did Marx fail to remember the Hegelian point that *the self is historical,* as opposed to a fixed essence or something already existing in a presocial state of nature. Stirner, however, posits an "I" that is every bit as ahistorical as Feuerbach's *Man.* The ego to which Stirner incessantly refers is not that of a particular person; it is a general category, a pure abstraction residing outside place and time. Despite his many discussions of historical topics, Stirner never thinks historically; his usage of the past is exclusively designed to report those alien events which have befallen the "me" (or, quite inconsistently, the *Mankind*) that is inexplicably ever the same.

When Stirner does borrows something from the Hegelian historians, it is their "upside down" depiction of a world in which "material history" appears to be produced by "ideal history." Thus, Stirner's thoughts on the uprisings of workers have as their reference the "idea" of revolt, which he discusses without bothering to study the history of the actual struggles of the working classes. What the workers have done in America, Belgium, and England is of no interest to him; nor does he care whether the political regime is absolutist or constitutionalist, even though historical experience proves that both the bourgeoisie and the proletariat strongly prefer representative government, the capitalists in order to dominate the state, the wage-earners to gain an opportunity to organize.

In keeping with the general tenor of the Young Hegelian movement, Stirner represents the disunity of thought and action. Because he foolishly assumes his self is given, not made, Stirner does not realize that he must actively develop his qualities; "nor does he need to worry about the conditions of the world, which in reality determine the extent to which an individual can develop." Similarly, adds Marx, the egotistical radicalism of Stirner amounts to nothing more than the substitution of rhetoric for action. "The difference between revolution and Stirner's rebellion is not, as Stirner thinks, that the one is a political and social act whereas the other is an egoistical act, but that the former is an act whereas the latter is not an act at all."

Stirner, in common with the other Young Hegelians, grounds his project of liberation in a speculative philosophy which is unequal to the task assigned it. Henceforth, Marx suggests, our studies should be less in philosophy than in social and economic history. Once we have achieved a theoretical understanding of our situation based on empirical research, it will be evident that our unfreedom has been caused by collective forces which can only be removed by action taken in common. No one can be free alone, nor does anyone have reason to desire the isolation that diminishes rather than enhances the self.

If Stirner posits the need to choose between one's own and the social good, that is because his thought is an expression of the very bourgeois outlook he despises. For it is capitalism which sets us against one another and communism which will end the false dichotomy pitting the person against society. "Communist society," as Marx sees it, far from demanding the diminution of persons, is the "only society in which the genuine and free development of individuals ceases to be a mere phrase." Communism in Marx's sense will not be a grim spectacle of scarcity spread evenly, as in pre-industrial visions of socialism; rather, Marx's is a communism of abundance in which everyone wins and no one is reduced to getting his own by taking from someone else. Such a communism will not signal the ultimate triumph of the state but its dissolution, because a classless society has no need for the state.

Like a Phoenix rising from the ashes, anarchism has always had a way of regenerating itself after suffering the most devastating defeats. Routed by Marxists, the anarchists have repeatedly reasserted themselves through the expedient of relocating their intellectual shop inside Marxist thought. Left communism, as we have seen, is one example; the political writings of Jean-Paul Sartre (1905–1980) are another. It is arguable that when Sartre began to address political questions at the end of World War II, anarchism finally found its philosopher. For the Marxism conjured up by Sartre, the most famous philosopher of his day, was permeated by anarchist notions.

Take the example of Sartre's understanding of "permanent revolution," a concept used by Marxists and anarchists alike, each school defining it in accordance with its general outlook. To Marx in the early months of 1850, to Trotsky in the early twentieth century, "permanent revolution" meant combining two revolutions into one, in the sense of taking whatever steps are necessary to ensure that what begins as a bourgeois revolution will end with the proletariat in power, actively cajoling the workers of other countries to follow its example. Anarchists have a very different understanding of permanent revolution; to them it usually means that no society should ever be permitted to settle down into an institutionalized routine stifling the "spontaneity" of its individual members. Even the relatively conservative Proudhon held that "in history there is permanent revolution," and all the more so did Bakunin and the Surrealists who hated normality and relished upheaval.

The positions Sartre had held as an "existentialist" prepared him to adhere to the anarchist meaning of "permanent revolution" when he joined the political left. It had been his view during his existentialist phase that individuals are "authentic" only if they accept the burden of redefining themselves anew each day, without taking refuge in what they were the day before. Later, applying these lessons to society as a whole in *What is Literature?* (1947), he drew the political conclusion that a free society would reinvent itself day in and day out. There would be a "constant renewal of frameworks and the continuous overthrowing of order once it tends to congeal" in the world he envisioned—a "society in permanent revolution."

Sartre's conviction that revolution is an act of "will," not a response to the maturation of socio-economic conditions, further illuminates his relationship with Marxism and anarchism, and clearly stems from his existentialist starting point. Who we are hinges not on environmental circumstances in *Being and Nothingness* (1943), but on what we choose to make of that which is given. Our willed actions rather than our surroundings define us. By extension, the political Sartre readily concluded that the question of revolution comes down to willing and doing, never to waiting. But would his emphasis on "will" place him in the camp of the Leninists, for whom the will in question was that of the vanguard elite, or of the anarchists, for whom it was the will of the masses?

A Leninist in spite of himself in *The Communists and Peace* (1955), Sartre returned to the anarchist fold five years later in his *Critique of Dialectical Reason* (1960). When he wrote on revolution in 1955, Sartre did not believe the workers could act for themselves. However identical their interests, the proletarians are so isolated from one another by modern social conditions that he who places his trust in "spontaneity" waits in vain. Hence the party must impose a "collective will" upon the workers that transforms them from a passive mass into an active class. Dissatisfied with his own argument, Sartre spent the next several years studying the history of the French Revolution, and found in the storming of the Bastille a perfect example of what he wanted, a group fusing itself into cohesion through its own acts, without having recourse to leaders. In the *Critique* the events of July 14, 1789 figure prominently as an example of collectively self-willed revolution. Sartre's final position resembles nothing so much as Stirner's notion of a social group brought into existence by an act of will, subject each day to reconsideration; or Proudhon's call for a society run by a series of renegotiable contracts.

Whatever one may think of Sartre's anarcho-Marxist argument, it is difficult to deny that his thoughts are more lively and provocative than those set forth by his principal enemy, the brain-dead French Communist Party. The last round in the philosophical battle goes to the anarchists, no matter that all previous rounds were easily won by the Marxists.

ART: WHAT IS TO BE CREATED?

Creating is as primary to the anarchist tradition as theorizing is to the Marxist. Frequently anarchists had no use for the purveyors of theories, and when they did turn to intellectuals for inspiration, it was usually to those who preached the anti-intellectualist doctrine that philosophy and science are life-negating, whereas art is life-affirming. Montmartre in the early 1890s was a hotbed of anarchist-artists who hated all forms of "scientific" and inartistic socialism. Some decades later the Surrealists carried inside the Communist Party their revolutionary design for transforming society into a work of art, only to recoil in disgust when confronted with the unbudging Stalinist doctrine of "socialist realism." Within the realm of art the anarchists repeatedly outdid the Marxists, but in the process they wantonly glorified violence and opened a rift within their own ranks between artists and workers.

Montmartre was a haven for prostitutes, bohemian individualists, and for those artists who disdained the respectable academies and feared having their work embalmed in museums. Nearby stood Sacré Coeur, symbol of church, state, and reaction—a perfect counterpoint to Montmartre where the Paris Commune had begun in 1871 when two Versaillaise generals were killed. Surrounding Montmartre were those working class quarters, such as the faubourg Saint-Antoine, in which craftsmen and artisans produced furniture, shoes, and the like, while abjuring parliamentary politics and supporting anarchists on some occasions, right-wing extremists on others. Both artists and artisans have historically been strongly drawn to the anarchist cause, never more conspicuously so, nor in closer physical proximity, than in Paris during the first half of the 1890s.[10]

Despite geographical contiguity and overlapping ideological concerns, there was little communication between artists and workers. Some young anarchist poets tried but largely failed to emulate the earthy language of such early modern writers as Villon or Rabelais. Anarchist publishers experimented in the *argot* dialect of the lower classes, which was drawn from the criminal underclass of the city. By and large, however, the publishers' high-brow use in newspapers of this low-brow language is probably just another example of the recurring fascination of anarchist intellectuals (e.g., Stirner and Bakunin) with criminals and outcasts; it is doubtful that the workers and petty bourgeois paid much attention to such efforts to cross the barriers erected by occupation and social class. Only the poster art of the anarchists reached a large audience, the frequenters of the dance halls and cabarets of Montmartre, relatively few of whom were artisans.

In any case the anarchism of the workers was in many respects the direct opposite of that espoused by the artists. Conventional in their morality, the handicraftsmen were scandalized by the bohemian life style, the scant regard for family, and the search for free love that characterized the milieu of the artists. The bohemian individualism of the artists, moreover, was radically at odds with the drive for proletarian solidarity in trade union organizations which was the objective of the syndicalist movement, organized by Fernand Pelloutier and lasting from the mid-1890s until World War I. Although the syndicalists rejected Proudhon's condemnation of unions and strikes, they upheld his imperatives that the workers must manage their own affairs and ignore political parties.

Nor did the artists endear themselves to the workers when they likened work to drudgery and sought fulfillment in play and the free flight of the imagination. At the center of syndicalist thought was the Proudhonian belief that even under existing oppressive conditions, life in the workshop is its own reward. For tactical reasons having to do with admission to the antianarchist Second International, the syndicalists were willing to coat their documents with a veneer of Marxist rhetoric. Never, however, did they accept Marx's view that labor will be unrewarding until after the revolution. And if they could not abide Marx on the question of labor, all the less could they tolerate the artists who objected to labor on principle.

Pelloutier's position on art was essentially the same as that stated by Proudhon decades earlier. Content, not form, was what mattered; artists were to offer realistic depictions of social reality or, better yet, inspirational images of what a workers' society would look like. Kropotkin made much the same point when he praised Raphael's frescoes on city walls as noteworthy examples of the possibilities of popular art. Quite predictably, the avant-garde artists of Montmartre held a diametrically opposite view. The Symbolist poets, in particular, scorned the authors of novels, especially Emile Zola and the Naturalists, because an artist should do more

---

[10]For Montmartre in the early 1890s I have relied heavily upon Richard Sonn, *Anarchism and Cultural Politics in Fin de Siècle France* (Lincoln: University of Nebraska Press, 1989).

than pander to a mass audience. No doubt the French Symbolists would have agreed with Oscar Wilde's comment that "art should never try to be popular. The public should try to make itself artistic." To make matters worse, the novel records reality when it is far more fitting that we rebel against all that exists.

Unlike the anarcho-syndicalists who stressed content over form and placed their emphasis on the audience, the avant-garde of Montmartre put form first and wrote primarily for themselves. The French counterpart to Wilde's "art is individualism" is the statement that Symbolism is "individualism in art." Sound takes precedence over meaning in a Symbolist poem; signifiers become so much a world unto themselves that their referential functions are suspended. Which is to say, a Symbolist poem is more about the poetic process than about the world. This kind of poetry, the Symbolists believed, is a rebellion against reality and a bold assertion of the poet's self. To the Symbolists, art and anarchism are much the same, whereas art and socialism are "at the antipodes." Art cannot survive the socialist practice of chaining the artist to a social and political movement.

One of the most disturbing sides of the anarchist-artists of Montmartre was their apologetic response to terrorism. The incidence of bombings and other violent acts from 1892 to 1894 was the highest in the history of the Third Republic. Usually the work of a single person, never the outcome of a conspiracy, a bombing was a purely expressive and symbolic act, an instance of "propaganda by the deed." Anarchist writers and poster artists, propagandists by the word and the drawing, displayed great concern for the perpetrators and little or none for the victims of terrorism. It was a sign of the times when the anarchist poet Laurent Tailhade, asked his opinion of a bombing, replied, "What do the victims matter if the gesture is beautiful?" Beauty is beyond good and evil, the anarchist-artists implied; so is saintliness, which is also to the point, because the artists depicted the condemned terrorists as martyrs. In vain one searches in the posters and words of the artists for recognition of the utilitarian, inartistic principle that revolutionary violence is inexcusable when unfocused and ineffectual.

The belief that violence is, in and of itself, uplifting and redeeming had long been part of the anarchist heritage. "The passion for destruction is a creative passion!", Bakunin had suggested in a striking phrase that is all too easy to duplicate in anarchist writings. Even Proudhon, normally so eager to avoid conflict, could on occasion write that "war is divine." Against such a backdrop, it is impossible to place Georges Sorel solely under the fascist rubric to which he eventually adhered (See Chapter 8). Admittedly, his *Reflections on Violence* (1906) is more an abuse of the syndicalist movement than a faithful, authorized statement of its principles. Yet the vitalist and irrationalist philosophy he called upon to eulogize violence on a grand and glorious scale is akin to that invoked by Bakunin, whose anarchist credentials have never been in doubt.

Sorel admired the determination of the syndicalists "to create today the ethic of the producers of the future." But what he admired even more in syndicalist pronouncements was the progression from "propaganda by the deed" to "direct action," from bomb-throwing to the "general strike," from individual to collective acts of violence. Syndicalism was in general an updated restatement of Proudhon, coated over with phrases borrowed from Marx; hence Sorel seasoned his irrationalist cult of creative destruction with Marxian social categories. Neither capitalism nor socialism mattered to Sorel; only the terminology of social classes in conflict was suitable for his purposes. It was his hope that the "myth" of the general strike might rouse the workers to fight a total war against the bourgeoisie. By no other means could heroic values be reborn in a modern world infested with the humanitarian values espoused both by liberals and socialists. Just as the artist-anarchists of Montmartre had praised the beauty of individual terrorist acts, so did Sorel look forward to the "sublime" experience of viewing one fanatically inspired collective group fighting another in a battle to the finish.

The Surrealist movement born in 1924 bore many resemblances to the Symbolist school which had flourished from approximately 1885 to 1895. Surrealists no less than the earlier Symbolists hated the "realism" of novels and lauded the unreality of poetry. Symbolists loved to write about "dreams" and "dreaming"—words the Surrealists gladly inherited, adding a Freudian account of the primacy of dreams in the life of the "unconscious" mind. When the Surrealist leader André Breton (1896–1966) wrote that "Imagination alone offers me some intimation of what *can be,*" he was simply repeating a theme of Symbolism and, more generally, of romanticism. The novelty of Breton's position lay in the techniques he and his coterie developed to free the imagination: recital of dreams; spontaneous poems, drawings, and actions; improvised speeches; texts written in a state of hypnosis. By these methods the Surrealists hoped to abolish the gap between "the real and the imaginary, . . . the communicable and the incommunicable," the conscious and the unconscious.

In the beginning Surrealism was vaguely anarchistic, to the limited extent that it had a political outlook. Breton exhorted his companions to "lay waste to the ideas of family, country, religion"; his position was one of relentless hostility to work and to duty. Before long, however, he realized that if the Surrealist faithful were "to transform the world" or "to change life," they would have to adopt a political theory and join a political organization. It is all very well for the Surrealists to cry out that "poetry must be made by all, not by one"; but by what means are we to arrive at a society which is the living embodiment of art? How can Surrealism liberate the worker along with the artist?

Breton's answer is that Surrealists must become Marxist revolutionaries. Accordingly, he now criticizes his past writings for paying too much attention to mind, too little to the socio-economic environment. "Our fate," he announced in the *Second Manifesto of Surrealism* (1930), is to give "our allegiance completely, without any reservations, to the principle of historical materialism." His new understanding is that "the *liberation of the mind,* the express aim of Surrealism, demands as a primary condition . . . the *liberation of man.*" Freedom had from the start been a theme of Breton; but it was only when he decided that everyone must be free that he signed on as a Marxist and placed his bets on a proletarian revolution.

So it was that the Surrealists entered the Communist party, only to leave it a few years later or to be thrown out. The marriage between Surrealism and Stalinism was never more than one of convenience, and soon each party was suing the other for divorce on the grounds of irreconcilable differences. With the exception of Louis Aragon, the Surrealists were unwilling to abandon their former beliefs upon entering the Communist party. Most were horrified by the dedication of the Soviet Union to work, duty, family, country, and economic competition. Nothing was more abhorrent to a Surrealist than Russian State capitalism, unless it be the "cretinizing" doctrine of "socialist realism" which stifles the imagination, replacing its protests against reality and visions of a liberated existence with Stalinist homilies, apologetics, and propaganda.

For their part, the members of the Communist party saw the Surrealists for what they were: artists playing at politics or, far more dangerous, anarcho-Marxists trying to subvert Communism from within. It is no accident that Breton eventually took up with Trotsky, the prophet outcast who in the 1930s, with his attacks on bureaucracy and lamentations at the grave of the revolution betrayed, sounded ever more like an anarcho-Marxist. One other sign of Breton's anarchist heritage may be discerned in his habitual allusions to the Paris Commune, long forgotten by orthodox Marxists but a living memory for all who cherished the black flag, no matter that they kept it in the closet.

When Jean-Paul Sartre launched an envenomed assault on Breton in *What is Literature?*, the reading public experienced something rare and perhaps unprecedented. Here, instead of the usual anarcho-Marxist attack on an orthodox Marxist, was one anarcho-Marxist attacking another. Sartre spied a hidden fascist impulse lurking within the ranks of these supposed libertarians: "Don't the punitive expeditions of the Surrealists resemble the pranks of the young royalist henchmen [of the *Action française*]?" The refusal of the Surrealists to enter into a rational discussion and their "scattered acts of violence" give to the "dogmatic texts of the Surrealists a purely formal but disturbing resemblance to the political writings of Charles Maurras." It is difficult to dismiss Sartre's charge out of hand, given Breton's notorious sentence in the *Second Surrealist Manifesto:* "The simplest Surrealist act consists of dashing down into the street, pistol in hand, and firing blindly, as fast as you can pull the trigger, into the crowd."

Sartre's quarrel with the Surrealists revolves around what he regarded as their reckless misappropriation of Freud. In *Being and Nothingness* he had held that psychoanalysis properly employed is the path to an understanding of "human reality." Unfortunately it is the abuse of Freud, the resort to his name to excuse irresponsibility, which is commonplace in our age. Nothing is more characteristic of our warmed-over romanticism, Sartre believed, than the claim that our actions are the outcome of passions and neuroses beyond our control. If he objected to the unwillingness of private individuals to assume responsibility for their everyday lives in *Being and Nothingness,* all the more did Sartre denounce the public and political Surrealists in *What is Literature?* for excusing anything and everything done in the name of allowing free play to the instincts and the "id."

In fact, argues Sartre, there is no bundle of drives, no unconscious mind, dwelling within me and dictating my actions. There is nothing but what I have chosen to be, what I have made of myself through my actions, each an exercise in self-definition. The trouble is, I do not remember and may not wish to recall the original choice by which I related myself to the world and to my fellow human beings. Existential psychoanalysis is a method of interpreting the meaning of my seemingly most meaningless acts and of recovering my personal history, so that, with the assistance of the analyst, I can understand who I am and assume control of my life. Nothing is gained, however, when we posit the notion of "the unconscious" to explain human acts. "How," asks Sartre, "could the [internal Freudian] censor discern the impulses needing to be repressed without being conscious of discerning them?" Psychoanalysis does not take the unconscious and render it conscious; rather, it transforms consciousness into knowledge—into self-knowledge, to be exact. By this means analysis enables me to turn my life's work into a responsible project. In direct contrast, the Surrealists' use of "the unconscious" is an escape from one's self into the comforts and excuses of irrationalism.

Unfortunately Sartre could not leave well enough alone. In his 1961 introduction to Frantz Fanon's *The Wretched of the Earth,* Sartre is guilty of the same irresponsible position on political violence of which he had accused the Surrealists in 1947. Fanon, a psychiatrist by training, believed the European settlers had imposed a "colonial neurosis" upon the peoples of the Third World. The conclusion Sartre drew from Fanon's book was that since all Europeans benefit economically from colonialism, all are "racists" and "executioners." Hence, a black person who kills a white person is automatically justified. Violence committed by the exploited, in Sartre's view, is therapy, freedom, and creativity. Violence is "man recreating himself."

Why Sartre came to uphold such an extreme view is not entirely clear. Perhaps he was tormented by memories of the indictment he had levelled against the Surrealists—his slashing charges that because of their aloofness from genuine political commitments, their failure to reach the workers, and their obsession with scandalizing the bourgeoisie, the Surrealists "remain the parasites of the class they insult." Was he not guilty of the same faults and did he not need to prove his mettle by definitively placing revolution above art and literature?

One thing seems certain. Sartre no longer believed, as he had in 1947, that European literature could ever be "the reflective self-consciousness of a classless society." It was not to the French proletariat and socialist intellectuals but to the wretched of the earth that the later Sartre turned for a revolution that would be as unlettered and inartistic as it was to be creative and indiscriminate in its destruction. Bakunin, surely, would have understood. So would Emile Henry, the Montmartre terrorist of the 1890s whose justification of throwing his bomb at no one in particular was that "there are no innocent bourgeois."

FINAL THOUGHTS

In May of 1968 the French students rummaged through the closets of their parents, dusted off the black flags, and proudly displayed them. For a month anarchism revisited its past glories as persons from every walk of life, many of whom had read no anarchist authors, joined the consciously anarchist student leaders in chanting demands for self-management. Soon thereafter the black flags disappeared, never to be seen again. After coming to light so unexpectedly and burning so brightly, the anarchist lamp was extinguished. What made these strange events possible?

No one expected anarchism to make another appearance on the stage of history at so late a date as 1968. The conventional wisdom was that anarchism had been an ideology of economically backward countries in the nineteenth century—Spain, Italy, Russia, and, to a lesser extent, France. The larger the peasantry and petty bourgeoisie, the stronger the anarchist movement. Using this standard explanation, one can readily understand that Proudhon caught on when he did; one cannot, however, explain the anarchist outburst in 1968, after twenty years of unprecedented growth and prosperity in a new France bearing little economic resemblance to its former self.

We can, perhaps, gain an appreciation of the sudden reemergence and equally rapid disappearance of anarchism if we remember that the historical mission of anarchism, whatever its social roots, has always been to challenge centralized political organizations. The French state in 1968 was still the highly bureaucratic apparatus against which both the anarchists and Karl Marx had raised their fists in the nineteenth century. And the Communist party in France was still the top-heavy, plodding, excessively centralized and authoritarian structure it had more or less been from the start. Both the state and the organization set up to overthrow it were Jacobin to the core.

Anarchism and anarcho-Marxism, therefore, were far from outdated in 1968. If Germany has been the classic home of Social Democracy, and Spain the host of anarchism, then France is the country which more than any other has been the sponsor of various anarcho-Marxist hybrids—syndicalist, Surrealist, Sartrean, some Trotskyist spin-offs, and otherwise. Against the backdrop of rigid Communist orthodoxy and a rich legacy of anarcho-Marxist protest, one can understand why most of the French student leaders quoted Rosa Luxemburg or the Surrealists more frequently than Bakunin; or why they cited Marx rather than Pelloutier to refute the Jacobin Communist party. As for the larger public, it quoted no one but that did not prevent a great many persons from joining the rebellion against the Jacobin, overcentralized state.

A few years after 1968, the French intellectuals began to repudiate their Marxist past, and the French state began to cede some of its activities to civil society. Under the new dispensation, anarchism and anarcho-Marxism quickly lost their *raison d'être*. Having lived parasitically off the body of the Marxism it despised, anarchism died unnoticed and unmourned when Marxism faded away. Only if anarchism finds its own independent reason to be can it be reborn.

BIBLIOGRAPHY

Breton, André. *Manifestoes of Surrealism.* Ann Arbor: University of Michigan Press, 1972.

Cole, G. D. H. *Marxism and Anarchism, 1850–1890.* London: Macmillan, 1969.

Dolgoff, Sam, ed. *Bakunin on Anarchism.* Montréal: Black Rose Books, 1980.

Joll, James. *The Anarchists.* Cambridge, MA: Harvard University Press, 1964.

Lichtheim, George. *Marxism in Modern France.* New York: Columbia University Press, 1966.

Marx, Engels, Lenin. *Anarchism and Anarcho-Syndicalism.* New York: International Publishers, 1972.

Plekhanov, Georgi. *Anarchism and Socialism.* Westport, CT: Hyperion Press, 1981.

Nadeau, Maurice. *The History of Surrealism.* Cambridge, MA: Harvard University Press, 1989.

Sonn, Richard. *Anarchism and Cultural Politics in* Fin de Siècle *France.* Lincoln: University of Nebraska Press, 1989.

Thomas, Paul. *Karl Marx and the Anarchists.* London: Routledge & Kegan Paul, 1980.

Ulam, Adam. *The Unfinished Revolution.* New York: Vintage Books, 1964.

Woodcock, George. *Anarchism: a History of Libertarian Ideas and Movements.* New York: Meridian Books, 1962.

Chapter
13

Student Rebellion in the Late 1960s: America and France

The more I make love, the more I feel like making the revolution; the more I make revolution, the more I feel like making love.

Slogan of French students

Make love, not war.

Slogan of American students

THAT REMARKABLE YEAR, 1968

Rarely do historians or other social scientists agree on anything, but they are united in their judgment that 1968 was one of the most eventful years of the twentieth century. This was the year when Martin Luther King, Jr., and Robert Kennedy were assassinated; the year when the Vietnamese Communists launched the Tet Offensive; it was another year in the ongoing Chinese Cultural Revolution; and in August the world witnessed with sorrow the invasion of Czechoslovakia by Soviet troops who succeeded in ending Alexander Dubček's quest for a "communism with a human face." Not least significantly, 1968 was the year when student rebellions became matters of the utmost political importance.

Especially significant for anyone interested in the politics of student revolt are the events occurring throughout May of 1968 in Paris and later that summer in Chicago at the time of the Democratic National Convention. Both in America and in France the students of 1968 carried their rebellions out of the classrooms and into the streets, where they challenged the legitimacy of regimes professedly liberal and democratic. Mayor Richard Daley's response was to turn the police loose on the students, with the result that the agents of law enforcement, with Daley's blessing, engaged in what the Kerner Commission later termed a "police riot." Students, delegates to the Convention, passers-by, members of the press were clubbed and beaten indiscriminately and with conspicuous glee by the police, who had carefully covered their badges so that they could not be held accountable for their actions. Few who remember those days in August of 1968 can forget some of the more nauseating scenes: Daley screaming "Kike" at Abraham Ribicoff when the Senator objected to the barbarity of the police; Hubert Humphrey ignoring the noise outside his hotel and kissing the TV set when nominated for the Presidency; and Humphrey, again, speaking with vapid optimism about "the politics of joy" at a time of the most profound disenchantment with American public life.

Possibly the French events of May 1968 were even more stunning than what was to follow in Chicago, three months later. Not since the Franco-Prussian War and the Paris Commune of 1871 had France, the country of revolutions, been the site of such a major upheaval. David Caute has characterized May 1968 in France as "the greatest popular insurrection ever experienced by a capitalist democracy in time of peace."[1] As always, Paris was the center of the rebellion, but on this occasion the people of a provincial city briefly outdid the sophisticated residents of the capital. In Nantes, a modest-sized town rarely associated with radical politics, the students, peasants, and workers banded together during the last week of May, and ran the city with an impromptu alternative government. "Had the scenario [played out at Nantes] unfolded in the capital city rather than a faraway province," Bernard Brown dispassionately observed in 1974, "the outcome of the May Revolt might well have been a revolution."[2] American students discredited the legitimacy of an elected government; French students went further: they triggered a set of events which, in the judgment of some social scientists, nearly toppled the entire structure of French politics.

These remarkable events may have originated in the academy, but that does not mean the typical professor was well prepared to comprehend them. Arguably it was the social scientists—the very persons trained to explain political events—who were least ready for the raucous unraveling of the political structures of America and Europe. Throughout the 1950s and well into the 1960s, the best known sociologists and political scientists propounded the thesis of the "end of ideology." Seymour Lipset, to take one example, affirmed that the "fundamental problems of the industrial revolution have been solved"; major social upheavals, he held, were no longer possible, now that the "workers have achieved industrial and political citizenship." Admittedly, social struggle will continue, but only in a mitigated, harmless form; future fights will occur "without ideologies, without red flags, without May Day parades."

Lipset disdained "those intellectuals who must have ideologies or utopias to motivate them to political action."[3] Obviously his target was the Marxists. It never occurred to him how thoroughly Marxist (minus the radicalism) was his own analysis: he, too, assumed that without an oppressed proletariat, radicalism cannot flourish. The year 1968 proved both Lipset and the Marxists dramatically mistaken.

Better to look to Plato's *Republic* than to Lipset's *Political Man* for a prediction that democracy would one day yield events of the kind that shocked everyone in

---

[1]David Caute, *The Year of the Barricades: a Journey Through 1968*, p. 212.
[2]Bernard E. Brown, *Protest in Paris: Anatomy of a Revolt*, p. 152.
[3]Seymour Martin Lipset, "The End of Ideology?" in *Political Man: the Social Bases of Politics*, ch. 13.

1968. No friend of democracy, Plato feared that its egalitarian dynamic would result in students who made light of their teachers, and in teachers too ambivalent about their authority to exercise it convincingly. If for no other reason than that he was not immune to Greek prejudices, Plato also warned that democratic equality would encourage women to question their social status; and, indeed, in 1968 the Women's Movement in America was born of the New Left. Finally, it was Plato's conviction that youths would be everything, elders nothing in a democratic society, and that the most mature persons would ape the ways of youngsters instead of providing models for youths to follow. Here, too, Plato was uncannily prescient; the late 1960s marked the emergence of a "Youth Culture," and during those heady days it was not unusual to see elders, ashamed of their age, mimicking the clothes and lifestyle of students.

As is incumbent upon a social scientist, Plato dug beneath the surface in search of the underlying conditions fostering a conflict between generations. His explanation was that young persons rebelling against their elders were in truth simply living out the secret, repressed desires of their parents. Oligarchical fathers and mothers skimp and save, deferring their gratifications as they painstakingly accumulate and then tenaciously safeguard the family fortune. Longing to consume but denying their desires, parents suffer from a divided self. In their spendthrift children, who are as preoccupied with present satisfactions as their parents are with living for the future, the repressed side of the older generation successfully fights its way to the forefront of consciousness. Nothing, then, is more natural than for repressed, puritanical parents to produce anti-authoritarian, "liberated" children.[4]

Brilliantly insightful, Plato's analysis is nevertheless seriously inadequate in at least one respect. Hostile to democracy, he could only see destruction and the denial of principled action in the upsurge of youth. Completely missing in his account is the intense idealism of the student rebels of the late 1960s. When Kenneth Keniston interviewed students involved in the antiwar activities of the New Left, he found that many among their numbers were the children of idealistic parents who, in the judgment of their offspring, had failed to live up to their principles.[5] This is a far cry, indeed, from Plato's grasping, selfish oligarchs and their irresponsible sons.

However one views the student revolts of 1968, there is no denying that they took place in many countries, including America, Belgium, England, France, West Germany, Italy, Japan, Mexico, Poland, Spain, and Yugoslavia. The question arises, Was the rebellion of students one phenomenon with varying national manifestations, or was it a different event in each country? Was it one long story with many chapters, or many short stories bound together in a single volume?

Insofar as there was an international student culture and an awareness on the part of students in one country of the political activities of their counterparts in other nations, one may justifiably speak of student rebellion as a general phenom-

---

[4]*Republic,* Book VIII and the beginning of Book IX.
[5]Kenneth Keniston, *Young Radicals: Notes on Committed Youth.*

enon. Rock music then as now united students speaking varying tongues; marijuana, too, was popular with students of differing nationalities;[6] and undergraduates traveling across Europe could count on being offered lodging in the dormitories of foreign universities. On every campus there were posters of Che Guevara and demonstrations against the policy of the American government in Vietnam. To be a student was to be a member of an international community.

"The Berkeley model was copied at Berlin university a few years later, with Paris following suit soon afterwards," wrote Daniel Cohn-Bendit, the most conspicuous figure in the Paris revolt of May, 1968. Possibly so, and it is decidedly true that throughout the hectic year, 1968, students were attentive to the television coverage of the rebellions taking place in countries other than their own. What they saw was a constant repetition of events, most obviously so, perhaps, in the invariable radicalization of the student moderates on one campus after another the moment the university called in external police forces to end the occupation of administrative offices. Everywhere one encounters the same pattern: a student takeover of buildings, a list of non-negotiable demands, a violent response from student-hating police, followed by a mobilization of the entire campus.

There is, then, a prima facie case to be made for the proposition that the rebellion of students was everywhere the same. But as any anthropologist knows, similar events and symbols may have different meanings and contrasting consequences in varying cultural contexts. A comparative analysis is needed to decide whether there was one general and international student revolt or a series of such revolts, each with its unique national characteristics.[7]

Hence we shall attempt a comparative study of what may be the two most dramatic episodes of student rebellion in the late 1960s, the American and the French examples. For a preliminary indication of how alike on the surface and yet dissimilar on a closer view the two cases were, we need only cite two slogans, one American, the other French. In the United States the best known motto of those years was "Make love, not war." In France one of the many slogans on the walls of the Sorbonne in 1968 read: "The more I make love, the more I feel like making the revolution; the more I make the revolution, the more I feel like making love." On both sides of the Atlantic the sexual revolution was in full swing; but in America love was linked by students with the politics of protest against the war in Vietnam, whereas in France love was associated with a rich tradition of revolutionary politics. All our subsequent efforts to compare and contrast student rebellion in France and America may be regarded as embellishments of this initial hint.

---

[6]For virtually all Americans students, smoking a "joint" was a standard ritual of a college education. Hence Bill Clinton was just like his classmates when, by his own admission, he smoked marijuana; he may, however, be the only person of his generation to smoke the "weed" without inhaling.

[7]It is difficult to find a comparative study of 1968. Books on student rebellion address the situation in this or that country, or offer a panoramic overview of events in many countries. Neither approach is comparative in method.

AMERICA AND FRANCE: THE SIMILARITIES

In 1962 Tom Hayden and other founding members of the Students for a Democratic Society (SDS) met at Port Huron, Michigan, and drafted a statement of principles. The Port Huron Statement opens with these words: "We are people of this generation, *bred in at least modest comfort,* housed now in universities, looking uncomfortably to the world we inherit [italics added]." Exploitation is not the theme of this manifesto of the New Left; alienation is—the alienation felt by students who frankly admit that they are the beneficiaries of privileged circumstances. In France as well, the rebels of the New Left sprang from the ranks of the affluent. The initial uprising of May 1968 took place at the University of Nanterre, which drew its student body from the western, wealthy areas of Paris.

Prior to 1968 academics had designated the poor and deprived as candidates for the role of earth-shakers; or social scientists scoured the ranks of the "relatively deprived" when searching for potential trouble-makers, and every so often a sociologist or political scientist would dust off Tocqueville's finding that groups whose expectations have been raised, then dashed, are prime candidates for initiating political uprisings.[8] The year 1968 overturned all these standard hypotheses. Any list of the similarities between student revolts in France and America must include this unexpected item: in both countries it was not the "wretched of the earth" (Fanon) but the affluent of the suburbs who rebelled. Deprived neither absolutely nor relatively, with everything to look forward to, the students chose nevertheless to take to the streets.

A second characteristic common to all the student movements is that the undergraduates and graduates, along with their untenured allies among the faculty, rebelled against the university before taking their movement into the streets of the major cities. Underlying the complaints of the students was the enormous growth of universities since World War II, the attendant overcrowding of classrooms and dormitories, the impersonal instruction, the preponderant weight given to research over teaching in decisions of tenure, and the relative underfunding of the humanities as contrasted with the rich governmental backing of the sciences following the Russian launching of Sputnik, the first human-made satellite, in 1957. Add to this list of grievances the insistence of college administrators upon playing the role of parents in sexual matters. Many a campus revolt that ended with a grandiose call to pull down the national government began as a modest protest against a university policy of refusing students permission to entertain friends of the opposite sex in their dormitory rooms.

Though all the foregoing complaints were voiced in America, the students in France had even stronger reasons to object to their lot. The number of students attending French universities more than quadrupled from 1950 to 1968; the comparative figures are equally staggering: there were two university students in France for each student attending an English or West German university. The

---

[8]Tocqueville, *The Old Regime and the French Revolution,* Part III, ch. 4.

physical plant and teaching facilities, unfortunately, simply did not keep pace with the mushrooming student population. Students found themselves squeezed into overcrowded lecture halls; they were required to take rigid, repetitive, mechanical exams; and usually were taught by junior faculty, if taught at all. Supposedly the library of the Sorbonne served 30,000, but in fact it could seat only 300. Many students decided that attending class was not worth the trouble, and bought mimeographed copies of lecture notes. They knew their absence would go unnoticed or would be deliberately overlooked by a faculty preoccupied with its research activities. Most students prior to 1968, in France as in America, were far from being exponents of revolutionary doctrines. But the widespread disenchantment of rank and file students before the disruptions at the Sorbonne, Columbia University, San Francisco State, and other centers of higher learning was of enormous use to the minority of ideologically committed students once hostilities erupted.

C. Wright Mills was dead long before 1968, but his *The Sociological Imagination* inspired the leading student radicals on both sides of the Atlantic. Tom Hayden learned from Mills how to criticize the pattern of thinking and research prevalent in the university, and so did Daniel Cohn-Bendit. It was Mills' contention that sociology and political science in America were irrelevant at best, harmful at worst. Many publications of social scientists involve the collection of data on the part of investigators who have not asked themselves what question they are attempting to answer. Studies of voting were popular with political scientists seemingly for no reason other than that votes are amenable to statistical treatment; certainly the typical finding that wealthy persons are likely to vote Republican does not constitute an intellectual breakthrough, Mills noted. Down then with the hyper-empiricists who cannot see the forest for the trees. The Port Huron Statement restates Mills' contention that empiricism, American-style, prevents scholars from dealing with the big issues.

The sociology of Talcott Parsons, continued Mills, stands at the opposite extreme; it is theory divorced from reality and devoid of substance, but rich in the proliferation of high-sounding jargon. By talking about the "functional prerequisites" of any and all social systems, Parsons managed to avoid dealing with the problems of any specific society. When Cohn-Bendit sarcastically remarked that the "two great 'hopes' of French sociology are the jargon of Parsons and the cult of statistics," he was repeating the charges C. Wright Mills had earlier levelled against American sociology. Cohn-Bendit used Mills, an American sociologist, to denounce the growing influence of American sociology in the French universities.

So far the argument of Hayden and Cohn-Bendit has been that the universities failed to address the problems besetting society. This is not to say, however, that the spokespersons of the New Left in America and France regarded the universities as "ivory towers," hopelessly far removed from the surrounding social and political environment. On the contrary, both Hayden and Cohn-Bendit criticized the academy for serving all too effectively, and too uncritically, an undemocratic, technocratic, and managerial social order, itself allied by the profit motive to the warfare state. Supposedly teaching and research are "value-free"; in truth, wrote Cohn-Bendit, the university "churns out the trained personnel that is so essential for bureaucratic capitalism. The system needs an ever increasing number of engineers, technicians, scientists, administrators, and sociologists to organize production." Cohn-Bendit offered arguments in 1968 that paralleled those stated six years earlier in the Port Huron Statement: the specialization of education mirrors specialization in the corporation, and, in the words of Hayden and his cohort, "leaves little room for sweeping thought."

By 1968 the ranks of student protestors had swollen to prodigious proportions. Few among their numbers were as articulate or as intellectually sophisticated as Tom Hayden and Daniel Cohn-Bendit, but all had learned to dismiss the notion that the university was politically neutral. The research conducted on campus, funded by the government and supportive of the ongoing war in Asia, was morally outrageous in the eyes of many students and not a few professors. Little training in critical versions of social theory was needed for students to comprehend the link between chemists and napalm. On almost every campus, American students demanded removal of the ROTC, and eventually their growing political awareness led them to denounce their schools as slum lords, eager exploiters of the local poor.

By way of summary, the New Left was born within the university and reached its climax in the riot-torn streets of Chicago and Paris. Before it moved beyond the university, the student movement was already genuinely radical insofar as its critique of higher education, both in France and in America, was a resounding condemnation of the role the university plays in the larger socio-political order.

There is another reason why the proponents of the New Left, both American and French, spent considerable time addressing the situation of the university before entering the national political arena. Members of other ideological movements, left, right, and center, separated their private lives, sexual relationships, and leisure activities from their public selves. Not so the New Left faithful who adamantly maintained that "the personal is political." If one of the major problems of modern society, as the young radicals believed, is that it artificially compartmentalizes our lives into discreet, unconnected segments; if we therefore suffer from a divided, diminished, and alienated self, as they contended, then it follows that political activists must find a way to unite the public and private dimensions of their existence. The solution, the youthful leftists were convinced, is to begin with what is nearest us, our immediate and everyday surroundings—for them the universities—and to transfigure the ordinary circumstances in which we live before venturing to change the world.

The authors of the Port Huron Statement sought to find through politics "a meaning in life that is personally authentic." Only if "fraternity" replaces "egoistic individualism" can we hope to put an end to "personal alienation." "Politics has the function of bringing people out of isolation and into community"; hence political activity is "a necessary, though not sufficient means of finding meaning in personal life." To understand Hayden's politics, it is clear, one must not forget his fascination with Albert Camus and the existential theme of "authenticity." Another source is, yet again, C. Wright Mills, who in the Chapter 13 of *The Power Elite* warned that the "publics" of America were rapidly disintegrating into "a society of masses."

The vision of "atomized individuals turned into vital groups" through the redeeming activism of radical politics may also be detected in Cohn-Bendit's treatise, *Senile Communism: the Left-Wing Alternative.*[9] He, too, may have derived such notions from Mills, but a source closer to home is the political writings of Jean-Paul Sartre, still a widely read author in the late 1960s. It was Sartre's claim in his *Critique of Dialectical Reason* (1960) that isolation is a "social product of cities." Take the example, he suggests, of several Parisians waiting for a bus. Their objective is the same but it in no way unites them; they are together but do their best to distance themselves from one another. To Sartre the only positive fusion of individuals is in the formation of spontaneous groups, as happened during the Revolution on the occasion of storming the Bastille. It is not surprising that Sartre in 1968 sided firmly with the students mingling in the streets, nor is it unexpected that the students should warmly embrace him—especially since, in a gesture characteristic of the period, Sartre played the student rather than the teacher of Cohn-Bendit.

One other feature common to the student politics of France and America was the attack on the reigning "consumer society" and the related effort to establish a cultural alternative, a "counter-culture." Poster-art and graffiti written on the walls of the Sorbonne were a means by which the French students communicated to their classmates and to the public at large their hostility to consumerism. "Commodities are the opium of the people," read one poster; a second, more menacing, message read, "Merchandise—we'll burn it." A third asked the political question, "Are you consumers or real participants?" No sooner did the student insurrection of 1968 spill over from the Sorbonne to the nearby national theater, the Odéon, than the director, almost immediately, joined the movement and heeded its call to transform the Odéon into a center for "creative revolution," meaning a revolution both cultural and political. The students who liberated the national theater explained their action with these words: "Since the National Assembly has become a bourgeois theater, all bourgeois theaters should be transformed into National Assemblies."

It was the Situationists in France who were primarily responsible for the poster-art which denounced consumerism and the advertising industry. Jerry Rubin in America expressed much the same message when he sang the praises of theft and arson. Rubin, Abbie Hoffman, and the Yippies objected not only to the passive and manipulated consumerism of leisure time, but were equally opposed to the work ethic that alternated with shopping binges in the lives of middle-class Americans. "Freedom is the end of work," Hoffman announced, adding in his inimitable fashion, "Our goal is full unemployment." Many of the same messages emanated from the Lower East Side Motherfuckers, a New York group which borrowed ideas from the avant-garde artistic movements of Italy and France—Dada, Surrealism, Futurism, and Situationism. Seemingly there is no tendency of the New Left that did not appear on the walls of the Sorbonne during May of 1968, and so it is that one message took direct issue with the work ethic: "People who

---

[9]Daniel & Gabriel Cohn-Bendit, *Obsolete Communism: The Left-Wing Alternative* (New York: McGraw-Hill, 1968), pp. 16, 63, 79. For reasons which will be become clear later in this essay, *Senile Communism* is a better translation.

work are bored when they don't work; people who don't work are never bored." On both sides of the Atlantic, young persons yearned for a new culture, a new way of life, to counter and replace the old culture.

Back to nature, back to the arts and crafts of yesteryear, were motifs frequently voiced by the proponents of the counter-culture. Marx had scornfully denounced the artisans of the modern world as "petty bourgeois," that is, he regarded them as pitiful lower-middle-class leftovers from an earlier phase of economic history, the period preceding the triumph of the bourgeoisie, with its factories, machines, collective production, and economies of scale. The late 1960s was a time when many a son or daughter of upper-middle-class origins consciously sought to carve out a living through the very arts and crafts that Marx and technocrats had consigned to the dust bin of history. Pride of workmanship, quality over quantity of production, and the theme that "small is beautiful" were the concerns of significant numbers of young persons, who hoped to escape from the doldrums of "alienated labor."

Students and "drop outs" feared the consequences of technology and lamented the entire historical record of scientific advance, from early modern to contemporary times. Francis Bacon's aspiration, the conquest of nature, had been fulfilled, but at the cost of polluting the earth and removing humans from their home in the ecological order. Machines, chemicals, and weapons were turning against their creators, and humans were discovering that they may have burned behind them the bridges back to Mother Nature. In the hope that it was not too late, some young Americans fled to rural communes, where they would live off the land without using the machinery employed by commercial farmers. Nature, peace, love were their slogans. Native Americans were their heroes because "Indians" understood that humans belong to the land, the land does not belong to humans. French students, more familiar than their American counterparts with the rigors of rural existence, did not idealize the farm, but they did speak vaguely about the need to be at one with the universe, and the Situationists were second to no one in their determination to cast off the technocratic straight-jacket. Guy Debord, one of the leading Situationists, devoted his influential *Society of the Spectacle* (1967) to a spirited attack on the social consequences of the "incessant spread of technical rationality."

Any list of the affinities between the French and American students must include their enthusiasm for democracy combined with their repudiation of the institutions of representative government. Cohn-Bendit sang the praises of the students who in May "asserted their right to enter their own university, and to run it themselves for the benefit of all." All the more did he admire the brief period when the people of Nantes practiced self-rule. "Act with others, not for them," was his advice to all political activists. It was a professor teaching at the University of Michigan, Arnold Kaufman, who invented the phrase "participatory democracy"; it was a student, Tom Hayden, attending the same school who wrote that phrase into the Port Huron Statement. Intended in 1962 to serve as a supplement to representative government, "participatory democracy" had by 1965 evolved in some minds into an alternative to conventional notions of democracy. The longer the Vietnam war lasted, the more unpopular it was, and the more disgusted students became with elected representatives deaf to their constituencies. The great fault of the American and European democracies, the youthful protestors concluded, was that they were undemocratic and would continue to be so until the public learned to take seriously the idea of self-government.

Most obvious of all, the American and European New Lefts were alike in their contempt for the Old Lefts. In the eyes of the student radicals, the support of Willy Brandt and Harold Wilson for the American war in Asia permanently discredited the German Social Democrats and the British Labour party. As for France, the young activists regarded the Communist party as one of the most conservative, antirevolutionary forces within the country. "The communists fear revolution," Sartre shouted to the press during the events of May. He and the students were correct: the party was so preoccupied with the next election that it did all it could to wrap itself in patriotism and law-and-order politics.

The American situation was roughly similar to that in Europe. The democratic socialists of the older generation of American intellectuals, with their constant rehashes of stale polemics pitting Trotskyites against Stalinists, with their need to prove their loyalty by Cold War rhetoric, advocacy of the warfare state, and applause of the American venture in Vietnam, had made themselves part of the problem, not the solution. Liberal Democrats were equally unwilling to criticize anything done in the name of anticommunism, which is why the young radicals rejected the alliance of socialist left and liberal center advocated by such established leftists as Irving Howe and Michael Harrington. The crowning blow came with the revelation that the CIA had funded various liberal organizations, including the National Student Association. When the liberal ship sank beneath the waves, it took down with it the old leftists who had gone along for the ride. In general, the Old Left of each country accepted the corporate economy and hitched its aspirations to the modern state, economic planning, and bureaucratic administration —the very forces which the youngsters rejected as conservative and undemocratic.

Nothing mattered more to the young rebels, American and French, than to avoid repeating the mistakes the Left had been committing for the past half-century. Unlike the Bolsheviks, the students maintained that the end does not justify the means. Resort to means that contradict the end inevitably destroys the end, or so the youthful rebels contended, pointing to the dismal failure of the Russian revolution. "We find violence to be abhorrent," wrote the authors of the Port Huron Statement. Cohn-Bendit and his comrades agreed that inhumanity cannot foster a regenerated humanity.

Democracy was both end and means to Hayden and the SDS; their organization aimed to build a more democratic world, and in the meantime was itself to be the very image of democracy in action. How seriously they took their rhetoric is proven by their unwillingness to bring meetings to a close; marathon sessions were not unusual because anyone and everyone could and did speak interminably. Oscar Wilde once remarked that socialism would take too many evenings; exhausted members of the SDS began to wonder whether the same might be true of democracy.

The French students agreed that the new world must be visible here and now, in embryo, in the groups leading the way to the future. Hence this slogan, scrawled on the walls of the Sorbonne in May 1968: "We lead a marvelous life. We sleep; we eat; we don't touch money; no one thinks of it. *This is already the society we want to create* [italics added]." It was completely in keeping with the new notions of leftist politics that an atmosphere of carnival and festival pervaded the Latin quarter during the days following the student takeover of the Sorbonne. Nonstop, a jazz band played its music in the streets, to the dismay of the Old Left, to the delight of the New. The Old Left had sacrificed the present to a future forever just out of reach; the New Left, therefore, adopted as one of its ideals the repudiation of all idealism which sacrifices life to ideas, the real and lived present to the unreal and unlived future.

As was so often the case, Cohn-Bendit proved to be the person who most effectively summarized the viewpoint of the student radicals:

> The real meaning of revolution is not a change in management, but a change in man. This change we must make in our own lifetime and not for our children's sake, for the revolution must be born of joy and not of sacrifice.[10]

Senile Communism closes with these words: "Make the revolution here and now. It is your own. *C'est pour toi que tu fais la révolution.*"

One of the ways in which leftist means have historically defeated leftist ends is through the emergence of a "new class." Some students of the late 1960s had read Robert Michels' *Political Parties* (1911); others had come across *The New Class* (1957) by Milovan Djilas; and all students were familiar with the rock lyrics of the day: "Meet the new boss; same as the old boss." Djilas, at one time the second ranking member of the Yugoslav Communist party, showed how the revolutionary party, officially dedicated to forging a classless society, had itself become a privileged elite:

> The heroic era of communism is past . . . The epoch of practical men has set in. The new class has been created. It is at the height of its power and wealth, but it is without new ideas. It has nothing more to tell the people. The only thing that remains is for it to justify itself.[11]

Decades earlier, Michels proved that the German Social Democratic party, despite its egalitarian rhetoric, was profoundly oligarchical. "The party," wrote Michels, "is no longer regarded as a means for the attainment of an end, but gradually becomes an end-in-itself." Consequently, "the socialists might conquer, but not socialism, which would perish in the moment of its adherents' triumph."[12]

So anxious were American and French student activists to prevent the growth of a new class within their movement that they attacked not certain forms of leadership but leadership as such. Even more pleasing to Cohn-Bendit than the presence of 35,000 demonstrators in the Champs Elysées was their capacity to manage affairs "without any leaders at all." At the end of his book he affirms his conviction that "the revolutionary cannot and must not be a leader." In his judgment "democ-

---

[10]Cohn-Bendit, *Obsolete Communism*, p. 112.
[11]Milovan Djilas, *The New Class* (New York: Praeger, 1957), pp. 53–54.
[12]Robert Michels, *Political Parties* (New York: Free Press, 1962), pp. 338–355.

racy is not suborned by bad leadership but by the very existence of leadership." True to his word, Cohn-Bendit did not object to the manner in which the students set about coordinating their rebellion: to prevent the advent of a "new class," the entire steering committee changed hands every twenty-four hours.

Directly paralleling the situation in France was the mounting hostility to leadership within the American SDS. On one occasion Tom Hayden sat with the audience rather than with his challenger during a debate, which led his opponent to quip: "You're such a grass root, Tom, that I don't know whether to debate you or water you." By the late 1960s hostility to leadership within the SDS had assumed proportions that alarmed Hayden: workshops questioned the need for chairpersons; the position of national secretary was deliberately left vacant; political literature never reached the mailbox because no one volunteered to stuff envelopes and it was unthinkable that anyone should have the audacity to issue the necessary order. Full circle was reached when members of the student movement accused Hayden of being too much the leader.

It is far easier to know what the New Left was against than what it favored. The students of America and France were antihierarchical, antibureaucratic, antimanagerial, anticonsumer society, antiwork ethic, antiwar, anti-Old Left. Perhaps the positive content of their ideologies will come to light when we explore the contrasting cultural contexts in which they played their parts as rebels with a cause.

AMERICA AND FRANCE: THE DIFFERENCES

"Make love not war" was the slogan of the American students; "make love and revolution" was that of the students attending the Sorbonne. In the United States the student rebellion of the late 1960s was yet another episode in a recurring pattern of political protest that is one of the defining characteristics of the American political tradition. Young Americans, for all their impassioned attacks on the "system," spoke relatively sparingly of revolution and incessantly of protest and reform. In direct contrast, the French students spoke endlessly of revolution. Out to destroy tradition, the young men and women of France were nevertheless reenacting a script of revolutionary utterances and symbolic gestures that had been written as early as the French revolution, and rewritten time and again throughout the nineteenth century. France's tradition is one of revolutions; America's is one of renewals. Similar on the surface, student rebellions in France and America are on a closer look markedly different; and the pattern of their differences follows exactly the contrast between the political cultures of the two countries.

A quick perusal suffices to show that American and French students invoked strongly contrasting ideologies, even as they launched similar-sounding salvos against the bureaucratic "establishment." Visitors to France in May of 1968 were bound to notice the conspicuous, prominent, prideful display of red and black flags, symbols of Marxism and anarchism, respectively. The question in Paris was never whether but rather what kind of revolutionary a disenchanted student should be. This is less than surprising, given the long history of the capital of France as the Mecca of revolutionaries of every stripe. Is there a place other than

Paris where one could find, until recently, a restaurant run by an anarchist whose customers paid only if they wished, and then as much or as little as they saw fit?

Everything in France, Marxism and anarchism counted for little or nothing in the American student movement. If the Progressive Labor Party, a Leninist group, captured the SDS in 1969, that only proves how vulnerable a disorganized social movement is to takeover by a few disciplined fanatics. The rank and file of SDS continued to go their own way, leaving the few members of the Leninist vanguard to lead no one but themselves. Tom Hayden thought nothing more essential than for the student radicals to "speak American";[13] and socialism, he realized, was not American but European. As for anarchism, it likewise is largely irrelevant to American history, and therefore was weakly represented among the students. Typically, an anarchist in the United States has been first generation, just off the boat (e.g., Emma Goldman or Johann Most). Anarchism as a political movement has a rich European history, especially in Italy, Spain, and France, but it lacks indigenous roots in the United States.

Mere traces of anarchism are the most one can detect in the American counter-culture. Possibly the Motherfuckers and the Yippies borrowed anarchist themes from the French Situationists, but neither group had more than a minuscule membership. Of the many persons in America who were aware of the antics of Hoffman and Rubin, few had heard of Situationism or thought of the two clown princes of youthful rebellion as representing anything but themselves. Only the French Situationists understood the analogy between their position and that of a handful of Americans, but they rejected Rubin on the grounds that his predilection for drugs signalled his entrapment in consumerism. Taking revolution seriously, the Situationists had no use for psychedelic acid trips or for Zen mysticism, either. Rubin, apparently, was counter-revolutionary in French eyes, and the same was true of a great deal of the American counter-culture, because it reeked of apolitical self-indulgence.

What, then, are the intellectual sources upon which the founders of the SDS drew? Jefferson and Tom Paine in the remote past, John Dewey more recently, were favorites of the New Left during the early days. Hayden and his cohorts, advocates of participatory democracy, proponents of a sense of political community that begins with what is closest at hand and then reaches out to the entire society, quite naturally felt inspired when they read Dewey's words: "To be realized [the ideas of democracy] must affect all modes of human association, the family, the school, industry, religion." Decades before C. Wright Mills bemoaned the decline of publics, the venerable Dewey had warned that "the Public will remain in eclipse" until the era when society is democratically restructured into a "Great Community." These words appear in Dewey's *The Public and its Problems,* one of the books Hayden consulted before drafting the Port Huron Statement.

In earlier American history Hayden admired the tradition of civic republicanism, the belief of Jefferson, Paine, and also of the Anti-Federalists that it is not enough for citizens to vote every so often. The "fullness of integrated personality"

---

[13]See James Miller, *"Democracy Is in the Streets"* (New York: Simon & Schuster, 1987), p. 54.

which Dewey saw as resulting from self-rule was already—in Hayden's view—the goal of the American founders, for whom the notion of popular sovereignty entailed active political involvement of the citizenry in shaping their lives according to their own choices. "Each generation," wrote Jefferson, has a "right to choose for itself the form of government it believes most promotive of its own happiness." Against the likes of Edmund Burke, Jefferson categorically rejected the claim that the present generation is bound to uphold the agreements of its predecessors: "The dead have no rights. They are nothing." Fiery Tom Paine agreed: "Every generation is, and must be, competent to all the purposes which its occasions require. It is the living, not the dead, that are to be accommodated." Jefferson was unmoved by the argument that his philosophy was bound to stir up rebellions; "I hold that a little rebellion now and then is a good thing, and as necessary in the political world as storms in the physical . . . It is a medicine necessary for the sound health of government."[14]

Why should the Students for a Democratic Society look to Europe for ideological succor when everything they needed was plentifully supplied by the American political tradition? The ethos of civic republicanism, initiated by the founders, received a new impetus from Jacksonian democracy, with its theme that it was up to the "common man," now armed with the vote, to root out the disease of political corruption. So deep did the waters of civic republicanism run that Eugene Debs shied away, as much as he could, from the words "socialism" and "proletariat," preferring republican rhetoric about the civic virtues and redemptive powers of the "people."[15] Regarded as another chapter in the long American story of civic and democratic protest and renewal, the radicalism of the SDS was as American as apple pie.

Louis Hartz, in his well-known study of *The Liberal Tradition in America* (1955), argued that both socialism and conservatism of the European variety, both genuinely left and right-wing ideologies, were missing from the history of America, the country in which even the most passionate conflicts have typically been fought out between different varieties of liberals, each side claiming to be the true defender of individual rights and constitutional government. By and large the case of the student radicals of the late 1960s confirms the thesis of Hartz, provided allowance is made for the tradition of civic humanism which figures nowhere in his account. Legal proceduralism, economic individualism, the rags to riches dream of Horatio Alger, and the natural rights doctrine of Locke, do not constitute the entirety of the American political culture. The other side of the American creed is the belief in the sturdy yeoman farmer, ready to perform his civic duty, mixing his avarice with occasional doses of fraternity, determined to restore the republic to its

---

[14]Merrill Peterson, ed., *The Portable Thomas Jefferson* (New York: Penguin, 1988), pp 417, 560. Paine, *Rights of Man* (New York: Penguin, 1988), p. 42.

[15]Marxism has been even more out of place in America than other forms of socialism. Marx himself seems to have acknowledged this when, determined to kill the First International rather than have Bakunin control it, he accomplished his purpose by moving it from Europe to New York. Later Marxists coined the expression "American exceptionalism" to express their frustration that the world's most capitalistic society had the smallest Marxist political movement.

pristine origins whenever corruption threatens the body politic. Tom Hayden appealed to this civic and democratic tradition, and updated it for modern circumstances with the assistance of John Dewey. Hayden wanted to restore the lost dream of American democracy, as had so many reformers and protestors before him.

Throughout 1968 the French students waged intense ideological battles pitting one Marxist sect against another, opposing anarchists to Marxists, and uniting all student radicals, despite their fierce disagreements, against the reactionary Communist Party. This wealth of ideological positions was not duplicated in the United States; instead, the American students accepted the national faith in liberal and democratic ideals while vehemently stressing the enormity of the gap between ideals and reality. Usually politics in America involves the bargaining of various interest groups, each too focused on its immediate objectives to think much about fulfilling any high-sounding ideals. Every so often, however, there is an outburst of moral outrage, sparked by the conviction that the ideals of the American creed receive nothing more than lip service.[16] Hypocrite! is a charge Americans frequently make, because they assume that everyone knows what is unquestionably right, and yet some persons refuse for selfish reasons to abide by their professed belief in the "self-evident truths" enunciated in the Declaration of Independence and the Constitution.

The era of student rebellion was preceded by three other historical episodes when significant numbers of Americans rose up to demand that the contradiction between ideals and reality be erased. During the Revolutionary War, the age of Jackson, the Populist and Progressive eras, and finally, the late 1960s, American politics was caught up in moral crusades quite unlike the politics as usual of interest group bargaining. All four periods featured reaffirmations of democratic ideals and claims that the will of the people had been stifled by bureaucracy, hierarchy, specialization, and irresponsible power. Appeals to the public were issued by pamphlets at the time of the Revolution, by the penny press in the Jacksonian period, by magazines and the mass press when the Progressives held sway, and by mass demonstrations against the Vietnam war in the 1960s.

Attacks on large scale organization and on any and all obstacles to popular rule are ingredients common to all four periods of ideological fervor. The colonists believed the British empire was overwrought, and they complained that to finance this excessive structure the King and parliament had decided to squeeze more taxes from Americans without their consent. To make matters worse, the English turned to their military to enforce the new arrangements; and theirs was a professional army, the presence of which was a sign of corruption and a portent of despotism in republican thought, which called for a citizens' militia. Jacksonians fought the national Bank, which they deemed an antidemocratic monster, a frightening threat to their threefold program of placing the people above aristocrats, diligent

---

[16]See Samuel P. Huntington, *American Politics: the Promise of Disharmony* (Cambridge, MA: Harvard University Press, 1981). The next several paragraphs of my essay are indebted to his account. One of the shortcomings of his book is that he obscures the distinction between Populism and Progressivism. Another is that he omits abolitionism and the New Deal.

labor above leisured inaction, and equality of opportunity above monopoly and privilege. Politically, the Jacksonians championed the popular will against the caucus system; culturally, they opposed military academies, specialized education, and the gentlemanly ideal of the liberal arts. Literary scholars fare poorly in Jacksonian commentary, on the grounds of their learned snobbery. Whatever decreases the distance between different ranks of society is good, on a Jacksonian view; whatever accentuates differences is bad.

Through trust-busting and direct primaries, the Populists and some of the Progressives hoped to bring economic magnates and bosses of political machines to heel, thereby restoring the flagging democratic process. The exposures of muckraking journalists, forerunners of the "investigative reporters" of our age, prepared the way for the programs of Progressive reformers, who, like the student rebels of the 1960s, hailed from upper-middle-class families. Approximately half a century after the Progressive era, President Eisenhower opened the fateful 1960s with his famous warning against the threat to democracy posed by the growing influence of the "military-industrial complex." His was a most unexpected comment coming from a conservative military man, not to mention how incongruous it is that Ike should use a phrase sounding remarkably similar to C. Wright Mills' notorious reference to "the power elite."

None of these four incandescent periods of American history is especially remarkable for the originality of its passionately asserted political ideas[17]; all featured the civic republican theme of the need for a renewal, a rededication to the first principles of the republic.[18] Like their radical forebears, the students at the end of the 1960s concluded that something was fundamentally amiss in American democracy. How else, they wondered, could one explain that despite the plummeting popularity of the war, the government continued to pour young men, all underprivileged and many black, into the jungles of Vietnam where they would lose their lives to prop up a corrupt regime? Days of rage would eventually erupt in America, but not before the passing of months and years of mounting frustration with a government that called itself democratic and yet ignored the will of the people.

The theme of saving the republic, to the extent that it figured at all in France, was wielded by de Gaulle, the man the students loved to hate. Within the circles of the politically most active French students the debates were between, first, different types of anti-anarchist Marxists; secondly, between Marxists and anarchists; thirdly, between Marxists of one or another hue of "orthodoxy" and varying challengers bearing anarcho-Marxist insignia. The entire history, almost, of French left-wing politics was replayed in miniature throughout the month of May. Prior to the Bolshevik revolution one looked to Germany for the largest Marxist party, the Social Democrats; to Italy and Spain for large scale anarchist movements; but it is

---

[17]It is arguable that the some of the Progressives, Herbert Croly for one, did break new ground in envisioning a modern state to carry out their reforms. See Eldon J. Eisenach, *The Lost Promise of Progressivism* (Lawrence: University of Kansas Press, 1994).

[18]This same rhetoric of renewal and restoration of the republic was sounded again during the months leading up to the ouster of Richard Nixon from the Presidency.

in France that one found a bountiful assortment of radical ideologies, ranging from anarchism to Marxism to various anarcho-Marxist hybrids, such as the syndicalist movement at the turn of the century or the Surrealists somewhat later. Walking in 1968 down the boulevards of Paris, built in the nineteenth century to facilitate crowd control, was to stroll down the memory lane of French leftist politics.

Among the Marxist students, the Trotskyists were omnipresent but split into squabbling factions. All Trotskyists agreed that although Stalin and the bureaucracy had betrayed the revolution, the day might yet come when the Soviet Union would make good on its claim that it was a workers' society. Of the more prominent Trotskyist factions, one saw Cuba and Vietnam as the beacons of hope, while a second group regarded Castro as petty bourgeois and damned the Cuban and Vietcong regimes on the grounds that they were unrepentantly Stalinist. It was to the organization of the workers of industrial nations that the latter group turned when planning to overthrow the state; consistently enough, these Trotskyites were deeply involved in the strike activities at Nantes, where they hoped to follow the classic revolutionary tactic of establishing a "dual power"—that is, an alternative government modelled on the Jacobin clubs and the soviets of the French and Russian revolutions. Arrayed against Trotskyists of every flavor were the French Maoists, explicitly Stalinist in orientation but convinced the Communist Party was not Stalinist enough.

Overwhelmingly, however, the student movement of 1968 belonged not to Marxists intent on salvaging the Russian revolution, but to young anarchists and anarcho-Marxists who remembered the martyrdom of their intellectual forebears at the blood-soiled hands of the brutal Bolsheviks. Cohn-Bendit's *Senile Communism* begins with a discussion of the student rebellion but ends with a brief history of how Lenin and Trotsky betrayed the revolution, long before the triumph of Stalin. As early as 1918, virtually at the outset of the revolution and well in advance of Stalinism, wrote Cohn-Bendit, the revolution was lost because Lenin and Trotsky made extermination of anarchists one of their highest priorities.

When the workers and sailors of Kronstadt rose up to defend the principle that "all power to the [democratic] soviets" should not mean "all power to the [centralized] party," Trotsky called upon his Red Army to crush them. Again, it was the Red Army under Trotsky's leadership which destroyed the military force assembled by the young Ukrainian, Makhno: another showdown between anarchism and Bolshevism, another loss for the cause of libertarian as opposed to authoritarian socialism. "Makhno's defeat," declared Cohn-Bendit, "spelled the defeat of the revolution; Trotsky's victory, the victory of the bureaucratic counter-revolution." Down, then, with the French Trotskyist students; up with the anarchists who must vindicate their fallen predecessors.

The very title of the book Daniel Cohn-Bendit wrote in conjunction with his brother Gabriel, a professor at the University of Nantes, was meant to tweak the nose of Lenin. *State and Revolution,* Lenin's tract of 1917, pictured workers running offices within twenty-four hours of the takeover of the state; *Left-Wing Communism: An Infantile Disorder,* written after the Bolshevik triumph, was Lenin's attempt to bury *State and Revolution* and to chide as adolescent anyone who repeated his earlier remarks in favor of workers' control. Cohn-Bendit, on behalf of the left-wing communism of Rosa Luxemburg, Anton Pannekoek, and the French students of 1968, decided to return insult for insult: if he and his kind were "infantile," then Lenin was surely "senile."

Cohn-Bendit shared with the Situationists an anarchism that was as receptive to Marx as it was hostile to Marxism. There was nothing to be said for what the Communist parties had made of Marx; but Cohn-Bendit and such Situationist figures as Guy Debord, Raoul Vaneigem, and Mustapha Khayati freely pillaged the writings of Marx, especially his early discussions of "alienation" and some of his later tomes as well, with their references to the "fetishism of commodities." In *The Society of Spectacle* Debord decried the movement from "being" to "having" to "appearing" in advanced industrial societies. Similarly, Khayati's *On the Poverty of Student Life* condemns the "totalitarian spectacle," the reduction of the human being to the status of an "admiring spectator . . . consuming unreservedly and uncritically." Anyone familiar with Marxian rhetoric will detect in all these discussions a heavy dose of the concept of "false consciousness."

Common to all these anarcho-Marxists was the ideal of a "nonauthoritarian and nonhierarchical socialist society," based on "horizontal relationships" and the self-governance of workers' control. Their goal, as stated in one Situationist text, was "the formation of workers' councils making decisions democratically at the rank-and-file level, federating with each other by means of delegates revocable at any moment, and becoming the sole deliberative and executive power of the entire country." Time and again, they recalled earlier efforts to achieve the same end, in the Paris Commune of 1871, the Russian revolutions of 1905 and 1917, the Spanish revolution of 1936, and the Hungarian uprising of 1956. This time, armed with lessons learned from past defeats, they would win.

The French students of 1968 reiterated the themes voiced in all previous clashes between anarchists and "authoritarian" Marxists. Anything that Proudhon and Bakunin had argued against Marx, syndicalists against parliamentary socialists, Rosa Luxemburg against Lenin, Surrealists against Stalinists, was certain to reappear sooner or later in the polemics of the students. If the students believed that the revolutionary movement—the means—must itself exemplify in miniature the future society—the end—they learned these lessons from Bakunin and Rosa Luxemburg. If Lenin in *What is to be Done?* placed "organization" above "spontaneity," then Bakunin, Luxemburg, and the Surrealists stressed spontaneity, and so did the French students following in the revolutionary footsteps of their illustrious forebears. Likewise the conviction of Cohn-Bendit and the Situationists that the workers must act for and organize themselves, as opposed to having a vanguard act for them, was a direct repetition of Bakunin, Luxemburg, and many another anarchist or anarcho-Marxist.

When Cohn-Bendit and the Situationists spoke of the virtues of federal organization, they were reissuing the proposals of Proudhon and Bakunin, just as their enthusiasm for the general strike of May 13 harkened back to the era of syndicalism. Even the odd boast of the most prominent students that theirs was a revolutionary movement unguided by a revolutionary doctrine becomes rhetorically significant when understood, in the first instance, as a revisitation of Bakunin's elevation of action over theory; and, in the second instance, as a response to

Lenin's assertion that "without a revolutionary theory there can be no revolution-ary movement." To which we may add that the very notion that students can be a source of revolutionary change dates back to Bakunin. In general, the constant harking back to the theme of workers' councils, of self-management or *autoges-tion*, as it was called in 1968; the incessant references to the Paris Commune of 1871; the occasional fascination of the New Left with outlaws; the view of revolu-tion as an act of will, not of circumstances; of permanent revolution and of revolu-tion as unending improvisation—all these items on the agenda of 1968 are just so many variations on the standard themes of the anarchist tradition.

The International Situationists were, far and away, the most colorful and prominent of the anarcho-Marxist groups deeply involved in the events of May, 1968. Their concerns and proposals were overwhelmingly the same as those addressed by André Breton and the Surrealists throughout the 1920s and 1930s. Once again there were protests against the diminution of the human spirit in a cap-italist society with a highly developed division of labor, specialization, and worship of commodities; once again artists called for a socialist society as devoted to free creativity and play as the Soviet Union was to work and authority from the top down. "We have made Paris dance," wrote one Situationist writer on May 30; we have substituted a self-activated and self-sustained people's "festival" for the previ-ous society of passive "spectacle." The graffiti and posters on the walls of the Sor-bonne were the inspiration of the Situationists: "Power to the imagination!" "Under the cobblestones, the beach!" "Take your desires for reality." "It is forbid-den to forbid." Just as the Surrealists had searched for the holy grail of a society constantly made and remade according to the urges of unfettered artistic imagina-tion, so did their Situationist offspring in the late 1960s speak of creative revolution and of a society in which each person would be a creative artist.

Dedicated to revolutionary change, the Situationists felt close to the Surreal-ists of the past but somewhat removed from the American rebels of their present. The Situationists sensed, quite rightly, that student protestors in the United States were noisy reformers, not revolutionaries. Mustapha Khayati, keen to see himself and his peers as part of an international student movement, praised the American New Left as best he could. Still, he expressed disappointment that his counterparts in the United States had built a "movement which remains largely attached to two relatively incidental aspects of the American crisis—the blacks and Vietnam."[19]

The sharp contrast between the reformist New Left of America and the revo-lutionary New Left of France went well beyond empty posturing. In France alone among the industrial democracies did what began as a student rebellion evolve into a series of strikes—a general strike—called for by workers. By contrast American laborers, especially the "hard hats" of the construction industry, positively hated the students whom they regarded as privileged traitors, unwilling to fight for their country and untroubled to see working-class youths dying in their stead. In France, moreover, one professional middle-class group after another went on strike. Final-

---

[19]Mutsapha Khayati, "On the Poverty of Student Life," in Ken Knabb, ed., *Situationist International Anthology*, p. 329.

ly, only in France, and specifically at Nantes, did a situation of "dual power" arise—supposedly the harbinger of revolution, as everyone knew who had the slightest familiarity with French and Russian history or with the polemics of the Left.

We may conclude that during the period of French and American student radicalism the events were much the same in the two countries, as were many of the specific admonitions and proposals set forth by young leftists. But the host ideologies which served the students as they explained those events and articulated their responses were as dissimilar as the history and culture of the French is from that of the Americans. Similar events, different meanings, and—we are about to see—different consequences.

THE LEGACY OF 1968

To the political actor, history almost always turns out to be a record of unintended consequences that he or she does not comprehend until after the event, when it is too late; to the political scientist or historian, the historical record is a web so intricately spun that a given cause sets off an endlessly complicated set of effects. If hindsight is always clearer than foresight, if a retrospective look has its rewarding moments of insight and self-recognition, that is in part because memory suppresses the fullness of the past. What follows should be understood as nothing more than a brief, incomplete, and deliberately oversimplified account of the consequences of the student rebellions of the late 1960s.

Perhaps the easiest place to begin is with the electoral consequences, which fall into a distinctive pattern, namely, the triumph of the conservatives. In France the Gaullists won victories of massive proportions in June 1968 and continued to fare well despite the departure from politics of the General himself in 1969. In America the Democratic party, badly split by the Vietnam war and the challenge from the New Left, lost the Presidency to Richard Nixon. Later, Ronald Reagan came to the fore and profited handsomely from what the students he despised had done. "Under the administration of President Reagan," observes one pundit, "it was neoconservatives who reaped the benefits of what the New Left, before its sudden collapse, had helped to sow—the delegitimation of liberal corporatism and the ideal of the welfare state."[20] The same is true of England: the New Left deeply divided the Labour party and inadvertently helped bring about the rise of Thatcherism and the decline of the welfare state.[21]

Identical in immediate electoral results, America and France go their separate ways when we consider the long-term systemic consequences of the turbulent politics of the late 1960s. For the Americans the outcome over the long haul has been, first, a revision of the electoral system yielding unexpectedly mixed or even straightforwardly pernicious results; and, second, the rise of the ecological and the

[20]Miller, *"Democracy is in the Streets"*, p. 321.
[21]See Samuel Beer, *Britain against Itself: the Political Contradictions of Collectivism* (New York: Norton, 1982).

Women's movements. In keeping with the larger history of reform movements in the United States, the story of the legacy of the late 1960s dwells sometimes on the glories but more frequently on the frustrations of reform politics. For France, in contrast to America, the eventual aftermath has proven to be, arguably, a significantly improved pattern of socio-political arrangements.

Before 1968, the French schools suffered from excessive distance between professors and students and from the arbitrariness of having one professor occupy a "chair," from which he barked out orders to other professors and made all major decisions. Within research laboratories, hospitals, and business organizations it was the same as in the university: in each unit a patron accountable to no one ruled the roost. This personalistic arbitrariness, Michel Crozier argued in a book published several years preceding the events of 1968, alternated with governance through highly impersonal bureaucracies, which were rule-bound, rigid, and staffed by personnel sharing the general inability of the French to resolve their conflicts in face-to-face discussions.

Essentially Crozier's analysis was an updated version of Tocqueville's *Recollections* and *The Old Regime and the French Revolution*. For both men the problem was the incapacity of their compatriots, numbed by endless social and political struggles, to resolve their problems through communication and bargaining. Identifying with groups only to gain protection against other groups, the French are—in Crozier's words—"simultaneously extremely conservative as members of . . . groups, and very progressive and creative anarchists as individuals within their own personal domains."[22] Unable to speak to or deal with management, the workers take to the streets when there is a labor dispute, not because they are genuinely radical and out to overthrow the state, but rather to force the state to intervene and to do for them what they and the managers are unwilling to do for themselves. Throughout the post–World War II era, the French have staged mock-radical demonstrations which are taken too seriously by outsiders who invariably fail to recognize that they are witnessing a scripted and ritualized game.

The year 1968 marks a turning point in French history because those who took to the streets did not seek the intervention of the state. *Autogestion,* self-management, power to make decisions at the local level, was the demand not simply of students but of persons drawn from every possible calling: doctors, lawyers, accountants, engineers, scientific researchers, statisticians, journalists, actors, film directors, and museum curators. Even the soccer players joined in, chanting "Soccer for the soccer players!" At last France was ready for the emergence of a civil society, related to but independent of the state, a social order with resources of its own for solving its problems. France would remain a republic but was henceforth to be a more liberal society and polity, displaying a greater capacity for local initiative than in the past. The anarchist slogans and black flags of the students did little to foster anarchism but proved to be a considerable boon to prospects for a more liberal France.

---

[22]Michel Crozier, *The Bureaucratic Phenomenon* (Chicago: University of Chicago Press, 1964), p. 289.

And America? The Democratic party's response to the events of 1968 was a concerted effort to make liberal democracy more democratic. Never again, it was felt, should a candidate be nominated, as Hubert Humphrey was, without contesting a single primary. New regulations were passed such that party regulars could no longer decide the nomination; the rank and file members, more than ever before, would be represented at the Convention, and the candidates would be forced to run the gauntlet of a seemingly unending succession of primary elections. This was the "new politics," invented by the Democrats but a fact of life for both parties after its enactment into state laws. By now we know the price that has been paid for this "reform": public boredom with seemingly interminable presidential campaigns, the inability of all but the most wealthy persons to run for office, and a politics of presidential selection in which the debased currency of vicious personal attacks has supplanted anything vaguely resembling a discussion of the issues. Steps taken to reform political parties have hastened their decomposition, and weakened parties have spelled a new low in public life.

Liberal and democratic reformers of the late 1960s, in their quest for greater democracy, also revived the Populist and Progressive initiative and referendum. Come the 1970s these political devices were used with noteworthy success by conservatives to roll back property taxes. Propositions 13 and 2½ in California and Massachusetts effectively crippled the public school system, which from the founding of America has been regarded as the guarantee of an enlightened citizenry and, more recently, as the source of an able and competitive work force.

On the positive side, the ecological movement got its start from the "back to nature" aspect of the counter-culture. And the contemporary version of the Women's movement has its origins in the late 1960s. It was from their experience as student radicals that women learned how to organize politically. It was from their distinctly second rate status within the student movement that women learned the necessity of organizing.[23] Young women responded with rage to Stokeley Carmichael's comment that "the only position for women in the Movement is prone." Eventually women became wary of Tom Hayden as well, and decided that the best way to be heard was to have their own organization. Quite accurately, we equate the late 1960s with sexual liberation; yet it is equally true that the women of that period began to realize that sexual freedom and freedom for women are far from being one and the same.

When all is said and done, more was said than done in the late 1960s. True, at Nantes there was a situation of "dual power" for several days—but only because the gendarmes had been called to Paris. Throughout May, France was more in limbo than in a state of revolution; not for a moment during the hiatus of authority did the army budge from its loyalty to de Gaulle. There was less, then, to the

---

[23]An unsubstantiated, possibly apocryphal report has it that when German student radicals seized administrative buildings on campus, the males wrote the radical pamphlets while the females did the radical laundry.

events in France than meets the eye; and less, too, than what stirs the memory to questionable parallels with earlier social explosions. "Dual power" in Nantes was probably more a remembrance of things past than a door to the future.

How odd that 1968 should bring France closer to liberal democracy of the kind Americans take for granted; how fitting that 1968 should give birth in the United States to new "causes" and to reform legislation leaving reformers wondering whether they have lost more than they have gained.

BIBLIOGRAPHY

Aron, Raymond, *The Elusive Revolution.* London: Pall Mall, 1969.

Brown, Bernard, *Protest in Paris: Anatomy of a Revolt.* Morristown, NJ: General Learning Press, 1974.

Caute, David, *The Year of the Barricades: A Journey Through 1968.* New York: Harper & Row, 1988.

Cohn-Bendit, Daniel & Gabriel, *Obsolete Communism: The Left-Wing Alternative.* New York: McGraw-Hill, 1968.

Debord, Guy, *Society of the Spectacle.* Detroit: Black & Red, 1970.

Huntington, Samuel P., *American Politics: the Promise of Disharmony.* Cambridge, MA: Harvard University Press, 1981.

Keniston, Kenneth, *Young Radicals: Notes on Committed Youth.* New York: Harcourt, Brace & World, 1968.

Knabb, Ken, ed., *Situationist International Anthology.* Berkeley: Bureau of Public Secrets, 1981.

Lipset, Seymour Martin & Altbach, Philip, eds., *Students in Revolt.* Boston: Houghton Mifflin, 1969.

Miller, James, *"Democracy is in the Streets": From Port Huron to the Siege of Chicago.* New York: Simon and Schuster, 1987.

Roszak, Theodore, *The Making of a Counter-Culture.* New York: Doubleday, 1969.

Touraine, Alain, *The May Movement: Revolt and Reform.* New York: Random House, 1971.

Chapter *14*

Multiculturalism and the Politics of Identity

During my life, I have seen Frenchmen, Italians, Russians . . . ; but I must say, as for man, *I have never come across him anywhere.*

Joseph de Maistre

*I*n recent years the conflict of ideologies in America has centered on the issue of multiculturalism. Caught in the middle of charges and counter-charges, the onlooker stares at the combatants in bewildered silence, wondering what to make of all the talk about "political correctness," puzzled by the dismantling of college courses on Western civilization, uncertain whether the debate is about anything important. On those rare occasions when the smoke of polemical excess clears for a moment, one sees that the issue is whether democracy will find a way to govern justly a society that is both more enriched and more divided than ever before by a multiplicity of ethnic and racial identities.

UNVEILING THE PROBLEM

For two centuries the favorite tactic of polemicists locked in ideological battle has been to "unveil" their opponents, as eighteenth-century thinkers said, or to "unmask" the enemy, in an expression much favored during the nineteenth century and still popular today. Marx and Marxists, in particular, have thrived on showing that behind the mask or veil of universalistic liberal ideology lies the class interest of the bourgeoisie. The historical roots of this kind of thinking may be found in writings of such figures of the French Enlightenment as Holbach and Helvétius, who lit up the eighteenth century with incendiary books charging that the rhetoric of the Catholic and supposedly universal Church was in truth nothing more than a rationalization of the reactionary interests of the priestly caste. Because the thought of the Enlightenment leads directly to nineteenth century liberalism, we may safely conclude that the game of unveiling or unmasking is by no means the monopoly of Marxian socialists; on the contrary, it has proven equally useful to liberals whenever they have found themselves on the outside, looking to attack the status quo.

Once liberalism was triumphant, such philosophers as John Stuart Mill, T. H. Green, and John Dewey sought to formulate principles allowing the new regime to be more than the embodiment of an ideology masking the privileges of some persons and the disadvantages of others. Theirs would be a liberalism that is legitimate because just, and the same may be said of the leading liberal philosopher of our time, John Rawls. Not the least striking feature of the writings of Professor Rawls is the manner in which he has transformed the imagery of veils and veiling from pejorative to positive usage. In a reformulation of the theory of the social contract, Rawls posits a hypothetical "original position" in which the members of a society convene to choose the principles of justice that shall govern their relations. To avoid bias, all persons shall be placed behind a "veil of ignorance" so that no one knows his or her talents, social class, ethnic affiliation, religious beliefs, gender, or sexual orientation. Doubtless Rawls would join with anyone wishing to unveil the racism that long hid behind the forms of liberal democracy in South Africa; but he is no less insistent that it is through a procedure of deliberate veiling that we learn what it takes to build a just liberal order, one wherein liberal rhetoric is not "false consciousness" or the rationalization of the interests of the powerful but the promulgation of the principles of a society that is fair to all and treats each person with respect.

Barely had Rawls published *A Theory of Justice* in 1971 than an entire scholarly industry mushroomed around his book and began production of a seemingly inexhaustible output of commentaries and criticisms. Almost from the first, questions were raised about the faceless, attributeless beings found behind the "veil of ignorance." Liberals longing for a sense of community wanted something more than the procedural republic outlined by Rawls. These communitarian critics effectively pointed out that justice is not everything, that it does not answer our need for friendship and other such emotionally satisfying relationships; but none of their criticisms challenged fundamentally the liberal edifice constructed by Rawls.

The subsequent criticisms launched by the multiculturalists, in marked contrast, most certainly do strike at the foundations of Rawls' political philosophy. It is the contention of the multiculturalists that our ethnic identities are precisely what constitutes our being, such that to strip us of our self-understandings as African Americans, Asian Americans, or Hispanic Americans is to rob us of our dignity and, indeed, of our very selves. Whether we are denuded by the philosophical abstractions of Rawls or deluded by the more popular notion of the "American way of life," our group identities are lost along the way. Particularly for oppressed ethnic and racial minorities the outcome is unacceptable, since in their case all talk about rights of individuals or about a shared American creed means the triumph of the culture of the powerful majority over the cultures of the vulnerable minorities. Multiculturalists therefore insist upon pulling the veil off the "veil of ignorance"; behind it they find ignorance both of the emotional depths of our ethnic identities and of the deleterious consequences for minorities of all concepts which dissolve our group identities, whether by counting us one by one or by universalizing us into oneness. "I" is rooted in an ethnic and immediate "we"—not in the ethereal and remote "we" of "we the people of the United States." Such is the multicultural argument.

Two recent events dealing with veiling and unveiling in the literal sense, one happening in France where it received enormous attention, the other in Boston where it was mentioned in the *Boston Globe,* seem to be cases in which life somehow imitates philosophy. Throughout 1989 the French found themselves embroiled in a debate over whether three Muslim girls should be permitted to wear traditional Islamic head scarves in the classrooms of their middle schools. What made the question so controversial was the strength of the historically sanctioned belief in France that the schools have a mission to sustain the idea of a "republic one and indivisible." Many of the French, including some of the most progressive in their numbers, feared the scarves as threats to the integrity of the republic, some commentators going so far as to issue warnings against the danger that France, if it abandoned its unifying republican tradition, might go the way of some English-speaking countries wherein each ethnic group asserts its "right to be different." Lingering in the background throughout the controversy were the disdain of the French far right for Muslim immigrants, and the ambivalent memories of French liberals of the days when their compatriots in Algeria forced Muslim women to remove their veils.

Eventually the courts ruled in favor of the Muslim girls, which would seem to sustain the claims of many observers that France is slowly evolving in the direction of America.[1] It is worth noting, however, that the French outcome runs parallel to America as it has been, not as multiculturalists want it to be. On the basis of repeated experiences in this country over the last several years it is not far-fetched to imagine that if the same incident occurred in America, multiculturalists would demand that Islamic studies be added to the curriculum, a proposal which might be granted with a minimum of controversy because almost everyone, feasibly, could agree that American youths will be ill-prepared to enter the world if they know nothing about Islamic peoples. Many multiculturalists presumably would not stop there, however; they would teach American and Western history as so many chapters in an unrelenting tale of imperialism. School boards would soon be intently watching the Disney version of *Aladdin,* while members debated whether the portrayal of Arabs fosters cultural stereotypes.

Muslim veils are badges of identity. When the Boston Symphony Orchestra puts up a veil, it is to hide identity. The judges of musicians auditioning for positions in the BSO sit behind a veil hiding the ethnic identity and gender of the candidates. Presumably without reading a page of Rawls, these judges appreciate the

---

[1]These words were written during July, 1994. Shortly thereafter new evidence came to light proving that the tradition of the "republic one and indivisible" dies hard. The Minister of Education announced his intention to ban Islamic head scarves. Paraphrasing Rousseau's comments on the "general will," he maintained that "the national will must not be ignored." The Minister of Interior, who also knew his Rousseau, then commented that "we cannot have government by judges. This is an affront to popular sovereignty." Clearly, the question how far the French are willing to move away from their old notions of republicanism remains to be answered.

advantages for fairness that can be gained from constructing a veil of ignorance. That at least was the case until the BSO hired a "diversity consultant" who immediately plunged the symphony into the disharmonious world of multicultural politics. According to a column appearing in the April 24, 1994, edition of the *Boston Globe*, the consultant issued a memo asking the staff of the BSO to reflect upon an inventory of "Workplace Cultural Diversity Comfort/Discomfort Indicators." Among the purported warning signs of nondiversity, against which the members of the BSO were urged to be on guard, the following items were listed: "uncomfortably segregated coffee [and] lunch breaks," "reticence of culturally diverse employees to give suggestions," "tolerance of ethnic/gender jokes in the workplace," "organizational literature [and] marketing imagery that is . . . not representative of all ethnic and cultural groups," "a majority culture view that everything is fine in your organization and no cross-cultural strains exist." Opponents of the multicultural agenda charge, not surprisingly, that "diversity consultants" create the very racial and ethnic tension they are hired to alleviate.

Since 1989 the climate of opinion in Europe and even more so in America has changed remarkably. In 1989 the French were looking forward to celebrating the bicentennial of the Declaration of the Rights of Man and Citizen (August 26, 1789). At the same moment communism was crumbling from within and the peoples of the former Soviet empire were calling for democratic regimes, which led Edgar Morin to suggest in *Le Monde* on June 9 that the eighteenth-century French slogan of "liberty, equality, fraternity" had once again become the "star of the future." It was also during the summer of 1989 that an American writer, mulling over the significance of East European strivings to establish democratic governments, announced "the end of history"; the historical drama of worldwide ideologies in conflict, he suggested, had been settled once and for all, and decided in favor of liberal democracy.[2]

Liberals, it seems, have an unfortunate habit of proclaiming themselves victorious and their challengers defunct. Just as writers in the 1950s prematurely proclaimed "the end of ideology" within the Western democracies, so in the early 1990s the cheerful note of the end of global confrontations of ideologies was no sooner sounded than events in Eastern Europe led to the onset of a deep pessimism about the prospects of liberal democratic government. The breakup of communism has meant less a return to the liberal glories of 1789 than a repeat performance of the worst days of 1848, that turbulent year when German liberalism died at the hands of a brutal nationalism. Rather than move onward to liberal democracy, the peoples of post–communist Eastern Europe have rekindled the ferocious national animosities that were held in check but not eliminated by the fallen communist regimes. As events in what was once called Yugoslavia attest, it is not liberal democracy but murderous national hatreds and genocide that have emerged from the ruins of communism.

The expectations so popular in 1989 of liberal democracy everywhere triumphant have given way in some circles to the question whether democracy is pos-

---

[2]Francis Fukuyama, "The End of History," *The National Interest* (Summer 1989), 3–18.

sible anywhere. Can America meet the multicultural challenge it currently faces? By some estimates whites will be a minority in California by the year 2000, and the same may be true of the country at large by 2050. Many current immigrants are of Asian or Latin American origin, or they are blacks from Haiti—this at a time when it is undeniable that the plight of African Americans has not improved over the last several decades. Racism and a new wave of nativism threaten to pull us apart.

At the very time when persons of good will should unite to combat a revival of Know Nothingism, the liberals and radicals of America are fighting one another in an inflammatory "culture war." At universities and colleges, in public elementary and secondary schools, battles rage over the curriculum. Radicals want to dissolve American history into a series of ethnic histories; such liberals as Arthur Schlesinger Jr. insist that "the disuniting of America" will result if the radicals have their way.

The ongoing debate over the curriculum is far from "academic"; it involves nothing less than the future of liberal democracy. Will America too be "balkanized," as some critics, the example of Eastern Europe in mind, charge? Or are we moving on to a new phase of democratic history, one more sensitive to differences and respectful of diversity than anything previously seen? Does the politics of identity signal the demise or the fulfillment of liberal democracy?

THE REVOLT AGAINST UNIVERSALISM

"All men are created equal," reads the Declaration of Independence. When Jefferson wrote these words more than two centuries ago, he did so as a good son of the Enlightenment. Throughout the eighteenth century the most advanced thinkers constantly spoke in a universalizing language, whether by attributing natural rights to all persons, postulating a utilitarian actor everywhere the same, formulating an ethics based upon universalizing the maxim of one's actions, or championing the cause of "humanity" against its priestly and despotic detractors.

Nothing is more characteristic of the present age than our insistence upon unmasking such universal rhetoric. Who is this "all" of which the Declaration of Independence speaks, we ask? Definitely it did not include the slaves; nor did it refer to Native Americans. And what of women? Were they meant to be included under the expression "all men"? How can that be, when females were not viewed as being the genuine equals of males?

Nor do we stop after pointing out that the "all" of the Declaration does not mean all; the next step is the multicultural one taken by many Native Americans and their sympathizers. Even if "all" did in fact mean everyone, that still would not save the way of life, the distinctive culture, of the Native Americans. The rights of each and of all citizens of the United States do not solve the problem of the Native Americans; likewise the Quebeckers worry that the rights of all Canadians will eventually entail the demise of their group right to *survivance*.

This revolt against universalism, however novel it may sound, has behind it a pedigree some two centuries in the making. Before the end of the era called the Enlightenment, the attack on universalism was already in full swing. Examinations of the past cannot answer all our present day questions, but a historical review can place the present in sharper perspective.

Taking a look backward, it is obvious that those advocates of the politics of identity who nowadays speak of themselves as "postmodernists" are employing a mistaken label. The multicultural program of today, far from marking the onset of a new and postmodern world of ideas, is but another chapter in the continuing story of the ideological debates of modernity which commenced with the French Revolution. It may be easier to decide what to keep and what to discard from the multicultural agenda if we understand the strengths and vulnerabilities of previous versions of the argument.

Today, attacks on universalistic ideals are delivered mainly from the left; historically, however, it has been the far right that has upbraided the cosmopolitan ideals of the Enlightenment. "During my life," wrote Joseph de Maistre, "I have seen Frenchmen, Italians, Russians . . . ; but I must say, as for *man,* I have never come across him anywhere."[3] Maistre was an arch-reactionary who blamed the excesses of the French Revolution on the *philosophes,* the cosmopolitan intellectuals of the eighteenth century who, regarding themselves as "the party of humanity," frequently set forth their hopes in universalistic language. As Maistre saw matters, humans are group-beings who become destructive the moment they are uprooted from their natural collective habitat by doctrines of natural rights that speak incessantly of individuals and humanity but rarely of family and nationality. Even Protestantism was anarchical insofar as it promoted an individualistic outlook; much better was the corporate structure of Catholicism, wrote Maistre, who would have French political authorities defer to the Pope.

Across the Channel, Edmund Burke expressed similar hostility to the *philosophes* in his famous conservative tract, the *Reflections on the Revolution in France* (1789–1790). What made Burke's arguments less extreme than Maistre's was that in England, unlike France, there was a constitutional tradition to preserve. No sooner, therefore, did Burke denounce universal and individual natural rights than he turned around and praised the traditionally sanctioned rights of Englishmen. Addressing an audience accustomed to the writings of John Locke, Burke also found it convenient to steal the idea of the social contract, adapting it to his own conservative purposes: "society is indeed a contract . . . , a partnership not only between those who are living, but between those who are living, those who are dead, and those who are to be born." In many fundamentals, however, there was no difference between Maistre and Burke: neither expressed anything but scorn for the reason of individuals, as opposed to the collective rationality they attributed to tradition; both took for granted, moreover, that an appreciation of the social and group-defined nature of human existence entailed a denunciation of individualism, universalism, and cosmopolitanism.

Kant is a leading target of multicultural radicals in America today for many of the same reasons that he has always been attacked by European conservatives. The reactionaries of yesteryear and the multiculturalists of our time understand moral-

---

[3]Jack Lively, ed., *The Works of Joseph de Maistre* (New York: Schocken, 1971), p. 80.

ity as the traditions, folkways, and mores of groups. In direct contrast, the "categorical imperative" of Kant centers on the individual who commands his or her self to "act as if the maxim of thy action were to become by thy will a universal law of nature."[4] Kant (like Rawls today) wanted to pull us out of our group contexts, the better to free us of our prejudices. It is typical of Maistre and Burke that in their reaction against the Enlightenment, they went so far as to praise prejudice. In Burke's words, "prejudice engages the mind in a steady course of wisdom and virtue, and does not leave the mind hesitating in the moment of decision—skeptical, puzzled, and unresolved." Because the *philosophes* were forever trying to destroy prejudice, Burke and Maistre saw fit to sing the praises of unreflective conviction.

Burke and Maistre stressed group identity as part of their campaign to discredit the heritage of the French Revolution. Marx also focused on groups, specifically on social classes, but he did so in order to finish the work of revolutionary transformation which the rebels of the late eighteenth century had started. No less than the reactionaries but for diametrically opposed reasons, Marx was out to discredit the Declaration of the Rights of Man and Citizen. In language that could just as well have been written by Maistre, Marx denounced the "unreal universality" of the rights stated in the famous document of August 26, 1789. Behind the veil of universal rights lurked the victory of the bourgeoisie over the aristocrats; soon, according to Marx, this same ideology of rights would give the bourgeoisie a second triumph, this time over the proletariat of the emerging capitalist order.

Consider another comparison and contrast between Marx and the European far right, namely, that after throwing out the "bourgeois" universalism of rights, Marx shouts the new universalizing slogan, "Workers of all countries, unite!" For all his focus on groups, Marx never relinquishes the cosmopolitan yearnings of the Enlightenment. "The workingmen have no country," he wrote in the *Communist Manifesto,* but his followers witnessed the day when the proletarians of various countries marched off to slaughter one another in the trench warfare of World War I. That illusion-shattering event proved that the right wing, in its glorification of national sentiment, outdid both liberals and socialists when it came to appreciating the most fundamental force in modern history, nationalism.

Let us admit that group and ethnic identifications are formative and immediate in a way that the universal ideal of "humanity" has never been nor ever will be. The question still remains, how should we understand the way in which we are "socially constituted"? Is there a German essence as some German romantics held; or was Herder, who preceded them in praising the *Volk,* correct in his view that nationality is a matter of traditions which are forever open to redefinition?

It was Johann Gottfried von Herder (1744–1803) who initiated the talk about the Volk which became an obsessive motif of German thought in the nineteenth century and beyond. But unlike later thinkers, Herder cited the Volk to criticize, not to repudiate, the humanitarian ideals of the Enlightenment. National identity,

---

[4]Immanuel Kant, *Fundamental Principles of the Metaphysic of Morals* (Indianapolis: Bobs-Merrill, 1949), p. 38.

to Herder, has nothing to do with physical inheritance or race; rather, our sense of "we" comes from a national culture forged by human actions over time, and by the shared language which links us together even as it fosters the growth of individual self-conscious personhood. Hence it was wrong for German princes to abandon their native tongue in favor of French; it was wrong, likewise, for German intellectuals to write in French or in frenchified German.

Nevertheless Herder upheld the worth of *Humanität* as wholeheartedly as he did the Volk. But humanity as he understood it was not an empty universal. Instead, humanity was the sum total of all the many unique national cultures, each such culture being composed as much of the mores of the common people as of the book-learning of the intellectuals. Not in the least did Herder have anything in common with those later champions of the Volk, the German romantics, who held humanitarian ideals in contempt and looked upon Germany as a favored nation. To Herder each culture has its worth, and no single European nation has a claim to superiority over the others, nor do the combined countries of Europe have a proper claim to precedence over non-European peoples. What arguably is best in multicultural arguments today sounds like variations on Herder's themes; what is worst sounds like an echo of the racial notions of some of the Volkish romantics.

Racial arguments have always been based on the arbitrary notion that mind is the expression of physical structure. In defiance or ignorance of all historical sensibility, racists posit mental traits and characteristics that are fixed once and for all times. Thus Gobineau, the famous racist ideologue, author of the *Essay on the Inequality of Races,* held that leadership, energy, and superiority are the permanent characteristics of whites; stability and fertility pertain to the yellow races; sensuality and art to blacks. How strange it is that some spokespersons for blacks today make the same racist arguments which whites formerly made against blacks. Several recent black authors see Africans and African Americans as inherently superior because they are genetically endowed with bountiful quantities of melanin, the factor accounting for skin pigmentation; whites, we are told, in order to compensate for low levels of melanin, have spread death and destruction everywhere. Such arguments have no scientific basis, nor, obviously, do they provide hope for overcoming the legacy of racism; their only significance is to offer a striking example of how one form of fanaticism breeds another.

Down to their anti-Semitic details, current arguments for black superiority duplicate the worst kind of nineteenth-century Volkish ideology. A much more promising way to deal with our present day politics of ethnic identity would be to return to something resembling Herder's notion of the Volk. No one has ever conjured up a richer or more subtly textured "feel" for the ways in which individual identity is molded by group and national contexts than Herder. But never did he speak of a German essence, eternally given and immutable. The culture of a people, in his historical view, is constantly being made and remade; a people defines its culture as much as culture defines a people.

American political thought has always spoken as profusely about the citizen as it has remained reticent about the state, which should make us feel comfortable with Herder, foe of the German administrative state and advocate of the people. In foreign affairs, too, Americans second Herder, albeit unknowingly, when they show humanitarian concern for persons living in foreign lands who suffer from hunger or political oppression. The "we" with which we identify expands or contracts many times in a single day, sometimes withdrawing to a unit as small as the family, at other times reaching out to persons on the opposite side of the globe. Humanitarianism and cosmopolitanism can part company with universalism and thrive all the better.

In one respect, however, Herder did not foresee our multicultural dilemma: although sensitive to the complex variations which can coexist in a single culture, Herder associated multiculturalism with the Hapsburg-style absolutist and dynastic state which he despised. As is always the case, we can only go so far in gaining insight from past thinkers; in the end, it is up to us to find our own answers.

THE REVOLT AGAINST SCIENCE

Enlightenment-bashers, were they to bother to read the *philosophes*, would soon discover that many of the finest minds of the eighteenth century were skeptical about universalizing modes of thought. One of the most frequently repeated arguments of the *philosophes* was that what passes for a rigorous exercise in reasoning frequently amounts to little more than projecting ourselves into what is unfamiliar, alien, other. Montesquieu, for instance, lamented that so many historians "want to modernize all the ancient ages." Rousseau registered a similar complaint:

> Despite three or four hundred years during which the inhabitants of Europe have inundated the other parts of the world, and continually published new collections of voyages and reports, I am convinced that we know no other men except the Europeans; furthermore, it appears, from the ridiculous prejudices which have not died out even among the intellectuals, that under the pompous name of the study of man everyone does hardly anything except study the men of his country.[5]

Few multiculturalists realize that when they indict social science as ethnocentric and tainted by complicity in imperialism, they are rehashing arguments first made more than two centuries ago by the *philosophes* they hold in contempt.

There is, to be sure, a major difference between the position of Montesquieu or Rousseau and that of the multiculturalists of today. Montesquieu was a founder and pioneer of sociology, Rousseau was calling for the training of anthropologists (to use the terminology of a later age). Both writers believed the development of social science, if properly pursued, could minimize prejudice and provide openings to build a more humane world. In sharp contrast, it is common for multiculturalists, especially if they adopt the additional label of postmodernists, to denounce anthropology as an undertaking inherently ethnocentric and politically compromised.

Here again, a look at the historical record may prove enlightening. A brief review of the history of the social sciences, we shall argue, reveals that their rise

---

[5]Rousseau, *Discourse on Inequality*, footnote J in Roger Masters, ed., *The First and Second Discourses* (New York: St. Martin's Press, 1964) p. 210.

was, indeed, tied to empire-building, and that their practitioners were guilty as charged of a failure to appreciate non-Western cultures. It is true that all too often social science has codified and justified ethnocentrism instead of combating it. But it is equally true that the best social science has had some success in fostering an appreciation of cultures originally strange and alien. To abandon the dream of Rousseau and Montesquieu is to destroy an important means of coming to terms with the problems facing the citizens of a multicultural society.

There is no denying that the rise of anthropology and sociology in England during the nineteenth century was disproportionately the achievement of thinkers associated in one way or another with British imperial rule in India.[6] Sir Henry Maine, for example, besides writing such works as *Ancient Law* and *Village Communities of East and West,* held the post of Legal Member of the Council in India. Typically Maine and his cohort resorted to a conceptual scheme of social evolution when studying history. One of the enticements attracting them to the notion of stages-of-development, clearly, was that it permitted them to justify empire without abjuring their liberal faith. Locke had said that although children have natural rights, parents must act for them until they reach their maturity. In the same manner, argued Victorian social scientists, the advanced country of England must act the parent toward its subjects in India, a nation they regarded as immature and childlike.

None other than John Stuart Mill, commenting on the British empire, hailed his country as "the power which . . . has attained to more of conscience and moral principle in its dealings with foreigners than any other great nation." Normally one thinks of *On Liberty* as an unlikely source for justifications of despotism, but when the discussion turns to non-Western peoples, Mill holds that "despotism is a legitimate mode of government in dealing with barbarians, provided the end be their improvement." While conceding that the Chinese are a civilized people, Mill insists that if ever China is to be improved, "it must be by foreigners."

At least two complaints may be lodged against Mill and Maine. The first is that, despite their credentials as good liberals, they are in danger of advocating Locke for England but Filmer for the British empire. An English child was subject to paternal authority for a specified number of years; no such limitation applied to the number of years a people could be subjected to English rule. Self-interest could and did easily corrupt the British into postponing indefinitely the date when the native population of India had reached its "maturity." In the ever expansive meantime the English would govern India according to procedures sufficiently paternalistic to vindicate Filmer's *Patriarcha,* the pamphlet Locke had refuted.

The second complaint is that Mill, Maine, and all theorists of social evolution were profoundly ethnocentric in their assumption that a people is civilized insofar as its culture approaches that of England. In the remote past England had been as India is in the nineteenth century; in the remote future India will evolve into a society similar to that of Victorian England. Never, in the foregoing account, do Mill or Maine study the culture of India in Indian terms; never do they ponder the

---

[6]See J. W. Burrow, *Evolution and Society: A Study in Victorian Social Theory* (Cambridge: Cambridge University Press, 1966).

possibility that Indian culture has its own merits. Despite their dismissal of the eighteenth-century notion of a universal human nature, the Victorian social scientists refused to question their new assumption of a universal scheme of social development. From hindsight it is clear that the new version of universalism, like the old, masked a bias: in this case, a belief that Western superiority is self-evident.

During the 1950s American social scientists struggled to come to terms with the breakup of the colonial empires and the concomitant emergence of a plethora of new non-Western nations. To do so they revisited the type of nineteenth-century social theory we have just discussed. "Modernization theory" was the label they affixed to repackaged thought shipped in from the previous century. No longer, it is true, was a scheme of stages of social and political development used to rationalize empire. But in other respects the tainted old wine was no better for being placed in new bottles. Failing to learn from the errors of the previous century, thinkers in the 1950s repeated the mistake of assuming that all nations should follow the Western course of evolution.

The result was that some of the most vital forces at work in the world were ignored or written off as irrelevant "survivals" from an earlier era. Muslim fundamentalism, a force to be reckoned with, was overlooked by social scientists four decades ago because religion was not taken seriously in the works of the nineteenth-century authors from whom "modernization theory" was cribbed. Marx saw religion as an opium the people would cease to need the moment they organized into militant organizations of workers. For Max Weber, the famous German sociologist, religion played a noteworthy part in the rise of capitalism, but his progeny assumed he regarded modern society as inherently secular. Saint-Simon and Comte, the founders of French sociology, similarly regarded religion as a dying force. As conservatives, Saint-Simon and Comte yearned for a faith that would pacify the masses; but they misunderstood their historical situation so completely as to deem it necessary to conjure up a new faith. All the foregoing comments about religion could be repeated for ethnic identity. Neither religion nor ethnicity figured significantly in the social theories of the nineteenth century; hence both were omitted from meaningful consideration in the theories of modernization of the mid-twentieth century.

When Western thinkers did get around to expressing doubts about the consequences of modernization, it was because they opposed the spread of democracy in Europe and feared the ascendancy of the peoples of Asia, Africa, and Latin America. Such outstanding historians of Western culture as Jacob Burckhardt and Johann Huizinga devoted their writings, in one way or another, to bemoaning the rise of a mass culture—or, rather, to lamenting the destruction of "true" culture, which on their view is always aristocratic and elitist. "Mass culture," they held, is a self-contradictory expression, for wherever the masses dominate there is no culture. Ortega y Gasset, in his *Revolt of the Masses* (1930), took the argument a step further: he denounced the rise of new nations ("mass-peoples") outside the Western orbit as adamantly as he voiced his disdain for the growth of popular government in Europe:

> The frivolous spectacle offered by the smaller nations today is deplorable. Because it is said that Europe is in decadence and has given over ruling, every twopenny–half-penny nation starts skipping, gesticulating, standing on its head or else struts around

giving itself airs of a grown-up person . . . Hence the panorama of "nationalisms" that meets our view everywhere.

It is commonplace nowadays for radicals to accuse liberals of failing to face up to their ethnocentric and antidemocratic prejudices. No one can accuse Ortega of hypocrisy.

What, then, of the idea of a social science? Are the postmodernists correct when they proclaim that all attempts to understand alien cultures are futile at best, exercises in imperialism at worst? Should we confine ourselves to studying our particular nation or culture, of better yet, our subculture and ethnic group? Was Spike Lee justified in declaring Norman Jewison unfit to make a film about Malcolm X; and what of the claims that Lee himself was too middle-class and white-minded to tell the story of the slain black leader: is this comeuppance or a point well taken?

One need only think of the example provided by Tocqueville to realize how mistaken it would be to abandon social science because of its past sins. *Democracy in America,* possibly the greatest book ever written on the United States, was the work of a Frenchman, which shows the fallacy of supposing that only a native can understand a given culture. Admittedly, when Tocqueville visited America his objective was not purely the anthropologist's quest to understand a foreign culture. His larger design was to prepare the French equivalents of Burckhardt and Ortega for a more democratic future. Himself a Count, Tocqueville's natural affiliation was with the aristocratic liberalism that loved checks and balances but hated popular suffrage and feared the cultural consequences of "the revolt of the masses." Not the least of Tocqueville's accomplishments is that the second volume of his monumental work displays the glories no less than the deficiencies of a democratic culture. For instance, where Burckhardt had dismissed journalism with an aristocratic sneer, Tocqueville noted the vital role that the popular press plays in a democracy. Where Burckhardt had wept over the decline of poetry, Tocqueville observed that the rise of the novel did not entail the demise of literature. The coming of democracy marks the transformation, not the obliteration, of literature and the arts.

The postmodernists are right to point out that social scientists are themselves part of the field they investigate; right also to say that no one can view history from the outside, *sub specie aeternitatis.* But they are wrong to imply that in the absence of complete objectivity we are reduced to total subjectivity. All knowledge is gained through peering upon the world from the viewpoint provided by a particular historical situation, but it is possible to enlarge one's perspective and to enhance one's self-awareness through careful exercises in comparative analysis. By studying America, Tocqueville raised himself above the French aristocratic liberals who refused to come to terms with the dawning age of democracy. Especially for someone today who is sympathetic to multiculturalism, it is essential to take Tocqueville's example to heart and to strive to reach beyond one's own culture, both to understand others and oneself.

In our present day predicament it is natural to turn to Tocqueville not only for vindication of the idea of a social science, but also for a proposed remedy to the problems facing a multicultural society. America, Tocqueville wrote to a French friend, is "a society formed of all the nations of the world"; yet its people are "a hundred times happier than our own." How so? Because in America the many different peoples are all citizens, active participants in public affairs. Civic education was the solution proposed by Tocqueville.

MULTICULTURALISM AND LIBERALISM

Readers of Arthur Schlesinger, Jr.'s *The Disuniting of America* are likely to conclude that multiculturalism is a fundamental denial of the American liberal creed. Many of the multiculturalists explicitly invite the same conclusion; some postmodernists, in particular, have announced with apparent pride that their lifework is to unmask liberalism as an ideology protective of racism and ethnocentrism. Nevertheless, there are good reasons to interpret the multicultural debate as the latest example of the never-ending process of liberal self-criticism.

Pull the veil off a few multiculturalists while they are preoccupied with unmasking a liberal, and what do we find? In most cases ex-liberals flailing against their past. Who but a person reared on the bread and butter of interest group liberalism can dismiss all concern for the common good with the ease of the multiculturalists, who are forever supporting the claims of this or that ethnic group while ignoring the larger social and political order, except to denounce it? The unspoken assumption of multiculturalism is Adam Smith's "unseen hand," which assures the cohesion of society even as its various members go their separate ways, with never a thought for the public interest. Likewise, the professors in the humanities who denounce Shakespeare as sexist or racist, or who deny there are grounds to place *Macbeth* above Madonna in artistic worth, are less the iconoclasts they take themselves to be than the latest offspring of Jacksonian democracy, which was suspicious of elitist institutions of higher education and especially hostile to the snobbery of professors of literature. What greater triumph for the Jacksonian persuasion can there be than for departments of English to lead the way in denying the value of Shakespeare?

Now reverse the procedure. Remove the veil from a liberal who is busily denouncing the multiculturalists, and one finds a person disturbed by how much he or she shares with the enemy. In the name of freedom of expression liberals lash out with anger against codes on campus outlawing not just public "hate speech" but ethnic jokes spoken in private conversation; yet these same liberals, faced with the problem of spousal abuse, support state intervention in the private sphere. Back and forth the contemporary liberal moves—depending on the immediate issue—between affirmation and denial of the time-honored commitment of liberalism to the sanctity of privacy. Fighting for the right to an abortion or against statutes outlawing sodomy, liberals reassert the claims of individuals to decide private matters for themselves. But since wife-beating is intolerable, liberals favor laws reaching into the home. Sometimes liberals find themselves in uncomfortable agreement with a central contention of multiculturalists, to wit, the claim that the traditional liberal ideals of an inviolable private space and a right to say anything too often serve to protect terrible abuses.

By no means is the affinity between liberals and their multicultural opponents limited to a few specific and recent issues. On the contrary, the multiculturalists are the unwanted offspring of a style of liberal thinking long in the making. To underscore the significance of the differences between contemporary liberals and multiculturalists one must first note their similarities, the most important being their mutual rejection of individualist philosophies, whether of the natural rights or the utilitarian variety, in favor of a view of persons as social and group beings.

Around the turn of the twentieth century, the English philosophers T. H. Green and L. T. Hobhouse offered theoretical defenses of the transformation of liberalism from the old doctrine of laissez faire to the new vision of a welfare state. Before long the influential John Dewey was reiterating their position to Americans. All three were quick to dismiss notions of humans in a state of nature, after which they denied the plausibility of the Benthamite calculator, supposedly everywhere and always the same. Individualism is in fact the product of a certain kind of social order, one that is distinctively modern, noted the new liberals. The "self-evident truths" of which the America founders spoke were not in the least evident during the Middle Ages; human reality is social and historical, concluded Dewey as had his English predecessors.

Much like Marx, the welfare liberals dismissed the supposedly universal and natural laws of classical political economy as little more than the increasingly outmoded norms of a passing social order. In the modern industrial world it is corporations, not individuals, that are in competition, and these corporations are public actors which should be subject to public control. Welfare liberals, in short, insisted that the classical liberal conception of "the private" is far too broad, because it encompasses many social activities and organizations that are of public significance. As liberalism moved from its laissez-faire to its interventionist phase, the sphere of "the private" shrank significantly.

So far a multiculturalist has no reason to disagree. Even more to the liking of the radicals of today are the statements of Green and his successors denying the plausibility of John Stuart Mill's distinction between self-regarding and other-regarding actions. Out to make the case for state intervention in the economy, the early welfare liberals stressed that individuals are not social atoms, each an entity unto itself. Rather, personhood is a social acquisition, and hence the state must remove the formidable social obstacles poverty places in the way of the development of personality. This new stress on the "positive" freedom to be a full member of the community was matched, however, by a curtailment of the freedom to do as one pleases in the private sphere. In Mill's libertarian argument a man or woman is free to be a drunk, so long as no one else gets hurt; Green, by contrast, noted that the drunkenness of one person inevitably affects the lives of his or her family and neighborhood. The philosophers of the welfare state agreed that the putatively "self-regarding" acts of a socially constituted self are bound to have an "other-regarding" dimension. Accordingly, the old liberal distinction between private and public was called into question—by the liberals themselves. Welfare liberalism both diminished the extent of the private sphere and underscored the instability of the public/private distinction.

The closer we move from the late nineteenth and early twentieth century universe of Green, Hobhouse, and Dewey to the contemporary welfare state, the more blurred becomes the distinction between public and private. In *Haven in a Heartless World: The Family Besieged* (1979), Christopher Lasch traces the growing reach of the state into the previously sacrosanct home; and shows the considerable extent to which the rise of American social science proceeded hand in hand with efforts to administer programs for reforming the family environment of the poor. For the best of motives, the very liberals who have always been the most staunch advocates of the right to privacy, now do their utmost to enter the homes of their fellow citizens. Under such circumstances it is difficult to know what is private and untouchable, what public and amenable to state intervention.

Let us apply the foregoing discussion to the contemporary debate over campus codes of speech prohibiting ethnic jokes told in everyday, "private" conversation. Multiculturalists defend such legislation; they argue that socially constituted humans are denied their very identity when subjected to comments ridiculing their persons on the basis of race, gender, or ethnicity. The liberals who oppose the codes, having long since abandoned Mill's distinction between private and self-regarding acts, on the one hand, public and other-regarding acts, on the other, are denied a foundation on which to build a systematic defense of their position. No longer able to contend that speech is one thing, harmful acts quite another, they must settle for the unsatisfying tactic of arguing over what constitutes the lesser of two evils: restricting speech or tolerating the intolerance which demeans even when it does not destroy.

Each ethnic group seeks self-definition but cannot escape the definitions foisted upon it. As Rousseau observed long ago, "social man always lives outside himself and knows how to live only in the opinion of others; it is from their judgment alone that he draws the sentiment of his own existence." Deweyite liberals, no less than multiculturalists, agree with Rousseau. A liberal may reject Frantz Fanon's call to violence but must concede the possibility that, even when not overtly oppressed, the natives suffer from a debilitating "colonial neurosis" inflicted upon them by the imperialist power. When the psychologist Robert Coles interviewed the first black children to enter the public schools of the American South, he reported that they had so thoroughly internalized racism as to regard themselves as inferior.[7] The liberals of yesteryear drew a line in the sand when it came to racist acts. Now that line is gone and efforts to draw a new line of demarcation somewhere in the terrain of nonviolent racism have failed. At any time a liberal outraged by racist innuendo may pass over into the ranks of the multiculturalists and demand strong restrictions on all manifestations of bias, however covert and bloodless.

Liberals cannot separate themselves from multiculturalists through retreating to a philosophically indefensible doctrine of universal and self-evident individual rights; hence they seek to show that their multicultural opponents, for all their talk

---

[7]Robert Coles, *Children of Crisis: a Study of Courage and Fear* (Boston: Atlantic Monthly Press, 1964).

about groups, misunderstand the nature of ethnic identity. At a time when doubts have been raised whether something as basic as gender is not, in part at least, a social construct, liberals remark on the oddity of insisting that ethnic identity is fixed forever. Social identities in contemporary society depend on contexts which are multi-layered and in a constant state of flux. David Hollinger has perceptively commented that "a New Hampshire resident of French-Canadian ethnicity may learn, by moving to Texas, that he or she is actually Anglo." Not so long ago, he adds, Americans were as rigidly typecast according to the religious categories of Catholic, Protestant, or Jewish as now they are sorted out and labelled Euro- or Asian American. Similarly, Donald Horowitz has noted that "an Ibo may be . . . an Owerri Ibo or an Onitsha Ibo in what was the Eastern region of Nigeria. In Lagos, he is simply an Ibo. In London, he is a Nigerian. In New York, he is an African." One's defining group ties, in short, are frequently in the eye of the external beholder.

Or such defining social characteristics are decided by one's own negotiable interests. The third generation, it has been suggested, is as concerned to rediscover its roots as the second generation was to escape them. Occasionally an ethnic group may choose to suppress forever, and with no harmful consequences, the first term of its formerly hyphenated identity, as German Americans did when World War II broke out.

All too readily the advocates of identity politics slide from an open philosophy of the socially constituted self to a closed dogma of the socially determined self. They take full account of the ways the world molds the self but neglect the deeds through which the self leaves its mark on the world. Sentencing us to life imprisonment in an ethnic cell, the ideologues of identity condemn us to a self-fulfilling prophecy of noncommunication. Liberals, simply by refusing to rule out the possibility of dialogue, hold out a modicum of hope.

One other conviction distinguishes the liberals from their challengers in the ongoing debate about social identity. Whereas ardent spokespersons for the multicultural position never address the question how a nation of nations, a culture of subcultures, is to cohere, liberals have focused their efforts on finding an answer. Twenty-two years after publishing his *Theory of Justice,* an embattled but determined John Rawls returned to the arena of disputation with his conciliatory *Political Liberalism* (1993). How can a liberal order be saved, not all of whose members believe in liberalism? What common conviction is possible in a society composed of a myriad of groups professing different and sometimes sharply conflicting beliefs? These are the concerns Rawls addressed in his second book.

Rawls reminded his readers at the outset of his new book that Western societies during the early modern period were in a similar fix. Deep religious conflicts threatened to tear nations apart, yet reconciliation was eventually achieved through a constitutional agreement to disagree. Much the same idea can be applied to our circumstances. No longer does Rawls espouse the comprehensive liberalism of his first book, because to do so would exclude persons holding other comprehensive doctrines. Now he settles for a lesser, a strictly "political" liberalism, an agreement to play by the public rules so that at the end of each contest between parties pursuing fundamentally different ends, the next debate can be scheduled in good faith by opponents who respect one another. To arrive at those rules, he remains convinced, there still is no better way than temporarily to divest ourselves of our ethnic garbs while attending a hypothetical convention conducting its meetings behind a veil of ignorance. Ethnicity will not be endangered by this procedure, the point of which is to ensure a society that is just to persons of all social identities.

The "American creed" is another source of commonality in an extraordinarily diverse population. All the great European students of the United States—Tocqueville, James Bryce, and Gunnar Myrdal, among others—were impressed by the shared American belief in representative government and individual rights. Multiculturalists would have us believe that the hidden meaning of the doctrine of individual rights is the loss of group rights and identity. Neither identity nor group rights are threatened, the liberals respond. It is in the nature of the creed that groups may retain their separate identity as long as they wish, provided they remember that the second term of their hyphenated identities—Asian-American, Latina/o-American, and so on—implies obligations befitting citizens.

As for the second claim, the suggestion that the insistence on individual rights signals the denial of group rights, liberals again are not at a loss for words. Any student of public life in America knows that the bargaining of interest groups pervades our politics, and agrees with the verdict rendered by Grant McConnell decades ago: "individual rights today [1966] derive from group rights, from membership in corporations, labor unions, farm organizations, and pressure groups."[8] In America, it is in the nature of things that blacks should pursue their rights through groups. Consequently liberals refrain from condemning exclusively black organizations as separatist; such organizations, many liberals concede, may indeed be necessary, just as they once were for the Irish and other disadvantaged groups.

Liberals are attentive to the common ground that makes it possible for persons to live together in a highly diverse society. They support and cherish a multitude of cultures, on the condition that cultural pluralism continues, politically, to be a form of liberal pluralism. An open society cannot be sustained if its component groups are hermetically sealed and refuse to interact with one another.

It is all to the good that current debates have served to remind Americans that their supposedly universal creed of rights is more accurately understood as a national and particular faith. Knowing that, we may still want to struggle against "abuses of human rights" in foreign countries, despite the claims of tyrannical rulers that their actions flow from time-honored mores. Surely a growing sense of relativity should not, for instance, discredit those Americans and Europeans who speak out against the genital mutilation of Masai women.

The greatest threat is not that we shall arbitrarily project our ideology of rights upon other countries but that xenophobia may gain renewed strength in America, a nation of immigrants. More people are moving across borders today than ever before; more than ever before the persons entering America do not have white skins. It is better for America to respond by incorporating everyone into its rhetor-

---

[8] Grant McConnell, *Private Power and American Democracy* (New York: Vintage, 1970), p. 354.

ically universal ideology than to follow a policy of sorting persons by skin pigmentation or other physical characteristics. The "American dream" of freedom for all has coexisted with the American nightmare of racism. Still, that dream continues to be the best hope for the future.

BIBLIOGRAPHY

Barber, Benjamin. *An Aristocracy of Everyone: The Politics of Education and the Future of America.* New York: Ballantine, 1992.

D'Souza, Dinesh. *Illiberal Education: The Politics of Race and Sex on Campus.* New York: Free Press, 1991.

Duster, Troy. "They're Taking Over! and Other Myths about Race on Campus," *Mother Jones,* Sept./Oct. 1991, pp. 30–33.

Fuchs, Lawrence. *The American Kaleidoscope: Race, Ethnicity, and the Civic Culture.* Middletown, CT: Wesleyan University Press, 1990.

Glazer, Nathan & Moynihan, Daniel Patrick. *Beyond the Melting Pot: The Negroes, Puerto Ricans, Jews, Italians, and Irish of New York City.* Cambridge, MA: M. I. T. Press, 1964.

Hollinger, David. "Postethnic America," *Contention,* Fall 1992, pp. 79–96.

———. "How Wide the Circle of the 'We': American Intellectuals and the Problem of the Ethnos since World War II," *American Historical Review,* April 1993, pp. 317–337.

Jacoby, Russell, *Dogmatic Wisdom: How the Culture Wars Divert Education and Distract America.* New York: Doubleday, 1994.

Kimball, Roger. *Tenured Radicals: How Politics Has Corrupted Our Higher Education.* New York: Harper & Row, 1990.

Schlesinger, Jr., Arthur. *The Disuniting of America: Reflections on a Multicultural Society.* New York: Norton, 1992.

Taylor, Charles. *Multiculturalism and the Politics of Recognition.* Princeton: Princeton University Press, 1992.

Todorov, Tzvetan. *On Human Diversity: Nationalism, Racism, and Exoticism in French Thought.* Cambridge, MA: Harvard University Press, 1993.

Chapter
15

Whither Liberal Democracy?

*Go into the London Stock Exchange . . . and you will see
representatives from all nations gathered together . . . Here Jew,
Mohammedan, and Christian deal with each other as though they were
all of the same faith.*

Voltaire

*E*very so often a political essay stirs up such a flurry of commentary that there
can be no doubt it speaks to the moment, expressing the hopes, doubts, or fears of
many persons. Within recent memory two such essays have appeared, the first during the summer of 1989, the second exactly four years later; the first announcing
the good news that liberal democracy was about to become universally triumphant,
the second bearing the sad tidings that doctrines of constitutional government and
individual rights are in worldwide retreat, endangered even in the United States by
the new-fangled ideology of multiculturalism. The essays in question are Francis
Fukuyama's "The End of History" (1989) and Samuel Huntington's "The Clash of
Civilizations?" (1993).[1] Perhaps we can arrive at a fitting finale to this edition of
Contemporary Political Ideologies by explaining why the prospects of liberal
democracy are neither as bright as indicated by Fukuyama nor as bleak as one
might conclude after reading Huntington.

Fukuyama wrote on the eve of the collapse of communism. When one communist regime fell after another during the months following the publication of his
essay, he stepped forth as the man of the hour. Americans were happy to learn from
events that they had been right all along about Bolshevism; and it pleased them

---

[1]Fukuyama, "The End of History," *The National Interest* (Summer 1989), 3–18. Huntington, "The
Clash of Civilizations?" *Foreign Affairs* (Summer 1993), 22–49. Huntington's follow-up comments
about multiculturalism in American education may be found in "If Not Civilizations, What?", *Foreign
Affairs* (Nov.–Dec. 1993), 186–194.

enormously to discover in Fukuyama's essay a vindication of their belief that liberal democracy is the sole viable socio-political regime and the one destined to enjoy universal success. Only the American movie producers had misgivings about the startling decomposition of communist regimes, because with the unravelling of the Soviet Union they had lost their favorite villains.

It took a mere year or two before script writers in Hollywood discovered they could replace scheming KGB personnel with dedicated Muslim fundamentalists. And it took not much longer for the eminent political scientist Samuel Huntington to replace the clash of ideologies, liberal versus Marxist, with a confrontation of civilizations, the West versus the rest. More and more the world is divided, in his opinion, into exclusionary civilizations, each the source of deep-seated identities based on culture and religion, compared to which the rallying cries of ideology fail to reach below the surface. In his view even nationality is secondary, because Muslims identify primarily as Muslims, not as members of this or that nation; they come to the assistance of other Muslims wherever they live, whatever their nationality—or so Huntington would have us believe.

The retreat of the West from its past colonial adventures is an old story. The new story, Huntington notes, is the vulnerability of the once revolutionary native governments to overthrow from within. During the course of kicking out the colonists, the Western-educated but anti-Western natives had adopted such European ideologies as socialism and nationalism, the better to turn these doctrines against their former masters. Today popular fundamentalist movements want nothing to do with anything of Western origin, and loudly condemn their rulers for betraying the faith of their fathers. No one can say with confidence that the political regimes of Algeria, Egypt, and Turkey are secure.

Civilizations, in Huntington's estimation of the contemporary situation, are "to die for"; they reach across national boundaries in ways that threaten war; they erect barriers of incomprehension and sow the seeds of animosity between one people and another. Where communism was inclusionary, the various civilizations—Islamic, Confucian, Slavic-Orthodox, Hindu, Western—are exclusionary. Liberals were sometimes able to enter into dialogue with communists on the best way to secure freedom and equality for all; they cannot do so with those who dismiss liberalism out of hand on the grounds that it is Western. It is a sign of the times that at a meeting of a Human Rights Conference, a coalition of Confucian and Islamic states rejected "Western universalism" and informed Europeans and Americans in no uncertain terms that the standards of liberal democrats are nothing more than the culture-bound norms of a particular civilization.

Not even in America is the survival of liberal democracy assured. Affirmative action and multiculturalism, Huntington warns, may lead in the United States to results similar to those we daily witness in televised reports on the horrors occurring in Eastern Europe. "Countries like the Soviet Union and Yugoslavia that bestride civilizational fault lines tend to come apart." "If the United States becomes truly multicultural and pervaded with an internal clash of civilizations, will it survive as a liberal democracy?"

What is right and what is wrong in the arguments of Fukuyama and Huntington?

WHITHER LIBERAL DEMOCRACY?

Fukuyama, arguably, represents some of the most unfortunate of the recurring trends in liberal thought. He is not the first but he may well be the most recent liberal spokesperson to replace necessary self-criticism with gratuitous self-congratulation. And he also belongs to a long line of liberals who have arbitrarily and dangerously decided that, if not God, then at least history is on the side of liberal democracy.

Throughout the nineteenth century and into the first years of the twentieth, a great many liberals took for granted that only constitutional regimes can be socially and economically progressive. John Stuart Mill, for example, never abandoned the standard of utility because he was convinced that nations governed autocratically can only be regressive and stagnant, most visibly in the economic sphere. He could afford to place all his bets on utility because it never occurred to him that an authoritarian government, such as that emerging in Germany, could have a great—and devastating—future. Secure in his belief that constitutional government is useful, autocratic government useless, Mill revised the utilitarian philosophy of his father but did not abandon it.

Mill's argument about progressive constitutionalism and regressive authoritarianism was one he uncritically inherited from the eighteenth-century Enlightenment. Montesquieu (1689–1755), for instance, had noted that Protestant, tolerant, and constitutional countries, such as Holland and England, were economically powerful whereas Catholic, intolerant, and authoritarian Portugal, Spain, and Italy were economically in decline. From such a starting point Montesquieu and the other *philosophes* pleaded for the reform of France, a Catholic country with an absolutist political regime. Which is to say, the "Whig interpretation of history," as Mill's viewpoint came to be called,[2] performed an important mission in Montesquieu's day. But by the age of Mill it had degenerated into shallow liberal self-congratulation.

Fukuyama's essay resembles a return to the Whig interpretation after a hiatus of some seventy or so years. For decades, European and American social scientists, faced with the success of the Bolsheviks in advancing Russia to the status of a great power, substituted discussions of "modernization from above" for the old doctrine of the inherently stagnant character of authoritarian government. The moment the Soviet Union collapsed Fukuyama set forth a new-sounding version of the old Whig story. Once again Westerners were invited to believe theirs is the only way, as if the histories of modern Russia, Germany, and Japan had never happened, as if the eventual fall of reprehensible regimes ensured that none would ever rise again.

Serving as backdrop to Fukuyama's essay is the Whig interpretation of history; standing in the foreground, directly under the floodlights, is the "end of ideology" thesis of some liberals of the 1950s. By mid-century such leading social scientists such as Daniel Bell and Seymour Martin Lipset had shed the socialist sympathies of their youthful days and settled into their mature years as confirmed liberals. It was, however, to their ingrained Marxist habits of thought that they turned for assurance that the liberal democracies of America and Europe would henceforth

---

[2]Herbert Butterfield, *The Whig Interpretation of History* (New York: Norton, 1965).

be stable regimes. Their Marxist past trained Bell and Lipset to search for a prole-tariat; their liberal present applauded the finding that no such class existed. In soci-eties with mixed economies, welfare states, and workers who regard themselves as members of the middle class, there is an end to the dangerous upheavals of revo-lutionary politics.

Fukuyama's claim that his theme of the "end of history" has nothing in com-mon with the earlier writings on the "end of ideology" is doubly mistaken. He is wrong, in the first instance, to assert that his talk of the triumph of liberal ideology is fundamentally different from earlier discussions of the decline of ideologies. He forgets that what Bell meant by the end of ideology was in reality the demise of revolutionary doctrines in the West and the triumph of the nonrevolutionary liber-al ideology which regards it as a matter of principle that principles should be dis-cussed as little as possible, means addressed more frequently than ends, compro-mise and bargaining substituted for barricades. Both the "end of history" and the "end of ideology" amount to proclamations of the victory of liberal ideology, with the difference that Fukuyama projected upon the entire world what Bell had more sensibly confined to the industrial democracies.

Another proof that Fukuyama's "end of history" amounts to little more than reheated "end of ideology" is that Karl Mannheim in 1929 and Maurice Merleau-Ponty in 1947 explicitly contended that with the impending demise of revolution-ary doctrines, history was about to come to a grinding halt. Mannheim and Mer-leau-Ponty were as disturbed by the nonexistence of a revolutionary proletariat as Bell and Lipset were later cheered by the same. It is from the downtrodden class, Mannheim believed, that progressive ideals and utopian aspirations emerge: take away the proletarian credentials of the workers, admit them to full citizenship, and therewith you have ended history. In Mannheim's words, "the disappearance of utopia brings about a static state of affairs in which man becomes no more than a thing." Merleau-Ponty agreed, adding, "after that there can be no more dreams or adventures."[3]

Fukuyama could have profited from recognizing the affinity between his posi-tion and the earlier "end of ideology" literature. Specifically he surely would have recognized that, Mannheim and Merleau-Ponty notwithstanding, history did not come to a halt when the revolutionary proletariat failed to materialize. Why, then, should anyone expect world history to end because of the collapse of communism in 1989?

Nor, in spite of the predictions of Bell and Lipset, did ideology come to an end in the late 1950s; instead, America and Western Europe went up in ideological flames in the late 1960s. Why, then, should Fukuyama invite the reader to con-clude that, after the fall of communism, there will be no new challenges to liberal democratic convictions? Today, Fukuyama's "The End of History" reads as a mere period piece, the period which began in 1989 and barely lasted beyond the year of its birth.

---

[3]Mannheim's *Ideology and Utopia* was originally published in 1929; Merleau-Ponty's *Humanism and Terror* in 1947.

If there is a lesson to be drawn from the Fukuyama episode it is that liberalism is at its worst whenever it declares itself the inevitable endpoint of history. Few things sound more presumptuous today than the self-assured and chauvinistic conviction of the British in the nineteenth century that one day all peoples would be the functional equivalent of good Victorians (see Chapter 14). Fukuyama's view of history is based upon a shocking failure to examine the history of liberalism, the doctrine which is at its best when it is skeptical, piecemeal, embarrassed by total visions, and wary of universal claims.

Liberalism is likewise at its best when it opens itself to an understanding of other cultures, as opposed to declaring its present the future of all nations. We have nothing to lose and much to gain from rejecting Fukuyama's optimism, which is as culturally-bound as it is naive.

Huntington would have us believe his essay on "The Clash of Civilizations?" is a gritty, tough-minded exercise in facing up to unpleasant realities. The much vaunted "new world order" did not emerge in the wake of communist self-destruction. Rather, we have a new world disorder in which nations are brought closer together than ever before by the media, yet divided more sharply than in the past by cultural differences. Undeniably the chemistry of this unstable combination is potentially explosive. Insofar as Huntington has alerted us to the new challenge, his essay is most welcome. The same cannot be said of those parts of his presentation which threaten to aggravate rather than remedy our difficulties at home and abroad.

What is least satisfying in Huntington's argument is that on the domestic front he seizes upon the most extreme version of multiculturalism, using its excesses to rationalize the growing reaction against immigrants that has brought into prominence the far right wing of European politics and may do the same in America. Then, turning to the world stage, he discusses cultures as if they were eternally fixed and inflexible—the very same notion he denounces at home when the most fanatical multiculturalists foreclose in advance the possibility of communicating and compromising across the barriers of ethnic, racial, and religious differences. Let us elaborate.

To read Huntington on the subject of civilizations is to revisit the old days when "national character" was studied without reference to the history of how that character became implanted, and without mention of the ongoing process by which a way of life is redefined from one time period to another, depending on changing circumstances and the success or failure of the leaders who respond to new challenges. All too frequently Huntington seems to be transplanting the worst of the old literature on national character to the larger units he calls civilizations.

At his worst Huntington simply takes the most extreme representatives of non-Western civilizations at their word, never bothering to measure what they say against the record of what they do. As the Bosnian case testifies, there has been more talk of rallying to the Islamic cause across national borders than actual commitments of Muslim troops. Nation–states are still so much the primary units in world politics that they manipulate civilizations far more frequently than civilizations control nations. Saddam Hussein discovered his religious ardor only when he was about to lose a war fought against him by a coalition of Western and Islamic powers. Similarly, the decision of the Serbian forces to initiate their offensive campaign against Croatia and Slovenia, as Jeane Kirkpatrick has shrewdly observed, "should settle the question of Serbian motives and goals, which are territorial aggrandizement, not holy war." In general, we would do well to remember that the major conflicts of the twentieth century have been fought within, not between, civilizations.

Some of the civilizational exclusivity and separatism on which Huntington dwells is his own mental invention. He treats Latin America as a civilization unto itself, no matter that the words "Latin" and "America" indicate it is a branch of Western civilization. Nor does he offer an adequate rationale for regarding orthodox-Slavic Russians as bearers of a non-Western civilizational standard, not to mention how unthinkable it is that Russia, in its current dilemma, could in any meaningful sense assume the role of a "second Byzantium," even if it so desired. Why, moreover, does he call China by the straightforward appellation "Confucian" after half a century during which its leaders have broken with the past; and does Huntington actually expect Taiwan and mainland China to lock their arms in a Confucian embrace?[4]

Islamic fundamentalism, perhaps the most remarkable new factor in world politics, is historically of recent origins and may well be more indicative of Muslim fears about the future than of certainty about the divine right of their tradition. Out of power, Muslim fundamentalists can thrive on the poverty of the masses; in power, they learn that many of their followers want Sony more than soil, market shares more than holy wars, jobs more than righteous unemployment. From the moment Muslims enter the world marketplace, they must temporarily set religious and cultural differences aside, so that mutually beneficial bargains may be struck.

One is reminded of what Voltaire wrote in his *Lettres philosophiques,* published in 1734:

> Enter the London stock exchange, that more respectable place than many a court; you will see the deputies of all nations gathered for the service of mankind. There the Jew, the Mohammedan, and the Christian deal together as if they were of the same religion, and apply the name of infidel only to those who go bankrupt. . . . On leaving these peaceful and free assemblies, some go to the synagogue, others go to drink; one goes to have himself baptized; another has his son's foreskin cut off and Hebrew words mumbled over him; others [Quakers] go to their church to await the inspiration of God with their hats on their heads; and all are content.

If we apply Voltaire's words about the London stock exchange to the international market place of our day, we discover reasons to hope that all is not lost in today's contentious and violent world.

The more we make an effort to learn about the civilizations of the non-Western world, the better the prospects for avoiding internecine strife. Muslims, like Jews and Christians, come in different varieties, of which fundamentalism is but

---

[4]See the comments of Fouad Ajami, Jeane Kirkpatrick, *et. al.,* in the September–October, 1993 edition of *Foreign Affairs.*

one. Applying stereotypes to Muslims, treating their identities as hermetically sealed, failing to learn how to translate Arabic into English and English into Arabic can only force upon Muslims the very rigidity Huntington fears. Enlightenment universalism may be dead, but Enlightenment cosmopolitanism continues to be meaningful insofar as it is grounded in studies of the concrete "humanity" which Johann Herder (1744–1803) came to know when he immersed himself in the many cultures which together compose the human world. On one occasion Herder explained in telling and moving terms why he studied foreign tongues: "I encompass the spirit of each people in my soul!—Reward sufficient, I think, to rouse our diligence in the study of many languages."

In a sequel to his essay about the civilizations of the world Huntington offers comments about the situation in his own American and European back yard. It comes as a disappointment that he apparently sees nothing disturbing and much that is reasonable in the mounting reaction against immigrants arriving from the non-Western portions of the globe.[5] One would think that if America is to show the world an example of how a single socio-political unit can accommodate persons of disparate ethnic and cultural backgrounds, it must meet this latest challenge. Instead of addressing the vital question our polity faces, he settles for ringing the multicultural alarm bell, without making the slightest effort to distinguish between destructive and constructive educational programs for recognizing the dignity of different cultural heritages.

Americans neither can nor ought to impose their outlook upon the world, but they should continue talking about "human rights" violations whenever that is the best way to counter wanton, institutionalized acts of oppression and violence. It is also fitting that Americans should strive to set an example of the virtues of liberal democratic government. We cannot be such exemplars, however, unless we address the problems of racism, slums, ghettoes, and all the social evils which both the politicians and the public seem increasingly determined to ignore. Representatives of non-Western cultures hold our flawed record against the principles for which we stand. They expect our liberal democratic concerns to begin at home, and so should we.

BIBLIOGRAPHY

Francis Fukuyama, "The End of History," *The National Interest,* Winter 1989/90.

Samuel P. Huntington *et. al., The Clash of Civilizations? The Debate.* New York: A *Foreign Affairs* Reader, 1993.

Olivier Roy, *The Failure of Political Islam.* Cambridge, MA: Harvard University Press, 1994.

---

[5]"If Not Civilizations, What?", p. 189.

Index

Absolutism, 26
Action. *See* Praxis
Adams, Brooke, 88
Adams, Henry, 88
Africa, 217, 305
  black separatist platform, 212
  national liberation movement, 190,
    206, 210
Albania, 95, 125, 137, 138, 139, 185,
  236
Algeria, 205, 214, 236, 314
Alienation, 1
America
  Latin America. *See* Latin America
  United States of America. *See* Unit-
    ed States
American Civil War, 150, 187, 205,
  211
Anarchism, 195
  art and, 264–269
  Fascist aspects of, 266–267, 268
  Marxism, reaction to, 244–264
  New Left philosophy, 284,
    287–290
  organization, debate with Marxists
    regarding, 245–251
  Paris Commune of 1871, debate
    with Marxists regarding, 251–257
  France, in May 1968, 269–270
  student movements, in, 284,
    287–290
  theory and practice, debate with
    Marxists regarding, 258–264
  violence and terrorism and,
    266–267, 268, 269
Antiabortion legislation, 91, 241

Anticommunism, 174, 188, 189–190,
  240, 281
Anti-Semitism, 127, 248, 302
  extremist movement in United
    States, 186–192
  Italy, in, 154
  Muslim fundamentalism, 235
  Nazism, 159–160, 161, 162, 164,
    165, 169, 171, 173–174
Anti-Tax Vigilante Group, 192
Apter, David, 43
Arab Emirates, 206
Arab nation, 220, 232
Aragon, Louis, 268
Argentina, 221
Aristide, Jean-Bertrand, 231
Aristotle, 8, 81, 142
Armenia, 207–208, 209
Aron, Raymond, 14
Aryan Nation party, 192
Austria, 185
Austro-Hungarian Empire, 198, 201,
  204, 205
Authoritarianism, 85, 145, 156, 160,
  315
  Anarchists and Marxists, debate
    regarding, 245, 247, 248
  basis of authority, 7
  definition of, 80
  Fascism. *See* Fascism
  future of, 183–184
  Iran, in, 234–236
  Marxist theory of, 180
  modernization theory, 180
  Nazism. *See* Nazism
  personality theory, 182

psychological interpretation of, 180–181

religious fundamentalism and, 232, 233, 234

Soviet Union, in, 121, 142, 143

Azerbaidjan, 207–208, 209

Babbitt, Irving, 88

Bacon, Francis, 55, 280

Bagehot, Walter, 84

Bakunin, Mikhail, 245, 246, 247, 248, 249, 251, 253–254, 255, 258, 263, 265, 266, 269, 270, 289, 290

Barzun, Jacques, 159

Bavaria, 208

Behavior, religion affecting, 223

Belgium, 73, 185, 205, 220, 241, 254, 262, 274

Bell, Daniel, 66, 315–316

Belleville Manifesto, 53–54

Bentham, Jeremy, 31–33

Bernstein, Eduard, 59–60, 152

Berth, Edouard, 153

Bismarck, Otto von, 80, 157, 160, 163, 202, 203, 246, 251

Black Panthers, 214–215

Black separatism, 211–216

Blanc, Louis, 53

Blanqui, Louis, 53, 252

Boff, Leonardo, 226, 228

Bosnia-Herzegovina, 210, 317

Brandt, Willy, 281

Brazil, 224

Breton, André, 267, 268, 290

Britain. See Great Britain

Brooke, Rupert, 221

Brown, Bernard, 273

Bruck, Möeller van den, 157, 159, 162

Bryce, James, 311

Bulgaria, 125, 136, 138, 205, 208, 209

Burckhardt, Jacob, 305, 307

Burke, Edmund, 80–84, 88, 145, 159, 285, 300, 301

Bush, George, 92, 93, 240

Byelorussia, 208, 209

Calhoun, John, 88

Calvin, John, 232, 233

Campanella, Tommaso, 55

Camus, Albert, 278

Canada, 210

Capitalism
development of, 22–23
Lenin's theory of, 110–111
Marx, critique by, 99–101
political movements, as basis for, 12
problems inherent in, 74–76
resurgence of, 66–74
trends in, 75–76

Caribbean countries, 236

Carmichael, Stokeley, 293

Carnegie, Andrew, 90–91

Castro, Fidel, 139, 214, 288

Catholic church, 223–231, 232, 300, 315

Caute, David, 273

Cedras, Raoul, 231

Censorship, 233, 235

Chapin, Morris H., 240

Charismatic leadership, 7, 233, 235

Chartism, 52–53

Checks and balances theory, 4, 90, 145, 306

Child labor, 47, 53

Chile, 224, 225

China, 69, 95, 139–140, 141, 142, 236, 237, 304, 318

Christian Democratic parties, 72–73, 137

Christian Identity, 192

Christianity, 27, 158, 187, 195, 215, 217, 218, 223–224, 261
fundamentalism, 231–234, 238–241
liberation theology, 224–231

Church
Nazi Germany, position in, 178, 180
politics, influence on, 223–224

Citizenship, 218

Civilizations, Huntington's theory of, 314, 317–319

Civil liberties, 27–28

Civil Rights Act of 1964, 213
Clark, John Henrik, 215
Class struggle, 104–105, 172,
    227–228, 253
Cobden, Richard, 46–47
Cohn-Bendit, Daniel, 275, 277–279,
    281, 282–283, 288–289
Cohn-Bendit, Gabriel, 288
Coles, Robert, 309
Colombia, 224
Colonies
    German expansionism, 175
    independence, demand for,
        205–206
    racial attitude toward, 204, 304–305
Comintern (Third International),
    119–120, 180, 246, 250, 255
Command economy, 118, 121, 123
    crisis of, 125, 128, 138, 142
Communication, ideology and, 10
Communism
    collapse of, 132–143, 198, 206, 314,
        315
    decline of, 126–127
    definition of, 97
    socialist parties and, 72
    society, concept of, 107–108
Communist parties, transformation of,
    70, 72
Communitarianism, 56, 97–98, 170,
    172, 174, 176–177, 182, 183, 188,
    219
Comte, Auguste, 305
Concordat, 178
Consent theory, 35
Conservatism, 79–93
Conspiracy theories, 190–192
Constitutionalism, 38–39
Constitution
    British conservatives, attitude of,
        86–87
    Greek city-states, 21–22
    introduction of, 45
Constitution of United States. *See*
    United States Constitution

Consumerism, 28
Contract, freedom of, 28–29
Contract theory, 83
Corradini, Enrico, 153, 154, 156
Cosmopolitanism, 216–219, 300, 301,
    303, 319
Coughlin, Charles E., 187–188
Counterideology, 2
Crimea, 209
Criteria of ideology, 16–18
Croatia, 137
Crozier, Michel, 292
Cuba, 139, 141, 142, 214, 215, 288
Czechoslovakia, 125, 135, 137, 138,
    205, 208, 209

Dadaism, 279
Daley, Richard, 272
Darwin, Charles, 90, 233
Debord, Guy, 280, 289
Definitions
    authoritarianism, 80
    capitalism, 65
    class, 104–105
    communism, 97
    conservatism, 79
    cosmopolitanism, 216–217
    democracy, 21
    dialectic idealism, 104
    dialectic materialism, 104
    dictatorship of the proletariat, 107
    end of ideology, theory of, 273
    ideology, 2
    infrastructure, 105
    lumpenproletariat, 102
    nationalism, 198
    national syndicalism, 151–152
    orthopraxis, 227
    participatory democracy, 280–281
    permanent revolution, 263
    philosophy, 3
    self-regarding act, 42
    socialism, 65
    superstructure, 105, 106
    surplus value, 101

syndicalism, 151–152
theory, 3
utopia, 11–12
Democracy
development of concept, 21–23
liberalism. *See* Liberalism
socialism. *See* Socialism
welfare state. *See* Welfare state
Democratic centralism, 113, 118, 119
Democratic National Convention
(Chicago 1968), 272–273
Democratic socialism, 56–59, 128
Denmark, 185, 220
DePugh, Robert, 191
Dewey, John, 284, 285, 286, 296,
308–309
Dialectic idealism, 104
Dialectic materialism, 104, 111, 113
Diderot, Denis, 157
Dilthey, Wilhelm, 158
Discrimination, 27–28
biological, 159, 173–174, 199, 302
Disraeli, Benjamin, 46, 87
Djilas, Milovan, 282
Dreyfus, Alfred, 154
Dubček, Alexander, 272
Duke, David, 192
DuPont, Pierre, 240

Eastern Europe, 135–138
East Germany. *See* Germany
Economic determinism, 105
Economic liberalism. *See* Capitalism
Economic man, 91
Education
American conservative approach to,
91, 92
black separatist movement and,
211
Fabian socialism, 57
liberal philosophy, 44
religious fundamentalism doctrine,
233
Stalinism concept of, 118, 126
Utopian socialism on, 56
welfare state, duty of, 64

Egalitarianism, 55, 74, 75, 97, 179,
217
conservative response to, 81
issues involved in, 7–8
property rights and, 8
Soviet concept of, 121–122
Egypt, 205, 206, 235, 236, 238, 314
Eisenhower, Dwight, 189, 190, 287
Elitism
conservative philosophy, 80, 84–86,
87, 89
Lenin's party organization as, 113
Plato on, 7, 273–274
Stalin's party organization as,
117–118
El Salvador, 224
Encyclopedists, the, 13
End of history, theory of, 298, 316
End of ideology, theory of, 273, 315,
316
Engels, Friedrich, 98, 99, 100,
107–108, 114, 152, 247–248,
251–252
Enlightenment, 4, 148, 150, 151, 152,
153, 156, 157, 295, 299, 301, 303,
315, 319
Entitlements, 8, 62, 64
Environmentalism
association with socialism, 72
Greenpeace, 12
legacy of student movement,
291–292, 293
parties representing, 73
Epicurean philosophy, 27
Equality. *See* Egalitarianism
Equal Rights Amendment, 92
Estonia, 135, 205
Ethics
communist ethic, 97
Ethiopia, 210
Ethnicity defined, 199–200
Ethnonationalism
African-American, 211–216
fundamentalism, link with, 210
Soviet Union, in, 135–138,
208–211

European Common Market, 220
European revisionism, 59–62, 152
Evangelicals, 231–234, 238–241
  women, role of, 233, 241
Expansionism, 175
Extremism, 183–192. *See also* Nazi
  right-wing extremism

Fabian socialism, 57–59
Faisceau, 153
Falkland war, 221
Falwell, Jerry, 239
Fanon, Frantz, 269, 276, 309
Farrakahn, Louis, 215
Fascism, 147–148
  anti-Semitism and racism in, 154,
    159–160, 161, 162, 164, 165
  communism, on, 151
  intellectual roots of, 148–166
  liberalism, response to, 148–149
  Marxists and, 148–151
  significance and consequences of,
    164–166
  syndicalism and, 151–156
  violence, attitude toward, 149–151
"Fellow travelers", 189, 190
Feminism, 72, 274, 291–292, 293
Feuerbach, Ludwig, 261, 262
Fichte, Johann, 157, 162, 202
Filmer, Robert, 163, 165, 304
Finland, 205, 208
First Amendment, 27–28
First International, 100, 151, 245, 246,
    247, 248, 251, 252
Förster-Nietzsche, Elizabeth, 155
France, 254, 315
  Anarchism in, 269–270
  Christian Democratic parties, 72,
    73, 137
  communist party, 70
  health programs, 64
  liberalism, expansion of, 44–48
  mixed economy of, 65, 66
  nationalism in, 153, 200, 205
  New Left movement, 272–294
  radical democrats in, 52–54

Revolution of 1789. *See* French
  Revolution of 1789
  socialist party, 71
  socialization, abandonment of, 71
  student movement in, 272–294
  student rebellion in, 272–275, 293
Franco, Francisco, 145, 156
Franco-Prussian War, 273
Frankfurt School, 149
Franklin, Benjamin, 13, 90
Free-market economy,
  Adam Smith's theory of, 29–31
  bases of, 69
  Christian Democracy favoring, 73
  European revisionism, changes in,
    60–62
  liberals' and conservatives' attitudes
    toward, 73, 74
  principles of, 28–29
French Revolution of 1789, 39, 148,
    157, 158, 163, 174, 201–202, 204,
    264, 300, 301
  intellectuals, role of, 13
Freud, Sigmund, 268, 269
Friedman, Milton, 68–69
Friedrich, Carl, 148
Fukuyama, Francis, 313–317
Fundamentalism, 92
  background of, 231
  characteristics of, 232–234
  Islamic, 185, 234–238
Futurists, 155, 156, 279

Gambetta, Jules, 53–54
Gandhi, Mohandas K. (Mahatma),
    213
Garvey, Marcus, 212, 214
Gasset, Ortega y, 305, 306, 307
Gaulle, Charles de, 201, 287, 291, 293
Gentile, Giovanni, 165
Georgia, 208, 209, 211
Germany, 46, 125, 135, 137, 138, 208,
    274
  Christian Democrats in, 72, 73
  health programs, 64
  liberalism in, 162–164

mixed economy of, 65
nationalism, 153, 160, 200
Nazism. *See* Nazism
social democratic parties, 61, 71
traditional nationalism, 202–203, 205
unification of, 136, 183–184, 203
Gingrich, Newt, 92
Glasnost, 129–130
Globalists, 93
Gobineau, Joseph Arthur de, 302
Goldman, Emma, 284
Goldwater, Barry, 93
Gompers, Samuel, 88
Gorbachev, Mikhail, 92
    economic reforms, 132–133
    ethnic problems, 132–138
    ideology of, 128–131
    institutional reforms, 125, 127, 131–134
    Marxism, liquidation of, 127
    perestroika, extent of, 129–130, 209
    Stalin, criticism of, 123, 128–129
Grass-roots action, 127, 129
Great Britain, 262, 274, 300, 304, 315
    conservative party and its ideology, 74, 80–87
    Fabian socialism, effect of, 57–59
    Falkland war, 221
    intellectuals, role of, 13–14
    Labour Party, 61, 71, 86, 281
    liberalism, expansion of, 44–48
    medical care programs, 64
    mixed economy, 65, 66
    nationalism in, 203–204, 205
    radical democrats, 52–54
    right-wing extremists, 185
Great Depression
    extremist movements during, 187–188
Greece, 205, 220
Greek city-states, 21–22, 217
Green, Thomas Hill, 296, 308–309
Guatemala, 224
Guevara, Che, 275
Gulf War, 238

Gutierrez, Gustavo, 225, 228

Haig, Alexander, 240
Haiti, 299
Haller, K.L. von, 163
Hamilton, Alexander, 89
Harrington, Michael, 281
Hartz, Louis, 211, 285
Hate groups, 191–192
Havel, Vaclav, 137
Hayden, Tom, 276, 277, 278, 280, 281, 283, 284–285, 286, 293
Hayek, F.A., 68
Hegel, Georg W.F., 99, 103–104, 106, 157, 158, 163, 258, 259, 260, 262
Helvétius, Claude-Adrien, 295
Henry, Emile, 269
Herder, Johann Gottfried von, 157–158, 159, 202, 301–303, 319
Hezbullah (Party of God), 235
Hindenburg, Paul von, 171
Hitler, Adolph, 147, 148, 149, 151, 156, 163, 164, 165–166, 168, 169, 170, 171, 172, 177, 178, 184, 188, 190, 203
    philosophy of. *See* Nazism
Hobbes, Thomas, 216
Hobhouse, L.T., 308–309
Hoffman, Abbie, 279, 284
Holbach, Paul-Henri Triry, baron d', 295
Holland, 185,205,315
Hollinger, David, 310
Hong Kong, 141
Horowitz, Donald, 310
Howe, Irving, 281
Huizinga, Johann, 305
Humphrey, Hubert, 273, 293
Hungary, 125, 135–136, 137, 138, 205, 208, 209
Huntington, Samuel, 313, 314, 317–319
Hussein, Saddam, 317

Idealism

philosophic idealism, 5
Identification, 11
Identity politics, 299, 300, 310
Ideological conservation, 2
Ideology defined, 2
Imperialism, 114. *See also* Capital-
    ism
India, 206, 210, 304
Individual
    liberal doctrine regarding, 25–26,
        150
    liberation theology, approach to,
        228–229
    Marxist theory, 150
    Nazi doctrine regarding, 176
    preconceptions as to, 4
    society, relationship between, 6–7
    state intervention, effect on, 40–41
    Stoic view on, 27
Individual motivation theory, 4
Individualism. *See* Individual
Indonesia, 210, 236
Instability, 74–76
Intellectuals
    attitude toward, 13–14
    economic liberalism, controversy
        involving, 90
    Europeanists and Federalists, 220
    Iranian fundamentalism and,
        235–236
    role of, 13–14
    superiority as basis for authority, 7
Intelligentsia, 118
Intercommunalism, 214
Internationalism, 220, 221
Iran, 205, 206, 232, 233, 234–236, 238
Iraq, 205, 235, 236, 238
Ireland, 204, 220
Islam. *See* Muslim fundamentalism
Isolationism, 93
Israel, 205, 212, 232, 235
Italy, 65, 66, 204, 270, 274, 284, 287,
        300, 315
    anti-Semitism in, 154
    communist party, transformation of,
        70, 72

Fascism, 121, 147, 148, 154–155,
        166
    nationalism in, 153, 154, 205
    national syndicalism in, 151–153,
        165
    unification of, 205

Jackson, Jesse, 215
Jacobins, 147, 158, 164, 165, 247, 249,
        251, 253, 255, 257, 270, 288
Jacksonians, 286–287, 307
Jahn, Friedrich Ludwig (Father), 161
James, William, 148
Japan, 65, 66, 93, 141, 175, 274, 315
Jaruzelski, Wojciech, 136, 137
Jefferson, Thomas, 7, 13, 284, 285,
        299
Jewison, Norman, 306
John Birch Society, 190, 191
Johnson, Lyndon, 214, 216
Jordan, 206, 236

Kant, Immanuel, 163, 300–301
Kashmir, 210
Kaufman, Arnold, 280
Kautsky, Karl, 150, 248–249, 254–257
Kedourie, Elie, 200
Kemp, Jack, 240
Kennan, George, 142
Kennedy, John F., 214
Kennedy, Robert, 272
Keniston, Kenneth, 274
Kerner Commission, 272
Keynes, John Maynard, 62–64, 69
Keynesian economics, 62–64
Khayati, Mustapha, 289, 290
Khomeini, Ruhollah (Ayatollah
        Khomeini), 234–236
Khrushchev, Nikita, 122, 208
Kim, Il Sung, 139
King, Martin Luther, Jr., 212, 213,
        215, 216, 272
Kipling, Rudyard, 204, 205
Kirkpatrick, Jean, 318
Know-Nothing party, 186–187, 190,
        299

Kohl, Helmut, 203
Kropotkin, Peter, 254, 260, 261, 265
Ku Klux Klan (KKK), 187, 190, 192
Kuwait, 206

Lagarde, Paul, 157, 158, 161–162
LaHaye, Tim, 239
Laissez-faire capitalism, 26
Langbehn, Julius, 157
Lasch, Christopher, 309
LaRouche, Lyndon, 191
Lassalle, Ferdinand, 246
Latin America, 73, 305, 318
    economic modernization, 225–226
    liberation theology, role of, 224,
        228, 229
Latvia, 205, 208
Leadership
    American conservative doctrine,
        89–90
    charismatic leadership, 233, 235
    China, role in, 139–140
    collective leadership, 123
    communist leadership, crisis of,
        135–141
    conservative theory as to, 84–86
    Lenin's doctrine, 111, 113, 115
    Nazi principle, 176, 177
    New Left on, 282–283, 284–285
    North Korean leadership, charac-
        teristics of, 139
    Stalinist doctrine, 115, 117–119
Lee, Spike, 306
Legitimization, 9
Lenin, Vladimir Ilyich, 17, 95, 108,
        110–115, 117, 119–120, 142, 149,
        206, 288, 289, 290
    Anarchists, reaction to, 246, 248,
        249–251, 254–255, 256–257,
        258
Leninism, 110–115, 195, 284
    nationalism, position on, 206
LePen, Jean-Marie, 184–185
Liberalism
    cosmopolitan nature of, 218–219
    economic liberalism. See Capitalism

Fascism, response to, 148–149
    Germany, in, 162–164
    radical democracy and, 54
Liberal democracy, prospects for,
        313–319
Liberation theology
    background of, 224–226
    base ecclesiastical communities,
        230
    collective sin principle, 228–229
    future of, 230–231
    history, view on, 227
    orthopraxis, orthodoxy distin-
        guished, 227
    overview, 224
    poor, role of, 228
    social service principle, 229–230
    society, analysis of, 227–228
    Theological Education by Exten-
        sion (TEE), 229
Liberty Lobby, 191
Libya, 205
Lippmann, Walter, 88
Lipset, Seymour Martin, 186, 273,
        315–316
List, Friedrich, 162
Lithuania, 135, 205
Locke, John, 285, 300, 304
    democracy, concept of, 22
    individual consent theory, 35
    property, view on, 8
    representative government, organi-
        zation and functions, 37–38
    understanding, nature of, 6
Lovett, William, 52
Lumpenproletariat, 102
Luther, Martin, 245, 246
Luxembourg, 220
Luxemburg, Rosa, 248–250, 270, 289

Macaulay, Thomas Babington, 44
McCarthy, Joseph, 189–190
McConnell, Grant, 311
Machiavelli, Niccolò di Bernardo, 152
Madison, James, 6, 89
Maine, Henry, 28–29, 304

Maistre, Joseph de, 300, 301
Majoritarianism, 37–38
  conservative doctrine, 87
  democratic socialists and, 56–57
  radical democrats' platform, 52
Makhno, Nestor, 288
Malcolm X, 214–216, 306
Malthus, Thomas, 99
Managerial revolution, 181–182
Manipulation, 9–10
Mann, Thomas, 164
Mannheim, Karl, 12, 316
Mao, Tse-tung, 139, 140
Maoism, 139–140
Marinetti, Filippo Tomasso, 155
Marsden, George, 239
Marx, Karl, 3, 48, 98–104, 106–108,
     111, 114, 115, 128, 142, 149, 150,
     152, 155, 162, 163, 172, 180, 206,
     227, 244, 245, 246–248, 251–253,
     255, 256, 257, 258–260, 261–263,
     265, 266, 270, 280, 289, 295, 301,
     305, 308
Marxism, 195
  Anarchism, reaction to, 244–264
  capitalism, economic analysis of,
     99–103
  communism. See Communism
  Communist Manifesto, 48, 98, 100,
     206, 246
  cosmopolitan nature of, 218–219
  criticism of, 59–60
  economy, socialization of, 23
  Fascists and, 148–151
  Frankfurt School, 149
  history, theory of, 103–106
  liberation theology, adopting,
     227–228
  nationalism, position on, 204–205,
     206
  Nazism, interpretation of, 180
  organization, debate with Anar-
     chists regarding, 245–251
  Paris Commune of 1871, debate
     with Anarchists regarding, 251–
     257

  religion, view on, 224
  revolution, theory of, 106–107
  Stalin and, 149
  student movements and, 287–289
  theory and practice, debate with
     Anarchists regarding, 258–264
  violence, attitude toward, 149–151
Mass society, 180–181, 183
Maurras, Charles, 151, 152, 153–154,
     164–165, 268
May Revolt (France 1968), 272, 273
Mazzini, Guiseppe, 203, 247
Mazowiecki, Tadeusz, 136
Meinecke, Friedrich, 158
Melville, Herman, 88
Merleau-Ponty, Maurice, 150, 316
Messianic spirit, 232, 235
Mexico, 197
Michels, Robert, 165, 282
Mikulski, Barbara, 191
Militia groups, 192
Mill, John Stuart, 17, 33–35, 249, 296,
     304
  industrialization, comments on, 51
  representative government, role of,
     37–38, 315
  self-regarding and other-regarding
     acts, 42–43, 308, 309
  state, role of, 40
Mills, C. Wright, 277, 278, 287
Minimum wage, 65
Minutemen, 191
Mises, Ludwig von, 68
Mitterand, Francois, 71
Mixed economy, 65–66, 69
Mladenov, Petar, 136
Modernization theory, 180, 182, 305
Mommsen, Theodor, 158
Montesquieu, Charles-Louis de
     Sécondat, 303, 304, 315
Moralism, 233
Moral Majority, 239–240
More, Thomas, 55
Morin, Edgar, 298
Morocco, 205, 210, 236
Most, Johann, 284

Movement, freedom of, 46
Muhammed, Elijah, 215
Müller, Adam, 157
Multiculturalism, 295
  liberalism and, 307–312, 313, 314,
    317
  liberal notions of the self, attitude
    toward, 296–298
  science, revolt against, 303–307
  universalism, revolt against,
    299–303
Muslim fundamentalism, 185, 210,
  232, 233, 234–238, 305, 314, 318
Mussolini, Benito, 147, 148, 149, 151,
  152, 154–156, 164, 165, 188
Myrdal, Gunnar, 311

Napoleon Bonaparte, 157, 201
Napoleon, Louis, 251
National Front party, 185
Nationalism, 156, 195, 298, 301
  British and American nationalists,
    203–204
  challenge to, 220
  characteristics of, 198–201, 314
  development of, 198
  France, in, 153
  French Revolution, effect on,
    201–202
  fundamentalism and, 234, 236, 238
  Germany, in, 153, 160, 174–175,
    200
  Italy, in, 153, 154
  Nazi doctrine, 153, 160, 174–175
  overview, 204–206
  Soviet Union, in, 135–138, 198,
    208–211
  state, nationality distinguished
    from, 198
National Association for the Advance-
  ment of White People, 192
Nationality defined, 198–201
National Socialist White Peoples'
  Party, 192
National Student Association, 281
Nation-state, 174–175

  definition of, 198
Naturalists, 265
Natural leaders, 84–85, 89
Natural rights, 25, 45–46
  utility concept, replacement by, 33
Nazism, 121, 142, 315
  anti-Semitism as ideology, 159–160,
    161, 162, 164, 165, 169, 171,
    173–174
  communist movement, as response
    to, 151, 169
  development of, 147, 148, 169–172
  economic policy, 179–180
  Fascism and, 156
  history, use of, 158–159
  intellectual roots of, 159–162
  nationalism and, 160
  organizations promoting, 169–170
  principles of, 148, 155, 156,
    172–180
  program of, 147, 155, 162–164, 168,
    169
  propaganda machine, 148, 172
  return, possibility of, 183–184
  society, reaction of, 177–179
  synchronization theory, 168
  violence, attitude toward, 172
  Volk and, 159–162, 164, 176
Nechaev, Sergei Gennadevich, 248
Neo-liberals, 68–69
Neo-Marxism, 2
Netherlands, 220
New Deal, 91, 188
New Left in America and France, 274
  consumer culture, critique of,
    278–280
  democratic ideals and republican-
    ism in, 284–287
  differences between, 283–291
  leadership, attitude toward,
    282–283, 284–285
  legacy of, 291–294
  Marxism and Anarchism in,
    283–284, 287–290
  new class, concern about, 282–283
  Old Left, critique of, 281–282

origins of, 276–291
  Situationism and Surrealism in, 290
  university, critique of, 276–278
Newly industrialized countries, 74
Nicaragua, 224
Nietzsche, Friedrich, 152, 155
Nixon, Richard, 291
North, Gary, 239
North Korea, 95, 139
Nuremburg trials, 177

O'Connor, Feargus, 52
Oman, 206
Organic theory, 6–7, 81, 83, 86, 89
Organization of African Unity, 220
Organization of Afro-American Unity,
  214, 215
Organization of American States, 220
Origination of ideology, 3
Orthopraxis. *See* Praxis
Ottoman Empire, 204, 205
Owen, Robert, 56

Paine, Thomas, 284, 285
Palmer, R.R., 13
Pannekoek, Anton, 289
Papacy, 218
Paris Commune of 1871, 245, 264,
  268, 273, 289, 290
  Marxists and Anarchists, debate
    regarding, 251–257
Parsons, Talcott, 277
Paternalism, 85–86, 90, 178–179
Pauperization, 102–103
Peaceful coexistence, 122, 130
Pelloutier, Fernand, 152, 265, 270
Perestroika, 127–131, 209
Pericles, 21
Personal freedoms, 26–27
Personality theory, 182
Peru, 224, 225
Philosophy, ideology distinguished, 3
Place, Francis, 52
Plato, 3, 98
  equality, attitude toward, 273–274
  ideology, bases of, 5

political authority, basis of, 7
property, view on, 8
Plekhanov, Georgi, 260, 261
Pluralism, 6, 22, 131, 162, 311
  defined, 43–44
Poland, 125, 135, 136, 137, 138, 201,
  204, 205, 208
Political authority, 7
Pollution
  social cost of, 43
Popular sovereignty, 39–40
Populist party, 191
Populists, 286, 287, 293
Port Huron Statement, 276, 277, 278,
  280, 281, 284
Portugal, 220, 315
Postmodernists, 300, 303, 306, 307
Pragmatism, 148
Praxis (orthopraxis), 225
  defined, 227, 229–230
Primitive societies, 55
Progressive Labor Party, 284
Progressives, 286, 287, 293
Proletariat, dictatorship of, 107, 111
Property rights, 28
Proudhon, Pierre-Joseph, 55, 151,
  245, 246, 247, 248, 249, 252, 254,
  255, 259–260, 263, 264, 265, 266,
  270, 289
Psychoanalysis, 268–269

Rabelais, François, 265
Radicals, 52–54
  students as, 272–294
Rainbow Coalition, 215
Ranke, Leopold von, 158
Rashdoony, Rousas J., 239
Ratzinger, Joseph Cardinal, 226
Rauschning, Hermann, 156, 164,
  165
Rawls, John, 296, 297, 301, 310–311
Reactionary defined, 80
Reagan, Ronald, 70, 92–93, 291
Reformed capitalism, 62, 64–65
Regionalism, 220
Religion, 44, 80, 84, 89, 91, 106, 305

fundamentalism. *See* Fundamentalism

Islamic fundamentalism. *See* Muslim fundamentalism

liberation theology doctrines, 226–230

national consciousness, effect on, 199, 200

role of, 223–224

Renan, Ernest, 200

Representative government, 37–38, 86–87

introduction of, 45–46

radicals and liberals, reconciliation between, 54

Republic defined, 89

Revolution, 106–107

Bolshevik Revolution, 108, 110, 133, 150, 254

French Revolution. *See* French Revolution of 1789

Lenin's doctrine, 111, 114–115

perestroika as, 128–130

rising expectations of, 74

Ribicoff, Abraham, 273

Ricardo, David, 99

Right-wing extremism, 183–192

Robertson, Pat, 239, 240

Robespierre, Maximilien, 201, 256, 261

Rockwell, Lincoln, 192

Roman Empire, 217–218

Romania, 125, 137, 138, 205, 209

Roosevelt, Franklin D., 190

Rosenberg, Alfred, 150

Rousseau, Jean-Jacques, 219, 303, 304, 309

common ownership theory, 55–56

democracy, 39–40

political authority, source of, 39

social contract, 22

Rubin, Jerry, 279, 284

Rushdie, Salmon, 236

Russia. *See also* Soviet Union

liberalism, expansion of, 45

political movements in, 203

Saint-Simon, Claude Henri de, 305

Salazar, Antonio de Oliveira, 145, 156

Sartre, Jean-Paul, 263–264, 268–269, 270, 279, 281

Schlesinger, Arthur Jr., 299, 307

Scotland, 56

Second International, 150, 151, 249, 255, 265

Secret police, 117, 123, 126, 129, 138, 149

Self-determination, 174, 200–201, 205, 206, 212

Self-government, 200

Self-interest, 29, 31, 97

enlightened self-interest, 33–35

Self-regarding and other-regarding acts, 42–43, 308, 309

Separatism, 211–212, 214–215

Serbia, 210, 318

Seton-Watson, Hugh, 198

Shaw, George Bernard, 57–58

Silone, Ignazio, 156

Situationists, 279, 280, 284, 289, 290

Slovenia, 137, 209–210, 318

Smith, Adam, 22, 29–31, 53, 54, 99, 307

Social cost, 43

Socialism, 70–72

democratic socialism, 56–59

ethics of, 55

Fabian socialism, 57–59

future of, 72, 314

state-managed economy, 22–23

Utopian socialism, 11, 55–56, 98, 99, 195

Social justice, 48

Social liberty, 28

Socrates, 14

Solidarity (Poland), 9, 135, 136, 137, 138

Sorel, Georges, 151, 152–155, 156, 162, 164, 266–267

Sources of ideology, 3

South Africa, 296, 297

Southern Baptists, 240–241

Southern Christian Leadership Conference, 213
Soviet Union, 69, 70, 98, 236, 270, 290, 300
  communist countries, changes in, 138–141
  dissolution of, 132–143, 198, 206, 314, 315
  free-market economy, 74
  governmental institutions, 125, 127, 131–134
  nationalism in, 135–138, 198, 208–211
  political pluralism, 131
  right-wing extremism in, 185–186
  role of, 142–143
Spain, 70, 210, 220, 254, 255, 270, 274, 284, 287, 315
Sri Lanka, 210
Stalin, Joseph, 13, 95, 110, 115–123, 129, 130, 139, 142, 148, 206, 209, 245, 251, 288
Stalinism, 115–123, 267–268
  nationalism, position as to, 206–208
  reasons for, 142
State
  Anarchist position, 247, 249, 253, 261
  Hegel on, 160–161
  Leninist position, 111
  Marxist position, 106–108, 247, 253, 256
State intervention, 40–41
  conservative position, 86
  limited intervention, 47
  radical democracy and, 53
Status quo, 15
Stirner, Max, 155, 245, 260, 261–262, 264, 265
Stoics, 27, 217
Student movements in America and France
  consumer culture, critique of, 278–280
  democratic ideals and republicanism in, 284–287
  differences between, 283–291
  leadership in, 282–283, 284–285
  legacy of, 291–294
  Marxism and Anarchism in, 283–284, 287–290
  new class, concern about, 282–283
  Old Left, critique of, 281–282
  origins of, 276–291
  rebellions, 272–275
  similarities between, 276–283
  Situationism and Surrealism in, 290
  university, critique of, 276–278
Student rebellions in America and France, 272–275
Students for a Democratic Society (SDS), 214, 276, 281, 283, 284, 285
Subjective economic condition, 105–106
Substitutism, theory of, 115
Sudan, 210, 236
Sumner, William Graham, 90–91
Supremacy, 175, 190, 192, 202, 204
Surplus value theory, 101
Surrealism, 245, 251, 263, 264, 267–268, 269, 270, 279, 289, 290
Sweden
  health programs, 64
Switzerland, 112, 199, 254
Symbolist poets, 265–266, 267
Syndicalism, 165, 250, 265, 266, 270
  defined, 151–152
  Fascism and, 151–156
  national syndicalism, 151–153, 165
Syria, 205, 235, 236, 238

Tailhade, Laurent, 266
Taiwan, 141, 318
Tariffs, 46
Terrorism
  Anarchist philosophy of, 266–267,268, 269
Thatcher, Margaret, 70, 74, 291
Theory defined, 3
Third World, 224, 229, 269
Thought, freedom of, 26–28

Tocqueville, Alexis de, 93, 134, 276, 292, 306–307, 311
Totalitarianism
  communist model, 125–126
  Fascism and, 148–149, 156
  fundamentalism and, 235–236
  Nazism and, 175, 176, 181
Trade, freedom of, 46–47
Trade unions, 61, 88, 106, 118, 183, 247, 249, 256, 258
  Nazi attitude toward, 172, 173, 178, 179, 181
  Solidarity (Poland), 9, 135, 136, 137, 138
Traditionalism, 232–234, 238, 241
Trotsky, Leon, 114, 150, 249, 250–251, 254–255, 257, 263, 268, 270, 288
Truman, Harry S, 190
Truth
  nature of, 6
  political authority, bases of, 7
  religious fundamentalism, interpretation by, 232
Tunisia, 185, 205, 236
Turkey, 201, 205, 207–208, 314
Types of ideology, 14–16
Tyranny, 89

Uganda, 197
Ukraine, 208, 209
Underclass, 72, 75
Union Party for Social Justice, 188
United States
  black separatism, 211–216
  conservatism in, 87–93
  Constitution of. See United States Constitution
  economic principles, 65–66
  education, 64
  extremist movements, 186–192
  health programs, 64
  Keynesian economics, 62
  New Left movement, 272–294
  political parties, emergence of, 45–46
  slavery, 44
  student movement in, 272–294
  student rebellion in, 272–275
  welfare services, 62, 64–65
United States Constitution
  conservative doctrine based on, 89–90
  First Amendment, 27–28
  Pilgrims' Constitution, 35
Universalist ethic, 217
Universal Negro Improvement Association, 212
Universal suffrage, 52
Uses of ideology, 9–13
USSR. See Soviet Union
Utilitarianism, 31–35
  economic man theory, 22
Utopian socialism, 11, 98, 99 107, 195
  ethics of, 55–56

Validity criteria, 16–18
Valois, Georges, 153
Vaneigen, Raoul, 289
Vatican Council, 224, 230
Versailles Treaty, 163, 169, 172, 173
Vietnam, 139, 142, 272, 275, 281, 286, 287, 288, 291
Villon, François, 265
Virgil, 55
Virtual representation, 85
Voltaire, François-Marie Arouet de, 157, 318
Voluntarism, 113
Voting rights, 213

Walesa, Lech, 135, 136, 137, 138
Wallas, Graham, 58
Webb, Sidney and Beatrice, 58
Weber, Max, 3, 305
Weimar Republic, 157, 161, 162, 163–164, 165
Welch, Robert H.W., 190
Welfare state, 8, 54, 62, 64–65
  conservative doctrine, 91
  free-market economy and, 62
  liberal doctrine on, 308–309
  positive state concept, 22–23

West Germany. *See* Germany
White Aryan Resistance, 192
White Patriot Party, 192
Wilde, Oscar, 265, 281
Will, human
    revolution, as factor in, 255,
        263–264
Wilson, Harold, 281
Wilson, Woodrow, 163, 193, 203
World War I, 154, 161, 169, 171, 175,
        177, 179, 186, 187, 189, 193,
        201, 203, 205, 211, 212, 221,
        265, 301

World War II, 165, 169, 179, 185–186,
        189, 190, 198, 203, 205, 206, 208,
        211, 220, 224, 263, 276, 292, 310

Yeltsin, Boris, 133, 134
Yippies, 279, 284
Youth Culture, 274
Yugoslavia, 135, 137, 138, 198, 205,
        206, 209, 211, 236, 241, 274, 298,
        314

Zhivkov, Todor, 136
Zola, Emile, 265